Studies in Economic History

Aims and Scope

This series from Springer provides a platform for works in economic history that truly integrate economics and history. Books on a wide range of related topics are welcomed and encouraged, including those in macro-economic history, financial history, labor history, industrial history, agricultural history, the history of institutions and organizations, spatial economic history, law and economic history, political economic history, historical demography, and environmental history.

Economic history studies have greatly developed over the past several decades through application of economics and econometrics. Particularly in recent years, a variety of new economic theories and sophisticated econometric techniques—including game theory, spatial economics, and generalized method of moment (GMM)—have been introduced for the great benefit of economic historians and the research community.

At the same time, a good economic history study should contribute more than just an application of economics and econometrics to past data. It raises novel research questions, proposes a new view of history, and/or provides rich documentation. This series is intended to integrate data analysis, close examination of archival works, and application of theoretical frameworks to offer new insights and even provide opportunities to rethink theories.

The purview of this new Springer series is truly global, encompassing all nations and areas of the world as well as all eras from ancient times to the present. The editorial board, who are internationally renowned leaders among economic historians, carefully evaluate and judge each manuscript, referring to reports from expert reviewers. The series publishes contributions by university professors and others well established in the academic community, as well as work deemed to be of equivalent merit.

All books and chapters in the Studies in Economic History book series are indexed in Scopus.

Jun Kajima

Shanghai under the Socialist System

The Impact of the Planned Economy and the Socialist Transformation

Springer

Jun Kajima
Faculty of Economics
Keio University
Tokyo, Japan

ISSN 2364-1797 ISSN 2364-1800 (electronic)
Studies in Economic History
ISBN 978-981-95-3224-7 ISBN 978-981-95-3225-4 (eBook)
https://doi.org/10.1007/978-981-95-3225-4

The original submitted manuscript has been translated into English. The translation was done using artificial intelligence. A subsequent revision was performed by the author(s) to further refine the work and to ensure that the translation is appropriate concerning content and scientific correctness. It may, however, read stylistically different from a conventional translation.

This Springer imprint is published by the registered company Springer Nature Singapore Pte Ltd.
The registered company address is: 152 Beach Road, #21-01/04 Gateway East, Singapore 189721, Singapore

To Hitomi

Acknowledgements

This volume is an English translation of*Shakaishugi taiseika no Shanghai keizai: keikakukeizai to kōyuka no impakuto* (社会主義体制下の上海経済——計画経済と公有化のインパクト), which was published in Japanese in 2018 by the University of Tokyo Press. The original Japanese edition was based on my doctoral dissertation, submitted to the University of Tokyo in 2010, as well as subsequent research. I am grateful to my supervisors during my undergraduate and graduate studies, namely Professors Banno Ryokichi, Okumura Satoshi and Yoshizawa Seiichiro. Additionally, Professor Tajima Toshio, who was the director of the Contemporary China Research Base at the Institute of Social Science at the University of Tokyo during my time there as a research associate, profoundly shaped the direction of this study.

I wish to express my appreciation to Professors Zhu Yingui, Debin Ma, and Richard von Glahn for being my host professors at, respectively, Fudan University, the London School of Economics and Political Science, and the University of California, Los Angeles when I was a visiting student/scholar. The transformative experiences at these institutions not only helped push my research in new directions but also fueled my motivation to publish an English version. Moreover, I want to offer my sincere thanks to my various colleagues and friends who supported my research through discussions, suggestions, and encouragement: Brett Sheehan, Carles Brasó Broggi, Dominic Berry, Feng Xiaocai, Gilles Guiheux, Hayashi Koji, Hirata Koji, Hong Shaoyang, Huangfu Qiushi, Izutani Yoko, Kajitani Kai, Kawai Shinichi, Kigoshi Yoshinori, Kubo Toru, Lin Chaochao, Lin Pan, Linda Grove, Matsumura Shiho, Marukawa Tomoo, Men Chuang, Minato Teruhiro, Mine Takeshi, Murakami Ei, Nakagane Katsuji, Peng Juanjuan, Robert Cliver, R. Bin Wong, Thomas G. Rawski, Tomizawa Yoshia, Uenishi Kei, Valeria Zanier, Wang Rui, Yukawa Kazuo, and Zhang Xinyuan. On a similar note, I would like to thank all of the staff and librarians who assisted me at the many universities, institutions, and libraries I visited for my research, especially the Shanghai Municipal Archives.

I want to express my gratitude to Professor Okazaki Tetsuji and Ms. Kawakami Juno (Springer Japan) for giving me the opportunity to publish my work as part of Springer's Studies in Economic History Series. I also want to thank the University of Tokyo Press for agreeing to permit Springer to publish the English edition. As for the English translation process, I am greatly indebted to Professor Andrew T. Kamei-Dyche for his proofreading work. Without his patient support, the English version would never have existed.

During the years I was working on this project, my wife, Hitomi, and my sons, Hiroshi and Tatsuki, gave me constant support and energy for life and work. I have no way to fully express my appreciation to them, but I hope the publication of this volume can repay their kindness even a little.

This study was supported by the Fuji Xerox Setsutaro Kobayashi Memorial Fund 2005 Fellowship (September 2005-August 2006), and a series of grants from the Japan Society for the Promotion of Science (JSPS), specifically a JSPS Grant-in-Aid for Young Scientists (B) "An Inter-regional Comparative Study of China's Fiscal System during the Planned Economy Era, 1949–1978" (Principal Investigator, April 2008-March 2011, JSPS KAKENHI Grant Number: 20730228), a Grant-in-Aid for Young Scientists (B) "A Comparative Study of the Relationships between Local Government and Enterprise in China during the Planned Economy Era, 1949–1978" (Principal Investigator, April 2011-March 2014, JSPS KAKENHI Grant Number: 23730321), and a Grant-in-Aid for Scientific Research (C) "A Comparative Study on the Influence of the Socialist Economic System on the Development of Chinese Enterprises" (Principal Investigator, April 2015-March 2019, JSPS KAKENHI Grant Number: 15K03570). The publication of the original Japanese edition was supported by a JSPS Grant-in-Aid for Publication of Scientific Research Results (Publication of Research Results, JSPS KAKENHI Grant Number: 17HP5095) for the fiscal year 2017.

Contents

1 Introduction 1
1.1 Setting the Issue 1
1.2 Literature Review 6
1.3 Perspectives and Methodology 12
1.4 The Structure of This Book 13
References 14

Part I The Shanghai Economy and the Formation of the Socialist System

2 Profile of the Shanghai Economy 21
2.1 The Emergence of "Shanghai Municipality" 22
2.1.1 From the Opening of the Port to the First World War (1843–1914) 23
2.1.2 From the First World War to the Second Sino-Japanese War (1914–1937) 25
2.1.3 The Second Sino-Japanese War (1937–1945) 26
2.1.4 Postwar National Government Period (1945–1949) 26
2.2 The Shanghai Economy in the Long Run 28
References 33

3 The Establishment of the People's Republic of China and Shanghai Enterprises 37
3.1 Shanghai Enterprises in 1949 40
3.2 The "New Democratic Economy" and State Contracts 45
3.2.1 The "New Democratic Economy" 45
3.2.2 Processing Orders 47
3.3 The Development of Processing Orders Under the "Adjustment of Industry and Commerce" 51
References 58

4 The Korean War and the Formation of the Socialist System 63
4.1 The Korean War and the Expansion of Processing Orders 64
4.1.1 Wartime Economic Control 64
4.1.2 Expansion of Processing Orders During Wartime 68
4.2 The Socialist Transformation in Shanghai 73
4.2.1 Changes in the Perception of Private Enterprises and Processing Orders 73
4.2.2 From Processing Orders to the Socialist Transformation 80
References 89

Part II The Socialist Fiscal System and Shanghai

5 Reform of the Fiscal and Taxation System 95
5.1 Reform of the Fiscal and Taxation System Before and After 1949 97
5.1.1 The Postwar Period of the Republic of China 97
5.1.2 The Early Years of the People's Republic of China 102
5.2 Tax Collection and the Fiscal Revenue of Shanghai 111
5.2.1 Tax Collection in Shanghai 111
5.2.2 Tax Revenue and Shanghai's Fiscal Structure 121
References 124

6 Local Government and Local Enterprises 129
6.1 The Socialist Transformation and Enterprise Revenue 130
6.2 The Fiscal Relationship Between the Shanghai Municipal Government and Local Enterprises 133
References 142

7 Interregional Comparison of Provincial-Level Local Public Finances 145
7.1 Perspectives and Methodology of the Interregional Comparison 146
7.2 Comparative Analysis of Local Public Finances in Provinces, Municipalities, and Autonomous Regions 151
7.2.1 Local Public Finances of Provinces, Municipalities, and Autonomous Regions 151
7.2.2 Fiscal Transfers Between Central and Local Government 153
7.2.3 Comparison of Local Fiscal Revenue and Expenditure Structure: The Ratio of Enterprise Revenue and Economic Construction Expenditure 160
References 163

Part III Industrial Development in Shanghai under the Socialist System

8 The Impact of the Heavy-Industry-Priority Strategy: The Textile and Machinery Industries 169
8.1 The Industrial Organization of Shanghai 170
8.2 The Development of the Textile and Machinery Industries 174
8.3 Performances Under the Socialist System: Investments and Profits 177
References 186

9 The Restructuring of Industrial Organization: The Rubber Processing Industry 189
9.1 The Rubber Processing Industry in Shanghai 191
9.1.1 The Birth and Development of Shanghai's Rubber Processing Industry 191
9.1.2 The Shanghai Rubber Processing Industry in the Postwar Period 193
9.2 The Influence of Governmental Economic Control in the Early 1950s 196
9.2.1 Governmental Control Over Raw Rubber Distribution 196
9.2.2 Governmental Monopolization of Product Sales Channels 198
9.3 The Socialist Transformation and the Restructuring of Industrial Organization 201
9.3.1 "Prosperity" Under Economic Control 201
9.3.2 Reorganization of the Rubber Industry Through the Socialist Transformation 203
References 206

10 The Material Distribution System: The Cement Industry 209
10.1 The Material Distribution System and Cement 211
10.1.1 The Material Distribution System 211
10.1.2 Management of Cement Production and Distribution 215
10.2 The Development of the Shanghai Cement Industry 218
10.2.1 Historical Background 218
10.2.2 The Socialist System and the Shanghai Cement Industry 220
10.3 The Demand and Supply of Cement in Shanghai 224
10.3.1 Demand 224
10.3.2 Supply I: State Distribution 228
10.3.3 Supply II: Self-Procurement by Shanghai 229
References 239

11 Regional Integration and Interregional Network: The Power Industry ... 243
11.1 The Power Industry in Shanghai ... 246
11.1.1 The Postwar Period ... 246
11.1.2 The Plan to Establish the United Power Company ... 250
11.2 Regional Integration in the Early Years of the PRC ... 253
11.2.1 The Outbreak of the Korean War and the Onset of Military Control ... 253
11.2.2 Regional Integration Through the Socialist Transformation ... 256
11.3 The Formation of Interregional Networks ... 259
11.3.1 Development of the Shanghai Power Industry During the Planned Economy Period ... 259
11.3.2 The East China Power Grid and the Shanghai Power Industry ... 262
References ... 268

12 Conclusion ... 273
12.1 The Reform and Opening-Up Policy and Shanghai's Economy ... 273
12.2 The Historical Significance of the Chinese Socialist System ... 276
12.2.1 The Emergence of Local Governments as Economic Entities ... 276
12.2.2 Regional Integration by Local Governments and Interregional Division ... 278
12.2.3 Central Control in Principle and De Facto Local Autonomy ... 280
References ... 283

Name Index ... 285

Subject Index ... 287

About the Author

Jun Kajima is a professor of economic history at the Faculty of Economics, Keio University. His research focuses on the economic history of modern China, especially the socialist system after 1949. He has published articles, chapters, and monographs on the economic history of China in English, Chinese, and Japanese. His publications include *Economic Development in East Asia during the Cold War Era: China and Taiwan* (co-edited with Toshio Tajima and Teruhiro Minato; Koyo shobo, 2024, in Japanese); "Light Industry: Socialist Industrialization and the Textile Industry," in Katsuji Nakagane, ed., *Studies on the Chinese Economy During the Mao Era* (Springer, 2022); *Shanghai's Economy under the Socialist System: The Impact of the Planned Economy and Socialist Transformation* (University of Tokyo Press, 2018, in Japanese); *Economic History of Modern China: An Approach Based on Statistical Data* (co-authored with Toru Kubo and Yoshinori Kigoshi; University of Tokyo Press, 2016, in Japanese); and *The Development of China's Cement Industry: Industrial Organization and Structural Change* (co-edited with Toshio Tajima and Zhu Yingui; China Social Science Press, 2011, in Chinese). He obtained his undergraduate degree from Saitama University, a master's from Tokyo Metropolitan University, and a Ph.D. in Letters from the University of Tokyo. He has been a visiting student at Beijing Normal University and Fudan University, a visiting senior fellow in the Department of Economic History at the London School of Economics and Political Science, and a visiting scholar in the Department of History at the University of California, Los Angeles.

Abbreviations

CCP	Chinese Communist Party (中国共产党)
GMD	Guomindang, or Chinese Nationalist Party (中国国民党)
PRC	People's Republic of China (中华人民共和国)
ROC	Republic of China (中华民国)

Chapter 1
Introduction

Abstract What was the historical significance of the socialist system formed in China over the course of the twentieth century? To seek to answer this question, this book focuses on Shanghai, the center of modern industry in China since the latter half of the nineteenth century, as a case region, and examines the influence of the introduction of the socialist system in the 1950s on the municipality's economy through a careful analysis of historical archives and other materials. This chapter introduces the theme, literature, perspectives and methodology, and structure of the book. The main issues this study pursues are, first, how the Shanghai Municipal Government's control system over the Shanghai economy developed and functioned, and second, how the Shanghai economy was transformed by the implementation of the socialist system. Through analyzing the case of Shanghai, this book explores the impact of the socialist system on the Chinese economy.

Keywords Socialist system · Socialist transformation · Planned economy · Industrialization · Chinese economy · Shanghai · Centralization-decentralization

1.1 Setting the Issue

What was the historical significance of the socialist system formed in China over the course of the twentieth century? This is the main question that this book seeks to answer. The emergence of socialist countries in the wake of the Russian Revolution of 1917 and the subsequent establishment of the Soviet Union came to represent a major element of the world economy in the twentieth century, since these countries composed the Communist bloc which divided the world economy with the Capitalist bloc during the Cold War period. Moreover, the government-led development ideology of socialism affected not only those countries that directly adopted socialist systems, but also the development strategies of post-colonial countries that became independent after the Second World War, such as India. Although by the end of the twentieth century most socialist countries had disappeared from the world, exemplified by the collapse of the Soviet Union in 1991, it is essential to examine the

J. Kajima, *Shanghai under the Socialist System*, Studies in Economic History,
https://doi.org/10.1007/978-981-95-3225-4_1

historical processes of constructing socialist systems in order to fully grasp the long-term development of the world economy in the twentieth century. This book aims to contribute to this understanding through considering the case of China.

Before beginning the discussion, it is necessary to clarify the definition of "socialist system" used throughout this book. Given the myriad views on the concept of socialism, there exists no common fixed definition.[1] Sometimes it has been understood primarily as an ideology, and at other times as primarily a form of socio-economic system. The current work defines a socialist system as an economic system which simultaneously combines the following three factors: (1) public ownership of the means of production, (2) distribution of resources via a non-market planned economy, and finally (3) monopolistic control of political power by a single party.[2] These elements can be articulated as distinctive features of a socialist system that clearly distinguish it from other economic systems, and correspondingly serve, therefore, as the minimum criteria necessary to treat socialist systems as a unique type of economic system. From this point of departure, this book focuses in particular on the unique institutional character of the socialist systems that existed in the twentieth century and their influence on the development of the Chinese economy and society.

Given this definition, it can be said that at present in the twenty-first century there exists no country that has all the elements comprising a socialist system, and that socialist systems are thus themselves already reduced to historical artifacts.[3] In the case of China, a socialist system was established through the implementation of the First Five Year Plan (planned resource distribution system) in 1953 and the subsequent socialist transformation (socialization of the means of production) in 1956, only to begin dissolving gradually since the start of the "Reform and Opening-up" (改革开放) policy in 1978. In other words, based on the criteria above, the Chinese socialist system only existed for approximately twenty-two years, from 1956 to 1978. Although the Chinese government declared the concept of a "socialist market economy" in 1992 and continues to describe the country itself as socialist today, it can no longer be considered a socialist system—and is consequently not treated as one in this book—due to the lack of two factors, namely (1) the socialization of the means of production, and (2) a planned resource distribution system.[4]

[1] On the variety of views on socialism, see Shiokawa (1999, pp. 1–25). To give but one example, János Kornai essentially regards countries controlled by communist parties as socialist countries, and analyzes the common political, economic, and social systems seen in these countries as elements of socialist systems (Kornai 1992, pp. 4–5, 9–11).

[2] Oka et al. (1976), Shiokawa (1999), Okumura (1999, p. 21), Mōri (1990), and Wada (1992).

[3] Wada (1992) and Shiokawa (1999) also regard socialist systems as a historical phenomenon rather than institutions that continue to exist in the contemporary world.

[4] The term "socialist market economy" refers to the mechanism by which the market exerts its basic functions for resource allocation under the macro-control of the government. It was introduced by Jiang Zemin (江泽民) at the 14th National Congress of the Chinese Communist Party (CCP) in October 1992 and the "Decision on Issues Concerning the Establishment of the Socialist Market Economic System" (中共中央关于建立社会主义市场经济体制若干问题的决定), which focused on (1) establishing a modern enterprise system, (2) building a unified national open market system, and (3) establishing indirect macro-control functions of the government, was

The reader may ask why the current work chooses to focus, then, on China as a case study in socialist systems. First, China represents an important case in terms of the great size of its economy and population, both of which experienced tremendous change in the wake of the socialist transformation. During the early modern Qing dynasty (1644–1912), China's traditional economy, in the wake of the country's great growth in territory and population at the time, came to represent a unique economic structure with particular institutions, such as a monetary system divided between employing silver bullion as interregional currency and copper cash as local currency, which makes it a unique case to have experienced a socialist system in the latter half of the twentieth century (Kuroda 1994; Okamoto 2013). According to Angus Maddison's estimates, in 1820, China's share of world GDP amounted to 32.9%, while its share of the world's population came to 36.6%.[5] Although the share of GDP had fallen to merely 5.2% in 1952 due to the industrialization of the Western countries, its share of world population in that same year remained an impressive 21.8%. Therefore, China serves as not only a special case, but a particularly important one in light of its scale, and it is worthwhile to investigate how this enormous economy and society was transformed through the implementation of a socialist system in the course of the long-term process of modernization that had commenced in the latter half of the nineteenth century.[6]

Moreover, China's case is also especially significant for understanding the development of East Asian countries after the Second World War. In the East Asian region countries experienced successive economic growth one after another as the late twentieth century wore on: Japan experienced rapid economic growth from the mid-1950s to the early 1970s; Taiwan, South Korea, and Hong Kong caught up as Asian Newly Industrializing Economies after the 1960s; and China rose after the aforementioned Reform and Opening-up Policy implemented in 1978. However, the political and economic circumstances of each East Asian country were different, and China's experience with a socialist system in the planned economy period marked it as clearly distinct from its neighbors. How to situate the trajectory of postwar Chinese development in the context of East Asian regional development, therefore, is a significant point of debate.

At this juncture, it can be instructive to consider how macro statistics illustrate the place of the planned economy period in the long-term process of Chinese modern economic development.[7] As Fig. 1.1 shows, China's modernization process since

adopted at the 3rd plenary session of the 14th Central Committee of CCP in November 1993. Amako et al. (1999, p. 459) and Katō and Uehara (2004, pp. 67–68).

[5] Maddison (2007, p. 44, Table 2.1, 2.2a). While Saito (2008, pp. 81–91) points out some problems with Maddison's estimates, they are helpful for demonstrating the general size and import of the Chinese economy. The percentage of the world population comprised by China remained approximately 22% from 1950 to 1980 (Kubo et al. 2016, p. 12).

[6] In addition, it is important to note that China had maintained a relatively stable socialist economic system for over 20 years, unlike other Asian and African socialist states. This is another reason why China's case is helpful for exploring the influence of a socialist economic system on an economy and society.

[7] The following description is based on Kubo et al. (2016, pp. 7–20).

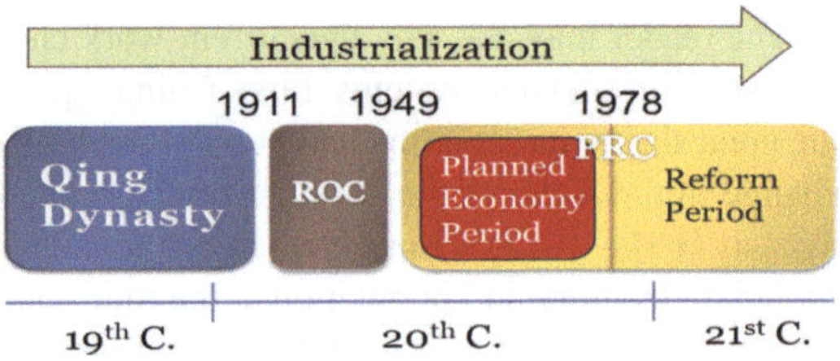

Fig. 1.1 Chinese economy since the latter half of the nineteenth century. *Source* Created by author

the latter half of the nineteenth century can be roughly divided into three periods: (1) early industrialization, from the opening of the ports in 1843 to the Republic of China (ROC) period (or Republican period, 1912–1949); (2) the socialist system during the planned economy period of the People's Republic of China (1949–1978); and finally (3) the dissolution of the socialist system and rapid economic growth of the Reform period (1978-).

As for the long-term performance of the Chinese economy, Fig. 1.2 shows China's real GDP and its growth rate from the 1930s to 2010, based on the estimates of Minami and Makino (2014). The characteristics of each era are immediately discernible: the relatively low growth rate in the Republican period (although only shown for the years 1932–1940 due to the lack of data); the relatively high growth with intermittent years of substantial minus growth in the planned economy period; and the high and stable growth in the Reform period. In particular, the rapid and continuous economic growth achieved during the Reform period stands out as impressive, while the planned economy period suffered some years of great minus growth due to radical policies and political destruction, most notably the Great Leap Forward (大跃进, 1958–1960) and the Cultural Revolution (文化大革命, 1966–1976). This "high but unstable growth" is a prominent characteristic of the planned economy period.

In terms of the industrial structure over the long run, Fig. 1.3 clearly shows a rapid expansion of manufacturing and mining after 1952. Agriculture, forestry, and fishery accounted for over 50% in 1933–1952, while even by 1952 manufacturing and mining only amounted to around 25%. However, it came to exceed 50% in 1960 and subsequently maintained the same level while agriculture, forestry, and fishery came to consistently decline after 1980. Yet when considering how the latter decline was paralleled by the increase in services over the same period, the bulk of the share comprised by manufacturing and mining did not change until 2010.

This transition in industrial structure was clearly the result of the industrialization policy known as the "Heavy-industry-priority Strategy" employed during the planned economy period. Turning to look at the shares of output value of manufacturing in China from 1933 to 1980, as illustrated in Fig. 1.4, it is clear that Chinese industry during the Republican period was centered on light industries, such as cotton yarn and weaving, while the heavy industry amounted to less than 20% of output in 1953. However, the intensive governmental investment in heavy industry based on the aforementioned economic strategy dramatically expanded the ratio of manufacturing gross output value comprised by heavy industry through the planned economy period. As a result, by 1980 the ratio had reached 60%. In short, China's industrialization was

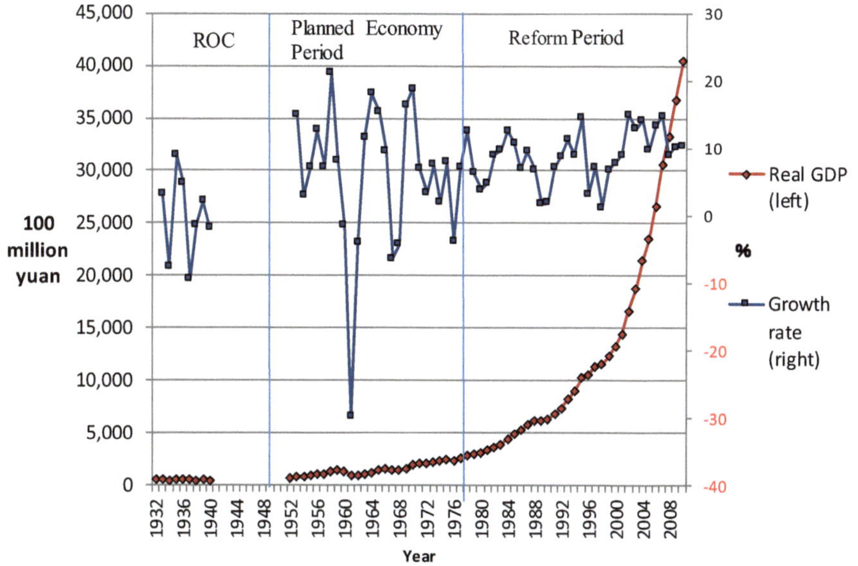

Fig. 1.2 Real GDP and growth rate of China, 1932–1940, 1952–2010. *Note* Real GDP calculated based on constant 1952 prices. *Source* Kubo et al. (2016, p. 17). Original data from Minami and Makino (2014, p. 360, Table 0.1)

substantially advanced by the "Heavy-industry-priority Strategy" carried out during the planned economy period.

As these macro statistics clearly illustrate, the planned economy period not only had some distinct characteristics but moreover can be seen as representing a significant period of transition in the long-term development of the modern Chinese economy. The "high but unstable growth" of the planned economy period reflects both the result and distortion of the intensive developmental policy implemented by the government. On the other hand, from the perspective of industrial structure, the period was one of transition from an agriculture-oriented society to a manufacturing- and mining-oriented one, serving as a bridge between the initial industrialization period prior to the Republican period and the rapid economic growth of the Reform period. This transition, bound up with China's socialist experience, shows why China provides such a fascinating and instructive case for comparison to other East Asian countries that experienced rapid postwar economic growth. The main purpose of this book is to explore the impact of the socialist system on the Chinese economy, through analyzing the processes of the Chinese socialist system's formation and dissolution as a historical phenomenon.

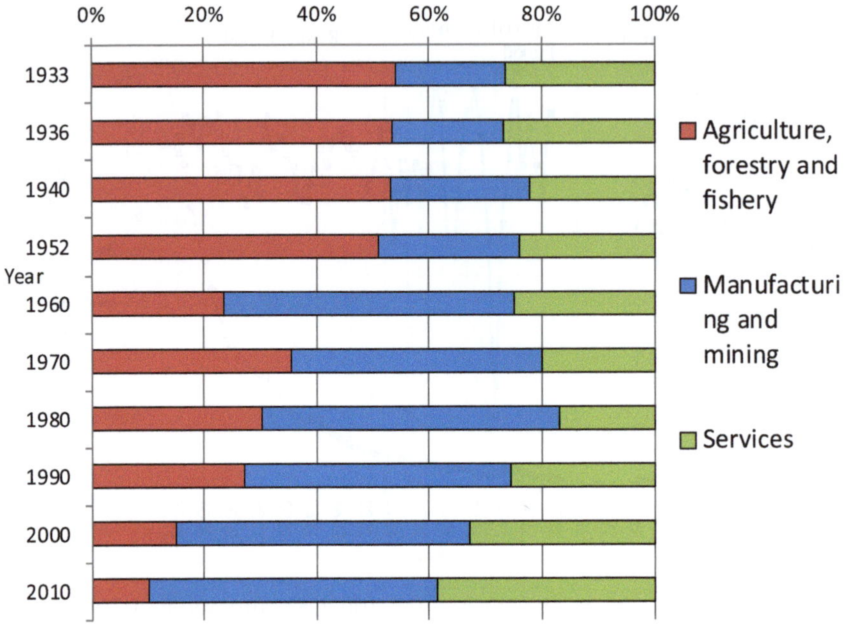

Fig. 1.3 Industrial structure of China, 1933–2010 (Shares of Gross Value Added at current prices). *Note* Breakdowns of "Manufacturing and mining" and "Services" are as follows: Manufacturing and mining: manufacturing, mining, construction, supply of electricity and gas, transportation, and communications. Services: wholesale, retail, finance, insurance, real estate business, governmental services, others. *Source* Minami and Makino (2014, p. 20, Table 0.8)

1.2 Literature Review

How has scholarship on the Chinese socialist system developed? First, it is important to note that research on China's socialist experience has not simply been continuously accumulated over time. The changing nature of China's economic system has itself greatly influenced this research situation. China's socialist system, since its formation in the 1950s, and especially since it was proclaimed to represent a unique socialist path in the late 1950s, attracted global attention as a new socialist system capable of replacing the Soviet model. However, due to the Chinese government's restrictions on information disclosure, efforts to shed light on the reality of the enigmatic Chinese socialist system from what limited information was available were mainly made in Japan, Taiwan, and the Western world during the planned economy period. Representative of these are the studies by Ishikawa (1960), Perkins (1966), Donnithorne (1967), and Lardy (1978). However, with the transition of the economic system in the wake of the Reform and Opening-up Policy in 1978, research interests both inside and outside China shifted to investigating the various issues involved in the economic development and system transition during this new era. The attention

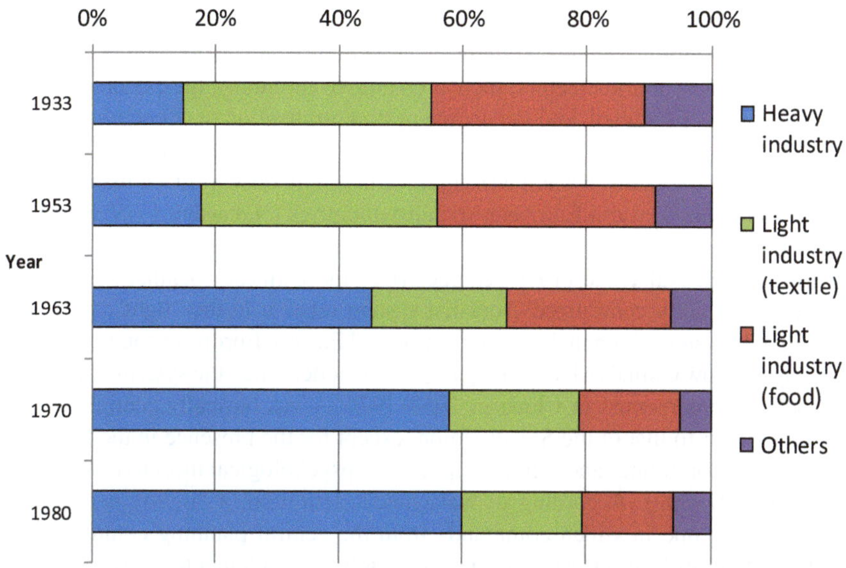

Fig. 1.4 Shares of gross output value of manufacturing in China, 1933–1980. *Note* "Heavy industry" is the sum of "metals and metal products," "machinery," and "chemicals and chemical products". *Sources* Kubo et al. (2016, p. 73) and Kajima (2022, p. 194)

accorded the planned economy period correspondingly decreased until the emergence of a new wave of studies focusing on it as the source of the initial conditions for the Reform period, as well as studies that employed the perspectives of modern Chinese economic history.

In light of these research trends, it is pertinent to revisit the characteristics of the Chinese socialist system as an economic system and the problems identified by previous studies. Generally speaking, a socialist system can be defined as a command economy based on the socialization of the means of production.[8] A command economy, in essence, is an economic system that mainly functions through being vertically controlled by the central government. In such a system, each ministry of industries in the central government exercises control over its own enterprises through governmental command. However, various complementary market factors such as currency, tax, finance, and contracts are also required, since in practice such systems tend to not perform well due to the flaws and rigidity inherent in central planning and vertical control. Even the Soviet Union's socialist system, established in the 1930s and often cited as a typical or archetypal command economy, retained these complementary factors. Therefore, a vertical control system orchestrated by the central government with complementary market factors can be posited as a basic style of command economy.

[8] Shiokawa (1999, pp. 109–116). The outline of the general nature of socialist systems below draws on Shiokawa's work.

According to this general definition of a socialist system, the factors that determine the differences among socialist systems in each country and era amount to the extent of complementary market factors, such as enterprise autonomy, the extent to which a private sector is permitted, and the degree of decentralization of economic management (Shiokawa 1999, pp. 112–114). On this point, many studies have pointed out that the Chinese socialist system was significantly more decentralized than were the Soviet Union and Eastern European socialist countries (Nakagane 1979; Shiokawa 1999).

In this vein, Nakagane (1979) characterizes the Chinese socialist system as a "loose" or "slackly centralized" socialist system relative to the "tight" or "tightly centralized" systems seen in the Soviet Union and Eastern European countries, while pointing out how China's Mao Zedong (毛泽东) model—i.e., the system of ideology and policy implemented in China in 1958–1976[9]—was basically centralized in a similar manner to that of the Soviet Union, except for the presence in the former of the People's Communes and a great emphasis on psychological incentive (Nakagane 1979, pp. 297–309). According to Nakagane's definition, a "tightly centralized" system means one in which commands from the central planning committee can reach the bottom level effectively, and ultimately be implemented (irrespective of the result), while reports from the bottom level can also reach the central government effectively. In other words, it is a system which entails the clearly institutionalized communication of information and execution of commands. Conversely, a "slackly centralized" system has no such institutionalized communication routes for information, and central commands are not completely implemented.

Nakagane also insists that the Chinese socialist system was "decomposed" in reality, rather than "decentralized," by highlighting some cases in which enterprises and/or local governments sometimes even neglected central commands (Nakagane 1979, p. 302). In a "decomposed" system, local governments and enterprises did not acquire their autonomy legally/officially (that is to say, their authority was not "decentralized" in character), but they made decisions and behaved as individual entities under a nominally centralized system.

Here, it is important to note that the objects of decentralization in socialist systems could be separated into two distinct groups: enterprises under the control of a central ministry, and local governments that served as regional authorities (Schurmann 1966, pp. 175–176; Nakagane 1979, p. 298). This engendered, therefore, two types of centralized/decentralized relationship: one being the relationship between central ministries and their respective enterprises, demarcated by industrial sector, and the other being that between the central government and local governments, demarcated by administrative level.

To provide a basic framework for considering centralization/decentralization in a socialist system, Brus (1973) divides all economic decisions into three groups: (1) basic macro-economic decisions which determine the general direction of economic

[9] According to Nakagane (1979, p. 265), the Maoist model became prominent in the CCP during the "Yan'an period" around 1940, the Great Leap Forward period in 1958–1959, and the Cultural Revolution period in 1966–1968.

development: the rate of growth of national income, the shares of investment and consumption in national income, the distribution of investment outlays between sectors and branches, the principles of distribution of the consumption fund between different social and vocational groups, etc.; (2) current (or sectional) decisions: the size and detailed structure of output of a given branch or enterprise, the sources of supplies and direction of sales, the structure of personnel and form and methods of remuneration inside a branch or an enterprise, etc.; (3) individual decisions: the composition of the consumer-goods basket in the framework of household income, the choice of profession and occupation, etc., (Brus 1973, p. 7). On this basis, he argues that the scope of the "centralization versus decentralization" issue in a planned economy is, in principle, limited to the second group of decisions, but it is important to note that this classification is essentially based on the relationship between the central industrial management ministry and its subordinate companies.[10]

On this point, Ellman (1979) stresses the significance of the autonomous behavior of local governments like provincial administrations and others below them, rather than the relationship between the central ministries and their respective enterprises, in the Chinese socialist system, while nonetheless admitting the primary significance of central planning. Many other studies also insist on the importance of local-level autonomy in the Chinese socialist system; for example, Ishihara (1990) highlights the process of decentralization between the central government and local governments by analyzing the Chinese economic management system from the 1950s to the 1970s. Chō (1998) also regards local governments as a distinct unit from the perspective of the political system, labeling it a "multilayered centralized regime."[11]

Tajima (1990, 1994, 2000), meanwhile, characterizes the Chinese socialist system as a "regional economic system"—in which each level of local government controlled its respective domain based on the regional socialization of property rights and resources—by paying attention to the "administrative level-based control system" of local state-owned enterprises, and by exploring the relationships between local fiscal structure and local industries. Of course, as Lardy (1978) pointed out in his research on the decentralized policy in the latter half of the 1950s, it is necessary to note that the primary position of the central government on resource distribution was maintained even as decentralization proceeded. Nevertheless, it is evident that the key distinguishing characteristic of the Chinese socialist system was local government-based decentralization rather than central or enterprise-based decentralization.

---

[10] Brus argues that the reason why the issue of "centralization versus decentralization" in a planned economy is limited to the second group of decisions is that, in a socialist planned economy, at least the decisions of the first group must be made by the central planning authorities, constituting a minimum degree of centralization, while the decisions of the third group are basically made by individuals, constituting a minimum degree of decentralization (for although the central government may influence individual decisions, it does not make decisions on their behalf). Brus (1973, pp. 7–8).

[11] Shū (1997) pointed out that China's state governing system had relatively static institutions of political economy, which he characterized as constituting a "divided state," as well as dynamic interaction between said institutions and each political and economic unit, which he called "organized confusion."

In light of this distinct character of the Chinese socialist system, two more questions arise, namely (1) why was the Chinese socialist system locally decentralized, and (2) how did this arrangement function as a system, and what effect did it have on China's existing (pre-1949) economic structure?

On the first question, some scholars, for example Gurley (1976), see the nature of the system as characteristic of Mao Zedong's model, which had pursued an independent Chinese socialist system distinct from that of the Soviet Union. On the other hand, Kosugi and Okumura insist that it was the result of Mao Zedong's "People's War" strategy, which had its origins in the CCP's guerrilla war style—itself based on achieving regional self-sufficiency during the Second Sino-Japanese War[12]—developed to fight against the US and Soviet Union superpowers (Kosugi 1988; Okumura 1999, pp. 154–155). They argue that the reason why China's leaders adopted a locally decentralized socialist system was to develop their own nuclear weapons and proceed with spontaneous industrialization at relatively low cost during the circumstances in which China found itself without foreign aid due to the Sino-Soviet Union conflict that commenced in 1956. Comparing these two arguments, the war strategy factor appears more persuasive than does an appeal to ideology.

As for the second question, unlike the first this issue has yet to be thoroughly explored. The discussion in previous research of the war strategy factor only serves to explain the reason why a locally decentralized socialist system was adopted, so how it actually functioned as a system, and the effects it had on China's economic structure, remain to be properly studied. To explore these issues, it is necessary to employ a long-term view, including drawing on a case study of a given region to examine the situation before and after the implementation of the socialist system.

However, previous studies on the Chinese socialist system and Chinese economy have lacked this perspective. Recall that research on the Chinese socialist system has followed a bumpy trajectory and not proceeded in a continuous manner. Initially, in the planned economy period, particularly from the latter half of the 1950s, the Chinese socialist system received extensive attention from researchers all over the world because the Chinese government asserted that it was pursuing an independent model of socialist system distinct from that of the Soviet Union. At the same time, due to the Chinese government's restriction on the outflow of information pertaining to its domestic economy, researchers outside of mainland China, such as those located in Japan, Taiwan, and Western countries, made strenuous efforts to lift the veil of mystery and reveal the real situation of the Chinese economy by drawing upon the limited information available to them through the 1960s to 1970s (Ishikawa 1960; Perkins 1966; Donnithorne 1967; Lardy 1978). However, the Reform policy after 1978 prompted researchers to turn their attention to the transitions of the economic system and rapid economic growth at the time. As a result, research on the planned economy period experienced a decline, with the exception of some studies focusing on the initial conditions of economic growth after 1978, or on historical continuities and discontinuities before and after 1949 from the viewpoint of economic history.

[12] Selden (1971) is a classic study of the CCP's guerrilla war style.

The studies produced at this time have distinct benefits but also shortcomings. For example, studies published in China offer detailed information on the outline of institutions and policies from the viewpoint of said institutions, but they lack an analysis of the influence of the changes experienced by those institutions and/or economic policies (Zhongguoshehuikexueyuan jingjiyanjiusuo 1978; He and Wang 1984; Miki 1971; Nambu 1991). On the other hand, studies outside of China focus on statistical analysis on the macro economy as well as the institutions, but due to a lack of information they are limited to exploring micro-economic entities and the relationship between them. Moreover, the most significant problem with these studies is they set the start point of analysis at the establishment of the PRC in 1949 and, therefore, they lack any consideration of continuities and discontinuities in the system before and after 1949. On this point, some Chinese economic studies which regard the planned economy period as the initial condition or historical origin of the rapid economic growth after 1978 suffer from the same problem (Nakagane 1992, 1999, 2012; Shiraishi 2016).

In this sense, the transformation of historical studies on 1950s–1960s China since the 2000s due to the disclosure of post-1949 historical official records in mainland China is a welcome development.[13] Some newer studies sought to explore a longer-term treatment of the development of the Chinese economy across the 1949 and 1978 divides by concentrating on a fixed locale, such as a regional case study of Sichuan (Bramall 1993), case studies of specific industries (Tajima 2005, 2008; Tajima et al. 2010), or treatments of economic policy (Kubo 1996) and market economy (Katō and Kubo 2009; Nakagane 2010). However, heretofore no study comprehensively explores the impact of the implementation of the socialist economic system. Historical studies often regard the 1950s in China as heralding the end of the development of modern private enterprises and the market economy since the latter half of the nineteenth century.[14] Even newer studies on long-term developments in the Chinese economy have also proven unable to bridge the pre- and post-1949 divide fully due to the lack of information and research available on the planned economy period.

Meanwhile, economic history studies of the PRC have developed in the mainland (Wu 1999; Wu and Dong 2001). These studies, however, likewise cannot address the above issues since they do not fully make use of the results of previous research on the economic history of the Republican period and studies of the Chinese economy during the planned economy period that were produced in Western countries, Japan, Taiwan, and Hong Kong.[15]

[13] For example, Izutani (2000, 2001, 2002, all included in Izutani 2007), Zhang (2006), Gui (2006), and Sun (2006).

[14] In the context of previous research on the development of Chinese modern private enterprises since the latter half of the nineteenth century, the completion of the socialist transformation in 1956 is regarded as the end of this development; see Kajima (2008; 2012).

[15] On this point, see Kajima (2007).

1.3 Perspectives and Methodology

This book aims to shed light on the structure and workings of the Chinese socialist economic system, with its regionally decentralized features under an originally centralized institution, and to explore the impact of the socialist transformation on the Chinese economy and society. In order to pursue this objective, the book adopts, first, a historical perspective, tracing the situation before and after the implementation of the socialist economic system in the 1950s, and second, a regional perspective. In particular, the book focuses on the relationship between local governments and enterprises.

As touched on above, Brus (1973) discussed centralization and decentralization in socialist systems by focusing on the relationship between the central ministries for each industry and the respective state-owned enterprises under their control. On this point, Kornai (1980) also explores the relationships between a government and enterprises, and identifies what he calls a "shortage economy" as a specific feature of socialist systems. A "shortage economy" means one in which there is a chronic excess of demand over supply, a primary factor of which he identifies as being the "soft budget constraint" of state-owned enterprises. Managers of state-owned enterprises in socialist economic systems were required to archive production quotas assigned by the government; therefore, they would often make efforts to maintain raw materials and labor forces for production to the greatest extent possible under a "soft budget constraint" situation, which enabled them to exceed budget limitations via governmental subsidies and a negotiable credit system. As a result, the insatiable demand for input goods lead to chronic shortages, or a "shortage economy." Such a characteristic is often seen as a symbol of a socialist system's inefficiency in distribution of production factors.

These discussions serve to illustrate the importance of examining the relationship between government and enterprises when analyzing socialist economic systems. Moreover, if indeed the Chinese socialist economic system was characterized by decentralized features in its central and local government relationships, then the key to understanding the economic activities in said system is the relationships between local governments and local enterprises in a given region, which is why this book adopts just such a perspective.

As a case region, this book focuses on Shanghai, which has been the center of modern industry in China since the latter half of the nineteenth century. The main points this study pursues are, first, how the Shanghai municipal government's control system over the Shanghai economy developed and functioned, and second, how the Shanghai economy was changed by the implementation of the socialist economic system.

The first reason for choosing Shanghai as a case study is that not only was it the locus of China's modern economic development from the late nineteenth century through to the Republican period, but moreover the rate of private enterprises was relatively high at the time of the implementation of the socialist system. Although Northeast China was also important for the PRC government in 1949 due to the succession of Japanese heavy industry inherited from Manchukuo, almost all of the enterprises there had already been nationalized by that time.[16] As discussed above, the socialization of the means of production was one of the distinguishing features of a socialist system, and correspondingly, Shanghai, which prior to 1949 already had many private enterprises, was significantly impacted, relative to the rest of the country, by the implementation of the socialist system.

The second reason is that Shanghai was the Chinese city that experienced the greatest impact of the transition in international relations before and after 1949. As discussed below, the development of Shanghai up until 1949 had been based on the expansion of foreign trade in the wake of the opening of ports and the influx of modern technology and institutions, especially in the foreign settlement. The Chinese economy during the Republican period was strongly tied to the world economy, and modern Shanghai was both a product and symbol of this link. On the other hand, the Korean War and the Cold War in East Asia restrained the economic relationships between China and capitalist countries, and affected the building process of the Chinese socialist economic system in the 1950s. Therefore, exploring the case of Shanghai represents an effective way to shed light on the impact of such international changes on China.

Of course, Shanghai is a distinctive city in terms of its economic scale; neither can it be said to be a typical city, which has implications when it comes to discussing the relationships between local governments and enterprises. Nevertheless, this book focuses on Shanghai due to the relatively large impact of the socialist transformation the city experienced. It is the author's position that a thorough consideration of Shanghai's case will help bring about new insight into the impact of the socialist economic system on China and the role therein in modern Chinese economic history.

1.4 The Structure of This Book

This book consists of three parts comprising a total of twelve chapters. Part I summarizes the general structure of Shanghai's economy and how the socialist economic system developed in Shanghai in the first half of the 1950s. Chapter 2 draws on macro statistics to give an overview of the long-term changes in Shanghai's economy, while Chapters 3 and 4 explore the process of the building of the socialist economic system in Shanghai by focusing on the PRC government's policy toward private enterprises.

Part II discusses China's fiscal and taxation policy during the planned economy period and the impact thereof on Shanghai's local fiscal structure. Chapters 5 and 6 explore how Shanghai's taxation and local fiscal structure changed before and after 1949, and how these were shaped by the socialist transformation in 1956. Chapter 7 provides a regional comparison by utilizing the author's database of provincial-level local public finance in order to clarify Shanghai's position within China as a whole.

[16] On the high rate of nationalization in Northeast China at the time of the founding of the PRC, see Okumura (2001).

Part III takes up the cases of several industries and explores various aspects of each industry under the socialist economic system. Chapter 8 compares Shanghai's textile and machinery industries, the former of which served as the core of Shanghai's modern industry until 1949, and the latter of which was the most supported industry after 1949 due to the PRC government's Heavy-industry-priority Strategy. Chapter 9 focuses on the rubber industry in order to illustrate the change in the originally decentralized industrial organization before and after 1949. Next, Chapter 10 takes up the cement industry to see the relationships between the central government's material distribution policy and the behavior of local enterprises, while Chapter 11 focuses on the power industry, which was characterized by centralized control and interregional cooperation. Finally, Chapter 12 turns to a discussion of the broader historical meaning of the Chinese socialist economic system.

References

English Language

Bramall, Chris. 1993. *In Praise of Maoist Economic Planning: Living Standards and Economic Development in Sichuan since 1931.* Oxford: Clarendon Press

Brus, Włodzimierz. 1973. *The Economics and Politics of Socialism: Collected Essays.* London; Boston: Routledge & K. Paul

Donnithorne, Audrey. 1967. *China's Economic System.* New York: F. A. Praeger

Ellman, Michael. 1979. *Socialist Planning.* 1st edition, Cambridge; New York: Cambridge University Press

Gurley, John G. 1976. *China's Economy and the Maoist Strategy.* New York: Monthly Review Press

Kajima, Jun. 2022. Light Industry: Socialist Industrialization and Textile Industry. In *Studies on the Chinese Economy During the Mao Era*, ed. Katsuji Nakagane, 187–204. Singapore: Springer, Singapore. https://doi.org/10.1007/978-981-19-5410-8_9

Kornai, János. 1980. *Economics of Shortage.* Amsterdam; New York; Oxford: North-Holland Publishing Company

Kornai, János. 1992. *The Socialist System: The Political Economy of Communism.* New York: Oxford University Press

Lardy, Nicholas R. 1978. *Economic Growth and Distribution in China.* Cambridge: Cambridge University Press

Maddison, Angus. 2007. *Chinese Economic Performance in the Long Run.* 2nd edition, Paris: Development Centre of the Organisation for Economic Co-operation and Development

Perkins, Dwight H. 1966. *Market Control and Planning in Communist China.* Cambridge, Massachusetts: Harvard University Press

Schurmann, Franz. 1966. *Ideology and Organization in Communist China.* Berkeley: University of California Press

Selden, Mark. 1971. *The Yenan Way in Revolutionary China.* Cambridge: Harvard University Press

Chinese Language

Gui, Yong. 2006. *Siyou chanquan de shehui jichu: chengshi qiye chanquan de zhengzhi chonggou 1949–1956* (私有产权的社会基础:城市企业产权的政治重构 1949–1956), The Social Foundation of Private Property Rights: The Political Reconstruction of Urban Enterprise Property Rights, 1949–1956). Shanghai: Lixin kuaiji chubanshe

He, Jianzhang and Wang Jiye. 1984. *Zhongguo jihuaguanli wenti* (中国计划管理问题, China Planning Management Issues). Beijing: Zhongguo shehuikexue chubanshe

Sun, Huimin. 2006. Shanghai lüshiye de gaizao yu xiaomie (上海律师业的改造与消灭(1949–1957), The Transformation and Elimination of Shanghai's Legal Profession: 1949–1957). In *Lianganfentu: Lengzhanchuqi de zhengjingfazhan* (两岸分途:冷战初期的政经发展, Parting Ways: Politics and Economics across the Taiwan Straits since 1949), ed. Chen Yongfa, 77–118. Taipei: Institute of Modern History, Academia Sinica

Wu, Chengming and Dong Zhikai, eds. 2001. *Zhonghuarenmingongheguo jingjishi di 1 juan 1949–1952* (中华人民共和国经济史 第1卷 1949–1952, Economic History of the People's Republic of China, Volume 1: 1949–1952). Beijing: Zhongguo caizhengjingji chubanshe

Wu, Li, ed. 1999. *Zhonghuarenmingongheguo jingjishi* (中华人民共和国经济史, Economic History of the People's Republic of China), Volumes I & II. Beijing: Zhongguo jingji chubanshe

Zhang, Xule. 2006. *Shanghai siying jinrongye yanjiu: 1949-1952* (上海私营金融业研究 (1949-1952), Research on Shanghai's Private Financial Industry: 1949-1952). Shanghai: Fudan University Press

Zhongguoshehuikexueyuan jingjiyanjiusuo. 1978. *Zhongguo zibenzhuyigongshangye de shehuizhuyigaizao* (中国资本主义工商业的社会主义改造, The Socialist Transformation of China's Capitalist Industry and Commerce). Beijing: Renmin chubanshe

Japanese Language

Amako, Satoshi et al., eds. 1999. *Gendai chūgoku jiten* (現代中国事典, Encyclopedia of Contemporary China). Tokyo: Iwanami shoten

Chō, Koui. 1998. *Chūgoku no jūsōshūkentaisei to keizaihatten* (中国の重層集権体制と経済発展, China's Multi-layered Centralized System and Economic Development). Tokyo: University of Tokyo Press

Ishihara, Kyōichi. 1990. 1970 nendai madeno chūgokukeizaikanri: shisutemu to jittai (1970年代までの中国経済管理——システムと実態, Chinese Economic Management up to the 1970s: System and Reality). In *Mōtakutōjidai no chūgoku: Gendaichūgokuron 1* (毛沢東時代の中国<現代中国論1>, China in the Mao Zedong Era: Discussions on Contemporary China No.1), ed. Mōri Kazuko, 146–185. Tokyo: Japan Institute of International Affairs

Ishikawa, Shigeru. 1960. *Chūgoku niokeru sihonchikusekikikō* (中国における資本蓄積機構, Capital Accumulation Mechanism in China). Tokyo: Iwanami Shoten

Izutani, Yōko. 2000. Shinchūgoku kenkokushoki no taimin'eikigyōseisaku: 'Minshukaikaku' 'sanhangohanundō' to kisengaishano kōshigōeika (新中国建国初期の対民営企業政策——『民主改革』・『三反五反』運動と汽船会社の公私合営化, The Policy of the People's Republic of China toward Private Enterprise in the Early Period after Its Foundation). *Shakaikeizaishigaku* (社会経済史学, Socio-Economic History) 66(4): 453–468, 485. https://doi.org/10.20624/sehs.66.4_453

Izutani, Yōko. 2001. Chūgoku no shakaishugika to chōsensensou: taishūundou wo tekotoshita sōdōintaisei no kōchiku (中国の社会主義化と朝鮮戦争——大衆運動を梃子とした総動員態勢の構築, China's Socialization and the Korean War: Construction of a Total Mobilization System Using Mass Movements as a Lever). *Rekishigaku kenkyū* (歴史学研究, Journal of Historical Studies) 755 (Special Issue): 145–153

Izutani, Yōko. 2002. Chūkajinminkyōwakoku kenkokushoki no kin'yuseisaku: kin'yugyō no shakaishugikaizou (中華人民共和国建国初期の金融政策——金融業の社会主義改造, Early People's Republic of China's Financial Policy - Socialist Transformation of the Financial Industry). *Ritsumeikan Studies in Language and Culture* (立命館言語文化研究) 13(4): 63–72

Izutani, Yōko. 2004. Chūkajinminkyōwakoku kenkokushoki no kokkaniyoru busshishōakukatei: menbōshokugyō niokeru taishū undō no tenkai wo chūshinni (中華人民共和国建国初期の国家による物資掌握過程——綿紡織業における大衆運動の展開を中心に, The Process of State Control of Materials in the Early People's Republic of China: Focusing on the Development of Mass Movements in the Cotton Spinning Industry). *Rekishigaku kenkyū* (歴史学研究, Journal of Historical Studies) 793: 18–36, 64

Izutani, Yōko. 2007. *Chūgoku kenkokushoki no seiji to Keizai: Taishū undou to shakaishugitaisei* (中国建国初期の政治と経済—— 大衆運動と社会主義体制, Politics and Economy in the Early Years of the People's Republic of China: Mass Movements and the Socialist System). Tokyo: Ochanomizu shobō

Kajima, Jun. 2007. Shohyō Zhang Xianwen nado hencho Zhonghuaminguoshi (Nanjing-daxue chubanshe, 2025nian): Dandaishi no nakano keizaishi jojutsu: Chūkaminkoku to chūkajinminkyōwakoku (書評:張憲文等編著『中華民国史』(南京大学出版社,2005年) 断代史のなかの経済史叙述——中華民国史と中華人民共和国史, Book Review: Zhang Xianwen et al., eds. 'History of the Republic of China' (Nanjing University Press, 2005) Economic History Narrative in the History of the Republic of China and the People's Republic of China). *Chūgoku kenkyū geppō* (中国研究月報, Monthly Journal of Chinese Affairs) 61(5): 11–17

Kajima, Jun. 2008. 1950 nendai chūgoku kenkyū no doukou to kadai: shakaikeizaishi wo chūshinni (1950年代中国研究の動向と課題——社会経済史を中心に, Trends and Issues in Research on the 1950s China: Focusing on Socio-Economic History). *Chikaki ni arite* (近きに在りて, Being Nearby) 53: 64–73

Kajima, Jun. 2012. Keikakukeizaiki no keizaishi (計画経済期の経済史, Economic History of the Planned Economy Period). In *Chūgoku keizaishi nyūmon* (中国経済史入門, Introduction to Chinese Economic History), ed. Kubo Tōru, 175–184. Tokyo: University of Tokyo Press

Katō, Hiroyuki, and Kubo Tōru. 2009. *Shinka suru chūgoku no shihonshugi* (進化する中国の資本主義, Evolving Chinese Capitalism). Tokyo: Iwanami shoten

Katō, Hiroyuki, and Uehara Kazuyoshi, eds. 2004. *Chūgoku keizairon* (中国経済論, Studies on Chinese Economy). Kyoto: Minerva shobō

Kosugi, Shūji. 1988. *Gendai chūgoku no kokkamokuteki to keizaikensetsu: Chōtaikoku shikou, teikaihatsu keizai, shakaishugi* (現代中国の国家目的と経済建設——超大国志向・低開発経済・社会主義, State Objectives and Economic Construction in Contemporary China: Superpower Aspiration, Underdeveloped Economy, Socialism). Tokyo: Ryūkei shosha

Kubo, Tōru. 1996. Kingendai chūgoku ni okeru kokka to Keizai: chūkaminkokuki keizaiseisakush-iron (近現代中国における国家と経済——中華民国期経済政策試論, State and Economy in Modern and Contemporary China: A Tentative Essay on Economic Policy during the Republic of China Period). In *Rekishi no nakano gendaichūgoku* (歴史のなかの現代中国, Modern and Contemporary China in History), ed. Tatsuo Yamada, 82–116. Tokyo: Keisō shobō

Kubo, Tōru, Kajima Jun, Kigoshi Yoshinori. 2016. *Tōkei de miru chūgoku kingendai keizaishi* (統計でみる中国近現代経済史, Economic History of Modern China: An Approach Based on Statistical data). Tokyo: University of Tokyo Press

Kuroda, Akinobu. 1994. *Chūka teikoku no kōzō to sekaikeizai* (中華帝国の構造と世界経済, Structure of the Chinese Empire and World Economy). Nagoya: The University of Nagoya Press

Miki, Takeshi. 1971. *Chūgoku kaifukuki no keizaiseisaku: Shinminshushugi keizairon* (中国回復期の経済政策——新民主主義経済論, Economic Policy in China's Recovery Period: New Democratic Economy). Tokyo: Kawashima shoten

Minami, Ryoshin, and Makino Fumio, eds. 2014. *Ajia chōki keizaitōkei 3: Chūgoku* (アジア長期経済統計3——中国, Asian Historical Statistics 3: China). Tokyo: Tōyō keizai Shinpōsha

Mōri, Kazuko. 1990. Shakaishugi no henyō to tonza shita chūgoku no kaikaku (社会主義の変容と頓挫した中国の改革, Transformation of Socialism and China's Stalled Reform). *Jinmin no rekishigaku* (人民の歴史学, People's History) 105: 8–15

Nakagane, Katsuji. 1979. Chūgoku: Shakaishugi keizaiseido no kōzō to tenkai (中国——社会主義経済制度の構造と展開, China: Structure and Development of the Socialist Economic System). In *Keizai taiseiron, dai 4 kan: gendaishakaishugi* (経済体制論 第IV巻 現代社会主義, Economic System Theory, Volume IV: Contemporary Socialism), ed. Masayuki Iwata, 263–313. Tokyo: Tōyō keizai shinpōsha

Nakagane, Katsuji. 1992. *Chūgoku keizairon: Noukoukankei no seijikeizaigaku* (中国経済論——農工関係の政治経済学, The Political Economy of Agro-industrial Relationships in Contemporary China). Tokyo: University of Tokyo Press

Nakagane, Katsuji. 1999. *Chūgoku keizai hattenron* (中国経済発展論, Economic Development and Transition in China). Tokyo: Yūhikaku

Nakagane, Katsuji, ed. 2010. *Rekishitekishiya karamita gendaichūgokukeizai* (歴史的視野からみた現代中国経済, Contemporary Chinese Economy from a Historical Perspective). Tokyo: Tōyō bunko

Nakagane, Katsuji. 2012. *Kaihatsu keizaigaku to gendai chūgoku* (開発経済学と現代中国, Development Economics and Contemporary China). Nagoya: The University of Nagoya Press

Nambu, Minoru. 1991. *Gendai chūgoku no zaiseikinyūseisaku* (現代中国の財政金融政策, Fiscal and Financial Policies of Contemporary China). Tokyo: Taga shuppan

Oka, Minoru, Miyanabe Noboru, Yamanouchi Kazuo, Takenami Shoichirō. 1976. *Shakaishugi keizairon* (社会主義経済論, Studies on Socialist Economy). Tokyo: Chikuma shobō

Okamoto, Takashi, ed. 2013. *Chūgoku keizaishi* (中国経済史, Chinese Economic History). Nagoya: The University of Nagoya Press

Okumura, Satoshi. 1999. *Chūgoku no gendaishi: Sensō to shakaishugi* (中国の現代史——戦争と社会主義, Modern History of China: War and Socialism). Tokyo: Aoki Shoten

Okumura, Satoshi. 2001. Chūgoku niokeru shihonshugi to shakaishugi: Tōhoku no ichi ni chūmokushite (中国における資本主義と社会主義——東北の位置に注目して, Capitalism and Socialism in China: Focusing on the Position of the Northeast). In *Kōza higashiajia kingendaishi 2: Higashiajia keizai no kiseki* (講座東アジア近現代史2 東アジア経済の軌跡, Lecture on Modern and Contemporary History of East Asia 2: The Trajectory of East Asian Economy), ed. Uemura Yasuo, Sakuradani Katsumi, Hori Kazuo, 109–138. Tokyo: Aoki shoten

Saito, Osamu. 2008. *Hikaku keizai hattenron: Rekishiteki apurōchi* (比較経済発展論——歴史的アプローチ, Comparative Economic Development: A Historical Approach). Tokyo: Iwanami shoten

Shiokawa, Nobuaki. 1999. *Genzonshita shakaishugi: Leviathan no sugao* (現存した社会主義——リケアイアサンの素顔, Socialism that existed: The Real Face of Leviathan). Tokyo: Keisō Shobō

Shiraishi, Maho. 2016. *Keikakukeizai no jisshōbunseki: Chūgokuno keizaikaihatsu* (計画経済の実証分析——中国の経済開発, Empirical Analysis of Planned Economy: Economic Development of China). Kyoto: Kyoto University Press

Shū, Shōhou. 1997. Shikirareta kokka, soshikisareta konran: Chūgoku niokeru kokka, shokuba, kojin (仕切られた国家・組織された混乱——中国における国家・職場・個人, Controlled State, Organized Chaos: State, Workplace and Individual) in *Gendai chūgoku* (現代中国, Modern China) 71: 87–98

Tajima, Toshio. 1990. Chūgoku no keizaihendō: Daiyakushin shōyakushin to keizaikaikaku (中国の経済変動——大躍進・小躍進と経済改革, Economic Fluctuations in China: Great Leap Forward, Small Leap Forward and Economic Reform). *Ajia keizai* (アジア経済, Asian Economy) 31(4): 41–60. http://hdl.handle.net/2261/7480

Tajima, Toshio. 1994. Chūgoku no kokuyūkigyōkaikaku to seihukan zaiseikankei (中国の国有企業改革と政府間財政関係, Reform of State-owned Enterprises and Inter-governmental Fiscal Relations in China). *Chūgoku kenkyū geppō* (中国研究月報, Monthly Journal of Chinese Affairs) 48(4): 2-31

Tajima, Toshio. 2000. Chūgoku no zaiseikinyū seidokaikaku: Zokuchiteki keizai system no keisei to henyō (中国の財政金融制度改革——属地的経済システムの形成と変容, Reform of China's Fiscal and Financial System: Formation and Transformation of Territorial Economic System). In *Gendai chūgoku no kōzōhendō 2 keizai: Kōzōhendō to shijōka* (現代中国の構造変動2 経済——構造変動と市場化, Structural Changes in Contemporary China, Volume 2, Economy: Structural Changes and Marketization), ed. Nakagane Katsuji, 73-106. Tokyo: University of Tokyo Press

Tajima, Toshio, ed. 2005. *20 seiki no chūgoku kagakukōgyō: Eiri kagaku tengen denka to sono jidai* (20世紀の中国化学工業——永利化学・天原電化とその時代, The Origins and Development of China's Chemical Industry), Institute of Social Science Research Series No.17, 165–205. Tokyo: Institute of Social Science, The University of Tokyo

Tajima, Toshio, ed. 2008. *Gendai chūgoku no denryoku Sangyō: 'Fusoku no keizai' to sangyōsoshiki* (現代中国の電力産業——「不足の経済」と産業組織, Electric Power Industry in Contemporary China: 'Economy of Shortage' and Industrial Organization). Kyoto: Shōwadō

Tajima, Toshio, Shu Yinki, Kajima Jun, eds. 2010. *Chūgoku cement sangyō no hatten: Sangyōsoshiki to kōzōhenka* (中国セメント産業の発展——産業組織と構造変化, Development of China's Cement Industry: Industrial Organization and Structural Change). Tokyo: Ochanomizu shobō

Wada, Haruki. 1992. *Rekishi toshiteno shakaishugi* (歴史としての社会主義, Socialism as History). Tokyo: Iwanami shoten

Part I
The Shanghai Economy and the Formation of the Socialist System

Chapter 2
Profile of the Shanghai Economy

Abstract This chapter aims to provide a context for the overall discussion, in the form of an overview of the process of development experienced by Shanghai's economy until 1949, while drawing on macro statistics to illustrate the structural changes Shanghai's economy underwent in the second half of the twentieth century. The development of Shanghai's economy through the Republican period was driven by various domestic and foreign private economic entities responding to China's expanding foreign trade after the opening of the ports. By contrast, after 1949, with the establishment of the Chinese Communist Party regime and the introduction of the socialist system, such private economic activities came under government control. The rapid development of Shanghai's heavy industry under the socialist system and the impact of the "Heavy-industry-priority Strategy" in the planned economy period changed the structure of Shanghai's industry, which had previously been centered on light industry in the Republican period. Furthermore, the significant decline in Shanghai's role as a foreign trade port triggered by the Korean War in the early 1950s meant that the conditions that had characterized Shanghai's economy up until the Republican period substantially transformed.

Keywords Shanghai economy · History of Shanghai · Shanghai Municipality · Heavy-industry-priority Strategy · Foreign trade

Wu Guozhen (吴国桢), who became the mayor of Shanghai after the Second World War (in office from May 1946 to April 1949), described Shanghai during his tenure as the "nerve center of China" (Pei et al. 1999, p. 30). What he was getting at was the notion that Shanghai was able to influence the entire Chinese economy, indicating the economic importance of Shanghai within China at the time. As touched on in the introduction, one of the reasons why Shanghai makes an excellent case study is its significant economic presence. But how did this come about in the first place? What historical processes caused the Shanghai economy to develop to such an extent, and what changes did its structure undergo through the course of the planned economy period after 1949? This chapter aims to provide a context for the overall discussion of the book, in the form of an overview of the process of development experienced

J. Kajima, *Shanghai under the Socialist System*, Studies in Economic History,
https://doi.org/10.1007/978-981-95-3225-4_2

by Shanghai's economy until 1949, while drawing on macro statistics to illustrate the structural changes it underwent in the second half of the twentieth century.

2.1 The Emergence of "Shanghai Municipality"

The process by which "Shanghai Municipality," the very subject of analysis in this book, came about as an administrative unit, is somewhat complex.[1] The origins of Shanghai as a city are said to date back to the establishment of a market on the banks of the Huangpu River in the tenth century, against a backdrop of the development of both the Lower Yangtze Delta and the market economy in China. In the mid-thirteenth century, at the end of the Southern Song Dynasty, Shanghai Town was established in Huating County (later Songjiang County). Shanghai Town was upgraded to a county in 1292 during the Yuan Dynasty, becoming Shanghai County, Songjiang Prefecture. In 1553, a county castle (a wall surrounding the county center) was built as a defensive measure against wokou/wakō (倭寇, so-called Japanese pirates), and it developed as an outer port of Suzhou, the leading economic center in Jiangnan.

A significant turning point for Shanghai was the establishment of Western concessions in the northern part of Shanghai County following the opening of the port, one of several opened as a result of the settlement that ended the First Opium War in 1843. After the establishment of the British concession in 1845, the US and France followed suit (the British and American concessions merged in 1863 and were thereafter referred to as the International Settlement). In these concessions, foreigners benefitted from extraterritoriality, and the area occupied by these concessions also expanded over time. Meanwhile, in parts of Shanghai County outside the concessions, attempts were made to form a city dominated by Chinese, and in 1927, Shanghai Special City (later renamed Shanghai City in 1930) was established by the Nanjing National Government of the ROC, creating a situation where foreign concessions and areas under Chinese government control coexisted. After the occupation of the concessions by the Japanese military during the Second World War, followed by the return of the concessions to the pro-Japanese Wang Jingwei regime (1940–1945), Shanghai City was finally established in 1945 as a single administrative unit, a situation that has persisted down to the present (Osaka shiritsudaigaku keizaikenkyūjo 1986, pp. 29–30).

However, the boundaries of Shanghai Municipality changed even after the establishment of the PRC in 1949. As of May 1949, the area comprising Shanghai City Municipality amounted to 636.18 km^2, including 20 urban districts (82.40 km^2) and 10 suburban districts (529.43 km^2).[2] However, in 1958, the incorporation of 10 neighboring counties (Jiading, Baoshan, Shanghai, Songjiang, Jinshan, Nanhui,

[1] The following description of the formation of Shanghai Municipality is mainly based on Osaka shiritsudaigaku keizaikenkyūjo (1986, pp. 19–23), Takahashi and Furumaya (1995, pp. 2–233), Onoe (1971, pp. 257–327), Miyata (2006, pp. 15–22), and Okamoto (2013, p. 206).

[2] As of May 1949, the city districts were Huangpu, Laozha, Xincheng, Jing'an, Jiangning, Putuo, Changning, Yimiao, Penglai, Songshan, Luwan, Changshu, Xuhui, Zhaobei, Beizhan, Hongkou,

Chuansha, Fengxian, Qingpu, and Chongming) belonging to Jiangsu Province into Shanghai Municipality increased the city's area to 5910.01 km^2, more than nine times its previous size.[3] At that time, all of the previous suburban districts were reorganized into suburban counties (i.e., counties belonging to the city), and after the merger and adjustment of the urban districts, a system resulted in which 10–12 urban districts (140.86 km^2) were surrounded by 10 suburban counties (Fig. 2.1). This structure essentially endured until the 1980s.[4]

The opening of the port in 1843 was a major milestone for the long-term development of Shanghai's economy. As mentioned above, Shanghai had been developing as a hub of domestic trade even before the opening of the port, and from the latter half of the eighteenth century in particular it had become a key point in the coastal trade networks (沿海市场圈) connecting the coastal regions of the Northeast, the lower Yangtze, and South China (Miyata 2006, pp. 15–22; Takahashi and Furumaya 1995, pp. 28–33). However, it is also true that the influx of modern technology and systems due to the opening of the port as well as the simultaneous expansion of foreign trade served to guide the unique development of Shanghai thereafter. The process of the development of the Shanghai economy from 1843 to 1949 can be roughly divided into four periods, each of which will now be outlined.[5]

2.1.1 From the Opening of the Port to the First World War (1843–1914)

It was not simply the case that after the opening of the port Shanghai's foreign trade immediately expanded dramatically; in fact, the entry of Western steamship companies at first could be said to have just strengthened the existing domestic coastal trade networks (Miyata, 2006). Rather, the full-scale development of foreign trade occurred after the 1880s, when the export of primary products grew in the wake of the drop in international silver prices. As a result, Shanghai formed the treaty port trade networks (开港场市场圈) that included in its hinterland the production areas of export primary products, establishing thereby its position as a hub of not

---

Beisichuan Road, Tilanqiao, Yulin, and Yangpu; meanwhile, the suburbs consisted of Xinshi, Jiangwan, Wusong, Dachang, Zhenru, Xinjing, Longhua, Gaoqiao, and Yangjing. Additionally, the area of Shanghai City included 24.35 km^2 of the water surface area of the Huangpu and Suzhou Rivers, which was itself later increased to 47.13 km^2 due to the incorporation of neighboring counties in 1958 (Shanghaishi tongjiju 1984, p. 51; 2001, pp. 3–5).

[3] In that year, the old suburbs were reorganized to create Pudong County, but it was abolished in 1961, with the rural area turned into Chuansha County and the urban suburbs into the Huangpu, Nanshi, and Yangpu districts. On top of this, in 1970 the suburbs expanded, whereupon the city area expanded to 6,185.48 km^2 (Shanghaishi tongjiju 2001, pp. 4–5).

[4] From the late 1980s, there was a notable trend of converting existing suburbs into city districts (Shanghaishi tongjiju 2001, pp. 4–5).

[5] The following description is based mainly on Onoe (1971, pp. 257–327), Shanghai shehuikexueyuan jingjisuo (1980, pp. 1–42), and Takahashi and Furumaya (1995).

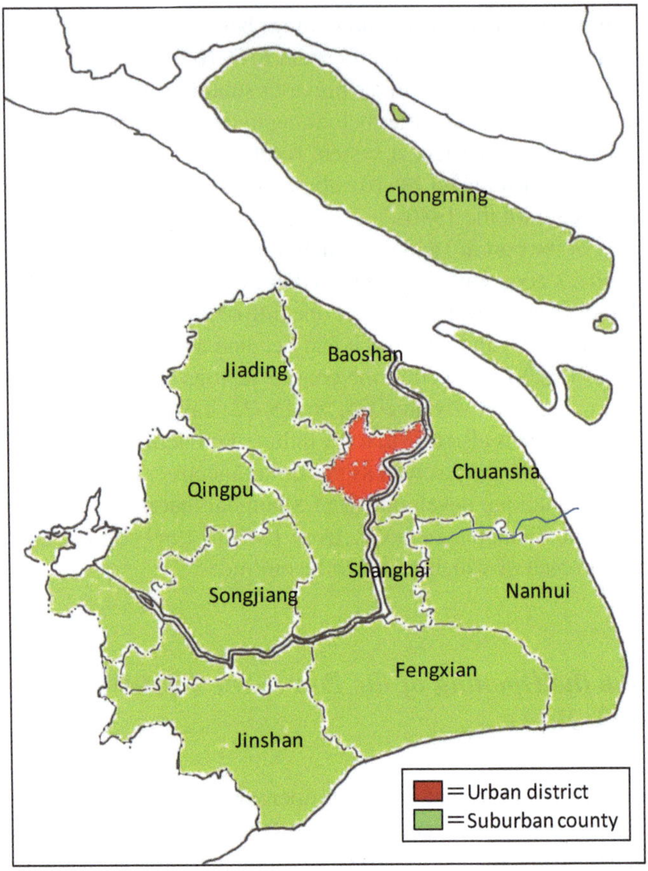

Fig. 2.1 Map of Shanghai Municipality, 1958. *Source* Based on Osaka shiritsudaigaku keizaikenkyūjo (1986, p. 229, Figure IV-1-12). Original map from Shanghai shehuikexueyuan shanghai jingjinianjian bianjibu (1983), opening matter

only domestic but also foreign trade in East Asia (Furuta 2000; Kigoshi 2012). Moreover, the Western concessions formed in Shanghai became a base for the inflow of modern technology and systems, and due to their relatively high security, they also absorbed many wealthy Chinese (landlords and merchants) and workers from the lower Yangtze Delta area, especially during the Taiping Rebellion (1851–64).

The emergence of modern industry in Shanghai was predicated on a foundation of the accumulation of commerce and finance centered on these port areas. It began with the construction of docks by foreign companies associated with the entry of the steamship industry, the latter development becoming even more substantial when the participation of foreign companies in manufacturing in the port areas was approved by the Treaty of Shimonoseki in 1895. On the other hand, modern factories built with Chinese capital were established under governmental leadership, examples being the Jiangnan Manufacturing Bureau (江南制造局), a state-owned military arsenal in 1865, and the Shanghai Machine Weaving Bureau (上海机器织布局), the first Chinese mechanical cotton industry enterprise founded and managed by private capital under government supervision, in 1880 (Hatano 1961; Suzuki 1992). At the same time, small private factories also appeared, such as the Fachang Machinery Factory (发昌机器厂), a private ship and machinery repair factory, initially established before 1863 and outfitted with modern equipment no later than 1869 (Xu and Huang 1998, pp. 44–45).

2.1.2 From the First World War to the Second Sino-Japanese War (1914–1937)

The turning point for Shanghai's industrialization was the outbreak of the First World War. When imports of industrial products from Europe were cut off and the prices of said products in China soared, a boom in private enterprise establishment, later called the "golden age," occurred in Shanghai. The center of the boom was the cotton industry, where Chinese companies rose through competition with Japanese-run cotton companies in China called zaikabō (在华纺). During the boom, companies representing Chinese private capital, such as Shenxin Textile Factory (established in 1915), were born. Moreover, private enterprises in various industries also emerged, mainly in light industry, such as flour milling, tobacco manufacturing, the chemical industry, matches, and cement. These industrial enterprises were basically import-substituting ones that made products for the domestic market, and their growth was deeply tied to the increase in income in the domestic agricultural sector that had arisen from a sustained increase in primary product exports and the expansion of industrial product demand. Shanghai's industrialization was also fueled by the supply of raw materials from the domestic agricultural sector. Such domestic trade, mainly between the lower Yangtze Delta (including Shanghai) and the middle and upper reaches of the Yangtze River, formed a strong economic relationship that some have referred to as the Yangtze River trade networks (长江市场圈) (Kigoshi 2012, Chapter 4).

The Nanjing National Government, which was established in 1927 and became the central government of China, based its operations on the gradual integration of the domestic economy centered around Shanghai, and so furthered Shanghai's industrial development, an aim that was also served by the recovery of tariff autonomy and the government's setting of protective tariffs on industrial products. The situation appeared to be threatened when international fluctuations in silver prices occurring after the onset of the Great Depression in 1929 greatly shook the Chinese economy, ultimately triggering a financial panic in Shanghai in 1934 (Shiroyama 2011, Part II). However, the currency reform by the National Government in 1935 brought about the transition from the silver standard as well as the unification of national currency in the form of the "Legal Tender Note" (法币, Fabi), and aided in driving economic recovery from the panic (Kubo 1999, Chapter 8). Despite the Northeast region being separated from the ROC due to the establishment of Manchukuo by

Japan in 1932, economic integration within the ROC, centering on Shanghai, had substantially progressed by 1937.

2.1.3 The Second Sino-Japanese War (1937–1945)

Not long after the Second Sino-Japanese War broke out in July 1937, Shanghai became a battlefield in the Battle of Shanghai (Aug. 13–Nov. 26, 1937), at the conclusion of which the entire city outside the concessions came under Japanese military occupation. Some of the facilities of private Chinese factories were relocated inland to Sichuan, Guizhou, Hunan, and so forth, along with the relocation of the National Government to Chongqing,[6] while other companies were either placed under the management of Japanese companies after being initially managed by the Imperial Japanese Army, or took refuge in the concessions where security was maintained by the Western countries. Those companies that took refuge in the concessions enjoyed a boom called "prosperity during the isolated island period" ("孤岛"时期的繁荣) due to favorable conditions such as the continuation of domestic and foreign trade along with the influx of refugees providing cheap labor.

However, when the Pacific War (1941–1945) broke out in December 1941, all areas of Shanghai, including the concessions, became subject to Japanese rule. British and American companies were placed under Japanese control, as were Chinese companies, the latter under the name of delegated management by Japanese companies and Sino-Japanese joint management. Moreover, during this time economic activities in Shanghai generally shrank due to the imposition of strict material control. Above all, the disruption of both foreign trade, which had characterized Shanghai's development since the opening of the port, and the domestic trade relations centered on the Yangtze River basin that had been formed before the war, were a major blow for the Shanghai economy.

2.1.4 Postwar National Government Period (1945–1949)

After the Second World War, Shanghai returned to its position as the center of the national economy. Although the territory of the ROC after the war was reorganized to include Taiwan and the Northeast region, in 1946 Shanghai's imports accounted for 85% of the national total, its exports 62%, domestic inflows 31%, and outflows 68% (Haiguan zongshuiwusishu tongjike 1947, pp. 124, 129). There were certainly

[6] During the relocation inland, the Shanghai Factory Relocation Supervision Committee (上海工厂迁移监督委员会) and the Shanghai Factory Union Relocation Committee (上海工厂连合迁移委员会) were established to oversee the process. The breakdown of the 146 private factories relocated inland is as follows: 66 in the machinery and metal industry, 4 in shipbuilding, 1 in steelmaking, 18 in electrical appliances, 5 in glass and ceramics, 20 in the chemical industry, 14 in culture and printing, 7 in textile dyeing, 6 in food, and 5 in other (Takahashi and Furumaya 1995, p. 207).

challenges: when it came to manufacturing, there were factors hindering recovery, such as a massive influx of United Nations relief supplies, a surge in imports due to the hasty trade liberalization policy of the National Government, and a short supply of electricity relative to the demand. However, on the other hand, there were also favorable conditions, such as an increased demand for postwar light industrial products, as well as the withdrawal of Japanese products, which had been competing with Chinese products before the war, from the market.[7]

Perhaps what most significantly hindered the recovery of Shanghai's economy in the postwar years was the National Government's monetary policy and the resulting inflation. First, the collection exchange rate of the reserve banknotes issued by the Wang Jingwei regime (issued in the central and southern regions centered on Shanghai during the war) with the National Government's Legal Tender Notes was set unfairly low, leading to a surge in prices in the old reserve banknote circulation areas (Kigoshi 2012, Chapter 7). Furthermore, as the civil war between the Guomindang (GMD, or Nationalist Party, 中国国民党) and the Chinese Communist Party (CCP, 中国共产党) intensified, the National Government increased the issuance of Legal Tender Notes due to increased military spending, triggering hyperinflation and plunging the Shanghai economy into chaos (Miyashita 1967, pp. 35–36). Although the National Government issued the Gold Yuan Note in August 1948 to replace the Legal Tender Note, it was unable to maintain the new currency's value, and consequently Shanghai faced military occupation by the CCP amid record hyperinflation.

The upshot of the processes covered in these four periods is that after the opening of the port, Shanghai had become the economic center of China through a combination of external factors, such as the expansion of foreign trade, the establishment of concessions, and the entry of foreign companies, and internal factors, such as the growth of domestic trade, the accumulation of commerce and finance, and the development of light industries. Although its economic development was certainly influenced by various political and military factors—such as the policies of successive Chinese governments, the Second Sino-Japanese War, and the Chinese Civil War between the Nationalists and the Communists—it was essentially shaped by the vigorous activities of private economic entities responding to domestic and international market trends. The private economic entities here included farmers producing primary products for export, Chinese merchants and foreign trading companies handling the export of domestic products and the import of foreign products, Chinese and foreign industrial companies producing goods mainly for the Chinese domestic market, and finally financial institutions supporting these activities financially. In this sense, the economic development of Shanghai from the start when the port was opened can be said to have embodied the mutual reactions of various economic entities that arose in the long process of the Chinese economy being incorporated into the world economy from the mid-nineteenth century to the mid-twentieth.

[7] Jin (2006, pp. 93–97); Shanghaishi gongshangxingzhengguanliju and Shanghaishi xiangjiaogongyegongsi shiliaogongzuozu (1979, p. 56); also see Chapter 9 of this book.

2.2 The Shanghai Economy in the Long Run

The previous section traced the development of Shanghai's economy up through the end of the Republican period. Having established its origins and character, it is now pertinent to turn to this book's main concern and begin clarifying how this economy was transformed through the introduction of the socialist system in the 1950s. By way of a first step to approach the issue, it is helpful to look at the long-term transition of the Shanghai economy by considering the available macro statistics. As already mentioned, Shanghai city as a single administrative division was only something that came into being after the Second World War, and the statistics used here are mainly those from after 1949, except for some that refer to the Republican period. Moreover, for a comparative perspective, this section will also consider data from the Reform period in the 1980s and beyond.

First of all, a sense of the economic scale and industrial structure of Shanghai can be gleaned from Table 2.1, which shows the nominal GDP as recorded in official statistics from the People's Republic of China. The ratio of Shanghai's GDP (the total value added produced in the area) to the national total GDP rose from 5.4% in 1952 to 10.9% in 1960, when the Great Leap Forward policy was underway (1958–60). Since 1990, the ratio has been declining, falling below 5%. This may seem somewhat surprising given the popular image of Shanghai's development since the 1990s, best represented by the development of the Pudong New District (浦东新区), but as far as the official statistics indicate in terms of GDP ratio to the national total, the situation of Shanghai's economy during the Reform period shrunk in comparison with what it had been during the planned economy period. Conversely, this means that Shanghai during the planned economy period occupied an extremely important position.

Secondly, regarding the industrial structure, secondary industry accounted for more than half thereof at 52.4% in 1952, with tertiary industry following at 41.7%. What is impressive is that secondary industry expanded further in the 1950s, reaching 77.9% in 1960, and consistently maintained levels over 70% until 1980. This expansion of secondary industry brought about a relative reduction in tertiary industry, including commerce and finance, which had characterized Shanghai's economy up to the Republican period, and after 1960 its share dropped to around 20%. These statistics support the assessment of Takahashi and Furumaya (1995), which described the change in Shanghai's economy from the Republican to planned economy periods as Shanghai having transitioned "from a multifunctional city to a production city" (Takahashi and Furumaya 1995, p. 249). The share of tertiary industry began to recover significantly only after entering the 1990s with the Reform period.

Table 2.2 provides a closer look at Shanghai's manufacturing industries, which served as the core of the economy's secondary industry. Here, the statistics primarily come from the 1933 figures based on Liu Dajun (刘大钧)'s "China Industrial Survey Report" (中国工业调查报告) and related research results. The figures in the table give the Gross Industrial Output Value, which is the total output value including intermediate goods production.

Table 2.1 Shanghai's regional GDP (nominal) and industrial structure, 1952–2010 (Unit: 100 million yuan)

Year	Shanghai	To national total (%)	Primary industry (%)	Secondary industry (%)	Tertiary industry (%)
1952	36.7	5.4	5.9	52.4	41.7
1957	69.6	6.5	3.9	58.7	37.5
1960	158.4	10.9	2.7	77.9	19.4
1965	113.6	6.6	5.7	73.0	21.3
1970	156.7	6.9	4.7	77.1	18.1
1975	204.1	6.8	4.0	77.2	18.8
1978	272.8	7.5	4.0	77.4	18.6
1980	311.9	6.9	3.2	75.7	21.1
1990	781.7	4.2	4.4	64.7	30.9
2000	4,771.2	4.8	1.6	46.3	52.1
2010	17,166.0	4.2	0.7	42.1	57.3

Sources Shanghai, 1952–2000: Shanghaishi tongjiju and Guojia tongjiju shanghai diaochazongdui (2009, pp. 68–69). 2010: Shanghaishi tongjiju and Guojia tongjiju shanghai diaochazongdui (2013, p. 60). National total, 1952–2000: Guojia tongjiju guominjingjizonghetongjisi (2010, p. 9). 2010: Zhonghuarenmingongheguo guojiatongjiju (2015, p. 58)

The first point to take note of in Table 2.2 is that the ratio of Shanghai's industries to the whole country in 1933 was as high as 48.1%. This figure was likely influenced by the nature of the original survey, which did not include small-scale factories such as handicrafts. However, it nevertheless illustrates Shanghai's prominent position in the modern Chinese industrial sector at the time. As for the situation after 1949, there was a gradual downward trend in the presence of Shanghai's industries vis-à-vis. the country as a whole. The ratio of Shanghai to the whole country decreased from 19.1% in 1952 to the high 10s after the mid-1950s, and by the 1970s it had dropped to less than 15%. Considering that Shanghai was biased toward secondary industry throughout the planned economy period, as shown in Table 2.1, and that, moreover, Shanghai's industrial production value was (despite some ups and downs) basically increasing through the period, this decrease in the ratio to the whole country has been understood as the result of concentrated investment in the inland areas represented by the Third Front Construction (三线建设) campaign and the decentralization of industrial bases (Kosugi 1988, pp. 194–198). Furthermore, after 1990, the ratio of Shanghai's industries to the country as a whole only further decreased. This was possibly influenced by the fact that Shanghai's industrial function expanded outwardly to neighboring Jiangsu and Zhejiang provinces during the same period (Seki 1997, pp. 24–28).

The ratio of light industry to heavy industry in industrial production, as shown in Table 2.2, confirms that Shanghai was a city that embodied China's industrial development during the Republican period centered on light industry, given the nearly

Table 2.2 Shanghai's gross industrial output value and the ratios of light and heavy industry, 1933–2010 (Unit: 100 million yuan)

Year	Shanghai	To national total (%)	Light industry (%)	Heavy industry (%)
1933	*10.5	48.1	79.3	18.3
1952	66.6	19.1	79.3	20.7
1957	118.8	16.9	71.0	29.0
1960	299.0	18.3	45.0	55.0
1965	230.8	16.5	56.1	43.9
1970	312.2	14.7	51.9	48.1
1975	420.4	13.1	48.5	51.5
1978	514.0	12.1	51.8	48.2
1980	598.8	11.6	55.3	44.7
1990	1,642.8	6.9	51.5	48.5
2000	7,023.0	8.2	41.3	58.7
2010	31,038.6	4.4	21.6	78.4

Notes *is a figure in the unit of Legal Tender Notes of the National Government, 100 million yuan. The figure only includes the data of factories which used motor power and employed over 30 staff and workers, and it also includes the data of foreign companies and companies in Manchukuo in Northeast region. The "Heavy industry" in 1933 includes "metallurgy and refining," "manufacturing of machine, metal and transformation appliances," "chemical industry," "building materials" and "water and electricity." The "Light industry" includes "textile industry," "garment industry," "leather industry," "rubber industry," "food industry," and "papermaking and printing industry." The breakdown of heavy industry and light industry after 1952 are unknown

Sources Shanghai 1933: Xu and Huang (1998, pp. 338–339). Original data from Liu (1937) etc. 1952–2000: Shanghaishi tongjiju and Guojia tongjiju shanghai diaochazongdui (2009, pp. 276–279). 2010: Shanghaishi tongjiju and Guojia tongjiju shanghai diaochazongdui (2013, p. 252). National total 1933: Huang (1989, p. 66), Note 1. Original data from Wu (1947, Chapter 3, Table 1); Wang (1947). 1952–2000: Guojia tongjiju guominjingjizonghetongjisi (2010, p. 40). 2010: Guojia tongjiju gongyetongjisi (2012, p. 21)

80% light industry ratio in 1933 and 1952. This light industry-centered structure changed significantly during the period of the Great Leap Forward policy in 1958–60, when, for example, the heavy industry ratio exceeded light industry for the first time in 1960 at 55.0%. Although the heavy industry ratio temporarily decreased in 1965, this structure, where light industry and heavy industry competed at around the 50% level, continued into the 1970s. This structural change in the rise of the heavy industry ratio is in line with the industrialization of China as a whole as outlined in the introduction. However, on the other hand, it is also important to note that light industry in Shanghai maintained a share of about 50% until 1990. Therefore, it would be best to understand Shanghai during the planned economy period as an industrial city that had both light industry, developed up to the Republican period, and heavy industry, where investment was intensively carried out under the socialist system.

What about foreign trade, which had characterized the development of Shanghai since the late nineteenth century? Table 2.3 shows the transition in Shanghai's imports and exports and the ratio thereof to China as a whole, including figures from the customs statistics for the Republican period from 1912 to 1936. The first point to note here is Shanghai's prominent position as a trading port during the Republican period, with its ratio to the country as a whole accounting for 40–50% of both imports and exports throughout the 1912 to 1936 era. On the other hand, after 1949, these values declined to reach 14.5% for exports and merely 0.5% for imports in 1952, and since then the ratio of trade value to China as a whole has remained dramatically and consistently much lower than was the case in the Republican period.

During the planned economy period, as will be described in more detail later, China was essentially prohibited from trading with the capitalist bloc due to the former's participation in the Korean War in 1950, whereupon its main trading partners shifted to the Soviet Union and Eastern Europe in the 1950s and 1960s (Kubo

Table 2.3 Shanghai imports and exports, 1912–2010 (Unit: 100 million US$)

Year	Import (A)	To national total (%)	Export (B)	To national total (%)
1912	#1.7	44.7	#2.1	43.2
1926	#3.6	41.9	#6.0	52.1
1936	*3.6	51.3	*5.6	58.8
1952	1.2	14.5	0.1	0.5
1957	4.5	28.3	0.4	2.5
1960	6.2	33.4	0.5	2.7
1965	7.7	34.3	0.6	3.0
1970	8.7	38.4	0.5	2.0
1975	22.2	30.6	1.1	1.4
1978	28.9	29.7	1.3	1.2
1980	42.7	23.5	2.4	1.2
1990	53.2	8.6	21.1	4.0
2000	253.5	10.2	293.6	13.0
2010	1,807.8	11.5	1,880.9	13.5

Note (1) #=Haikwan tael (海关两, 100 million tael), * =Legal Tender Note (100 million yuan). "To national total" in 1936 does not include Manchukuo, Northeastern region. (2) According to a note in the original source, the figures from 1952 to 1990 for Shanghai are based on the statistical standard of Shanghaishi shangwuweiyuanhui (上海市商务委员会, the former Shanghaishi waijingmaowei 上海市外经贸委), and those after 2000 are from the statistics of the Chinese Customs. Also, the figures for the national total before 1978 are from the statistics of Waimao yewu tongji (外贸业务统计), and those after 1980 are from the statistics of Chinese Customs

Source Shanghai 1912–1936: Hsiao (1974, pp. 175–176). 1952–2000: Shanghaishi tongjiju and Guojia tongjiju shanghai diaochazongdui (2009, pp. 152–153). 2010: Shanghaishi tongjiju and Guojia tongjiju shanghai diaochazongdui (2013, p. 141). National 1912–1936: Hsiao (1974, pp. 22–25). 1952–2000: Guojia tongjiju guominjingjizonghetongjisi (2010, p. 60). 2010: Zhonghuarenmin-gongheguo guojiatongjiju (2015, p. 356)

et al. 2016, pp. 142–147). The trade volume during the same period was modest, growing from exports of $823 million and imports of $1.18 billion in 1952 to $2.26 billion and $2.326 billion respectively in 1970 (Zhongguo duiwaijingjimaoyinianjian bianjiweiyuanhui 1984, IV-3). During this era, the ratio of China's export volume to the world's total export volume, as well as the ratio of the total amount of exports and imports to China's GDP, fell below the levels of the 1930s,[8] suggesting that trade as a whole was relatively stagnant. This situation began to improve with the increase in trade with Japan, the US, and Western Europe due to the rapprochement between the US and China in the early 1970s[9], but in the midst of all these changes in China's overall trade structure since 1949, Shanghai's position as a trading port declined significantly compared to the Republican period.

What is most notable about the trend in Shanghai's trade over time is the remarkable stagnation of its imports. While the ratio of exports to the national total fell in 1952 and then maintained a steady presence at 28.3–38.4% from 1957 to 1978, imports consistently remained at merely 1–3% from the early 1950s onward. This suggests that Shanghai during the planned economy period was largely assigned the role of serving as an export window for China. On the other hand, considering that the main items imported into Shanghai during the Republican period, especially in the 1930s, were industrial production goods and raw materials such as metals, ores, machinery, vehicles, paper, chemical products, dyes, and cotton,[10] the fall of imports also meant that Shanghai's industry during the planned economy period had limited access to industrial production goods and raw materials from overseas.

Since the Reform period in the 1980s, the growth of imports has been particularly noticeable compared to the increase in exports before the 2000s, when the amount of imports and that of exports came to reach almost the same level. However, the ratio of Shanghai to the national total for both exports and imports was around 10%, and so in no way had the city regained the presence it had during the Republican period.

In summary, a major shift occurred in the economic structure of Shanghai as well as China as a whole before and after 1949, as is evident through examining the long-term trends of Shanghai's economy. As already mentioned, the development of Shanghai's economy until the Republican period was driven by various domestic and foreign private economic entities responding to the new phase of China's expanding foreign trade in the wake of the opening of ports. By contrast, after 1949, with the establishment of the CCP regime and the introduction of the socialist system, such

[8] The ratio of China's exports to the world's total exports was 1.56% in 1930, 0.91% in 1950, 1.44% in 1960, and 0.72% in 1970. The ratio of total exports and imports to China's GDP was 14.9% in 1933, 9.7% in 1950, 10.5% in 1960, and 5.9% in 1970 (Kubo et al. 2016, p. 139, Table VII-1–2).

[9] The trade amount grew by about three times in just four years from 1970, with exports of $6.949 billion and imports of $7.619 billion in 1974 (Zhongguo duiwaijingjimaoyinianjian bianjiweiyuanhui 1984, IV-3).

[10] The breakdown of the top ten main imports of Shanghai in 1936 was metals and ores 11.3%, cotton 6.2%, machinery 5.9%, paper 5.4%, chemical products 5.1%, dyes 4.4%, vehicles about 4% (decimal point unknown), other textiles (excluding cotton products) 3.1%, tobacco leaves 2.6%, and timber 2.6% (Shanghai shehuikexueyuan jingjisuo and Shanghaishi guojimaoyixuehui xueshuweiyuanhui 1989, pp. 191–196).

private economic activities came under government control. The rapid development of Shanghai's heavy industry under the socialist system and the impact of the "Heavy-industry-priority Strategy" in the planned economy period changed the structure of Shanghai's industry, which had previously been centered on light industry in the Republican period, tremendously. Furthermore, the significant decline in Shanghai's role as a foreign trade port triggered by the Korean War in the early 1950s meant that the conditions that characterized Shanghai's economy up until the Republican period had substantially transformed.

After the Reform and Opening-up Policy began in 1978, the dismantling of the socialist system seems to have, on the one hand, returned the Shanghai economy to the structure that had characterized it during the Republican period. However, on the other hand, it is not necessarily clear from the analysis based on macro statistics how the introduction of the socialist system during the planned economy period specifically affected the Shanghai economy. The subsequent two chapters will take this up, examining how the socialist system was erected upon the structure of the Shanghai economy that had developed up until the Republican period.

References

English Language

Hsiao, Liang-lin. 1974. *China's Foreign Trade Statistics, 1864–1949*. Cambridge, Massachusetts: Harvard University Press

Chinese Language

Guojia tongjiju gongyetongjisi, ed. 2012. *Zhongguo gongyejingjitongji nianjian 2012* (中国工业经济统计年鉴 2012, China Industrial Economic Statistical Yearbook 2012). Beijing: Zhongguo tongji chubanshe

Guojia tongjiju guominjingjizonghetongjisi, ed. 2010. *Xinzhongguo liushinian tongjiziliao huibian* (新中国六十年统计资料汇编, Compilation of Statistical Data for Sixty Years of New China). Beijing: Zhongguo tongji chubanshe

Haiguan zongshuiwusishu tongjike, ed. 1947. *Zhonghuaminguo 35 nian haiguan zhongwaimaoyi tongjiniankan juan 1* (中华民国35年海关中外贸易统计年刊卷1, Republic of China 35th Year Customs Foreign Trade Statistics Yearbook Volume 1), Shanghai. In *Zhongguo jiuhaiguan shiliao: 1859–1948* (中国旧海关史料 (1859–1948), China Old Customs Historical Materials), Volume 146, ed. 2001. Zhongguo jiuhaiguan shiliao bianjiweiyuanhui. Beijing: Jinghua chubanshe

Huang, Hanmin. 1989. 1933 he 1947 nian shanghai gongye chanzhi de guji (1933和1947年上海工业产值的估计, Estimates of Shanghai Industrial Output in 1933 and 1947). *Shanghai jingjiyanjiu* (上海经济研究, Shanghai Economic Research) 1: 63–68

Jin, Zhihuan. 2006. *Zhongguo fangzhijianshegongsi yanjiu* (中国纺织建设公司研究 (1945–1950), Research on China Textile Construction Company, 1945–1950). Shanghai: Fudan University Press

Liu, Dajun. 1937. *Zhongguo gongyediaocha baogao* (中国工业调查报告, Report on a Survey of Chinese Industry), Volumes 1–3, Junshiweiyuanhui ziyuanweiyuanhui canlaoziliao No. 20. In *Minguoshiqi shehuidiaocha congbian* (民国时期社会调查丛编, Collection of Social Surveys during the Republic of China Period), Volume 2, Modern Industry. Fuzhou: Fujian jiaoyu chubanshe, 2010

Pei, Fei (Nataniel Peffer) and Wei Muting (Martin Wilbur) interviewed, Wu Xiuyuan translated, Gao Yunpeng proofread, Ma Jun annotated. 1999. *Cong shanghai shizhang dao "taiwan shengzhuxi": wu guozhen koushu huiyi* (从上海市长到"台湾省主席"(1946–1953年): 吴国桢口述回忆, From Mayor of Shanghai to 'President of Taiwan Province,' 1946–1953: Oral Memoirs of Wu Guozhen). Shanghai: Shanghai renmin chubanshe

Shanghai shehuikexueyuan jingjisuo. 1980. *Shanghai zibenzhuyi gongshangye de shehuizhuyigaizao* (上海资本主义工商业的社会主义改造, The Socialist Transformation of Shanghai's Capitalist Industry and Commerce). Shanghai: Shanghai renmin chubanshe

Shanghai shehuikexueyuan jingjisuo and Shanghaishi guojimaoyixuehui xueshuweiyuanhui, ed. 1989. *Shanghai duiwaimaoyi 1840–1949* (上海对外贸易1840–1949, Shanghai Foreign Trade 1840–1949), Volume I. Shanghai: Shanghai shehuikexueyuan chubanshe

Shanghai shehuikexueyuan shanghai jingjinianjian bianjibu, ed. 1983. *Shanghai jingji 1949–1982* (上海经济1949–1982, Shanghai Economy 1949–1982). Shanghai: Shanghai renmin chubanshe

Shanghaishi gongshangxingzhengguanliju and Shanghaishi xiangjiaogongyegongsi shiliaogongzuozu, ed. 1979. *Shanghai minzu xiangjiao gongye* (上海民族橡胶工业, Shanghai Native Rubber Industry). Beijing: Zhonghua shuju

Shanghaishi tongjiju, ed. 1984. *Shanghai tongjinianjian 1983* (上海统计年鉴 1983, Shanghai Statistical Yearbook 1983). Shanghai: Shanghai renmin chubanshe

Shanghaishi tongjiju, ed. 2001. *Shanghaishi guominjingji he shehuifazhan lishitongjiziliao: 1949–2000* (上海市国民经济和社会发展历史统计资料 (1949–2000), Historical Statistics on Shanghai's National Economy and Social Development: 1949–2000). Beijing: Zhongguo tongjichubanshe

Shanghaishi tongjiju and Guojia tongjiju shanghai diaochazongdui, ed. 2009. *Guanghui de liushizai: shanghai lishitongji ziliaohuibian 1949–2009* (光辉的六十载:上海历史统计资料汇编 1949–2009), Glorious Sixty Years: Shanghai Historical Statistical Data Compilation, 1949–2009). Beijing: Zhongguo tongjichubanshe

Shanghaishi tongjiju and Guojia tongjiju shanghai diaochazongdui, ed. 2013. *Shanghai tongjinianjian 2013 nian* (上海统计年鉴 2013年, Shanghai Statistical Yearbook 2013). Beijing: Zhongguo tongjichubanshe

Wang, Fusun. 1947. Zhanqian zhongguo gongyeshengchanzhong waichangshengchan de bizhongwenti (战前中国工业生产中外厂生产的比重问题, The Issue of the Proportion of Foreign Production in China's Pre-war Industrial Production). *Zhongyang yinhang yuebao* (中央银行月报, Central Bank Monthly), New Volume 2, Issue 3

Wu, Baosan, ed. 1947. *Zhongguo guomin suode: 1933 nian* (中国国民所得 (1933年), China's National Income: 1933), Volumes I & II. Beijing: Zhonghua shuju

Xu, Xinwu and Huang Hanmin, ed. 1998. *Shanghai jindaigongyeshi* (上海近代工业史, History of Shanghai's Modern Industry). Shanghai: Shanghai shehuikexueyuan chubanshe

Zhongguo duiwaijingjimaoyinianjian bianjiweiyuanhui, ed. 1984. *Zhongguo duiwaijingjimaoyinianjian 1984* (中国对外经济贸易年鉴 1984, China Foreign Economic Trade Yearbook 1984). Beijing: Zhongguo duiwaijingjimaoyi chubanshe

Zhonghuarenmingongheguo guojiatongjiju, ed. 2015. *Zhongguo tongjinianjian 2015* (中国统计年鉴 2015, China Statistical Yearbook 2015). Beijing: Zhongguo tongji chubanshe

Japanese Language

Furuta, Kazuko. 2000. *Shanghai network to kindai higashi ajia* (上海ネットワークと近代東アジア, Shanghai Network: The Economic Order in Late Nineteenth-century East Asia). Tokyo: University of Tokyo Press

Hatano, Yoshihiro. 1961. *Chūgoku kindaikōgyōshi no kenkyū* (中国近代工業史の研究, Study on Modern Chinese Industrial History). Kyoto: The Society of Oriental Researches, Faculty of Letters, Kyoto University

Kigoshi, Yoshinori. 2012. *Kindai chūgoku to kōikishijōken: kaikantōkei niyoru macro teki apurōchi* (近代中国と広域市場圏——海関統計によるマクロ的アプローチ, Inter-regional Trade of Modern China: A Macroeconomic Analysis of China Maritime Customs Statistics). Kyoto: Kyoto University Press

Kosugi, Shūji. 1988. *Gendai chūgoku no kokkamokuteki to keizaikensetsu: Chōtaikoku shikou, teikaihatsu keizai, shakaishugi* (現代中国の国家目的と経済建設——超大国志向・低開発経済・社会主義, State Objectives and Economic Construction in Contemporary China: Superpower Aspiration, Underdeveloped Economy, Socialism). Tokyo: Ryūkei shosha

Kubo, Tōru. 1999. *Senkanki Chūgoku 'jiritsu eno mosaku': Kanzeitsūkaseisaku to keizaihatten* (戦間期中国「自立への模索」——関税通貨政策と経済発展, China's Quest for Sovereignty in the Inter-war Period: Tariff Policy and Economic Development). Tokyo: University of Tokyo Press

Kubo, Tōru, Kajima Jun, Kigoshi Yoshinori. 2016. *Tōkei de miru chūgoku kingendai keizaishi* (統計でみる中国近現代経済史, Economic History of Modern China: An Approach Based on Statistical data). Tokyo: University of Tokyo Press

Miyashita, Tadao. 1967. *Shinchūgoku no tsūkaseisaku* (新中国の通貨政策, New China's Monetary Policy), Seimeikai Series V. Tokyo: Seimeikai

Miyata, Michiaki. 2006. *Chūgoku no kaikou to enkaishijō* (中国の開港と沿海市場——中国近代経済史に関する一視点, China's Opening of Ports and Coastal Market: A Perspective on Modern Chinese Economic History). Tokyo: Tōhō shoten

Okamoto, Takashi, ed. 2013. *Chūgoku keizaishi* (中国経済史, Chinese Economic History). Nagoya: The University of Nagoya Press

Onoe, Etsuzō. 1971. *Chūgoku no sangyō ricchi ni kansuru kenkyū* (中国の産業立地に関する研究, Study on Industrial Location in China). Tokyo: Institute of Developing Economies

Osaka shiritsudaigaku keizaikenkyūjo, ed. 1986. *Shanghai: Sekai no daitoshi 2* (上海 世界の大都市2, Shanghai: World's Major Cities 2). Tokyo: University of Tokyo Press

Seki, Mitsuhiro. 1997. *Shanghai no sangyō hatten to nihon kigyō* (上海の産業発展と日本企業, Industrial Development in Shanghai and Japanese Companies). Tokyo: Shinhyōron

Shiroyama, Tomoko. 2011. *Daikyōkōka no chūgoku: Shijō, kokka, sekaizeizai* (大恐慌下の中国——市場・国家・世界経済, China under the Great Depression: Market, State and World Economy). Nagoya: The University of Nagoya Press

Suzuki, Tomoo. 1992. *Youmu undou no kenkyu: 19 seiki kouhan no chūgoku niokeru kōgyōka to gaikō no kakushin nitsuiteno kousatsu* (洋務運動の研究——一九世紀後半の中国における工業化と外交の革新についての考察, A Study of the Westernization Movement in China in the Latter Half of the Nineteenth Century). Tokyo: Kyūko shoin

Takahashi, Kōsuke, and Furumaya Tadao, eds. 1995. *Shanghaishi: Kyodaitoshi no keisei to hitobitono ayumi* (上海史——巨大都市の形成と人々の歩み, The history of Shanghai: Formation of a Mega City and People's Steps). Tokyo: Tōhō shoten

Chapter 3
The Establishment of the People's Republic of China and Shanghai Enterprises

Abstract This chapter explores the process of the building of the socialist system in Shanghai by focusing on the People's Republic of China government's policy toward private enterprises, especially that pertaining to the processing orders (加工订货) issued from government agencies and state-owned enterprises to private industrial enterprises. Shanghai was a major hub for private enterprise in the Republican period, and even after the occupation of Shanghai by the Chinese Communist Party in May 1949 there remained a significant number of private enterprises. Therefore, the new PRC government considered Shanghai the most important target area for the implementation of its policies in this field, and how to deal with the private enterprises in Shanghai represented a key issue in the formation of the Chinese socialist system.

Keywords Private enterprises · Processing orders · Establishment of People's Republic of China · New Democratic Economy

As mentioned in the Introduction, the main elements that shape a socialist economic system are considered to be (1) public ownership of the means of production, (2) distribution by a non-market planned economy, and (3) monopolistic control of political power by a single party. In China, (3) was formed with the establishment of the Chinese Communist Party regime in October 1949, (2) with the start of the First Five Year Plan in 1953, and (1) with the completion of the socialist transformation, which comprised the collectivization of agriculture, the joint public-private operation of capitalist commerce and industry (i.e., semi-nationalization of private enterprises), and the cooperative operation of individual handicraft industries, in 1956. This chapter and the next will examine specifically how the socialist system was instituted in Shanghai.

It is now known that the introduction of a socialist system in China was not necessarily planned right from the establishment of the People's Republic of China. As will be discussed later, the CCP initially advocated a basic policy of what it called "New Democracy" (新民主主义), which tolerated the existence of capitalist

J. Kajima, *Shanghai under the Socialist System*, Studies in Economic History,
https://doi.org/10.1007/978-981-95-3225-4_3

economic elements such as private enterprises[1] and envisaged a relatively long-term relationship of coexistence with them. However, in mid-1953, this initial policy was dramatically changed by Mao shifting to instead propose the "General Line of the Transition Period" (过渡时期的总路线), which called for an immediate transition to a socialist system. Just three years later, in 1956, this led to the completion of a full-scale socialist transformation.

Several studies have pointed out that Mao's sudden proposal for a transition to a socialist system was strongly influenced by changes in the international environment at the time.[2] According to these studies, the most important factor informing the shift was the outbreak of the Korean War in 1950 and China's participation in said conflict. It has been suggested that Mao's heightened defense consciousness, triggered by the conflict with the US, became a turning point that led him to advocate a major shift from coexisting with private enterprises to transforming them.

Furthermore, the Korean War had a significant impact not only on the consciousness of the CCP's leadership, but also on the actual processes of forming a socialist system. Izutani Yoko, having analyzed the process of mass movements initiated by the CCP before and after the Korean War, and in particular the "Five Anti" (五反) campaign—a mass movement that aimed to expose the "Five Poisons" (五毒) of private enterprise, namely bribery, tax evasion, theft of state property, cheating on government contracts, and theft of economic information—from early 1952,[3]

---

[1] The term "private enterprise" (私营企业) is often used alongside "state-owned enterprise" (国营企业), particularly in the context of the classification of enterprises under a socialist system, and generally has the same meaning as what is commonly referred to as a "private company" (民间企业). In this book, both "private company" and "private enterprise" are used, but in those sections pertaining to the policies and statistics of the CCP, the term "private enterprise" is used in deference to the usage in the original historical sources.

[2] Mōri (1994) examines the international relations of the time and the changes in Mao Zedong's foreign perception, pointing out that the tension in international relations that began with the outbreak of the Korean War in June 1950 strongly stimulated Mao's defense consciousness and greatly influenced his choice of socialism. Similarly, Okumura (1999) regards the subsequent socialist system itself as a "total war posture" (总力战态势) intended to counter possible American "imperialist" incursions, based on heightened defense consciousness in the wake of the outbreak of the Korean War.

[3] Zhongguoshehuikexueyuan jingjiyanjiusuo (1978), which can be said to represent the official view of the CCP on the socialist transformation, views the policy of the Chinese government toward private enterprises from the establishment of the PRC to the completion of the socialist transformation in 1956 as constituting a consistent "use, limit and transform" (利用、限制、改造) policy. It holds that this policy entailed utilizing the positive effects of capitalist commerce and industry on the national economy and people's lives, while limiting their negative effects. However, the negative effects of capitalist commerce and industry, believed to be inherent in the classist nature of the systems in question, are portrayed as conflicting with government restrictions and thereby inevitably leading to a socialist transformation. In this framework, the emergence of the "Five Poisons" is seen as an inevitable result of the classist nature of capitalist commerce and industry. The 1978 text is a rewrite of an earlier work, namely Zhongyang gongshangguanliju and Zhongguokexueyuan jingjiyanjiusuo zibenzhuyijingjigaizaoyanjiushi (1962), and there was also a "Shanghai version" produced by Shanghai shehuikexueyuan jingjisuo (1980). The internal logic of this policy toward private enterprises since 1949 continued in subsequent generations to be the basic interpretation followed in the CCP official view on the socialist transformation, as seen in,

points out that the "Five Poisons," which had in previous studies been attributed to the bourgeois character of private enterprise, were in fact structurally produced by the government's economic control imposed during the Korean War (Izutani 2007). Moreover, she emphasizes the important role played by the "Five Anti" campaign in the government's efforts to control private enterprises. Although the pattern of control of private enterprises through mass movements such as the "Five Anti" campaign, and its predecessor the "Three Anti" campaign, had already been pointed out by Gardner (1969) and others,[4] Izutani's argument is much more persuasive since it analyzes the relationship between the movements and the actual economic situation during the Korean War.

Building on these previous studies, this chapter and the next will focus on the governmental policy for private enterprises in Shanghai, paying close attention to the changes before and after the Korean War, while examining the process by which the socialist system was implemented. While many studies dealing with the socialist transformation, including the aforementioned Izutani (2007), depict the process, through which private enterprises gradually lost their freedom of management and were placed under governmental control, mainly from the perspective of private enterprises themselves (e.g., Gui 2006; Sun 2006; Zhang 2006), the governmental

---

for example, "Chapter 6: The Establishment of the People's Republic of China and the Realization of the Transition to Socialism," by Zhonggong zhongyangdangshiyanjiushi and Hu (1991).

The interpretive perspective at play here has a significant problem in that various phenomena that occurred during the process leading to the socialist transformation—for example, the emergence of the aforementioned "Five Poisons"—are obscured by the abstract concept of classism, or inherent social class associations. This issue also characterized pioneering works by Japanese scholars, such as Furushima (1969) and Miki (1971). On the other hand, a series of studies conducted in the late 1970s by Uehara (1975–76), Tanaka (1978), and Zama (1978) voiced dissenting opinions against the official CCP perspective. These studies share a critical stance toward the so-called "1949 Proletarian Dictatorship Theory," which was the official CCP view at the time, and which saw the establishment of the PRC in 1949 as constituting the formation of a proletarian dictatorship. Through examining the policies toward private enterprises in the early days of the PRC, this new generation of scholars aimed to reexamine the process of what was termed "the growth and transformation of revolution" (革命の成長転化, i.e., the establishment of the proletarian dictatorship). This analytical perspective, which incorporated the effects of participation in the Korean War and the development of mass movements, sought to discuss the economic policies of the early PRC in a more multifaceted manner. However, on the other hand, it also resembled the framework of the aforementioned Zhongguoshehuikexueyuan jingjiyanjiusuo (1978) in that it presupposed a "revolutionary growth transformation" and viewed the socialist transformation as an inevitable outcome of this process.

Following this burst of 1970s scholarship, economic history studies such as Dong (1996) and Wu (1999), which placed more emphasis on the role of private economic elements in the early days of the PRC within the context of the economic history of modern China, and which sought to clarify the process of Chinese economic development after the establishment of the PRC, were published in mainland China in the 1990s. However, these studies also shared the same problem as earlier ones in the sense that they inevitably viewed the friction between governmental restrictions and private enterprises as a manifestation of class conflict.

[4] On the strengthening of control through mass movements, Gardner (1969) highlights the case of Shanghai, while Lieberthal (1980) examines that of Tianjin.

control and management system of private enterprises has not itself received analytical attention.[5] From the standpoint of this book, which aims to clarify the actual state of the Chinese socialist system, it is significant to understand how the government expanded, and managed private enterprises under, its control.

Therefore, this chapter and the following one will examine the implementation of subcontracting and ordering policies (加工订货, hereinafter referred to as "processing orders") from government agencies and state-owned enterprises to private industrial enterprises, focusing mainly on trends within the government itself. As discussed in the previous chapter, Shanghai was a major hub for private enterprise in the Republican period, and even after the occupation of Shanghai by the CCP in May 1949 there remained a significant number of private enterprises. Therefore, the new PRC government considered Shanghai the most important target area for the implementation of this policy, and how to deal with the private enterprises in Shanghai represented a key issue in the formation of the Chinese socialist system.

Both chapters will emphasize in their analysis how the central government's policy shift before and after the Korean War affected the implementation of policies in Shanghai. As mentioned in Chapter 1, the relationship between the central and local governments in policy implementation is one of the most important aspects to grasp in understanding China's socialist system. The chapters therefore focus on the Shanghai Municipal Bureau of Industry and Commerce Administration (上海市工商行政管理局), which was the supervisory body for the implementation of processing orders at the local level, in order to shed light on the actual situation within the local government as it carried out policies.

This chapter seeks to assess the actual situation of the occupation of Shanghai by the CCP and the process by which private enterprise policy was introduced up until the outbreak of the Korean War. Chapter 4 will then build on this by clarifying the change in policy that occurred after the outbreak of the Korean War, and the process leading to the socialist transformation of private enterprises.

3.1 Shanghai Enterprises in 1949

On May 27, 1949, the entire city of Shanghai was occupied by the People's Liberation Army of the CCP. The basic policy of the CCP at the time regarding the takeover and management of urban enterprises was to seize control of all "bureaucratic capital" enterprises (that is, enterprises considered to be related to the old Nationalist regime) along with public enterprises, while maintaining their respective organizational structures and mechanisms, as well as uniformly protecting all private enterprises and their property in order to alleviate the chaos that would inevitably

[5] For an overview of the history of management and control systems for industry and commerce, see Dangdai zhongguo de gongshangxingzhengguanli bianjiweiyuanhui (1991). Other relevant studies include Brugger (1976) and Kawai (1991), which focus on the management system within state-owned factories.

occur during the takeover.[6] The takeover and management of "bureaucratic capital" enterprises and public enterprises in Shanghai was mainly carried out by the Financial and Economic Takeover Committee (财政经济接管委员会), itself established by the Shanghai Municipal Military Control Committee (上海市军事管制委员会),[7] in a process that this section will now examine by dividing it into industrial, commercial, and financial aspects.[8]

The confiscation of manufacturing enterprises was carried out in a distinct manner that differed depending on whether the enterprise in question was a heavy or light industry. In the case of heavy industry, the most important component of the process was the confiscation of those enterprises that had formerly belonged to the National Government Resources Committee (国民政府资源委员会) in Shanghai.[9] The companies confiscated by the Financial and Economic Takeover Committee's Heavy Industry Department (财政经济接管委员会重工业处) by the end of July 1949 amounted to 45 units, including the Resources Committee (资源委员会), the Postwar Business Storage Committee (善后事业保管委员会), the Nationalist Party Navy Shipyard (国民党海军造船所), and other "bureaucratic capital" companies. Of these, 21 were engaged in production, and the remaining 24 were engaged in management and business. Major enterprises included the Asia Steel Company (亚细亚钢铁公司), Shanghai Steel Company (上海钢铁公司), Jiangnan Shipyard (江南造船所), Central Shipyard Preparatory Office (中央造船厂筹备所), Cold Cast Wheel Factory (冷铸车轮厂), Minhang General Equipment Factory (閔行通用

[6] Such a policy was indicated on April 25, 1949, immediately after the start of the PLA's all-out assault on the Yangtze River basin. See "CCP Central Committee Instructions on Taking Over the Cities in the South of the Yangtze River to the East China Bureau" (中共中央关于接管江南城市给华东局的指示), April 25, 1949 and "East China Bureau Instructions on Taking Over the Cities in the South of the Yangtze River (Excerpt)" (华东局关于接管江南城市工作的指示 (节录)), April 1, 1949, Zhongyangjuanbianjibu (1992, pp. 30–33).

[7] On how the Shanghai Municipal Military Control Committee managed seizures, refer to Zhonggongshanghaishiwei zuzhibu et al. (1991, pp. 6–12).

[8] The predecessor of the Shanghai Financial and Economic Takeover Committee was the East China Financial Affairs Office (华东财经办事处) established in 1947. This office was an organization set up in the East China region under the control of the National Government to organize people, goods, and finances to support the front line. It was likely preparing for the takeover and management of various cities south of the Yangtze River as the PLA was crossing the river in the spring of 1949. See Sun (1990, p. 20, note 1).

[9] This committee was established in April 1935 on the eve of the Second Sino-Japanese War, and played a crucial role in maintaining the National Government's resistance to Japan by actively promoting the nationalization of heavy industry. After the war, it mainly took over heavy industrial enterprises and mines in the former Japanese-occupied areas, and as a result, as of April 1947, it reputedly controlled more than 50% of the nation's electricity, 32.5% of the coal, 100% of the oil, 80% of the steel, the majority of the metal mines, and many parts of the machinery and chemical industries. Quanguo zhengxie wenshiziliaoyanjiu weiyuanhui gongshangjingjizu (1988, p. 8). As for the takeover of companies belonging to the Resources Committee, this took the form of an ostensible uprising (effectively a defection from the National Government and joining the CCP), and except for that portion that had already been moved to Taiwan, it successfully brought almost all of its equipment and personnel under control without loss. For more on this process, see Zheng et al. (1991), Chapter 14 "The Resources Committee Abandons Darkness and Welcomes Liberation on the Mainland," and Liu (1997, pp. 178–181).

机器厂), Central Electric Equipment Company (中央电工器材公司, including 4 factories), Central Radio Company (中央无线电公司), the Qiujiang Machinery Factory (虬江机器厂) and Wusong Machinery Factory (吴淞机器厂) belonging to the China Agricultural Machinery Company (中国农业机械公司), the Central Chemical Factory (中央化工厂), and Yaohua Glass Factory (耀华玻璃厂) (Sun 1990, pp. 22–23; Liu 1997, pp. 178–185).

As for light industry, the confiscation of the China Textile Construction Company (中国纺织建设公司) was particularly significant.[10] This undertaking was basically completed in mid-June 1949, with the company's 38 factories (17 cotton spinning factories, 5 wool spinning factories, 6 dyeing factories, 1 hemp spinning factory, 1 silk spinning factory, 1 knitwear factory, 1 bandage factory, and 6 textile machinery factories), 8 warehouses, and over 60,000 staff and workers all being confiscated, while the retention of the general manager, deputy general manager, and heads of various departments within the company, as well as the maintenance of the "current position, current salary, and current system" of all personnel were announced (Liu 1997, pp. 182–183). The total number of companies confiscated by the Light Industry Department (轻工业处) amounted to 52 factories, 10 warehouses, 17 business units, and 65,000 staff and workers in total across four sections, specifically the China Textile Construction Company, chemical industry enterprises, tobacco industry enterprises, and the Central Industrial Experimental Institute (中央工业实验所). This illustrates just how large the proportion of light industry represented by the China Textile Construction Company was.[11]

Through the above confiscation of heavy and light industrial enterprises, the total number of factories confiscated by the CCP regime in Shanghai amounted to 157, and in terms of production equipment, the government had come to control about 41% of the city's spindles, one-third of its machinery manufacturing equipment, and one-fifth of its steel refining equipment.[12] These gains would become, in turn, an important part of the foundation for the state-owned industry of the regime.

Moreover, some commercial companies that had existed since the Republican period were also confiscated, including Yangtze Construction Company (扬子建业公司), China Import and Export Trading Company (中国进出口贸易公司), Fu Zhong Company (孚中公司), Unified Trading Company (统一贸易公司), Jinshan Trading Company (金山贸易公司), Letai Company (利泰公司), China Petroleum

[10] The China Textile Construction Company, a state-owned enterprise, was established in 1945 to temporarily nationalize former Japanese-owned cotton factories when conflicts over the disposal of these factories arose between capitalists who had moved inland with the National Government in wartime and those who remained in Shanghai. For the process of the establishment of the China Textile Construction Company, its management status during the civil war, and its relationship with the National Government, refer to Kawai (1987, 1992, 2001) and Jin (2006).

[11] Sun (1990, p. 21). After the takeover and new management situation settled down in September 1949, the Light Industry Office (轻工业处) was reorganized into the East China District Financial and Economic Committee Textile Industry Department (华东区财政经济委员会纺织工业部), which also took control of the China Textile Construction Company's factories.

[12] Liu (1997, p. 185). The number of industrial enterprises seized, 157, matches the total of the "state-owned," "local state-owned," and "public-private joint venture" categories in Table 3.1, but the precise correlation is unclear.

Table 3.1 Number and production value of industrial enterprises of Shanghai in 1949, by ownership (Unit: 10 thousand yuan)

	Number of enterprises (A)	%	Production value (B)	%	Production value per enterprise (B)/(A)
State-owned	92	0.5	50,981	15.8	554
Local state-owned	50	0.2	2,310	0.7	46
Cooperative	1	0.0	30	0.0	30
Public and private jointly-owned	15	0.1	1,171	0.4	78
Private	20,149	99.2	267,352	83.1	13
Total	20,307	100.0	321,844	100.0	16

Source Zhonggongshanghaishiwei tongzhanbu et al. (1993, Table 2). The original source is "National accounts of Shanghai (industry), 1949–1957" (unknown author, publisher and year of publication), p. 6, 10. Note: Table does not include data for production cooperatives and individual handicrafts. "Production value" is a constant price based on the 1952 price, and is a value in new RMB converted from old RMB at the rate of 10 thousand old RMB to 1 new RMB

Company (中国石油公司), Liwei Automobile Company (利威汽车公司), Jialing Enterprise Company (嘉陵企业公司), China Cotton Industry Company (中国棉业公司), Yangtze River Industrial Company (长江实业公司), Xiangji Company (祥记公司), China Tea Leaf Joint Venture Company (中国茶叶联营公司), and the China Silk Weaving Production and Sales Joint Venture Company (中国丝织产销联营公司) (Sun 1990, p. 23). Based on these confiscated companies, state-owned specialized companies (i.e., state-owned enterprises that specialized in trading certain commodities) were established from September through December 1949, such as the Shanghai Grain Company (上海市粮食公司), Raw Cotton and Cotton Products Company (花纱布公司), Daily Necessities Company (日用品公司), Coal Industry Company (煤业公司), Construction Material Company (建筑器材公司), Native Products Company (土产公司), Salt Industry Company (盐业公司), Chemical Industry Raw Material Company (化学工业原料公司), Tea Leaf Company (茶叶公司), Silkworm Thread Company (蚕糸公司), Pig Bristle Company (猪鬃公司), and Trade Trust Company (贸易信托公司).[13] These state-owned specialized

[13] Shanghai Municipal Bureau of Industry and Commerce (authors Fu Dejin and Zhao Chongwen), "The Role and Function of Processing Orders in the Socialist Transformation of Capitalist Industry and Commerce in Shanghai" (加工订货在上海资本主义工商业社会主义改造中的地位与作用), in Zhonggongshanghaishiwei tongzhanbu et al. (1993, p. 842). This document is not a primary source, but rather a summary written later. Also see Sun (1990, pp. 66–67). The Trade Trust Company was an organization that accepted commissions from institutions, units, and public and private enterprises in various places as well as conducting proxy purchases and sales. It dealt in particular with businesses that state-owned specialized companies could not cover. For example, at the initial stage of the establishment of the PRC, there were no state-owned specialized companies for industrial equipment, so the Trade Trust Company mainly handled the proxy sale of products produced by state-owned factories and imported goods in this area. See "Decision on the Business Policy and Profit of State-owned Trust Companies in Major Cities and Leadership Relations by the

companies played a major role in the government's control of the market, and were one of the main institutions that placed processing orders for private industries.

In the financial industry, enterprises including the Central Bank (中央银行), Bank of China (中国银行), Bank of Communications (交通银行), China Farmers Bank (中国农民银行), Central Cooperative Bank (中央合作金库), Postal Savings Bureau (邮政储金滙业局), Shanghai City Bank (上海市银行), Xinhua Bank (新华银行), China Industrial Bank (中国实业银行), Siming Bank (四明银行), and China Commercial Bank (中国通商银行), were confiscated; among these, the Central Bank, Shanghai City Bank, China Farmers Bank, Central Cooperative Bank, and the savings business and some other components of the Postal Savings Bureau were incorporated into various departments of the newly established Shanghai Branch of the People's Bank. Aside from these, some other banks were able to continue management in so-called public-private joint operation form after the confiscation of any shares related to the previous Nationalist regime, with some private shares retained, and a board of directors consisting of government representatives and private representatives formed. Among these cases, the Bank of China maintained its role as a specialized foreign exchange bank, and the Bank of Communications became a bank specializing in financial supervision of public-private joint ventures. In addition, several banks such as the China Domestic Products Bank (中国国货银行), Jiangsu Provincial Bank (江苏省银行), Zhejiang Bank (浙江银行), and Chinese private banks (钱庄) were reorganized and abolished, while 19 "bureaucratic capital" insurance companies also disappeared, with the exception of the China Insurance Company (中国保险公司) and China Aviation Insurance Company (中国航联保险公司) (Liu 1997, p. 203).

In addition to these industrial, commercial, and financial enterprises, businesses were also confiscated in various other industries such as transportation, communication, and real estate, with the total number of business units confiscated and managed being claimed to amount to 411 (Zhonggongshanghaishiwei zuzhibu et al. 1991, p. 12). In this way, the Chinese Communist regime succeeded in taking control of the core of the Shanghai economy by confiscating both government agencies and their related companies from the Nationalist period.

However, it is also a fact that in 1949 the PRC government directly managed only a fraction of the Shanghai economy as either state-owned or joint public-private enterprises. Table 3.1 classifies the number and production value of industrial enterprises in Shanghai as of 1949 by ownership. As shown here, privately-owned industrial enterprises accounted for an overwhelming amount: 99.2% of the total number and 83.1% of the production value. The fact that state-owned enterprises far outstripped others in terms of production value per enterprise suggests that these were large-scale state-owned enterprises such as the Resource Committee enterprises and the China Textile Construction Company. On the other hand, the great bulk of Shanghai's

---

Central Ministry of Trade" (中央贸易部关于各大城市国营信托公司业务方针及资金利润，领导关系的决定), Zhongguoshehuikexueyuan and Zhongyangdanganguan (1995, pp. 146–147). The decision text is dated May 4, 1950, the publication date of the *Trade Bulletin* (贸易公报) of the Central Ministry of Trade (中央贸易部) where the article appeared, so the exact date of the decision itself is unknown.

industry was made up of countless private enterprises, including small and medium-sized ones. As for the situation by industry sector, as shown in Table 2.2 the ratio of Shanghai's total industrial production in 1949 was 88.3% for light industry and 11.7% for heavy industry. According to other literature that distinguishes the textile industry from other light industries, the textile industry accounted for 62.4%, other light industry 24%, and heavy industry 13.6% (Shanghai shehuikexueyuan jingjisuo 1980, p. 34). Based on these figures, it can be said that private enterprises still occupied a high proportion, especially in the core sectors of the textile and other light industries.

3.2 The "New Democratic Economy" and State Contracts

3.2.1 The "New Democratic Economy"

The issue of how to deal with private enterprises, which existed on such a large scale, was an extremely important task facing the PRC government. In order to understand the background to the CCP's approach to private enterprise policy, it is important to grasp the concept of the "New Democracy" (新民主主义) which served as the basic political and economic policy of the CCP at the time of the establishment of the People's Republic.

This "New Democracy" concept, originally proposed in Mao Zedong's "On New Democracy" (新民主主义论, Jan. 1940), was rooted in understanding the transition to socialism as occurring in two stages, namely a New Democratic Revolution followed by a full-fledged Socialist Revolution. China, which for Mao was a "semi-colonial, semi-feudal" (半殖民地半封建) society, needed to essentially rush through a democratic revolution before it would be ready to undergo a true socialist revolution. The democratic revolution was to be led by an alliance of revolutionary classes under the leadership of the working class, thereby distinguishing it from the "old" democratic revolution associated with the May Fourth Movement in 1919 (Nihon kokusaimondai kenkyūjo chūgokubukai 1974; Amako et al. 1999, pp. 585–586). This further served to distinguish China's trajectory from that of Europe: while the European industrial societies had become bogged down in their (bourgeois-democratic) "old" democratic revolution, China was to pursue its own path through its distinct "new" democratic revolution, and proceed right through to socialism. Based on this revolutionary theory, the CCP's seizure of power in 1949 was positioned as the New Democratic Revolution, and the society after the establishment of the PRC was thus considered a New Democratic society.

The "New Democratic Economy" was a related idea that essentially entailed applying the concept of New Democracy to the economy. New Democracy hinged on the foundational notion of an "alliance of the working class and revolutionary classes," and this was reflected in how the New Democratic Economy was characterized by the coexistence of multiple economic components. According to the provisions set out in the "Common Program of the Chinese People's Political Consultative Conference" (中国人民政治协商会议共同纲领), which served as a temporary constitution at the beginning of the establishment of the PRC, the New Democratic Economy would consist of five economic components: (1) a state-owned economy of a socialist nature, (2) a cooperative economy of a semi-socialist nature, (3) state capitalism, which was a collaboration of state capital and private capital, (4) a private capitalist economy, and (5) an individual economy of peasants and handicraft workers. Further, it stipulated that the state was to place various economic components under the guidance of the state-owned economy, encourage specialization and cooperation, and promote the development of the entire society and economy as a whole (Zhonggong zhongyang wenxianyanjiushi 1992, pp. 7–8).

What is particularly important to note here is the positioning of the "private capitalist economy." The Common Platform stated that "for all private economic enterprises that are beneficial to the national economy and the people's livelihood, the people's government should encourage their entrepreneurial spirit and assist their development" (Article 30): in other words, it recognized private entrepreneurialism and saw this as positive provided it contributed to the "national economy and people's livelihood." In this sense, in principle the existence and development of "private capitalism" was tolerated, if not encouraged, but on the other hand the requirement that such ventures be "beneficial" for the national economy and the people imposed a limitation and indicated that the free development of a private capitalist economy would not be permitted.

This kind of flexibility can also be seen in the provision regarding state capitalism, which was defined, recall, as a "collaboration of state capital and private capital." The provision stipulated that state capitalism needed to "encourage private capital to develop toward state capitalism under necessary and possible conditions" (Article 31), and while this vaguely encouraged private capital to cooperate with the state, just what "necessary and possible conditions" entailed was not clear. Furthermore, as will be discussed later, the methods of cooperation merely consisted of a list of various forms, such as "for example, conducting processing in the place of state enterprises, joint ventures with the state, management of state enterprises in the form of leasing, development of the state's natural resources, etc." (Zhonggong zhongyang wenxianyanjiushi 1992, pp. 7–8).

In short, the stance of the government at the time of the establishment of the PRC toward the "private capitalist economy" was one that expected the economy to show productivity while being subject to certain guidance by the government; in other words, therefore, the conceptual framework allowed various interpretations regarding the specific form in, and degree to which, private enterprise could develop.

3.2.2 Processing Orders

Under the New Democratic Economy, the core of the private enterprise policies in the early days of the PRC was "processing in the place of state enterprises," or processing orders, as mentioned above in Article 31 of the "Common Platform." Processing orders (either 加工订货 or 加工定货) was a concept that included two different forms of business activity, specifically, contract processing (加工) and ordering (订货).[14] Moreover, sometimes it included several different business forms such as purchasing (收购), unified purchasing (统购), and exclusive sales (包销),[15] and in a broad sense, the term was used as an inclusive concept that encompassed the entire plethora of business concluded among state agencies, state-owned enterprises, and private industries.

Contract processing was a system where state agencies and state-owned enterprises supplied raw materials and semi-finished products to private factories and entrusted the latter with processing them with specified standards, quantities, and deadlines. After delivering the finished product to the state-owned enterprise or state agency, the private factory was supposed to be paid a processing fee calculated based on wages, reasonable costs, business taxes on processed products, and reasonable profits. As for ordering, the state agency or state-owned enterprise would determine the standards, quality, quantity, reasonable price, and delivery deadline of a given product, and then under those stipulations order it from a private factory. The order price was supposed to be calculated based on reasonable production costs, taxes, and reasonable profits.[16] However, this "reasonable profit" was only stipulated to be "calculated based on the medium standard under reasonable management conditions

[14] Strictly speaking, "processing" and "ordering" should be distinguished, and in the descriptions of the time the terms were certainly used differently when indicating a specific business form. However, both were generally referred to under the category of "processing orders," so this chapter and the next will use the term "processing orders" in this inclusive sense.

[15] The general definitions of each business form were as follows: (1) Purchasing (收购): State-owned enterprises or other state entities purchase a certain amount of products from private factories on a temporary or regular basis, based on specific standards, quality, and prices. In this system, there is no prior contract, and therefore the production of private factories is not subject to governmental regulation in advance; (2) Unified Purchasing (统购): The state orders a state-owned commercial sector to uniformly purchase products that are of significant relevance to the state plan and the people's livelihood. Generally, free market sales by private factories are prohibited for unified purchase items; (3) Exclusive Sales (包销): A state-owned commercial sector stipulates the standards, quality, and reasonable prices of products to private factories, and undertakes the sale of some or all of said products within a certain period. Generally, free market sales by private factories are prohibited for exclusive sales items. The above is based on the descriptions given in Amano (1961, pp. 139–140), Miki (1971, p. 230), and Zhongguoshehuikexueyuan jingjiyanjiusuo (1978, pp. 180–181).

[16] Zhongguoshehuikexueyuan jingjiyanjiusuo (1978, pp. 180–181). As can be seen from the above definitions, the difference between contract manufacturing and ordering is that in contract manufacturing, state organizations and state-owned enterprises supply industrial raw materials (or semi-finished products), while in ordering, state organizations and state-owned enterprises are not involved in the procurement of raw materials. In other words, in the case of contract manufacturing, it is assumed that the government has a certain degree of control over the necessary raw materials, and the development of the system is greatly influenced by this control. On the other hand,

in the same district,"[17] and since no specific criteria were indicated, it came to cause many problems in the actual execution process, as will be described later.

In terms of the government's management system for the process of executing processing orders, at the time of concluding a processing order contract the contents of the contract in question had to be registered with the local industrial and commercial administrative agency in charge, which was then responsible for guiding proceedings once the contract was concluded.[18] In addition, the distribution and management of processing orders in each locale were supposed to be carried out with the assistance of local industrial and commercial/business associations, labor unions, and industry associations.

The agency responsible for guiding the contract and execution of processing orders in Shanghai was the Shanghai Municipal Bureau of Industry and Commerce (上海市工商局), later renamed the Shanghai Municipal Bureau of Industry and Commerce Administration (上海市工商行政管理局) in March 1953 (but for convenience hereinafter still referred to under the earlier name).[19] This bureau was established on

in ordering, private industry is itself responsible for procuring the raw materials, so the circulation and price of raw materials in the market become important elements.

[17] Chen Yun, "Current Economic Situation and Measures to Adjust Industry and Commerce, Adjust Tax Revenue" (目前经济形势和调整工商业，调整税收的措施), June 15, 1950, in Chen (1984, p. 106).

[18] Ibid. Regarding the order form for processing orders, the document states that "The Government Administration Council Finance and Economic Committee (政务院财政经济委员会) organizes the order forms for processing orders required by each state-owned enterprise and agency, distributes these order forms to public and private industries twice a year, concludes contracts, and enables public and private industries to execute production in a planned manner." However, considering the actual process of execution, the work involved in processing orders was highly complex and tedious, and the quantity of such orders was immense, so it is unclear whether the Government Finance and Economic Committee was really organizing and distributing them "twice a year" as intended.

[19] In terms of the overall structure and personnel composition of the Shanghai Municipal Bureau of Industry and Commerce, the bureau consisted of a secretariat, personnel office, research office, industrial and commercial management office, market management office, industrial and commercial registration office, and enemy property management office, with all manner of various departments and subordinate agencies set up under them. The number of staff was reported to be 411 as of the end of 1949. Shanghaishi bianzhiweiyuanhui bangongshi (1988, pp. 8–11). According to Shanghai gongshangxingzhengguanlizhi bianzuanweiyuanhui (1997, p. 245), the number increased to 789 in August 1950, and then decreased to 600 in March 1953 due to the transfer of some of the bureau's agencies to the newly established Commercial Bureau.

The first director was Xu Dixin (许涤新), a Marxist economist. Xu joined the Federation of Social Scientists (社会科学家连盟) in the 1930s, joined the CCP in 1937 while organizing the activities of the All-China Left-Wing Cultural Federation (中国左翼文化总同盟), and served as an editor of the *New China Daily* (新华日报) in the CCP's Southern Bureau (中共南方局) in Chongqing during the Second Sino-Japanese War. After the war, he became a member of the Shanghai Work Committee (上海工作委员会), organized within the Shanghai Delegates' Office of the CCP (中共代表团上海办事处), and was engaged in economic research as well as the "united front" policy with Shanghai's industrial and commercial entrepreneurs. He also wrote many works on the "New Democratic Economy" during this period, such as Xu (1947, 1949a, 1949b), and contributed greatly to the formation of its theoretical foundation. After the establishment of the PRC, he served as the director of the Shanghai Municipal Bureau of Industry and Commerce, as

September 13, 1949, by the Industrial and Commercial Office of the Financial and Economic Takeover Committee (财政经济接管委员会工商处) within the Military Control Committee, after the seizure and management takeover operations had settled down.[20] Its responsibilities included the management and development of Shanghai's public and private industry and commerce, as well as market management, among other duties. Its primary duty, however, was to maintain a balance in the overall industrial and commercial elements within the city.[21]

---

well as the deputy director of the East China Finance and Economic Committee (华东财政经济委员会) and the Shanghai Municipal Finance and Economic Committee (上海市财政经济委员会), and in addition was one of the leading figures for financial and economic policy in East China and Shanghai. Xu (2007, p. 1688).

Under Xu Dixin, the deputy directors of the bureau were Cai Beihua (蔡北华) and Yang Yanxiu (杨延修). Cai Beihua had joined the CCP in 1935 while studying in Japan. After returning to China, he became a reporter for the *New China Daily* in Chongqing from 1943 to 1946, during which time he came to know Xu. After the war, he was involved in the aforementioned "united front" policy under Xu in the Shanghai Work Committee, then moved to Hong Kong, where he served as the general editor of the magazine *Economic Guide* (经济导报) and as a member of the Finance and Economic Committee of the CCP Hong Kong Work Committee (中共香港工作委员会财经委员会). He enjoyed close relations with Shanghai's industrial and commercial entrepreneurs, and from January 1953 served as the director of the Shanghai Municipal Bureau of Industry and Commerce, replacing Xu. Xu and Cai could be said to have helmed Shanghai's industrial and commercial administration in the early days of the People's Republic. The details of Cai's life in this summary were based on the "Chronology of Cai Beihua's Life and Works" in Lin (2001, pp. 453–497).

On the other hand, Yang Yanxiu served as deputy director of the Shanghai bureau until the end of 1955, and then replaced Cai as the director, a post he held until December 1957. However, there is scant information about him, and he does not appear in biographical dictionaries such as Sheng (1991).

[20] In terms of the continuity with Shanghai's governmental organization during the National Government era, the Shanghai Municipal Bureau of Industry and Commerce is generally considered to have inherited part of the duties of the Shanghai Municipal Bureau of Social Affairs (上海市社会局), as seen in Shanghaishi bianzhiweiyuanhui bangongshi (1988, p. 5). The predecessor of the Shanghai Municipal Bureau of Industry and Commerce, the Industrial and Commercial Bureau of the Financial and Economic Takeover Committee, had absorbed 376 people from the old government institutions (including 197 from the Shanghai Municipal Bureau of Social Affairs, 26 from the Shanghai Bureau of Weights and Measures (上海市度量衡检定所, an affiliate of the Bureau of Social Affairs), and 153 from the National Supply and Marketing Cooperative's General Office for the Supply and Marketing of Goods (全国供销合作社物品供销总处), so in other words a considerable proportion of staff were retained from the Nationalist era. Shanghai gongshangxingzhengguanlizhi bianzuanweiyuanhui (1997, pp. 242–243).

[21] Regarding the official duties of the Shanghai Municipal Bureau of Industry and Commerce, this outline was based mainly on the description given in Shanghaishi bianzhiweiyuanhui bangongshi (1988, pp. 6–7). This source states that the description therein was written up based on the organizational regulations of each department compiled and printed by the Municipal Government in August 1948 on the one hand, and the "Explanation of the Current Municipal People's Government Organization" compiled and printed by the Municipal Government Secretariat in December 1948 on the other. The author of the present study was unable to acquire these original 1948 documents. In addition to guidance on processing orders, the tasks of the Shanghai Municipal Bureau of Industry and Commerce included management of peddlers and street vendors, management of contracts (between public and private enterprises, and between private enterprises), registration of commerce and industry, management of trademark registration, management of advertising, and so forth. Shanghai gongshangxingzhengguanlizhi bianzuanweiyuanhui (1997, p. 243).

As for the relationship between the Shanghai Municipal Bureau of Industry and Commerce and its superior institutions, the bureau operated within a complex hierarchical structure. It was fundamentally supposed to operate under the guidance of the Central Private Enterprise Bureau (中央私营企业局), which merged with the Central Foreign Enterprise Bureau (中央外资企业局) in November 1952 to become the Central Bureau of Industry and Commerce Administration (中央工商行政管理局) established within the Central Financial and Economic Committee (中央财政经济委员会, hereinafter abbreviated as Central Finance Committee).[22] However, it was also subject to oversight by the central industrial ministries (Ministries of Heavy Industry, Fuel Industry, Textile Industry, Food Industry, Light Industry) as well as the Industrial Department of the East China Military and Political Committee (华东军政委员会工业部) at the Greater Administrative Region (大行政区) level for industrial production; similarly, in terms of commercial matters, it was subject to oversight by the Central Ministry of Trade (中央贸易部) and the Trade Department of the East China Military and Political Committee (华东军政委员会贸易部). In short, the Shanghai Municipal Bureau of Industry and Commerce was subject to vertical oversight under three distinct systems, namely private enterprise management, industry, and commerce. Furthermore, on top of all that, in terms of overall financial and economic policy it was subject to the guidance of the East China Financial and

Another important task for the bureau was the management of state-owned commercial companies, which began in March 1950 according to the central regulations. The Government Administration Council's "Decision on the Implementation of the Unified National State-Owned Trade" (关于统一全国国营贸易实施办法的决定, issued on March 14, 1950) states that "the trade departments of each greater administrative region and the people's governments of provinces and cities directly under the central government (直辖市) shall be subject to the dual guidance of the Central People's Government Ministry of Trade (中央人民政府贸易部) and the local People's Government Financial and Economic Committee (人民政府财政经济委员会)," but in the case of Shanghai, it is believed that the Shanghai Municipal Bureau of Industry and Commerce took over the role of the Financial and Economic Committee (which had not yet been established in Shanghai at the time). See Zhongyangrenminzhengfu fazhiweiyuanhui (1952, p. 325). This task continued until the Shanghai Municipal Bureau of Commerce (上海市商业局) was established in January 1953, to which the management of the specialized companies was transferred in March that same year.

[22] Shanghai gongshangxingzhengguanlizhi bianzuanweiyuanhui (1997, p. 243). Regarding the Central Private Enterprise Bureau (中央私营企业局), in July 1950, an instruction titled "Adjusting Public-Private Relations and Strengthening the Work of the Private Enterprise Bureau" (调整公私关系，加强私营企业局的工作) was issued under the name of Zhou Enlai, emphasizing enhancing the work of the Central Private Enterprise Bureau as well as coordination with local industrial and commercial administrative agencies and the private enterprise departments of various central departments. Zhou Enlai, "Adjusting Public-Private Relations and Strengthening the Work of the Private Enterprise Bureau," July 15, 1950, Zhongyangjuanbianjibu (1992, pp. 156–157). This document was also issued under the name of the Premier of the Government Administration Council as "The Government Administration Council's Instructions on Adjusting Public-Private Relations and Strengthening the Private Enterprise Bureau" (中央人民政府政务院关于调整公私关系，加强私营企业局的指示), date of issue unknown. The instruction also stipulates the following responsibilities for the Private Enterprise Bureau: (1) management of industrial and commercial reports by provincial and municipal industrial and commercial administrative agencies, (2) registration of private industry and commerce, (3) trademark registration, (4) management of public-private joint ventures, and (5) oversight of local industrial and commercial federations.

Economic Committee (华东财政经济委员会) at the greater administrative region level, and to that of the Shanghai Municipal Financial and Economic Committee (上海市财政经济委员会, established in July 1951) at the municipal level.[23]

3.3 The Development of Processing Orders Under the "Adjustment of Industry and Commerce"

The promotion of processing orders at the beginning of the establishment of the PRC was not only in line with the policy of New Democracy, which advocated the protection of private enterprises, but also represented a realistic response to the economic situation at the time. The economy in this early stage was characterized by inflation, which had continued on from the postwar National Government period. In response to this situation, the government took measures such as currency collection and price adjustment through the concentrated purchasing and selling of essential goods, while on the other hand, the "Decision on the Unification of National Financial

---

[23] On the other hand, to serve as a system of oversight below the municipal level, in June 1950 the Industrial and Commercial Guidance Liaison Group (工商辅导连络组) was organized jointly by the Shanghai Municipal Bureau of Industry and Commerce, the Shanghai Industrial and Commercial Federation Preparatory Committee (上海市工商联筹备委员会), and the Shanghai General Labor Union (上海市总工会). This group, which was responsible for reviewing processing orders, aimed to facilitate cooperation among government agencies and among industrial and commercial groups/labor unions in the implementation of said orders. Furthermore, in July 1950, under this group a total of 10 subgroups (加工订货审核小组) were established, one for each industry, such as cotton spinning and dyeing processing, heavy industry processing orders, daily necessities purchase orders, paper orders, grain processing, silk fabric processing, etc. Furthermore, several roving inspection subgroups (巡回稽查小组) were established as subordinate organizations of these subgroups, aiming to supervise and review more concretely the production plans and contracts of processing orders. At the same time, the Industrial and Commercial Guidance Office (工商辅导处) was established within the Shanghai Municipal Bureau of Industry and Commerce to serve as an agency responsible for holistic assessment of processing orders ("Summary of the Work of the Shanghai People's Government Bureau of Industry and Commerce in 1950 (Excerpt)" (上海人民政府工商局1950年工作总结 (节录)), January 1951, in Zhonggongshanghaishiwei tongzhanbu et al. (1993, pp. 97–98) and Shanghai gongshangxingzhengguanlizhi bianzuanweiyuanhui (1997, pp. 297–298). According to the latter source, the roving inspection subgroups were divided into seven categories: cotton spinning and dyeing, silk fabrics, heavy industry, daily necessities, department stores (miscellaneous goods), paper, and grain (p. 27).

Regarding the Industrial and Commercial Guidance Office, "Summary of the Work of the Shanghai People's Government Bureau of Industry and Commerce in 1950" records it as having been established in June 1950 (Zhonggongshanghaishiwei tongzhanbu et al. 1993, pp. 97–98), whereas another source gives the month as August that same year (Shanghai gongshangxingzhengguanlizhi bianzuanweiyuanhui 1997, p. 245). As for its role, this latter source states that it was responsible for "strengthening administrative management of specialized companies," but "How the Shanghai Bureau of Industry and Commerce Grasps Processing Orders" (上海工商局如何掌握加工定货), January 6, 1951, states that it was "responsible for the holistic understanding of processing orders" (Zhongguoshehuikexueyuan and Zhongyangdanganguan 1993, p. 657) and indeed, judging from its subsequent activities, it was in fact an organization strongly involved in the oversight of processing orders.

and Economic Policies" (关于统一国家财政经济工作的决定) was announced on March 3, 1950, promoting the securing of central financial income through the establishment of a nationwide financial and economic system.[24] Although these measures successfully brought inflation under control,[25] extreme deflationary policies then led to market turmoil and stagnation, plunging commerce and industry into recession. For example, by March 1950 cotton yarn production in Shanghai had fallen to 63.57% of what it had been in the same period of the previous year, while rolled cigarette production fell to 40.86%, and that of cement to 15.12%.[26]

The government, taking this situation seriously, put forward a new policy direction called the "Adjustment of Commerce and Industry" (调整工商业)—centered on modifying public-private relations, labor-capital relations, and production-sales relations—at the 3rd Plenary Session of the 7th Central Committee of the CCP (中共七届三中全会) in June 1950.[27] This new policy shift placed particular emphasis on processing orders for private industry, a matter which was considered "relatively important for both the national economy and private industry."[28]

---

[24] The specific measures taken were as follows: (1) unification of national tax revenue (aiming to increase central fiscal revenue by unifying the previously independent tax collection systems of each region under the central government); (2) organization of state-owned trade institutions (establishing nationwide specialized general companies for the purchase of important materials such as food, cotton, cotton yarn, cotton cloth, general merchandise (miscellaneous goods), the salt industry, the coal industry, and special products, under the guidance of the Central Trade Department); and (3) implementation of cash management within state organizations and state-owned enterprises (designating the People's Bank of China as the executing agency for cash management, stipulating that all cash and bills of state organizations, units, and state-owned enterprises should be deposited with it, as well as implementing transfer settlement through the bank for mutual transactions exceeding the limit amount among state organizations, units, and state-owned enterprises). Miyashita (1967, pp. 36–38) and Fujimoto (1971, pp. 39–42).

[25] Looking at the prices of rice, coal, and cotton yarn, it could be said that the rapid rise until March 1950 had converged, and that from April onward, except for a slight rise in cotton yarn, a certain level of stability had been maintained. Zhongguokexueyuan shanghaijingjiyanjiusuo and Shanghaishehuikexueyuan jingjiyanjiusuo (1958, pp. 448–563).

[26] The percentage of production reduction results from comparing the average production volume in March 1950 with that from January to March 1949. Furthermore, the ratio of unsold goods to production volume in cotton yarn was 66%, in rolled cigarettes 100%, and in cement an incredible 470% (a state of holding 3.7 times the production volume in stock), as reported by Xu Dixin ("Report on the Situation of Industry and Commerce in Shanghai," May 1950, in Zhongguoshehuikexueyuan and Zhongyangdanganguan 1996, pp. 377–378). The date and place of this report's issuance are unknown, but the possibility that it was made at the same meeting is quite high, as the document number (G128-1-26) cited in Zhongguoshehuikexueyuan and Zhongyangdanganguan (1996) matches that of "Summary of National Industrial Production at the Meeting of Directors of Industrial and Commercial Bureaus in Seven Major Cities" (七大城市工商局长会议汇总全国工业生产情况), 1950, on p. 372 of the same book.

[27] Miki (1971, p. 74). Prior to this, at the 7th meeting of the Central People's Government Committee (中央人民政府委员会第7届会议) held on April 13, 1950, it was proposed to shift the focus of fiscal and economic policy from balancing fiscal revenue and expenditure and stabilizing prices to "Adjusting Commerce and Industry" (Chen Yun, "Financial Situation and Food" (财政状况和粮食), April 13, 1950, in Chen (1984, p. 79).

[28] Chen Yun "Current Economic Formation and Adjustment of Commerce and Industry, and Adjustment of Tax Revenue Measures" (目前经济形成和调整工商业，调整税收的措置), June 15,

An editorial in the *People's Daily* dated June 8, 1950, gives the following as an expression of the government's position on processing orders at the time of implementing the "Adjustment":

> The proportion of industrial economy in the current Chinese national economy is only about 10%. This is the sum of public and private industries. If we do not adopt a policy of unity and development for private industry, which is beneficial to the national economy and people's lives, the speed of China's industrialization will soon decrease. Therefore, the state must provide the necessary assistance to private industry in terms of management scope, raw material supply, sales markets, working conditions, technical equipment, fiscal policy, financial policy, and so on, based on the overall policy of economic construction stipulated by the Common Program. Processing orders and product purchases for private industry by state agencies and state-owned enterprises are important forms of state assistance to private industry. This is precisely the method to help individual capitalism move towards state capitalism that is stipulated in Article 31 of the Common Program, and will gradually overcome the blindness in the production of private industry."[29]

Here, in line with the provisions of the Common Program (共同纲领, the provisional constitution of the PRC from 1949 until 1954), one sees highlighted the positive influence of private industry on China's industrialization, albeit with the reservation that it remain "beneficial to the national economy and people's lives," while processing orders are acknowledged as an "important form" of "assistance" to private industry. On the other hand, it is noteworthy that the text also refers to overcoming the "blindness" of private industry production through processing orders. In other words, the government also clearly intended to use processing orders to control the production of private industry, while maintaining the balance in the market for industrial products.

Just how were processing orders implemented in Shanghai under the "Adjustment of Commerce and Industry" policy? The main targets of processing orders at that time

---

1950, in Chen (1984, p. 106). Although processing orders were promoted as part of the "Adjustment of Commerce and Industry" policy shift, in actuality they had already been implemented in some areas immediately after the military occupation of Shanghai by the CCP. After the takeover and management transition had settled down, the Shanghai Military Control Committee (上海市军事管制委员会), and mainly the Heavy Industry Department (重工业处) and Food Department (粮食处) thereof, promoted processing orders to some industries—such as food processing, cotton spinning, shipbuilding, and some heavy industries—to support private industry and, above all, to materially support the "southward advance" (南进) of the People's Liberation Army, which was still ongoing at the time. The production carried out through such processing orders accounted for 10.0% of the total production value of private industry in 1949, as shown in Fig. 4.2 in the following chapter, but this was basically a provisional measure, and processing orders were systematically promoted only after being considered part of the "Adjustment of Commerce and Industry" policy. See Shanghai Municipal Bureau of Industry and Commerce Administration (authors Fu Dejin and Zhao Chongwen), "The Role and Function of Processing Orders in the Socialist Transformation of Capitalist Industry and Commerce in Shanghai," Zhonggongshanghaishiwei tongzhanbu et al. (1993, pp. 842–843).

[29] "How to Adjust the Relationship of Commerce and Industry" (如何调整工商业关系), *People's Daily* (人民日报), June 8, 1950, in Zhongguoshehuikexueyuan and Zhongyangdanganguan (1990, p. 746).

were the cotton spinning industry and the machinery manufacturing industry.[30] In the former, the amount of processing orders ordered by the Raw Cotton and Cotton Products Company, which was a state-owned company specializing in work with cotton products, from private factories in Shanghai from May to September 1950 amounted to 134,009 bales of cotton yarn and 1,571,159 bolts of processed cotton cloth. This was a significant increase compared to the amount of processing carried out throughout the East China region from August 1949 to May 1950, which totaled 44,929 bales and 973,802 bolts, respectively.[31] At that time, 37 out of 39 private factories in operation were receiving processing orders from state-owned enterprises and state organizations, either partially or entirely (Sun 1990, p. 60).

As for the machinery manufacturing industry, the orders placed by the East China Region Industrial Department (华东工业部) to the private machinery manufacturing industry over the three months of June, July, and August 1950 accounted for 60–80% of the production capacity of all private machinery manufacturing industries in Shanghai (Qian et al. 1957, p. 20).

In other industries as well, production by processing orders came to occupy a significant proportion of total production, encompassing 60% of rubber shoe production and all raincoat production in the rubber processing industry in 1950, while in the milling industry, processing orders in the second half of 1950 reached four times the self-production portion of each factory.[32] In the statistics for the second half of 1950, the processing order contracts reviewed by the Shanghai Municipal Processing Order Review Group (市加工订货审核小组) totaled 2436, with the number of private factories involved reaching as high as 1300.[33]

The results of processing orders under the "Adjustment of Commerce and Industry" policy in Shanghai are illustrated by Table 3.2, which summarizes the figures published at that time, and shows a marked increase in production in each industry.[34]

[30] At that time, Sun Xiaocun (孙晓村), a member of the Central Finance Committee, said, "Whether it is nationwide or just in Shanghai, the main targets of consignment processing and commodity ordering are the cotton industry and the machinery industry. When the situation of those two industries improves, their direct and indirect effects will reach more than 70% of the total industry." Sun Xiaocun "On the Public-Private Relationship in Processing and Ordering Procurement" (论加工定货收购中的公私关系), *Xinhua Monthly* (新华月报), June 3, 1950, in Zhongguoshehuikexueyuan and Zhongyangdanganguan (1993, p. 641).

[31] Xu Dixin, "Report on the Adjustment of Public-Private Relations and the Situation of Shanghai Industry and Commerce" (关于调整公私关系与上海工商业情况的报告), October 18, 1950, in Zhonggongshanghaishiwei tongzhanbu et al. (1993, pp. 78–80). On the development of processing orders for the cotton textile industry, see Izutani (2007), Chapter 3.

[32] Central Private Enterprise Bureau, "Some Issues in the Work of Processing Orders" (中央私营企业局加工订货工作中的一些问题), July 5, 1951,in Zhongguoshehuikexueyuan and Zhongyangdanganguan (1993, p. 659) (originally published in *Industrial and Commercial Situation Bulletin* (工商情况通报) no.15).

[33] Shanghai People's Government Bureau of Industry and Commerce, "Summary of the Work of the Shanghai People's Government Bureau of Industry and Commerce in 1950 (Excerpt)" (1950年工作总结 (节录)), January 1951, Zhonggongshanghaishiwei tongzhanbu et al. (1993, p. 98).

[34] The figures in Table 3.2 were released by the Shanghai Municipal Government, therefore it is possible that only thriving industries were listed in order to emphasize the effects of the policy. However, many of the industries in the table were Shanghai's major ones in the Republican period.

Table 3.2 Amounts of production and sale of main products in Shanghai, April and August 1950

Products	Unit	Production			Sale		
		April	August	Rate of increase (%)	April	August	Rate of increase (%)
Cotton yarn	Bale	60,453	67,902	12.3	52,977	76,184	43.8
Woolen yarn	Pound	276,697	385,871	39.5	212,765	428,201	101.3
Flour	Sack	99,738	523,032	424.4	406,472	644,560	58.6
Tobacco	Box	15,092	39,883	164.3	22,743	46,833	105.9
Matches	Box	1,122	4,293	282.6	2,837	4,824	70.0
Cement	Sack	53,448	116,504	118.0	29,192	114,279	291.5
Vegetable oil	Jin (500 g)	1,341,681	4,272,567	218.4	1,496,743	4,023,375	168.8
Soap	Box	33,323	106,497	219.6	33,193	76,933	131.8
Newsprint	Lian (500 sheets)	12,313	82,701	571.7	13,361	79,203	492.8

Source Zhongguoshehuikexueyuan and Zhongyangdanganguan (1993, p. 884). Original data from Shanghai Municipal Government "The Results of the Adjustment of the Relationships between Public and Private Commerce and Industry" (上海公私工商关系调整后的收获), in Chinese Institute of Industrial Economy (中国工业经济研究所). Shanghai Industry after the Adjustment of the Relationships between Public and Private Commerce and Industry (调整公私工商关系后的上海工业) (publisher unknown, October 1950). Note: "Rates of increase" are calculated by author

Further, consulting other sources that record the number of applications for opening or closing factories, the number of closure applications decreased significantly from June, with May as the peak, while the number of reopening applications, which were hardly seen before May, increased slightly (Zhongguoshehuikexueyuan and Zhongyangdanganguan 1993, pp. 887–889). In short, with the widespread development of processing orders, they came to play a significant role in the recovery of industrial production.[35]

However, on the other hand, government reports also drew attention to several problems that occurred during the execution of processing orders. What follows are some examples, in two categories.

a. Private enterprises' falsification of raw materials, diversion of public goods and expenses, and shoddy production

[35] However, no historical sources can be found that show that the processing fees and order prices of the processing orders, which were carried out as "assistance to private industry" at that time, were demonstratedly advantageous compared to market prices. That being said, it is clear that at least the quantitative expansion of processing orders (that is to say, the creation of demand by the government and state-owned enterprises) helped private industry to escape from recession.

A report issued by the East China Financial and Economic Committee to the Central Finance Committee, the Central Ministry of Trade (中央贸易部), and each local Financial and Economic Committee, states as follows:

> When public enterprises make processing orders and purchases, private factories always cut corners, falsify raw materials, and delay delivery, and there occur incidents such as the diversion of public goods and expenses. The delivered products which the Raw Cotton and Cotton Products Company ordered through processing orders to private factories did not meet the standards of quality. More than 180,000 bolts of processed cloth in Qingdao did not meet quality standards by 70%, and in Shanghai, too much starch was applied to the cloth, causing mold to grow. The Department Company [百货公司], a state-owned commercial enterprise dealing with miscellaneous goods], upon inspecting the warehouse, discovered phenomena such as insufficient drying of ordered rubber shoes, rubber parts being sticky, shoe parts turning yellow, toothpaste drying out and hardening, and sheets becoming crispy due to too much bleaching powder being used.[36]

The report highlights various instances where private enterprises were cutting corners and/or engaged in falsification. For private enterprises, the processing orders may have represented an opportunity to seek profit through engaging in business with public enterprises that lacked sufficient business experience. However, on the other hand, the fact that private enterprises were able to deliver even inferior products in the first place could also indicate the inadequacy of the system of management employed by the government agencies in charge of supervision.

b. Troubles in collaboration between the Shanghai Municipal Bureau of Industry and Commerce and state-owned enterprises/state organizations

A 1951 report from the Shanghai Municipal Bureau of Industry and Commerce states as follows:

> Based on the central regulations, the processing orders must be uniformly controlled by the local Bureau of Industry and Commerce, and must be able to promote cooperation and guidance to private commerce and industry in a well-planned manner. […] The public enterprises side recognized that state-owned enterprises do not need to obey the guidance of the Bureau of Industry and Commerce, and they did not pay much attention [to such guidance]. Through persuasion and the instructions of superior organizations, [such a bias] has already been overcome, but gradually another bias has occurred. Some units pushed all processing orders to the Bureau of Industry and Commerce, making the Bureau responsible for everything such as contracts, order forms, quality, standards, etc. In particular, the military's orders set [i.e., imposed] deadlines and prices [on the Bureau], and regarded the Bureau of Industry and Commerce as a rear support organization. Thus, the Bureau of Industry and Commerce became unable to bear the responsibility, and only after explaining that the Bureau of Industry and Commerce is only an intermediary organization to adjust public-private relations and not a corporate organization, was this difficulty finally resolved.[37]

---

[36] East China Financial and Economic Committee, "Report on the Phenomena and Policies Adopted in the Process of Rational Adjustment of Public and Private Relations after Price Stability" (华东财政经济委员会关于物价平稳后各地合理调整公私关系过程中产生的现象及采取的方针的通报), September 9, 1950, in Zhonggongshanghaishiwei tongzhanbu et al. (1993, pp. 75–76).

[37] Shanghai [Municipal] Bureau of Industry and Commerce "How Do We Control Processing Orders?" (如何掌握加工定货), January 6, 1951, in Zhongguoshehuikexueyuan and Zhongyangdanganguan (1993, p. 657).

The report shows how various problems emerged due to the unified management of processing orders by the Shanghai Bureau of Industry and Commerce. As can be seen from this example, when it came to the actual procedures of processing orders, the understanding of responsibilities was unclear even among state organizations, state-owned enterprises, and the bureau itself. Clearly the bureau, a department within the Shanghai Municipal Government, encountered various difficulties in managing processing orders uniformly.

As described above, the processing orders that were promoted as part of the "Adjustment of Commerce and Industry" achieved certain results in terms of the recovery of private enterprise production in Shanghai, but several problems occurred in the course of their operations. In response to this situation, Xu Dixin, the aforementioned director of the Shanghai Municipal Bureau of Industry and Commerce, stated the following at the first meeting of the second term of the Shanghai People's Representatives Conference (上海市第二届期第一次各界人民代表会议), which convened in October 1950:

> Representatives and comrades, the commerce and industry of Shanghai are already showing signs of improvement, but does this mean that everything is fine and that there are no problems at all? That's just not the case. As we move forward, difficulties still exist, and these difficulties are manifested in the following points. [...] First, in the adjustment of public-private relations, comrades in the state's economic sector have not yet been able to urge the transformation of private enterprises through this relationship, and some friends of private enterprises have inaccurate perspectives. They forget that there are "differences" among the five types of economies, they think that "considering both public and private" means "splitting fifty-fifty," and they interpret "treating all equally" as "egalitarianism." [...] As Vice Premier Chen Yun clearly stated, "The essence of the so-called adjustment of the relationship between public and private commerce and industry is to establish the leading position of the state economy on the one hand, and to allow the private capitalist economy to find its proper place under the guidance of the state economy on the other." We hope that our friends in the commerce and industry sector will firmly grasp this spirit.[38]

Here, Xu Dixin identified problems that the state's economic sector had encountered in dealing with various issues that had arisen in the course of pursuing the "Adjustment of Commerce and Industry" policy. He also reaffirmed the leading position of the state economy, while warning private commercial and industrial entrepreneurs to toe the line. However, in spite of such comments, the recognition of the "guidance of the state economy" in directing private enterprises at this point was not as strict as was the case in later periods. This was because the "Adjustment of Commerce and Industry" policy was predicated on the notion of providing assistance to private commerce and industry, rather than controlling them per se, and indeed the need for management and control of private enterprises by the government was not seen as particularly urgent. However, this situation was shortly to drastically change due to the overall situation of China's participation in the Korean War from October 1950.

---

[38] Xu Dixin, "Report on the Adjustment of Public-Private Relations and the Situation of Shanghai Industry and Commerce" (关于调整公私关系与上海工商业情况的报告), October 18, 1950, Zhonggongshanghaishiwei tongzhanbu et al. (1993, pp. 81–82). On the "five types of economies," see subsection 3.1, 3.2, 3.3 in this chapter.

References

English Language

Brugger, William. 1976. *Democracy and Organization in the Chinese Industrial Enterprise: 1948–1953*. Cambridge: Cambridge University Press

Gardner, John. 1969. The Wufan Campaign in Shanghai: A Study in the Consolidation of Urban Control. In *Chinese Communist Politics in Action*, ed. Doak A Barnett, 477–539. Seattle: University of Washington Press

Lieberthal, Kenneth G. 1980. *Revolution and Tradition in Tientsin: 1949–1952*. Stanford: Stanford University Press

Chinese Language

Chen, Yun. 1984. *Chenyun wenxuan* (陈云文选 (1949–1956), Selected Works of Chen Yun: 1949–1956). Beijing: Renmin chubanshe

Dangdai zhongguo de gongshangxingzhengguanli bianjiweiyuanhui, ed. 1991. *Dangdai zhongguo de gongshangxingzhengguanli* (当代中国的工商行政管理, Contemporary China's Industrial and Commercial Administration). Beijing: Dangdai zhongguo chubenshe

Dong, Zhikai, ed. 1996. *1949–1952 nian zhongguo jingjifenxi* (1949–1952年中国经济分析, Analysis of China's Economy: 1949–1952). Beijing: Zhongguo shehuikexue chubanshe

Gui, Yong. 2006. *Siyou chanquan de shehui jichu: chengshi qiye chanquan de zhengzhi chonggou: 1949–1956* (私有产权的社会基础:城市企业产权的政治重构 (1949–1956), The Social Foundation of Private Property Rights: The Political Reconstruction of Urban Enterprise Property Rights (1949–1956). Shanghai: Lixin kuaiji chubanshe

Jin, Zhihuan. 2006. *Zhongguo fangzhijianshegongsi yanjiu* (中国纺织建设公司研究(1945–1950), Research on China Textile Construction Company, 1945–1950). Shanghai: Fudan University Press

Liu, Songbin. 1997. *Zhongguo gongchandang dui dachengshi de jieguan: 1945–1952* (中国共产党对大城市的接管 (1945–1952), The Chinese Communist Party's Takeover of Large Cities: 1945–1952), Beijing: Beijing tushuguan chubanshe

Lin, Tonghua, ed. 2001. *Cai beihua wenji* (蔡北华文集, Cai Beihua Collection), Shanghai: Shanghai shehuikexueyuan chubanshe

Qian, hua et al ed. 1957. *Qinianlai woguo siyinggongshangye de bianhua* (七年来我国私营工商业的变化, Changes in Our Country's Private Industry and Commerce over the Past Seven Years). Beijing: Caizheng jingji chubanshe

Quanguo zhengxie wenshiziliaoyanjiu weiyuanhui gongshangjingjizu. 1988. *Huiyi guomindangzhengfu ziyuanweiyuanhui* (回忆国民党政府资源委员会, Recollections of the National Government Resources Committee). Beijing: Zhongguo wenshi chubanshe

Shanghai gongshangxingzhengguanlizhi bianzuanweiyuanhui, ed. 1997. *Shanghai gongshangxingzhengguanlizhi* (上海工商行政管理志, Shanghai Industrial and Commercial Administration Chronicle). Shanghai: Shanghai shehuikexueyuan chubanshe

Shanghai shehuikexueyuan jingjisuo. 1980. *Shanghai zibenzhuyi gongshangye de shehuizhuyigaizao* (上海资本主义工商业的社会主义改造, The Socialist Transformation of Shanghai's Capitalist Industry and Commerce). Shanghai: Shanghai renmin chubanshe

Shanghaishi bianzhiweiyuanhui bangongshi, ed. 1988. *Shanghai dangzhengjigou yange* (上海党政机构沿革 1949–1986, The Evolution of Shanghai Chinese Communist Party and Government Organizations 1949–1986). Shanghai: Shanghai renmin chubanshe

Sheng, Ping, ed. 1991. *Zhongguo gongchandang renmin cidian* (中国共产党人名大辞典, Dictionary of Names of Chinese Communist Party Members). Beijing: Zhongguo guojiguangbo chubanshe

Sun, Huairen, ed. 1990. *Shanghai shehuizhuyi jingjijianshe fazhan jianzhi: 1949–1985* (上海社会主义经济建设发展简史:1949–1985, A Brief History of Shanghai's Socialist Economic Construction Development: 1949–1985). Shanghai: Shanghai renmin chubanshe

Sun, Huimin. 2006. Shanghai lüshiye de gaizao yu xiaomie: 1949–1957 (上海律师业的改造與消灭 (1949–1957), The Transformation and Elimination of Shanghai's Legal Profession: 1949–1957). In *Lianganfentu: Lengzhanchuqi de zhengjingfazhan* (两岸分途:冷战初期的政经发展, Parting Ways: Politics and Economics across the Taiwan Straits since 1949), ed. Chen Yongfa, 77–118. Taipei: Institute of Modern History, Academia Sinica

Wu, Li, ed. 1999. *Zhonghuarenmingongheguo jingjishi* (中华人民共和国经济史, Economic History of the People's Republic of China), Volumes I & II. Beijing: Zhongguo jingji chubanshe

Xu, Dixin. 1947. *Guanliao zibenlun* (官僚资本论, Theory of Bureaucratic Capital). Hong Kong: Nanyang shudian

Xu, Dixin. 1949a. *Zhongguo jingji de daolu* (中国经济的道路, The Road of China's Economy). Hong Kong: Xin zhongguo shuju

Xu, Dixin. 1949b. *Gongshangyejia de chulu* (工商业家的出路, The Way Out for Industrialists and Businessmen). Hong Kong: Xinminzhu chubanshe

Xu, Youchun, ed. 2007. *Minguo renwu dashidian* (民国人物大辞典, Biographical Dictionary of the Republic of China). Revised and enlarged edition, Shijiazhuang: Huabei renmin chubanshe

Zhang, Xule. 2006. *Shanghai siying jinrongye yanjiu* (上海私营金融业研究 (1949–1952), Research on Shanghai's Private Financial Industry: 1949–1952). Shanghai: Fudan University Press

Zheng, Youkui, Cheng Linsun and Zhang Chuanhong. 1991. *Jiuzhongguo de ziyuanweiyuanhui: Shishi yu pingjia* (旧中国的资源委员会:史实与评价, Old China's Resources Committee: History and Evaluation). Shanghai: Shanghai shehuikexueyuan chubanshe

Zhonggongshanghaishiwei tongzhanbu, Zhonggongshanghaishi dangshiyanjiushi, and Shanghaishidanganguan. 1993. *Zhongguo zibenzhuyigongshangye de shehuizhuyigaizao: Shanghai juan* (中国资本主义工商业的社会主义改造 (上海卷), The Socialist Transformation of China's Capitalist Industry and Commerce: Shanghai Volume), Volume I & II. Beijing: Zhonggong dangshi chubanshe

Zhonggongshanghaishiwei zuzhibu, Zhonggongshanghaishiwei dangshiziliaozhengjiweiyuanhui, Zhonggongshanghaishiwei dangshiyanjiushi, and Shanghaishidanganguan. 1991. *Shanghaishi zhengquan xitong, difangjunshi xitong, tongyizhanzhanxian xitong, qunzhongtuanti xitong zuzhishi ziliao: 1949.5–1987.10* (上海市政权系统、地方军事系统、统一战线系统、群众团体系统组织史资料 (1949.5–1987.10), Historical Materials of Organizations of the Shanghai Municipal Government System, the Local Military System, the United Front System, the Mass Organization System: 1949.5–1987.10). Shanghai: Shanghai renmin chubanshe

Zhonggong zhongyangdangshiyanjiushi, and Hu Sheng, eds. 1991. *Zhongguo gongchandang de qishinian* (中国共产党的七十年, Seventy Years of the Chinese Communist Party). Beijing: Zhonggong dangshi chubanshe

Zhonggong zhongyang wenxianyanjiushi, ed. 1992. *Jianguoyilai zhongyaowenxianxuanbian: di 1 ce* (建国以来重要文献选编 (第1册), Selection of Important Documents Since the Founding of the People's Republic of China: Volume 1). Beijing: Zhongyang wenxian chubanshe

Zhongguokexueyuan shanghaijingjiyanjiusuo, and Shanghaishehuikexueyuan jingjiyanjiusuo, eds. 1958. *Shanghai jiefangqianhou wujiaziliaohuibian: 1921 nian – 1957 nian* (上海解放前后物价资料汇编 (1921年-1957年), Compilation of Price Data Before and After the Liberation of Shanghai: 1921–1957). Shanghai: Shanghai renmin chubanshe

Zhongguoshehuikexueyuan jingjiyanjiusuo. 1978. *Zhongguo zibenzhuyigongshangye de shehuizhuyigaizao* (中国资本主义工商业的社会主义改造, The Socialist Transformation of China's Capitalist Industry and Commerce). Beijing: Renmin chubanshe

Zhongguoshehuikexueyuan and Zhongyangdanganguan, eds. 1990. *Zhonghuarenmingongheguo jingjidanganziliaoxuanbian 1949–1952: Zonghe juan* (中华人民共和国经济档案资料选编1949–1952 (综合卷), Selected Economic Archive Materials of the People's Republic of China 1949–1952: Comprehensive Volume). Beijing: Zhongguo chengshijingjishehui chubanshe

Zhongguoshehuikexueyuan and Zhongyangdanganguan, eds. 1993. *Zhonghuarenmingongheguo jingjidanganziliaoxuanbian 1949–1952: Gongshangtizhi juan* (中华人民共和国经济档案资料选编1949–1952 (工商体制卷), Selected Economic Archive Materials of the People's Republic of China 1949–1952: Industrial and Commercial System Volume). Beijing: Zhongguo shehuikexue chubanshe

Zhongguoshehuikexueyuan and Zhongyangdanganguan, eds. 1995. *Zhonghuarenmingongheguo jingjidanganziliaoxuanbian 1949–1952: Shangye juan* (中华人民共和国经济档案资料选编1949–1952 (商业卷), Selected Economic Archive Materials of the People's Republic of China 1949–1952: Commercial Volume). Beijing: Zhongguo wuzi chubanshe

Zhongguoshehuikexueyuan and Zhongyangdanganguan, eds. 1996. *Zhonghuarenmingongheguo jingjidanganziliaoxuanbian 1949–1952: Gongye juan* (中华人民共和国经济档案资料选编1949–1952 (工业卷), Selected Economic Archive Materials of the People's Republic of China 1949–1952: Industrial Volume). Beijing: Zhongguo wuzi chubanshe

Zhongyang gongshangguanliju, and Zhongguokexueyuan jingjiyanjiusuo zibenzhuyijingjigaizaoyanjiushi, eds. 1962. *Zhongguo zibenzhuyigongshangye de shehuizhuyigaizao* (中国资本主义工商业的社会主义改造, The Socialist Transformation of China's Capitalist Industry and Commerce). Beijing: Renmin chubanshe

Zhongyangjuanbianjibu, ed. 1992. *Zhongguo zibenzhuyigongshangye de shehuizhuyigaizao: zhongyangjuan* (中国资本主义工商业的社会主义改造 (中央卷), The Socialist Transformation of China's Capitalist Industry and Commerce: Central Volume), Volumes I and II. Beijing: Zhonggongdangshi chubanshe

Zhongyangrenminzhengfu fazhiweiyuanhui, ed. 1952. *Zhongyangrenminzhengfu falinghuibian: 1949–1950* (中央人民政府法令汇编 (1949–1950), Compilation of Laws and Regulations of the Central People's Government: 1949–1950). Beijing: Renmin chubanshe

Japanese Language

Amako, Satoshi et al., eds. 1999. *Gendai chūgoku jiten* (現代中国事典, Encyclopedia of Contemporary China). Tokyo: Iwanami shoten

Amano, Motonosuke. 1961. *Gendai chūgoku keizairon* (現代中国経済論, Contemporary Chinese Economy). Kyoto: Minerva Shobō

Fujimoto, Akira. 1971. *Shinchūgoku no kokkazaisei no kenkyū* (新中国の国家財政の研究, Study on the Public Finance of New China). Tokyo: Yūhikaku

Furushima, Kazuo. 1969. Kokuminkeizai fukkōki niokeru tōseiseisaku to sonoseikaku (国民経済復興期における統制政策とその性格, The Control Policy in the Period of National Economic Recovery). *Shakai kagaku kenkyū* (社会科学研究, The Journal of Social Science), Institute of Social Science, University of Tokyo, 20(5–6): 1–36

Izutani, Yōko. 2007. *Chūgoku kenkokushoki no seiji to keizai: Taishū undou to shakaishugitaisei* (中国建国初期の政治と経済——大衆運動と社会主義体制, Politics and Economy in the Early Years of the People's Republic of China: Mass Movements and the Socialist System). Tokyo: Ochanomizu shobō

Kawai, Shin'ichi. 1987. Sengo chūgoku bōshokugyō no Keisei to kokuminseihu: Chūgokubōshokukensetsukōshi no seiritsukatei (戦後中国紡織業の形成と国民政府——中国紡織建設公司の成立過程, The Formation of China's Textile Industry after World War II and the National Government: The Establishment Process of The China Textile Industries Inc.,). *Kokusai kankeiron kenkyū* (国際関係論研究, Studies on International Relations) 6: 39–61. http://hdl.handle.net/2261/00076939

Kawai, Shin'ichi. 1991. *Chūgoku kigyō to soren moderu: Icchōsei no shiteki kenkyū* (中国企業とソ連モデル——一長制の史的研究, Chinese Euterprise and Soviet Model: A Historical Study of One Man Leadership System). Tokyo: Japan Association for Asian Studies

Kawai, Shin'ichi. 1992. Taisengo no chūgoku menbōshokugyō to chūbōkōshi (大戦後の中国綿紡織業と中紡公司, The China Textile Industries Inc., and cotton textile industry in China after World War II). *Journal of International Affairs*, Institute of International Affairs, Aichi University (愛知大学国際問題研究所紀要) 97: 323–349. https://aichiu.repo.nii.ac.jp/records/4569

Kawai, Shin'ichi. 2001. Chūbōkōshi to kokuminseihu no tōsei (中紡公司と国民政府の統制——国有企業の自立的経営方針とその挫折, The China Textile Industries Inc., and the National Government's Control: The Independent Management Policy of State-owned Enterprises and Its Failure). In *Sengo Chūgoku kokuminseihushi no kenkyū: 1945–1949 nen* (戦後中国国民政府史の研究1945–1949年, Studies on the History of the China's National Government after World War II: 1945–1949), ed. Mitsuyoshi Himeta, 209–234. Hachioji: Chuo University Press

Miki, Takeshi. 1971. *Chūgoku kaifukuki no keizaiseisaku: Shinminshushugi keizairon* (中国回復期の経済政策——新民主主義経済論, Economic Policy in China's Recovery Period: New Democratic Economy). Tokyo: Kawashima shoten

Mōri, Kazuko. 1994. Chūgoku no shakaishugi sentaku to kokusaikankyō (中国の社会主義選択と国際環境, China's Choice for the Socialization and International Environment). In *Higashi ajia to reisen* (東アジアと冷戦, East Asia and the Cold War), ed. Yamagiwa Akira, 259–283. Tokyo: Sanrei Shobō

Miyashita, Tadao. 1967. *Shinchūgoku no tsūkaseisaku* (新中国の通貨政策, New China's Monetary Policy), Seimeikai Series V. Tokyo: Seimeikai

Nihon kokusaimondai kenkyūjo chūgokubukai, ed. 1974. *Chūgoku kyūsantōshi shiryōshū 10 kan* (中国共産党史資料集 10巻, Collection of Historical Materials of Chinese Communist Party Volume 10). Tokyo: Keisō shobō

Okumura, Satoshi. 1999. *Chūgoku no gendaishi: Sensō to shakaishugi* (中国の現代史——戦争と社会主義, Modern History of China: War and Socialism). Tokyo: Aoki Shoten

Tanaka, Yoshiyuki. 1978. Kenkokushoki no keizaiseisaku: Chūgoku kakumei no seichōtenka no mondai niyosete (建国初期の経済政策——中国革命の成長転化の問題によせて, Economic Policy in the Early Years of the People's Republic of China: On the Issue of Growth and Transformation of the Chinese Revolution). In *Kōza chūgoku kingendaishi* (講座中国近現代史, Lectures on Modern and Contemporary Chinese History), Volume 7, ed. Nozawa Yutaka and Tanaka Masatoshi, 137–163. Tokyo: University of Tokyo Press

Uehara, Kazuyoshi. 1975–76. Kokuminkeizaifukkouki niokeru taishihonshugiseisaku (国民経済復興期における対資本主義政策, Capitalist Policy in the Period of National Economic Recovery). *Rekishi hyōron* (歴史評論, Historical Journal) 307: 1–18, 310: 57–69

Zama, Kōichi. 1978. Shakaishugi eno ikou to 'sanhan' 'gohan' undō (社会主義への移行と『三反』・『五反』運動, Transition to Socialism and 'Three Anti' and 'Five Anti' Movements). In *Kōza chūgoku kingendaishi* (講座中国近現代史, Lectures on Modern and Contemporary Chinese History), Volume 7, ed. Nozawa Yutaka and Tanaka Masatoshi, 165–198. Tokyo: University of Tokyo Press

Chapter 4
The Korean War and the Formation of the Socialist System

Abstract This chapter, building on Chapter 3, focuses on the policy of the processing orders given to private industrial enterprises, and examines the impact of changes in the situation after the Korean War on the CCP's private enterprise policy in Shanghai against the backdrop of the process of forming a socialist system. The Korean War broke out in June 1950, and China decided to enter the war on October 19 of the same year. This chapter is divided into two parts, with the first mainly analyzing the expansion of processing orders during wartime, from October 1950 up until the second half of 1951 when peace talks commenced, and the second taking up the development of governmental control over private enterprises after late 1951.

Keywords Korean War · Private enterprises · Processing orders · Public-private jointly-owned enterprises · Socialist transformation · General Line of the Transition Period

The Korean War broke out in June 1950, and China decided to enter the war on October 19 of the same year. There was significant debate among the leaders of the Chinese Communist Party until the last minute regarding entering the conflict, but ultimately the decision was made under the forceful leadership of Mao Zedong, and the Chinese People's "Volunteer Army" crossed the Yalu River on the China-North Korea border (Shu 1991). In short, even for the Chinese government itself, participation in the war was no certain thing and came as something rather unexpected.

This chapter, building on Chapter 3, will focus on the policy of processing orders given to private industrial enterprises, and examine the impact of changes in the situation after the Korean War on the CCP's private enterprise policy in Shanghai against the backdrop of the process of forming a socialist system. The Korean War saw peace talks commence on July 10, 1951, and after a period of "political negotiations without a ceasefire," an agreement was finally signed on July 23, 1953 (Kida 1993). Situating its analysis within this context, this chapter is divided into two parts, with the first mainly analyzing the expansion of processing orders during wartime, from

J. Kajima, *Shanghai under the Socialist System*, Studies in Economic History,
https://doi.org/10.1007/978-981-95-3225-4_4

October 1950 to the second half of 1951, and the second taking up the development of this system after late 1951.

4.1 The Korean War and the Expansion of Processing Orders

4.1.1 Wartime Economic Control

Participation in the Korean War forced a major change in the government's economic policy, and the new policy direction, in the words of Chen Yun, then Deputy Prime Minister and Head of the Central Finance Committee, was "War first, maintenance of the market second, and everything else third."[1] The "maintenance of the market" mentioned here specifically referred to the suppression of price increases, and demonstrated how the CCP regime wanted to avoid a recurrence of the inflation that had characterized the postwar National Government period, and which had only calmed down in March 1950, at all costs.

The background to the government's concern about price increases was not only the turmoil in the domestic economy resulting from the participation in the Korean War, but also the implementation of US trade restrictions on China.[2] The US government had already urged domestic oil companies to refrain from selling oil to China in 1949, and when the Coordinating Committee for Multilateral Export Controls (COCOM) was established from the end of 1949 to the beginning of 1950, it requested that participating countries strengthen export controls on the communist bloc, including China.

On top of this, once the Korean War broke out restrictions on trade with China became more substantial. After June 1950, measures such as export bans and the introduction of permit systems were gradually implemented for metals such as steel, silver, copper, lead, and zinc, natural resources such as petroleum, palm oil, rubber, and cotton, and equipment such as metal cutting machines, chemical equipment, transportation equipment, communication equipment, navigation equipment, and railway goods, targeting China, Macao, and Hong Kong, the last of which was an important transit trade port.[3] Furthermore, on December 3, 1950, all goods exported

[1] "Policy of Financial and Economic Work after the Start of the Korean War" (抗美援朝开始后财经工作的方针), November 15, 1950, Report at the 2nd National Financial Conference (第二次全国财政会议), in Chen (1984, p. 111).

[2] The following overview of the development of US export control policy toward China is based on "Customs General Administration Customs Statistics Annual Report, 1950" (海关总署海关统计年报 1950年), Zhongguoshehuikexueyuan and Zhongyangdanganguan (1994, pp. 447–448), Miki (1971, pp. 440–441), Mōri (1994b, pp. 102–103), and Katō (1992, pp. 123–178).

[3] The development of trade control after June 1950 was as follows. On June 28, 1950, a total embargo was initiated against North Korea, and at the same time, an export permit system for 11 items—including oil, rubber, palm oil, copper, diamonds, lead, and silver—was implemented for China and

to China, Macao, and Hong Kong were placed under control,[4] and thus the American embargo against China came to full fruition.

Against the backdrop of such trade restrictions, the government rolled out a series of material control policies. The "Directive on Price Fluctuation Issues" (关于防止物价波动问题的指示), promulgated on October 20, 1950, indicated that (1) goods relatively well-controlled by the government, such as food, cotton cloth, and coal, would be sold in the market by the government to stabilize the prices; (2) goods less controlled by the government, such as cotton yarn, petroleum, industrial equipment, and imported goods, would be intensively purchased by the government; and finally, (3) important industrial raw materials, such as rubber, steel, and copper, would be distributed based on industrial production needs.[5] The strengthening of material control was gradually pursued thereafter,[6] and particularly impactful among steps in this direction was the "Decision on the Unified Purchase of Cotton Yarn" (关于统购棉纱的决定) on January 4, 1951.[7] This decision stipulated that all cotton yarn and

Macao. Subsequently, in mid-August exports of 16 items—such as metal-cutting machines, non-ferrous metals, chemical products, chemical equipment, transportation equipment, communications equipment, and navigation equipment—were banned, and in September, the strengthening of cotton export control and the banning of exports of 20 items such as steel and railway goods were decided. At the same time, for Hong Kong, a ban on 10 items including rubber was decided on July 1, and a ban on 190 items was decided on August 12. Furthermore, in October 1950, when China decided to participate in the Korean War, the export limit for cotton was lowered, and limits were set for the export of copper and copper products, zinc and zinc products, and lead. In 1952, the CHINCOM (China Committee), which targeted China and North Korea, was established within COCOM (it later merged with COCOM in 1956). For more, refer to Amako et al. (1999, p. 890).

[4] Note that on December 6 of the same year, Japan was also ordered to impose a ban on exports to China, by the Occupation authorities (GHQ, the General Head Quarters of the Supreme Commander for the Allied Powers).

[5] Central Financial and Economic Committee of the CCP, "Instructions on the Issue of Preventing Price Fluctuations by the Central Financial and Economic Committee of the Communist Party of China" (中共中央财经委员会关于防止物价波动问题的指示), October 20, 1950, Zhongyangjuanbianjibu (1992, pp. 184–186).

[6] On November 14, 1950, the Central Ministry of Trade issued "Several Instructions on the Control of Speculative Commerce" (关于取缔投机商业的几项指示), and the crackdown on "speculative" commercial activities taking advantage of price fluctuations was intensified. Furthermore, in January of the following year, instructions were again issued regarding concentrated purchases of goods, mainly industrial equipment, which had become scarce due to restrictions on exports to China and which the government had relatively weak control over, for the purpose of collecting money by introducing goods into the market. See Central Ministry of Trade, "Price Policy and Basic Policy Direction after the Chinese Luna New Year" (中央贸易部旧年后物价政策及基本方针), January 13, 1951, and Central Ministry of Trade, "Instructions for Controlling Prices during the Chinese Lunar New Year Period" (中央贸易部春节期间掌握物价的指示), January 13, 1951," both in Zhongguoshehuikexueyuan and Zhongyangdanganguan (1995, pp. 68–70); and Central Trade Department, "Several Instructions on the Control of Speculative Commerce" (中央人民政府贸易部关于取缔投机商业的几项指示),November 14, 1950, Zhonggong zhongyang wenxianyanjiushi (1992, p. 466).

[7] Government Administration Council Finance and Economic Committee, "Decision on the Purchase of Cotton Yarn" (政务院财政经济委员会关于统购棉纱的决定), Zhongyangrenminzhengfu fazhiweiyuanhui (1953, p. 175).

cloth produced (excluding orders from governmental agencies and state-owned enterprises) by state-owned, public-private jointly-owned, and private factories would be purchased by the state-owned Raw Cotton and Cotton Products Company, effectively banning the market circulation of cotton products, one of the most important industrial products in China at the time.

In addition to the material control measures discussed above, financial control measures were also implemented.[8] In November 1950, almost immediately after deciding to enter the Korean War, the government took emergency measures to freeze public deposits (for a period of 40 days), further tightened cash controls for some unfrozen deposits, promoted cashless transactions among public institutions and state-owned enterprises, and strengthened inspections of on-hand funds. In December, it announced that financial controls would be strengthened from cash management to broader currency management. These financial controls and the development of mass movements in 1951–52, which will be discussed later, led to the culmination of the transformation of all private financial enterprises into public-private jointly-owned ones as early as December 1952, which was earlier than was the case in other industries.

Shanghai, being the economic center of China, was a major target area for these economic control policies. The Shanghai Military Control Committee and the Shanghai Municipal Government, following the central government's policies, promulgated the "Temporary Measures for Strengthening Market Management and Cracking Down on Speculation" (关于加强市场管理取缔投机的暂行办法) on December 18, 1950.[9] As for cotton products, a major manufacture, the Shanghai Cotton Yarn Supply Review Group (上海市棉纱供应审核小组) was jointly established by the Shanghai Municipal Bureau of Industry and Commerce, the East China Company of the Raw Cotton and Cotton Products Company (花纱布公司华东区公司), the East China Textile Administration (华东纺织管理局), and the Shanghai

[8] On the strengthening of financial control during the Korean War, see Izutani (2007, pp. 49–53), and Nambu (1991, pp. 609–612, 657–679). The following outline was based on both. While the government strengthened its control over currency, the People's Bank's business with private enterprises also expanded from 1951 onward and it led the re-organization of public-private jointly-owned banks, which had a relatively strong relationship with private enterprises at the time. In Shanghai, which was of course the financial center, on May 27, 1951, the so-called "Five New Banks" (新五行)—namely Xinhua (新华), China Industry (中国实业), Siming (四明), Commerce (通商), and Construction (建业)—were organized into the Five Banks Joint Management Office (五行联合总管理处). Furthermore, in July that same year, a separate management office for the Shanghai Bank (上海银行) was established, and in September, a joint management office of the "Five North Banks" (北五行)—consisting of Jincheng (金城), Continental (大陆), Salt Industry (盐业), Zhongnan (中南), and Union (联合)—was established, and the control over public-private jointly-owned banks was further strengthened.

[9] Shanghai Military Control Committee (上海市军管会) and Shanghai People's Government (上海市人民政府), "Temporary Measures for Strengthening Market Management and Speculation Control" (关于加强市场管理取缔投机的暂行办法), December 18, 1950, Zhonggongshanghaishiwei tongzhanbu et al. (1993, pp. 90–91).

Textile Union (上海市纺织工会) on January 10, 1951, and control over distribution was significantly strengthened.[10]

In addition, a notably unique feature of Shanghai's economic controls at the time was the control over purchases by government agencies outside of Shanghai. Shanghai, being a major industrial hub in China, was frequented by purchasing agencies from all over China for the purchase of industrial goods. On December 7, 1950, the Shanghai Municipal Bureau of Industry and Commerce promulgated the "Regulations on the Registration and Management of Units Purchasing Goods from Outside Shanghai" (关于外埠来沪采购物资单位登记管理办法), henceforth requiring agencies, units, and public enterprises (both state-owned and joint public-private enterprises) from other regions to register with the Shanghai Bureau. It mandated that processing orders, purchases, and sales of goods in Shanghai were to go through state-owned trading institutions.[11] This development can be seen as reflecting the troubles that had developed between the Shanghai Bureau and state-owned enterprises and state organizations discussed in the previous chapter.

The price trends and the effects of market control policies in the wake of the outbreak of the Korean War can be confirmed by examining the fluctuations in the wholesale prices of several major commodities in Shanghai, as shown in Fig. 4.1. The first thing to take note of is the sharp rise in raw rubber prices after June 1950. As will be discussed in Chapter 9, the supply of raw rubber in China was fundamentally dependent on imports, and the price surge at this time can be attributed to the impact of the US trade restrictions on China. Next, there was a notable increase in the composite index, but on the other hand, there was no sharp rise in major commodities such as rice, coal, and cotton yarn after June 1950. Rather, in the case of rice, there

---

[10] Zhonggongshanghaishiwei tongzhanbu et al. (1993, pp. 1472–1473). On January 28, 1951, the Shanghai Municipal Bureau of Industry and Commerce issued a "Decision on the Handling of Cotton Yarn Notes and Private Yarn," which required registration with the Bureau if cotton yarn was owned by anyone other than individuals and factories engaged in the cotton industry, while also imposing regulations on its sale. See Shanghai Municipal Bureau of Industry and Commerce, "Decision on the Handling of Cotton Yarn Notes and Private Cotton Yarn" (关于处理(纱布)栈单及私人存纱的决定), January 28, 1951, in Shanghai gongshangxingzhengguanlizhi bianzuanweiyuanhui (1997, p. 28). Some months later, on April 2, 1951, the Shanghai government issued a set of measures that restricted the trade in and circulation of copper, an important material; see Shanghai People's Government, "Temporary Measures for the Management of the Purchase and Transportation of Raw Copper" (上海市人民政府上海市管理铜料购运暂行办法), April 2, 1951, Huadong junzheng weiyuanhui caizhengjingji weiyuanhui (1951, pp. 748–749).

[11] "Regulations on the Registration and Management of Units Purchasing Goods from Outside Shanghai" (关于外埠来沪采购物资单位登记管理办法), promulgated on December 7, 1950, Shanghai gongshangxingzhengguanlizhi bianzuanweiyuanhui (1997, p. 27). The following related regulations were subsequently established as well: East China Military and Political Committee Financial and Economic Committee, "Regulations on Matters to be Noted by Each Purchasing Unit in Shanghai" (华东军政委员会财政经济委员会关于各采购单位在沪采购应注意事项的规定), December 26, 1950, and East China Military and Political Committee Trade Department, "Implementation Rules for Regulations on Matters to be Noted by Each Purchasing Unit in Shanghai" (华东军政委员会贸易部为执行华东财委关于各采购单位在沪采购应注意事项规定的实施细则), January 31, 1951, both in Huadong junzheng weiyuanhui caizhengjingji weiyuanhui (1951, pp. 671–676).

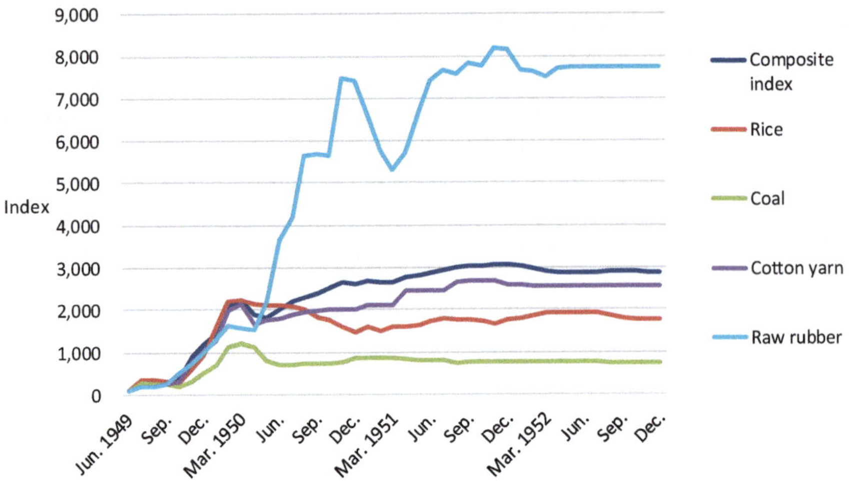

Fig. 4.1 Wholesale prices of major commodities in Shanghai, 1949–1952. *Note* The basis of all indices is Jun 1949 = 100. The details of each item are as follows: Composite index: covering major 47 commodities; Rice: nonglutinous rice, "Zhongbaijing" (中白粳), market price; Coal: bituminous coal, "Kailuan yihaoxie" (开滦一号屑), official price; Cotton yarn: 20 count "Lanfeng" (蓝凤), market price; Raw rubber: "Sanhao xingzhou hongxiangjiaozihuo 57.5 kg pack" (三号星洲红橡胶资货115斤装), market price. *Source* Zhongguokexueyuan shanghaijingjiyanjiusuo and Shanghaishehuikexueyuan jingjiyanjiusuo (1958, pp. 448–563)

was a downward trend in prices. From these points, it could be argued that the control policies intensively implemented by the government had a certain effect on the stabilization of prices in Shanghai. However, the development of such control policies was also to play a significant role for processing orders in wartime, which will be discussed next.

4.1.2 Expansion of Processing Orders During Wartime

Turning to consider the expansion of processing orders during wartime, the first point that can be confirmed is the quantitative expansion of processing orders from 1950 to 1951. Looking at Fig. 4.2, which shows the production by processing orders and the independent production and sales of Shanghai's private industry, it is clear that the production of processing orders in 1951 increased to 1.64 billion yuan, more than double what it had been in 1950. As a result, the total production of private industry (production amount of processing orders plus independent production and sales) can be seen to have also grown significantly, reaching 3.8 billion yuan in contrast to the stagnation of 1950, and the proportion of the increase in the production of processing orders (870 million yuan) reached 66.4% of the increase in the total production of private industry (1.31 billion yuan). These figures indicate that

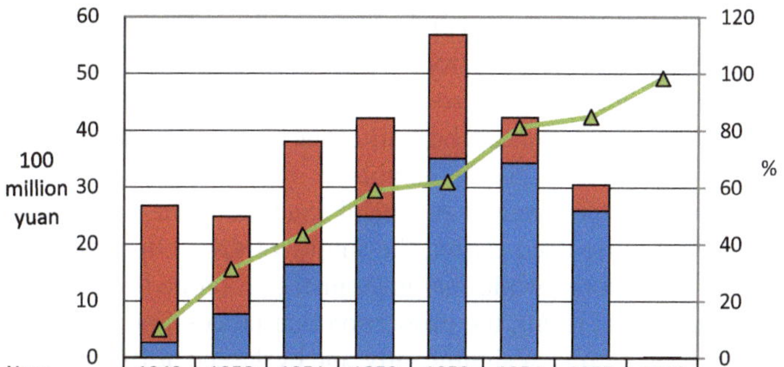

Year	1949	1950	1951	1952	1953	1954	1955	1956
Independent production and sales (left)	24.1	17.2	21.6	17.4	21.7	7.9	4.6	0.0
Processing orders (left)	2.7	7.7	16.4	24.8	35.1	34.3	25.9	0.1
% of total production comprised by processing orders (right)	10.0	31.0	43.1	58.8	61.8	81.2	84.8	98.4

Fig. 4.2 Production of processing orders and independent production and sales of Shanghai private industry, 1949–1956. *Note* (1) "Processing orders" include purchasing, unified purchasing, and exclusive sales. (2) Production calculated based on fixed price of 1952. All figures converted from old RMB to new RMB (10,000:1). (3) "% of total production comprised by processing orders" calculated as follows: processing orders/(processing orders + independent production and sales). *Source* Calculated based on Table 7 in "Statistics," Zhonggongshanghaishiwei tongzhanbu et al. (1993). Original data from Statistics of National Economy of Shanghai (Industrial Sector), 1949–1957 (1949-1957年上海市国民经济统计 (工业), author, publisher, and year of publication unknown), p. 85

the increase in the production of processing orders contributed significantly to the increase in the production of private industry. Moreover, the percentage that the production of processing orders comprised of the total production of private industry had steadily increased from 31.0% in 1950 to 43.1% in 1951.

The background to this increase in processing orders was the increase in demand for industrial products, particularly on the part of the military, during wartime. Industrial products needed by the military, especially raincoats, rubber shoes, canvas, towels, rice cookers, washbasins, water bottles, and other miscellaneous goods, were, aside from those produced by state-owned enterprises, generally procured via purchase or processing orders to private industry. Indeed, "After October [1950], under the influence of the expansion of the Korean invasion by American imperialism, the focus of public-private coordination shifted to cooperating and assisting in the control of goods by state organizations,"[12] and the role of processing orders shifted accordingly, changing from "assistance" to private industry, at the time just

[12] "Summary of the Work of the Shanghai People's Government Bureau of Industry and Commerce in 1950 (Excerpt)" (上海人民政府工商局1950年工作总结 (节录)), January 1951, Zhonggongshanghaishiwei tongzhanbu et al. (1993, p. 98).

following the establishment of the PRC (as seen in Chapter 3), to a means of procuring goods to support the war effort.

At the same time, in some industries private companies faced difficulty in obtaining raw materials on the market due to government economic control, resulting in a situation where private companies had to rely on government-commissioned processing for production. A typical example is the cotton spinning and weaving industry. As discussed earlier, the supply of raw cotton decreased due to the interruption of imports, while the government prohibited market circulation and made purchases. As a result, the proportion that processing orders represented in cotton fabric production grew significantly, and by the end of 1951, they had come to account for 50–80% of the total production volume of the industry.[13]

On the other hand, the expansion of processing orders during wartime, influenced by the difficult realities of wartime conditions, would also reveal the problems inherent in the execution process. The following examples drawn from documentary evidence help illustrate the reality of the situation.

a. Collusion between military-related public organizations and private enterprises through processing orders

The following is stated in a document sent by the East China Military and Political Committee Trade Department (华东军政委员会贸易部) to the Shanghai Municipal Bureau of Industry and Commerce on March 16, 1951:

> The document sent by the Shanghai Trade Trust Company (上海市贸易信托公司) on March 1, 1951, states the following: 'First, the Ordnance Department of the Central Military Commission (中央军事委员会军械部 [a department within the Central Military Commission's General Rear Service Department (中央军事委员会总后方勤务部) responsible for weapons and arms]) visited Shanghai to purchase gun straps and placed a total order of 20,000 pieces with our company, but private operators knew in advance that there would be a large number of orders. According to an investigation, Comrade Liu Chengyi (刘成义), the representative of the Ordnance Department of the Central Military Commission during the Shanghai visit, once stayed in the private First United Factory (私营第一联营厂), and our company's responsible comrade subtly asked him not to receive the factory's hospitality, but he still stayed at Room 402 of the Great East Hotel which the factory had reserved for his stay. [...] [this is followed by several more examples].' According to the investigation, the aforementioned purchasing units may have leaked purchasing figures [in exchange for] receiving entertainment from the private factory. This is not in line with the principles set by the East China Financial and Economic Committee, and furthermore, it makes it difficult for state-owned companies to control prices.[14]

[13] Shanghai Municipal Bureau of Industry and Commerce Administration (authors Fu Dejin and Zhao Chongwen), "The Position and Role of Processing Orders in the Socialist Transformation of Capitalist Industry and Commerce in Shanghai" (加工订货在上海资本主义工商业社会主义改造中的地位与作用), Zhonggongshanghaishiwei tongzhanbu et al. (1993, p. 848). Also, Izutani (2007), Chapter 3 points out that the control of raw materials in the cotton spinning and weaving industry had been progressing from an early stage.

[14] B182-1-222a. The Shanghai Municipal Bureau of Industry and Commerce reported the following as a result of its investigation into this matter:

> Comrade Liu, during his stay in Shanghai, made contact with a private factory (the so-called First United Factory), [whereupon said factory] lied to Comrade Liu, who was visiting

In the above case, the issue was a private factory offering entertainment for purchasing agency personnel from other regions and the resulting leakage of information related to processing orders. Clearly, barely had the system come to fruition before actors were developing means to circumvent it for their benefit. As mentioned earlier, despite the governmental control over the activities of purchasing agencies from other regions in Shanghai, issues like this persisted and were detrimental to the execution of processing orders.

b. Prevalence of processing orders without Shanghai Municipal Bureau of Industry and Commerce supervision

A report compiled by the Central Private Enterprise Bureau in July 1951 on the nationwide status of processing orders drew attention to the issue of the "unified management and distribution of processing orders." It stated,

> In order to encourage the development of private enterprises in a planned manner, and to prevent the state from suffering unnecessary losses, all government and state-owned enterprise processing order lists must only be distributed after being reviewed by the local People's Government Bureau of Industry and Commerce (人民政府工商局). On this point, we are still not doing well. Some state-owned enterprises, after finalizing the terms with private enterprises, merely send the contract to the Bureau for formal recording, and in extreme cases, they do not even report or record it.[15]

The same report also stated that such contracts had become rampant, which had in turn led to further problems, such as, (1) delays in delivery and decline in quality due to task assignments exceeding production capacity; (2) biases in contracts in favor of particular private factories; (3) the emergence of processing brokers (加工把头; a "把头" (head) was a labor supply contractor who controlled labor mediation, and here the term refers to brokers who mediated processing order contracts between state agencies and private factories); (4) the emergence of illegal private factories which had not obtained business licenses from the Bureau of Industry and Commerce; and finally, (5) the hiring of temporary workers, poaching of workers from state-owned factories, and other issues related to the fluidity of workers. Taken together,

---

Shanghai for the first time and was unfamiliar with the situation, that they could carry out mass production. In fact, the private factory thought it could raise prices and make a great profit if it accepted Comrade Liu's orders instead of the original orders allocated by the Trade Trust Company (贸易信托公司). Comrade Liu trusted what the private factory said, and despite our bureau's responsible comrades having pointed out the private factory's secret interests many times, he remained unmoved and accepted the [factory's] reception on the grounds that the Trade Association (同业公会) said it [i.e., the factory's claim] was true. At this point, our bureau and the Trade Trust Company recommended that he move to the guest house of the Third Field Army Logistics Department (第三野战军后勤部) as soon as possible, but because he had been dealing with the private factory for a long time, the leakage of task numbers was inevitable (B182-1-222b).

[15] Central Private Enterprise Bureau, "Some Problems in the Processing Order Work (Excerpt)" (加工订货工作中的一些问题 (节录)), July 5, 1951, Zhongguoshehuikexueyuan and Zhongyangdanganguan (1993, pp. 660–661).

these issues reveal the existence of shared interests between state organizations that needed industrial goods and private factories that were desperate to secure contracts, resulting from the rapid increase in demand for industrial goods during wartime. These problems occurred, moreover, against the backdrop of a context in which the formal contract process through each local Bureau of Industry and Commerce was unable to keep up with the expanding demand for processing orders.

c. Problems with processing fees and order prices in processing orders

A December 1951 report by the Shanghai Municipal Bureau of Industry and Commerce regarding processing orders for light industries stated,

> The contradiction between rational pricing and profiteering is the most prominent issue in the processing orders of 1951. We guaranteed a reasonable profit, firmly opposed profiteering, and calculated costs in various ways depending on the situation. Initially, when neither the state organizations which put in orders nor we ourselves understood the situation very well, and there was no cost data from public factories to refer to, we grasped the situation through meetings with private business persons in the same industry, referred to their comparative prices, and decided upon appropriate prices (this is a most primitive and unreliable method, and is now rarely used except when unavoidable). Once both the state organizations and we ourselves had some understanding of the cost particulars of the products, we made agreements, presented costs to each other, analyzed the data in detail, and studied and discussed with each other.[16]

This report illustrates how the setting of production costs, which was a crucial factor in determining the processing fees and order prices of processing orders, was being carried out in a trial-and-error manner. As discussed earlier, the basic principle of setting processing fees and order prices for processing orders was supposed to be calculated based on the "medium standard under reasonable management conditions in a general factory in the same district." However, this same report stated that,

> Even now, our guiding ideology is not clear enough regarding the standard [of what constitutes] 'reasonable profit' and a 'medium standard of reasonable management.' Therefore, when calculating specific costs, we are always inconsistent and inevitably the processing profits are too low [or too high].[17]

In other words, local organs like the Shanghai Municipal Bureau of Industry and Commerce struggled because they were only provided with general guidelines which required them to interpret vague concepts like "medium standard under reasonable management conditions," a situation compounded by their lack of knowledge about products, processes, and business practices.

---

[16] B182-1-226a. This "Summary" was a response to a request by the Central People's Government Ministry of Light Industry (中央人民政府轻工业部) for a summary of the 1951 processing order policy from the local Bureau of Industry and Commerce of each major city (received by the Shanghai Municipal Bureau of Industry and Commerce on December 4, 1951), and was submitted to the Ministry of Light Industry on February 15, 1952. For specifics, see B182-1-226b and B182-1-226c.

[17] Regarding the reference to processing profits being "too low" or "too high," there is evidence that in the original primary source "too low" was written first but then "too high" was added in afterward. It is unclear when this addition was made.

On the other hand, as the same report indicates, private companies also expressed dissatisfaction with the arbitrary processing fees and cost calculations by state-owned companies and government agencies. They did not often mince words when doing so. An opinion submitted to the government by nationwide representatives of private commercial and industrial businesspersons on October 15, 1951, ran as follows:

> The government's processing orders do not consider the profits of private enterprises and even cause losses to private enterprises. For example, department stores (百货公司) have taken advantage of others' difficulties, negotiating prices down during the slack season, and entering into long-term order contracts with private enterprises. The prices at that time were particularly low, but private enterprises had no choice but to accept them, and ultimately, they lost money. They had wanted to adjust the prices when the prices rose during the busy season to compensate for the losses during the slack season, but due to contract restrictions, private enterprises fell into great difficulties. They improved their management and finally lowered their costs, but the trading companies (贸易公司) immediately lowered the purchase prices, which was a "leek-cutting" (割韭菜) method, cutting the plant immediately after it has grown.[18]

It is difficult to examine the issue of price setting for processing fees and order prices during these war years based on concrete statistical data due to the lack of primary sources. However, from the standpoint of private enterprises, the setting of processing fees and order prices undoubtedly became an increasingly significant issue as the percentage of their production comprised by production through processing orders from state-owned companies and government agencies expanded. In this way, as processing orders expanded significantly during the war years, various issues inherent in the processing order system, and the impact thereof, became increasingly apparent.

4.2 The Socialist Transformation in Shanghai

4.2.1 Changes in the Perception of Private Enterprises and Processing Orders

Against the backdrop of the Korean War armistice talks that began in July 1951, the Chinese government attempted to tighten its control over society through mass movements.[19] On December 1, 1951, the Central Committee of the CCP (中共

[18] Government Administration Council Finance and Economic Committee (中财委), "Report on the Opinions of the Representatives of Industrial and Commercial Entrepreneurs Participating in the National Celebration and Policies toward Them" (关于参加国庆的工商代表反映的意见及处理方针的通报), October 15, 1951, Zhongguoshehuikexueyuan and Zhongyangdanganguan (1993, pp. 663–664).

[19] In fact, mass movements by the CCP, such as the "Campaign to Suppress Counterrevolutionaries" (反革命镇压运動), had already been implemented shortly after the establishment of the PRC, and the "Three Anti" and "Five Anti" movements mentioned elsewhere can be regarded as extensions of these earlier movements. For more on the development of such mass movements, see Izutani (2007,

中央) announced the "Decision on Implementing Simplification of Institutions, Increasing Production and Saving, and Opposing Corruption, Waste, and Bureaucratism" (关于实行精兵简政、增产节约、反对贪污、反对浪费和反对官僚主义的决定, heralding the official launch of the "Three Anti" movement (三反运动) against the "Three Evils" (corruption, waste, and bureaucratism) of the cadres of state organizations and state-owned enterprises (Izutani 2007, pp. 191–193). The crackdown on these "Three Evils" would later evolve into the "Five Anti" movement (五反运动) mentioned in Chapter 3, targeting the "Five Poisons" (bribery, tax evasion, theft of state property, cheating on government contracts, and theft of economic information) of private merchants and industrialists, who had built close relationships with the cadres of state organizations and state-owned enterprises amid the expansion of processing orders during the Korean War.

Concomitant with the tightening of control over private enterprises through mass movements, the leadership of the CCP began to recognize the need to reorganize private enterprises. On March 24, 1952, Bo Yibo (薄一波), one of the leaders of the central government, stated the following:

> The current difficulties mainly lie in private factories, especially small and medium-sized ones. For example, in Shanghai there are over 7000 small metal processing (五金业) factories with over 60,000 workers, but most of them are in a state of operation stoppage, work stoppage, and wage payment stoppage. On the other hand, those that have blindly developed during last year's improvements [in industrial production], such as [producers of] carbon paper and ink for cultural and educational supplies, and small-scale or handicraft industries in rubber processing and dyeing, produce many substandard and rough products, and now they have no market. Presumably, these industries will inevitably collapse. The Financial and Economic Committees of East China and Shanghai are currently organizing a special committee to advance the reorganization of the ranks (队列) in the economy in combination with the "Three Anti" [movement], studying which industries should be maintained, which should be downsized, and which can be eliminated.[20]

---

pp. 20–31). The "Campaign to Suppress Counterrevolutionaries" was primarily aimed at dealing with the remnants of the GMD forces and restoring social order, and the 3rd Plenary Session of the 7th Central Committee of the CCP (中共七届三中全会) in June 1950, when society was moving toward stability, stated a policy change with relatively lenient detection and punishment of those targeted under the movement. However, after the "Instructions on the Suppression of Counterrevolutionary Activities" (关于镇压反革命活动的指示) were issued by the Central Committee of the CCP in October 1950, the campaign rapidly turned more severe. The movement was carried out in conjunction with land reform in rural areas until the spring of 1951, and was broadly deployed in cities from the end of February 1951. In the course of this campaign, a considerable number of people were arrested in the tense situation during the Korean War, and the movement actively promoted the mobilization and organization of the masses. On this basis, the 3rd Session of the 1st Political Consultative Conference (政治协商会议第一届三次会议), which began on October 23, 1951, proposed the strengthening of the "Resist America, Aid Korea Movement" (抗米援朝运動), the Patriotic Production Savings Movement (爱国增产节约运動), and the Thought Reform Movement (思想改造运動).

[20] Bo Yibo, "Briefing on the Market, Industrial Production, and Tax Revenue Situation in East China in Mid-March" (关于3月中旬华东的市场、工业生产和税收情况简报), March 24, 1952, Zhongguoshehuikexueyuan and Zhongyangdanganguan (1996, p. 688). Moreover, Bo also reported to the central government on the specific situation of Shanghai's commerce and industry at the end of March 1952, emphasizing the importance of large enterprises from the perspective of

Behind this thinking among the CCP leadership was most likely the intention to respond firstly to the First Five Year Plan, which was to start in the following year (1953), and secondly to the situation of the rapid increase of small private industrial enterprises that had occurred against the backdrop of wartime military demand.[21] The Central Private Enterprise Bureau, the highest supervisory institution for private enterprise policy, stated in its report summarizing the first half of 1952 that,

> There are many closures in the commercial and industrial sectors, but these are mainly in industries that should be eliminated, or those with poor management and insufficient funds. [...] In the future, in order to adapt private enterprises to the large-scale economic construction of the state, based on the foundation of the victory of the "Five Anti" campaign we should take a step further to grasp the overall situation of private enterprises, and strengthen their management, supervision and transformation.[22]

As this report indicates, the government sought to promote a policy that would "eliminate" industries and enterprises deemed no longer useful, while working to enhance the "management, supervision and transformation" of private industry under the national goal of "large-scale economic construction," by which was meant, of course, the First Five Year Plan.[23]

---

securing employment for staff and workers. See "CCP Central Committee reply to Comrade Bo Yibo on Correcting the Neglectful Attitude toward Large Bourgeois Enterprises" (中共中央关于纠正对大资产阶级企业轻视的看法给薄一波同志的复示), April 5, 1952, and Bo Yibo, "Report on the Specific Analysis and Deployment of Shanghai's Industrial and Commercial Households (excerpt)" (对上海工商业户的具体分析和部署的报告 (节录)), March 31, 1952, attached to the aforementioned CCP Central Committee's reply, in Zhongyangjuanbianjibu (1992, pp. 281–283).

[21] Regarding the start of the First Five Year Plan, it had already been established by Mao's statement in February 1951 to the effect that it would entail "three years of preparation, and ten years of construction." In preparation for this large-scale economic development, a supervisory group for the formation of the First Five Year Plan was organized by six central leaders, including Zhou Enlai (周恩来), Chen Yun (陈云), the aforementioned Bo Yibo, and Li Fuchun (李富春) at the beginning of 1952. This group then created a "Five Year Plan Outline Draft" (五年计划轮郭草案) in August 1952, whereupon Zhou, Chen, and Li took it to the Soviet Union for consultation (Bo 1993, p. 286).

[22] CCP Central Committee endorsement of "The Central Private Enterprise Bureau's 'Comprehensive Report for the First Half of 1952'" (中共中央批转中央私营企业局 "1952年上半期综合报告), October 12, 1952; the original report from the Central Private Enterprise Bureau was issued on September 18, 1952, in Zhongyangjuanbianjibu (1992, pp. 369, 372).

[23] However, it should be noted that the concept of reorganizing private industry at this point in 1952 was not intended to eliminate all private enterprises. Bo Yibo's elimination proposal targeted some small and medium-sized factories, while he recognized the positive contribution of large factories to production. Even in the report of the Central Private Enterprise Bureau, the "transformation" of private enterprises being discussed strictly pertained to their management, and by no means constituted a socialist transformation of private enterprises (that is, the transformation of private enterprises into public-private jointly-owned ones) like what was seen later. Moreover, the report on the Planning Work Conference (计划工作会议) by the Central Finance Committee in March 1952 acknowledged the coexistence of the five types of economic components set out in the "Common Program." CCP Central Committee acknowledgement of "Report on the Government Administration Council Finance and Economic Committee (中财委)'s Planning Work Conference (excerpt)" (转发中财委计划工作会议的报告 (节录)), March 7, 1952, Zhongguoshehuikexueyuan and Zhongyangdanganguan (1993, p. 95).

How did this shift in the central government's perception of and approach to private enterprises affect the development of processing orders in Shanghai? Turning back to Fig. 4.2, it is clear that in Shanghai the production of processing orders amounted to 2.48 billion yuan in 1952 and 3.51 billion yuan in 1953, showing a stable increase. On the other hand, independent production and sales for those years totaled 1.74 billion yuan and 2.17 billion yuan, respectively. It is notable that the figure for independent production and sales in 1952 dropped significantly from the 2.16 billion yuan it had been in 1951, and that, as a result, the processing order ratio rose to 58.8% in 1952, indicating an increased dependence on processing orders in private industry. In 1953, the total production of private industry increased, reaching its peak during the 1949–56 era as the independent production and sales value recovered to the level of what it had been in 1951, but the production of processing orders grew even more, coming to comprise 61.8% of total production, exceeding even what it had been in 1952.[24]

This increase in the processing order ratio of private industry in 1952–53 reflects the temporary expansion of processing orders as a countermeasure to the "three stop" phenomenon of production stoppage, wage stoppage, and business stoppage in private industry triggered during the aforementioned "Three Anti" and "Five Anti" campaigns.[25] Although, in fact, there were few private entrepreneurs who

---

[24] At the beginning of 1953 when the First Five Year Plan was launched, the proportion that processing orders made up of private industrial production fell from 58% in the fourth quarter of 1952 to 48% in the first quarter of 1953. This was because the state-owned commercial sector refrained from processing orders in order to extract funds for key construction projects. However, afterwards it expanded again. Shanghai Municipal Bureau of Industry and Commerce (authors Fu Dejin and Zhao Chongwen), "The Position and Role of Processing Orders in the Socialist Transformation of Capitalist Industry and Commerce in Shanghai" (加工订货在上海资本主义工商业社会主义改造中的地位与作用), Zhonggongshanghaishiwei tongzhanbu et al. (1993, pp. 851–852).

[25] To facilitate this temporary expansion of processing orders, the government initially promoted the reorganization of the processing order system. Immediately after the formal start of the "Five Anti" campaign in early April 1952, under the guidance of the Shanghai Municipal Financial and Economic Committee, the Temporary Office for Processing Orders (加工订货临时工作办公室) was established by the joint efforts of the Shanghai Municipal Bureau of Industry and Commerce, the People's Bank (人民银行), the Shanghai Tax Bureau, the Shanghai Municipal Trade Union, and the industrial authorities. Shanghai gongshangxingzhengguanlizhi bianzuanweiyuanhui (1997, pp. 298–299).

Regarding the establishment of this Temporary Office for Processing Orders, the chronology section of Zhonggongshanghaishiwei tongzhanbu et al. (1993, pp. 1480–1481), states that the Processing Order Office (加工订货办公室) was established on March 25, 1952, and the Processing Order Committee (加工订货委员会) on April 6, 1952, which contradicts the description given in Shanghai gongshangxingzhengguanlizhi bianzuanweiyuanhui (1997, pp. 298–299). The details are unclear, but on the other hand, the description of the duties and functions of the Processing Order Office in the former source is similar to the duties and functions of the Processing Order Committee set out in B182-1-360a. It is unlikely that the Shanghai Municipal Bureau of Industry and Commerce would have suggested on the 31st of March the establishment of an organization with the same nature as the one already established on the 25th, and consequently it can be concluded that there was simply some confusion present in the description of the Processing Order Office given in Zhonggongshanghaishiwei tongzhanbu et al. (1993). Taking these points into consideration, the author of the present study decided to adopt the description given in Shanghai gongshangxingzhengguanlizhi bianzuanweiyuanhui (1997) instead for the establishment dates of both organizations.

were directly deemed illegal during the "Five Anti" campaign in Shanghai,[26] the campaign nevertheless exerted a significant psychological shock on business owners since it was conducted in the form of a mass movement and business owners had to contend with criticism from workers. On top of that, the rapid increase in workers' wages and welfare expenses through the "Five Anti" campaign clearly put pressure on the cash flow of private enterprises.[27] Moreover, much of the state's resources were

---

As for the role of the Processing Order Office, it served as an organization that oversaw temporary processing orders in collaboration with related departments and state-owned specialty companies, and was divided into three groups, namely heavy industry, textile industry, and light industry. On April 28, 1952, it was renamed the Shanghai Municipal Processing Order Committee (上海市加工订货委员会), with Fang Yi (方毅) as director, and Zhong Min (钟民) and Song Jiwen (宋季文) as deputy directors. This committee was a temporary organization established by the Shanghai Municipal Financial and Economic Committee in order to expand processing orders after the "Five Anti" movement. A primary source indicates that it was abolished after the production of private industry got back on track, but the actual date of abolition is unknown (B182-1–507). At the same time, in collaboration with the Processing Order Committee, a District Production Committee (区生产委员会) was established in each district of Shanghai to serve as an organization to unify the guidance of processing orders in that district. Furthermore, after the "Five Anti" movement, the Increase Production and Savings Committee (增产节约委员会) established within the enterprises themselves began to implement "dedicated funds" (专款专用) and "dedicated materials" (专料专用) monitoring systems to supervise raw materials and down payments supplied by the state. As a result, supervision of the implementation of processing orders was extended and strengthened at the grassroots level.

[26] The "Five Anti" campaign in Shanghai officially began on March 25, 1952, and had essentially ended by the end of June, with its formal conclusion announced on July 25. In Shanghai's "Five Anti" campaign, a total of some 164,890 commercial and industrial enterprises participated, of which 153,030 were subject to review and judgment. As for the breakdown of these judgments, there were 59,711 deemed law-abiding (39.0%), 69,730 essentially law-abiding (45.6%), and 18,362 semi-law-abiding/semi-illegal (12.0%), which altogether accounted for more than 96% of the total. The remaining 4512 deemed severely illegal (3.0%) and 715 completely illegal (0.5%) occupied only a small proportion of the total. Few enterprises had their direct assets confiscated or faced fines, with most instead being held responsible for "tax repayment and return of assets" (补税退财), in essence having to cover the portion of taxes they were deemed to have evaded and returning any income obtained illegally. For more on the "Five Anti" campaign in Shanghai, see Bo (1993, pp. 168–169) and Izutani (2007, pp. 194–196); and Shanghai "Five Anti" Campaign Special Compilation Group, "Shanghai 'Five Anti' Campaign," Zhonggongshanghaishiwei tongzhanbu et al. (1993, pp. 859–873). According to Bo (1993, p. 170), the start of the "Five Anti" campaign was first announced on February 10, 1952. However, as the campaign quickly became too radical, the CCP decided to postpone it and focus on the "Three Anti" campaign instead. Bo was dispatched to Shanghai on February 25, 1952, with the aim of inspecting and promoting the "Five Anti" campaign in Shanghai, but by that time the campaign had already become quite radical, having resulted in more than 200 arrests and 48 cases of capitalist attempted suicides (34 deaths of them). Witnessing this extremely tense situation, Bo suggested postponing the "Five Anti" campaign in Shanghai to the central CCP on the day he arrived in Shanghai (Shanghai "Five Anti" Campaign Special Compilation Group, "Shanghai 'Five Anti' Campaign," Zhonggongshanghaishiwei tongzhanbu et al. (1993, p. 871).

[27] Central Industrial and Commercial Administration Bureau, "The Issues and Opinions on the Funds and Processing Orders of Private Enterprises (Draft)" (中央工商行政管理局私营企业的资金及加工订货的问题与意见 (草稿)), March 1953, Zhongguoshehuikexueyuan and Zhongyang-danganguan (1993, pp. 714–715). One particular issue was the increase in production norm excess bonuses following the "Five Anti" campaign. For example, in the case of the Huasheng Electric Appliance Factory ("华生电气厂" written in the source, but it is perhaps "华生电器厂") in

devoted to the crackdown on illegal activities during the "Three Anti" and "Five Anti" campaigns, which caused the entire market to stagnate. This market stagnation affected industrial production; for example, 80% of private steel businesses and 90% of underwear manufacturing businesses had ceased operations by early April 1952.[28]

In response to this situation, the government implemented a short-term, intensive burst of processing orders. The number of factories targeted for processing orders in Shanghai reached 4003 in 54 industries by the end of April 1952, expanded to 7132 in May, and reached over 8200 in 82 industries in June.[29] During this period, processing orders accounted for 100% of the total production capacity in industries such as papermaking, matches, cement, high-end fountain pens, tires in the rubber industry, weaving, dyeing, cotton spinning, and hemp spinning; 80% of that in towels, sheets, various machine manufacturing, and electrolytic copper; and 60% of that in underwear and enamelware.[30] Furthermore, the amount of processing orders and purchases from March to June reached twice that of the same period in 1951, accounting for 81.5% of the total amount of private industrial business.[31] This dramatic but temporary expansion of processing orders was referred to as "artificial respiration" for private industry,[32] and as has already been seen, it achieved significant results in maintaining the production of private industry in 1952.

On the other hand, the development of processing orders during this period needs to be seen in the context of the overall policy of reorganizing private industry

---

Shanghai, the factory had set the production norm at a low level, and therefore when the workers worked to their fullest, they exceeded the prescribed amount of work by an average of 45.79% in 1952. As a result, the production norm excess bonus for 1952 amounted to 6.498 billion yuan (new RMB), which greatly exceeded the regular wage of 4.5 billion yuan. Moreover, according to statistics from 123 factories in Shanghai, despite a 7% decrease in business volume between 1951 and 1952, the income of staff and workers increased by 11%, and the total production norm excess bonus correspondingly increased by 14.5%, from 517.5 billion yuan to 592.9 billion yuan. The increased production norm excess bonuses as well as the wages and welfare expenses of private industry exceeded those of state and public enterprises. This increase in workers' wages and welfare expenses was one of the factors that led to a worsening of the financial condition of private industry.

[28] Chen Yun, "Market Situation and Public-Private Relations" (市场情况与公私关系), June 11, 1952, in Chen (1984, pp. 167–168); Shanghai Industrial and Commercial Administration Bureau (authors Fu Dejin and Zhao Chongwen), "The Position and Role of Processing Orders in the Socialist Transformation of Capitalist Industry and Commerce in Shanghai" (加工订货在上海资本主义工商业社会主义改造中的地位与作用), Zhonggongshanghaishiwei tongzhanbu et al. (1993, p. 849).

[29] Shanghai Industrial and Commercial Administration Bureau, op. sit., Shanghai Industrial and Commercial Administration Bureau (authors Fu Dejin and Zhao Chongwen), "The Position and Role of Processing Orders in the Socialist Transformation of Capitalist Industry and Commerce in Shanghai" (加工订货在上海资本主义工商业社会主义改造中的地位与作用), Zhonggongshanghaishiwei tongzhanbu et al. (1993, pp. 849–850).

[30] Song Jiwen, "Speech on the Issue of Processing Orders" (关于加工订货问题的讲话), May 19, 1952, Zhonggongshanghaishiwei tongzhanbu et al. (1993, p. 143).

[31] "Central Private Enterprise Bureau Comprehensive Report for the First Half of 1952" (中央私营企业局1952年上半期综合报告), September 18, 1952, Zhongguoshehuikexueyuan and Zhongyangdanganguan (1993, p. 907).

[32] Chen Yun, "Market Situation and Public-Private Relations" (市场情况与公私关系), June 11, 1952, in Chen (1984, p. 167).

discussed above. This policy was specifically manifested in the form of the selective distribution of processing orders. In a report on the temporary development of processing orders compiled by Shanghai's Industrial and Commercial Guidance Office in April 1952, it was clearly stated that,

> Processing orders must be linked to the future of industrial development — the layout of industry — and only then can we exert a guiding role in their production. Carrying out processing orders based on the future of industrial development — the layout of industry — not only achieves the goal of selectively assisting private enterprises, but also creates certain preparatory conditions for the future restructuring of the private economy (B182-1-360b).

Song Jiwen, who was the Deputy Director of the East China Military and Political Committee Finance Department (华东军政委员会财政部副部长) and the Deputy Director of the Shanghai Municipal Processing Order Committee (上海市加工订货委员会副主任), also made a similar statement at a round-table discussion of the Shanghai Municipal Committee's United Front Work Department (上海市委统一战线工作部, a liaison department between the CCP and other organizations, for example democratic parties) held on May 19, 1952.[33]

In response to this situation, the Shanghai Municipal Bureau of Statistics (上海市统计局) specifically compiled a plan for the reorganization of private industry, shown in Table 4.1, in August 1952. A glance at the table clearly shows how development was expected in heavy industries such as machinery manufacturing and metallurgy. In light industries, the cotton spinning and weaving industries were relatively important, while industries such as wheat flour (milling), rolled tobacco, and rubber (miscellaneous goods) that had accumulated to a significant degree in Shanghai up to the Republican period were positioned as targets for elimination. This showcases how the distribution principle of distinguishing between those industries deemed to have a future for development on the one hand and those seen as lacking this potential

[33] Song Jiwen listed four principles for processing orders, namely "(1) Those [enterprises] that are closely related to the state economy and people's lives and have a future for development should be supported; (2) Comprehensive factories (with good facilities, many workers, and products that conform to standards) should be given priority; (3) Based on the situation of supply, production, and sales, [it is necessary to] assess each situation and decide whether to support, maintain, or bring about a change in industry; and (4) Those [enterprises] that should inevitably be eliminated in the restructuring of the economy are generally not to be considered." Song Jiwen, "Speech on the Issue of Processing Orders" (关于加工订货问题的讲话), May 19, 1952, Zhonggongshanghaishiwei tongzhanbu et al. (1993, p. 143). These distribution principles were also mentioned in the instructions issued by the central government to Shanghai at the same time. These instructions stated, "(1) Those [enterprises] that are temporarily in difficulty, have a future [for development], and produce products that conform to standards should be given consideration through processing orders; (2) Famous private factories that are creditworthy and have a wide sales network should be encouraged to increase production (thus absorbing unemployed workers in that industry); (3) Organize small factories into joint ventures, expand existing organizations, and make the district production committee responsible for organization and guidance; and (4) In economic restructuring, regarding those [enterprises] that must be eliminated and have no room for processing orders, the government must solve the problem of worker reemployment (state-owned factories should absorb them, and those that cannot be absorbed by state-owned factories should be temporarily relieved by some means)" (B182-1-360c).

and thus being marked for elimination on the other was actively promoted during the development of processing orders at this time.

4.2.2 From Processing Orders to the Socialist Transformation

From the latter half of 1952, as private enterprises experienced a period of revitalization driven by the temporary expansion of processing orders, Mao Zedong began to mention the transition from "New Democracy" to socialism proper.[34] And as is well known, at the meeting of the Political Bureau of the Central Committee (中央委员会政治局) on June 15, 1953, he proposed the "General Line of the Transition Period" that clearly heralded the transition to socialism, and this then became official policy at the 4th Plenary Session of the 7th Central Committee of the CCP (中共七届四中全会) on February 10, 1954.

It generally accepted that a report on the "problem of state capitalism" authored by Li Weihan (李维汉) in May 1953 played an important role in informing Mao's "general line" proposal.[35] What is peculiar about this report is that it subdivided the concept of state capitalism, which had until then been a relatively ambiguous notion, into distinct stages arranged from elementary to advanced levels according to the form of policy in effect (and specifically, the extent to which the state participated in the economy in each model). Specifically, public-private jointly-owned enterprises were regarded as the "most advantageous form for transforming private enterprises and transitioning to socialism" and therefore constituted a "high-level form of state capitalism." Meanwhile, processing orders for private industry were positioned as a form that was "slightly inferior to public-private jointly-owned enterprises in terms of stability." Below this were still further forms, such as exclusive sales, unified purchases and sales, with purchases (i.e., a model in which the state only intervened in the economy by irregularly making purchases) set as the most widely used but lowest-level form (Zhonggong zhongyang wenxianyanjiushi 1993, pp. 223–224).

Moreover, based on this division of stages, the report set out the process whereby private factories were to be capitalized by the state, noting,

> the process of state capitalization of private factories, that is, the process of developing from a lower form of state capitalism to a higher form of state capitalism, is a process that gradually transforms their production relations and gradually moves towards socialism.

---

[34] Bo Yibo recalled in his memoir that Mao first spoke about the transition to socialism at a meeting of the Secretariat of the Central Committee (中央书记处) on September 24, 1952, Bo (1993, pp. 213–214).

[35] Li Weihan, "Report to the Central Committee and the Chairman on the Issue of Public-Private Relations in Capitalist Industry" ("关于资本主义工业中的公私关系问题"给中央並主席的报告), May 27, 1953, Zhonggong zhongyang wenxianyanjiushi (1993, pp. 222–224, 227) and Bo (1993, pp. 222–224). This report was based on surveys of private enterprises conducted in Wuhan, Shanghai, Nanjing, and other places in March and April of 1953.

Table 4.1 Plan for the reorganization of private industry in Shanghai, August 1952

	Heavy Industry	Light Industry	Textile Industry
1. Those with future for development	a. Machinery manufacturing (1) Cotton spinning machines (2) Papermaking machines (3) Machine tools (4) Hemp spinning machines (5) Cultural goods machinery (printing machine, etc.) (6) Civil engineering machinery (7) Automobile parts (8) Cold working machines b. Manufacture of electrical equipment (1) Cables (2) Switches (3) Electricity meters and testers c. Metal processing (construction, plumbing, linoleum, asbestos, etc.)	(1) High-grade fountain pens (2) Precision surveying instruments (3) Paper (4) Tires (5) Chemical raw materials (6) Dye of various colors (7) Pencils (8) Paraffin paper (蜡纸) (9) Raw materials for fragrances	a. Cotton spinning and weaving (spindles, 线锭) b. Woolen textile manufacturing (blankets for paper production) c. Hemp spinning

(continued)

Table 4.1 (continued)

	Heavy Industry	Light Industry	Textile Industry
2. Those with no need for development within short term; status quo to be maintained	a. Machinery manufacturing (1) Power equipment (engines and motors) (2) Fluid transport and mining machinery (3) Machinery for light industry and chemical industry (4) Sewing machines (5) Bicycles (6) Knitting machines b. Metallurgy and refining c. Manufacture of electrical equipment (1) Insulated wires (2) Generators (3) Enameled wires (4) Telephones (5) Transformers d. Iron and steel industry (1) Steelmaking (2) Rolling e. Nail manufacturing Round nails (元钉) f. Copper metallurgy and refining (1) Copper tubes (2) Fire-refined copper (3) Electrolytic copper g. Cement industry h. Textile goods manufacturing i. Metal processing (Extension pipes, set screws, iron locks(铁皮锁), copper buttons, miscellaneous parts)	(1) Pots (2) Enameled products (3) Soap (4) Phenolic resin (5) Rubber (industrial goods) (6) Chemical raw material (acid and alkali) (7) Printing ink (8) Varnish, paint, lacquer (9) Industrial leather (10) Household chemical products (toothpaste)	a. Cotton spinning and weaving (1) Spinning (纱锭) (2) Weaving (3) Textile printing b. Dyeing and weaving industry (1) All processes (2) White weaving (3) Color weaving (A and B ranks) c. Silk weaving industry (broad machines阔幅机, stranding wheel equipment打线车设备) d. Silkworm industry (1) Yarn reeling (2) Silk yarn e. Woolen textile industry (1) Woolen yarn (2) Woolen fabrics f. Knitting industry (electric sock knitting machines) g. Underwear manufacturing (All processes and weaving and sewing departments) h. Towel and sheet manufacturing (1) Use of electric power machinery (2) Bleaching and printing (3) Carpets (4) Pillowcases i. Handkerchief manufacturing (1) Electric power machinery (2) Printing j. Shirt and garment manufacturing (raincoats)

(continued)

Table 4.1 (continued)

	Heavy Industry	Light Industry	Textile Industry
3. Those to be reduced due to difficulty in supply of raw materials or sales	a. Machinery manufacturing Agricultural machinery (flour mills, oil presses) b. Shipbuilding Steamship and ship repair c. Manufacture of electrical equipment Cotton winding cords d. Copper metallurgy and refining (1) Electrolytic copper (2) Copper wires (3) Copper stems (铜梗) e. Metal processing Mill scale (轧皮), lighters, hooks, spinning and weaving, copper products, cash vaults, firefighting supplies, stationery, sewing supplies	(1) Rubber (household goods) (2) Leather (household goods) (3) Aluminum products (4) Dyes (sulfur black and sulfur blue) (5) Matches (6) Canned food (7) Cookies	a. Dyeing and weaving industry (1) Dyeing and finishing (2) Canvas (3) Cotton sewing threads b. Silk weaving industry (narrow machine狭幅机) c. Woolen textile industry (1) Camel wool weaving (2) Silk and cotton velvet d. Knitting industry (clothing goods) e. Underwear manufacturing (weaving and sewing) f. Towel and sheet manufacturing (human-powered machine) g. Handkerchief manufacturing (human-powered machine) h. Shirt and garment manufacturing (shirts)
4. Those to be gradually eliminated due to relatively small effect on state economy and people's lives and/or due to excess production capacity	a. Machinery manufacturing Cigarette and match making machines b. Copper refining industry Copper sheets c. Metal processing Candlesticks, fasteners, copper locks, wire drawing, (unreadable), box locks	(1) Leather (hand-crafted leather tanneries) (2) Rubber (miscellaneous goods) (3) Carbon paper (4) Pens (5) Oil expression (6) Flour (7) Cigarettes	a. Dyeing and weaving industry (color weaving, C rank) b. Knitting textile industry (hand-woven socks) c. Handkerchief manufacturing (sewing) d. Shirt and garment manufacturing (garment and children's clothing)

Source Based on the description of B31-2-193 included in Shanghaishi danganguan (2002)

Here, processing orders were no longer regarded as an important form of state aid to private industry, as was the case at the time of the establishment of the PRC, but rather as an important stage in the transition to socialism. The logic of the report was to formalize the understanding that the transition to socialism was specifically the process of transitioning from a system of processing orders to one of public-private jointly-owned enterprises.

In response to the policy changes at the central level, discussions about the transformation of private enterprises to public-private joint ownership in Shanghai also began. In the course of these discussions, one of the key documents that represented the perspective of Shanghai policymakers was the plan put forward outlining how this transformation was to occur in Shanghai, drawn up by the Shanghai Municipal Committee of the CCP (中共上海市委员会) on December 31, 1953.[36] For the specific process of this transformation to public-private joint ownership, the report proposed a sequence of heavy industry, textile industry, and finally light industry, with the reason for focusing on heavy industry being explained as follows:

> [Shanghai's] private heavy industry (mainly machinery and electrical machinery manufacturing) occupies a large share in the national machinery and electrical machinery manufacturing industry (the production volume of machine parts accounts for about half of the national total), has a high technical level, has a large potential production capacity, and has many small factories, and although the equipment is relatively old, the [mutual] cooperation ability is high, and a considerable number of factories are among the best in the country in terms of scale and quality, and have a significant influence on state economic construction and national defense construction. Looking at the current situation, if we do not actively promote public-private joint ownership, we will not be able to adapt to the demand arising from the development of the national economy day by day. First, without public-private joint ownership, we cannot promote technological reform. Old-fashioned products have already begun to be phased out, and it is inconvenient to have new [products'] blueprints from the Soviet Union and New Democratic states contracted to private industry. We can seek a proper solution to this problem only by changing the production relationship. Next, in the form of processing orders it is absolutely impossible to fully control and demonstrate the production capacity of private industry. The equipment at private factories is extremely uneven, and cannot be distributed uniformly; the technology is old and cannot be made to work together [i.e., is incompatible]. Therefore, it is difficult to distribute tasks fairly and rationally.... [omit]. The processing orders for the machinery and electrical machinery manufacturing industry in the first half of this year were close to 1 trillion yuan [equivalent to 100 million new RMB yuan], but 95% of them could not be completed on time. The chaotic situation of

[36] Shanghai Municipal Committee of the CCP, "Preliminary Opinions on the Socialist Transformation of Private Industry in Shanghai" (中共上海市委关于上海市私营工业进行社会主义改造工作的初步意见), December 31, 1953, Zhonggongshanghaishiwei tongzhanbu et al. (1993, pp. 263–267). This plan, which was recorded in the opinion paper on socialist transformation submitted to both the East China Bureau and the Central Committee, ambitiously aimed to transform the city's major factories, mainly in the heavy industries (primarily machinery and electrical machinery manufacturing) into public-private joint ownership, during the span of 1954 and 1955. Furthermore, the plan was to "use another two years to reorganize more than 5700 large factories in the city and transform them all into high-end forms of state capitalism by continuously using forms of production/sales joint ventures, production joint ventures, specialized companies, joint ventures, mergers, etc." The goal was to essentially complete the socialist transformation of Shanghai's private large-scale industry within the period of the First Five Year Plan, which was to end in 1957.

these factories' salaries and bonuses is also extremely serious (Zhonggongshanghaishiwei tongzhanbu et al. 1993, p. 265).

The point to note here is that, although the report focuses only on private heavy industry, it clearly articulates the need to address various management problems that were occurring in the process of carrying out processing orders in the context of the transformation of "production relationships" (that is, the transformation of private enterprises to public-private joint ownership). As discussed above, policymakers were aware of the many and varied problems that arose in the process of carrying out processing orders. To some extent, these problems could be said to embody the contradictions inherent in trying to enforce governmental control under the overall policy of New Democracy, which allowed for the existence of private enterprises. Mao Zedong's "General Line of the Transition Period" provided a new framework to replace the New Democracy, thereby offering, ostensibly, a direction for solving these problems at the field level. Whether the framework was actually effective, however, was another issue altogether.[37]

So it was that, with this change in the view of policymakers regarding private enterprises and the socialist transformation, the transformation of private enterprises into public-private joint ownership entities got underway in Shanghai. Before the promulgation of Mao's "general line," there were 82 public-private joint enterprises

[37] However, while there were opinions expressed emphasizing the promotion of public-private joint ownership, the main thrust remained the continuation of the processing order system. The same opinion paper, in addition to aiming for public-private joint ownership of large factories, also suggested that the socialist transformation of private industry be pursued through combining elements of state capitalism associated with the medium and low levels thereof, such as processing orders, depending on the overall situation. Shanghai Municipal Committee of the CCP, "Preliminary Opinions on the Socialist Transformation of Private Industry in Shanghai" (中共上海市委关于上海市私营工业进行社会主义改造工作的初步意见), December 31, 1953, Zhonggongshanghaishiwei tongzhanbu et al. (1993, pp. 266–267). Besides this, at the end of 1953, the Shanghai Municipal Financial and Economic Committee drafted the "Principles for the Calculation of Processing Profits and the Establishment of Standards for Private Enterprises" (上海市财政经济委员会对私营企业加工核算工缴利润和拟定规格标準的原则), December 1953, which set out the principles to be followed regarding the profits that private industry could earn through processing orders. The existence of this document itself suggests that the government was at this point still pursuing the management and control of private industry through processing orders. Zhonggongshanghaishiwei tongzhanbu et al. (1993, pp. 269–273). According to p. 269 of the same source, the "Principles for the Calculation of Processing Profits and the Establishment of Standards for Private Enterprises" included in the book is a revised draft that following its original drawing up by the Shanghai Municipal Financial and Economic Committee underwent numerous revisions by central departments. The date of "December 1953" written in the source is not the date when the Shanghai Committee sent the draft to the central government, but the date when the revised draft was published internally. Furthermore, in March 1954, the Government Administration Council Finance and Economic Committee (中财委) issued "Instructions on the Issue of Implementing Processing, Ordering, Unified Purchasing, and One-Hand Sales to Capitalist Industry" (关于对资本主义工业进行加工、订货、统购、包销问题的指示) to serve as a comprehensive instruction on the execution of processing orders at the central level. Zhongyangjuanbianjibu (1992), pp. 590–596. This too illustrates how the CCP and the government as a whole still saw processing orders as an important method for managing and controlling private industry as of at least the end of 1953 to the beginning of 1954.

in Shanghai (17 in finance, transportation, commerce, and cultural businesses, and 65 in industry). After 14 industrial enterprises were designated as "trial models of public-private jointly-owned enterprises" (公私合营试点) in December 1953, though, the target expanded to 151 in the second half of 1954 (Zhonggongshanghaishiwei tongzhanbu et al. 1993, p. 23).

However, a much more dramatic stage of the transformation of private enterprises into public-private joint ownership occurred in 1955–56. Some sense of this can be seen in Fig. 4.3, which shows the production of Shanghai's industrial enterprises organized by type of ownership. What is most impressive here is that while private industry production had been decreasing since 1954, and became almost negligible due to the completion of the socialist transformation in 1956, conversely the production of public-private jointly-owned enterprises rapidly expanded from 1954, and came to surpass state-owned and private enterprises in 1956. In short, this data illustrates how the socialist transformation of Shanghai was based on gradual progress up to 1954, and was then completed in a rush in 1955–56.

Moreover, an important point to consider is which governmental organization was responsible for managing the public-private jointly-owned enterprises that emerged through this rapid transformation. Table 4.2, which shows the change in the number of industrial enterprises in Shanghai by ownership, divides public-private jointly-owned enterprises into those that were "central jointly-owned" and those that were "local jointly-owned." It is readily apparent that the increase in the number of public-private jointly-owned enterprises after 1954 was due mainly to the increase in those

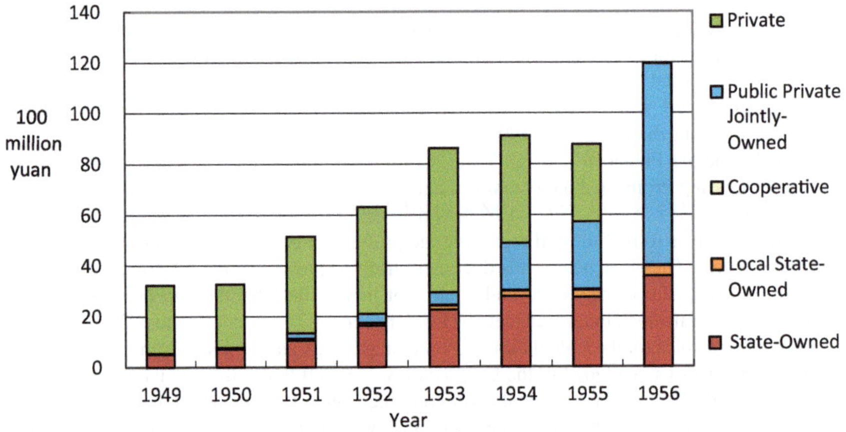

Fig. 4.3 Industrial enterprise output in Shanghai, by ownership type, 1949–1956. *Notes* (1) Table does not include production cooperatives and individual handicraft operations. (2) Production figures calculated based on fixed price of 1952; all figures converted from old RMB to new RMB (10,000: 1). *Source* Calculated based on Table 2 in "Statistics," Zhonggongshanghaishiwei tongzhanbu et al. (1993). Original data from Statistics of National Economy of Shanghai (Industrial Sector), 1949–1957 (1949–1957年上海市国民经济统计 (工业), author, publisher and year of publication unknown), p. 6, 10

in the "local jointly-owned" category. The number of such enterprises increased from 21 in the previous year to 201 in 1954, then to 333 in 1955, and then to the staggering number of 16,410 in 1956. On the other hand, the number of "central jointly-owned" enterprises also increased, from 42 in the previous year to 358 in 1956, but most of the leading private enterprises followed this path, since the total fixed asset amount of "central jointly-owned" industrial enterprises at the end of 1956 came to 696.05 million yuan, surpassing the 553.34 million yuan total of the overwhelmingly more numerous local jointly-owned enterprises (B31-1-32, p. 14).

The upshot of the transformation of private enterprises in Shanghai was that the countless small and medium-sized enterprises that had partly characterized Shanghai's industry since the Republican period came under the control of the Shanghai Municipal Government as "local public-private jointly-owned enterprises" affiliated with local government in 1956. This established, in other words, a foundation for regional integration centered on local government, with enterprises in the city all organized under the Shanghai Municipal Government.

This chapter and the preceding one examined the process of the formation of a socialist system in Shanghai, focusing mainly on private enterprise policy. In the course of the analysis thus far, several key points have emerged. First, it is important to be cognizant of the impact of the government's policy shift, due to the involvement in the Korean War, on private enterprise policy in Shanghai. The process of the development of private enterprise policy examined thus far can be summarized in four stages: (1) the development of processing orders as a form of "assistance to private enterprises" at the time of the establishment of the PRC; (2) the expansion of processing orders under a controlled economy due to participation in the Korean War, and the closer relationship between state-owned enterprises/government organizations and private enterprises; (3) the reorganization of private enterprises accompanied by the "Three Anti" and "Five Anti" campaigns; and (4) the transition to implementing the socialist transformation of private enterprises through public-private joint ownership, based on the "General Line of the Transition Period." During the course of

Table 4.2 Number and ownership of industrial enterprises in Shanghai, 1949–1956

Year	Central state-owned	Local state-owned	Cooperative (Processing factories)	Central jointly-owned	Local jointly-owned	Private	Total
1949	92	50	1	11	4	20,149	20,307
1950	108	48	3	17	7	20,707	20,890
1951	123	70	7	41	18	24,673	24,932
1952	132	89	7	46	19	25,548	25,841
1953	142	104	20	47	21	29,485	29,819
1954	152	118	23	43	201	27,983	28,520
1955	143	119	30	42	333	22,602	23,269
1956	149	130	43	358	16,410	6	17,096

Source B31-1-32, p. 11

this process, as previous studies have also identified (Mōri 1994a; Okumura 1999; Izutani 2007), participation in the Korean War was a significant turning point that directly led to the strengthening of control over private enterprises and the subsequent formation of a socialist system.

Second, the analysis focusing on the perspective of government policymakers revealed various problems in the implementation process of processing orders. At the level of the policymakers in Shanghai who were dealing with private enterprises, several significant problems—collusion between state-owned enterprises and private enterprises, processing orders being issued without going through the Shanghai Municipal Bureau of Industry and Commerce, and confusion over the setting of processing fees and order prices—were recognized from the beginning of the implementation of processing orders. Participation in the Korean War made these problems all the more apparent as the processing order system was significantly expanded, and the "Three Anti" and "Five Anti" campaigns that served as a political response to these problems in turn led the government to reorganize private enterprises. When Mao's "General Line of the Transition Period" proposal in 1953 formalized the promotion of a socialist transformation through public-private joint ownership, policymakers in Shanghai started to recognize that the problems with the processing order system could be solved through implementing public-private joint ownership. However, this change was not the result of merely adapting to the central government's shift in policy, but also indicated the seriousness of the problems surrounding the control over processing orders that were occurring on the ground.

Another point to note is that, as a result of the socialist transformation, most of what were originally private enterprises, especially many small and medium-sized enterprises that had developed up to the Republican period, were transformed into "local public-private jointly-owned enterprises" belonging to local governments (e.g., the Shanghai Municipal Government). This meant that, from the perspective of the Shanghai Municipal Government, most of the private enterprises that had been the target of processing orders were now placed under its own direct management. At the same time, it also meant that the government had to absorb the problems that had arisen in the course of implementing processing orders within the governmental system. The basic framework of the socialist system in Shanghai was formed by absorbing the existing economic structure of Shanghai, which had been built up to and developed through the Republican period, and remolding it into a socialist system through a process of transforming the means of production and reorganizing the mechanics thereof at the level of local government.

References

Chinese Language

Bo, Yibo. 1993. *Ruogan zhongdajuece yu Shijian de huigu* (若干重大决策与事件的回顾 (上), Review of Some Major Decisions and Events (Volume 1)). Beijing: Zhonggong Zhongyang dangxiao chubanshe

Chen, Yun. 1984. *Chenyun wenxuan* (陈云文选 (1949–1956), Selected Works of Chen Yun: 1949–1956). Beijing: Renmin chubanshe

Huadong junzheng weiyuanhui caizhengjingji weiyuanhui ed. 1951. *Huadongqu caizhengjingji falinghuibian* (華東区財政経済法令彙編 (上冊), The Compilation of Financial and Economic Laws of East China Greater Administrative Region, Volume 1). Shanghai: Huadong renmin chubanshe

Shanghai gongshangxingzhengguanlizhi bianzuanweiyuanhui, ed. 1997. *Shanghai gongshangxingzhengguanlizhi* (上海工商行政管理志, Shanghai Industrial and Commercial Administration Chronicle). Shanghai: Shanghai shehuikexueyuan chubanshe

Shanghaishi danganguan, edited and photographed. 2002. *Zhonghuarenmingongheguo jianguochuqi shanghaijingji huifudangan xuanji: 1949–1953 nian* (中华人民共和国建国初期上海经济恢复档案选集 (1949–1953年), Selected Archives of Shanghai Economic Recovery in the Early Years of the People's Republic of China: 1949–1953), Microfilm. Shanghai: Shanghaishi danganguan

Zhonggongshanghaishiwei tongzhanbu, Zhonggongshanghaishi dangshiyanjiushi, and Shanghaishidanganguan. 1993. *Zhongguo zibenzhuyigongshangye de shehuizhuyigaizao: Shanghai juan* (中国资本主义工商业的社会主义改造(上海卷), The Socialist Transformation of China's Capitalist Industry and Commerce: Shanghai Volume), Volume I & II. Beijing: Zhonggong dangshi chubanshe

Zhonggong zhongyang wenxianyanjiushi, ed. 1992. *Jianguoyilai zhongyaowenxianxuanbian: di 1 ce* (建国以来重要文献选编 (第1册), Selection of Important Documents Since the Founding of the People's Republic of China: Volume 1). Beijing: Zhongyang wenxian chubanshe

Zhonggong zhongyang wenxianyanjiushi, ed. 1993. *Jianguoyilai zhongyaowenxianxuanbian: di 4 ce* (建国以来重要文献选编 (第4册), Selection of Important Documents Since the Founding of the People's Republic of China: Volume 4). Beijing: Zhongyang wenxian chubanshe

Zhongguokexueyuan shanghaijingjiyanjiusuo, and Shanghaishehuikexueyuan jingjiyanjiusuo, eds. 1958. *Shanghai jiefangqianhou wujiaziliaohuibian: 1921 nian – 1957 nian* (上海解放前后物价资料汇编 (1921年-1957年), Compilation of Price Data Before and After the Liberation of Shanghai: 1921–1957). Shanghai: Shanghai renmin chubanshe

Zhongguoshehuikexueyuan and Zhongyangdanganguan, eds. 1993. *Zhonghuarenmingongheguo jingjidanganziliaoxuanbian 1949–1952: Gongshangtizhi juan* (中华人民共和国经济档案资料选编1949–1952 (工商体制卷), Selected Economic Archive Materials of the People's Republic of China 1949–1952: Industrial and Commercial System Volume). Beijing: Zhongguo shehuikexue chubanshe

Zhongguoshehuikexueyuan and Zhongyangdanganguan, eds. 1994. *Zhonghuarenmingongheguo jingjidanganziliaoxuanbian 1949–1952: Duiwaimaoyi juan* (中华人民共和国经济档案资料选编1949–1952 (对外贸易卷), Selected Economic Archive Materials of the People's Republic of China 1949–1952: Foreign Trade Volume). Beijing: Jingjiguanli chubanshe

Zhongguoshehuikexueyuan and Zhongyangdanganguan, eds. 1995. *Zhonghuarenmingongheguo jingjidanganziliaoxuanbian 1949–1952: Shangye juan* (中华人民共和国经济档案资料选编1949–1952 (商业卷), Selected Economic Archive Materials of the People's Republic of China 1949–1952: Commercial Volume). Beijing: Zhongguo wuzi chubanshe

Zhongguoshehuikexueyuan and Zhongyangdanganguan, eds. 1996. *Zhonghuarenmingongheguo jingjidanganziliaoxuanbian 1949–1952: Gongye juan* (中华人民共和国经济档案资料选

编1949–1952 (工业卷), Selected Economic Archive Materials of the People's Republic of China 1949–1952: Industrial Volume). Beijing: Zhongguo wuzi chubanshe

Zhongyangjuanbianjibu, ed. 1992. *Zhongguo zibenzhuyigongshangye de shehuizhuyigaizao: zhongyangjuan* (中国资本主义工商业的社会主义改造 (中央卷), The Socialist Transformation of China's Capitalist Industry and Commerce: Central Volume), Volumes I and II. Beijing: Zhonggongdangshi chubanshe

Zhongyangrenminzhengfu fazhiweiyuanhui, ed. 1953. *Zhongyangrenminzhengfu falinghuibian: 1951* (中央人民政府法令汇编 (1951), Compilation of Laws and Regulations of the Central People's Government: 1951). Beijing: Renmin chubanshe

Japanese Language

Amako, Satoshi et al., eds. 1999. *Gendai chūgoku jiten* (現代中国事典, Encyclopedia of Contemporary China). Tokyo: Iwanami shoten

Izutani, Yōko. 2007. *Chūgoku kenkokushoki no seiji to keizai: Taishū undō to shakaishugitaisei* (中国建国初期の政治と経済—— 大衆運動と社会主義体制, Politics and Economy in the Early Years of the People's Republic of China: Mass Movements and the Socialist System). Tokyo: Ochanomizu shobō

Katō, Yōko. 1992. *America no sekaisenryaku to kokomu 1945–1992: Tenki ni tatsu nihon no bouekiseisaku* (アメリカの世界戦略とココム 1945–1992: 転機にたつ日本の貿易政策, America's World Strategy and COCOM 1945–1992: Japan's Trade Policy at A Turning Point). Tokyo: Yūshindō kōbunsha

Kida, Shōjiro. 1993. Chūgoku to chōsensensō: Kyūsenkōshō wo megutte (中国と朝鮮戦争——休戦交渉をめぐって, The Korean War and Communist China Viewed from the Armistice Negotiations). *Asian Studies* (アジア研究) 39(3): 35–64. https://doi.org/10.11479/asianstudies.39.3_35

Miki, Takeshi. 1971. *Chūgoku kaifukuki no keizaiseisaku: Shinminshushugi keizairon* (中国回復期の経済政策——新民主主義経済論, Economic Policy in China's Recovery Period: New Democratic Economy). Tokyo: Kawashima shoten

Mōri, Kazuko. 1994a. Chūgoku no shakaishugi sentaku to kokusaikankyō (中国の社会主義選択と国際環境, China's Choice for the Socialization and International Environment). In *Higashi ajia to reisen* (東アジアと冷戦, East Asia and the Cold War), ed. Yamagiwa Akira, 259–283. Tokyo: Sanrei shobō

Mōri, Kazuko. 1994b. Reisen to chūgoku (冷戦と中国, Cold War and China). In *Higashi ajia to reisen* (東アジアと冷戦, East Asia and the Cold War), ed. Akira Yamagiwa, 85–109. Tokyo: Sanrei shobō

Nambu, Minoru. 1991. *Gendai chūgoku no zaiseikinyūseisaku* (現代中国の財政金融政策, Fiscal and Financial Policies of Contemporary China). Tokyo: Taga shuppan

Okumura, Satoshi. 1999. *Chūgoku no gendaishi: Sensō to shakaishugi* (中国の現代史——戦争と社会主義, Modern History of China: War and Socialism). Tokyo: Aoki shoten

Shu, Ken'ei. 1991. *Moutakutou to chōsensensō* (毛沢東と朝鮮戦争, Mao Zedong and the Korean War). Tokyo: Iwanami shoten

Unpublished Primary Sources

B31, Shanghaishi tongjiju dangan (上海市统计局档案, Shanghai Municipal Bureau of Statistics Archives)

B31-1-32, Shanghaishi tongjiju (上海市统计局) ed. "Shanghaishi guominjingjitongji1949–1956 nian" (上海市国民经济统计 1949–1956年, National Economic Statistics of Shanghai 1949–1956), October 1957

B31-2-193, "Shanghaishi siyinggongshangye paiduibiao shuoming" (上海市私营工商业排队表说明, Explanation of the Shanghai Private Industry and Commerce Queue Table), date of creation unknown

B182, Shanghaishi gongshangxingzhengguanliju dangan (上海市工商行政管理局档案, Shanghai Municipal Bureau of Industry and Commerce Archives)

B182-1-222a, Wu Xuezhi (吴雪之) "Weihanqingdiaocha zhongyangjunweijunxiebu dengdanwei caigouqingkuang bing xihanfuyou" (为函请调查中央军委军械部等单位采购情况並希函复由, For the letter requesting investigation of the procurement situation of units such as the Central Military Commission's Ordnance Department and hoping for a reply), March 16, 1951, from Huadong junzhengweiyuanhui maoyibu (华东军政委员会贸易部) to Shanghaishi gongshangju (上海市工商局)

B182-1-222b, Xu Dixin et al. (许涤新等) "Hanfu □yu zhongyang junweijunxiebu deng gedanweicaigouqingkuang qingchazhao" (函复□于中央军委军械部等各单位采购情况请查照, Reply to the letter requesting investigation of the procurement situation of units such as the Central Military Commission's Ordnance Department), March 24 or 26, 1951 (uncertain), from Shanghaishi gongshangju (上海市工商局) to Huadong junzhengweiyuanhui maoyibu (华东军政委员会贸易部)

B182-1-226a, "51 niandu qinggongye jiagongdinghuo gongzuozongjie" (51年度轻工业加工订货工作总结, Summary of Light Industry Processing Order Work in 1951), December 1951

B182-1-226b, Zhongyangrenminzhengfu qinggongyebu" (中央人民政府轻工业部) "Biansong jiagongdinghuo zongjiebaogao (编送加工订货综结报告, Sending Processing Order Summary Report), December 1, 1951

B182-1-226c, Shanghaishi gongshangju (上海市工商局) "Jisong 1951 niandu qinggongye jiagongdinghuogongzuo zongjiebao qingjianhe" (寄送1951年度轻工业加工订货工作综结报请鉴核, Sending the Summary Report of Light Industry Processing Orders in 1951 for Review), date of creation unknown

B182-1-360a, [Shanghaishi] gongshangju ([上海市]工商局) "Guanyu jinxing weichi shengchan jiagongdinghuodeng chubuyijian" (关于进行维持生产加工订货等初步意见, Regarding the Preliminary Opinions on Carrying Out Maintenance of Production and Processing Orders), March 31, 1952

B182-1-360b, [Shanghaishi gongshangju] ([上海市工商局]) "Jiagongdinghuo huifushengchang-ongzuo zongjie" (加工定货恢复生产工作总结, Summary of Work to Resume Production of Processing Orders), April 1952

B182-1-360c, "Zhongyang duiyu shanghai wuyuefen jiagongdinghuo ji shougougongzuo zhongyaozhishi" (中央对于上海五月分加工定货及收购工作重要指示, Central Important Directive on Shanghai's Processing Orders and Procurement Work in May, May 12, [1952], Gongyezu (工业组) ed. *Neibu cankao ziliao* (内部参考资料, Internal Reference Material), No. 1

B182-1-507, "Guanyu shanghai jiagongdinghuo guanlibanfa de shuoming" (关于上海加工定货管理办法的说明, Explanation of Processing Order Management Method in Shanghai), date of creation unknown, attached doccument to Xu [Dixin] (许[涤新]), Cai [Beihua] (蔡[北华]), Yang [Yanxiu] (杨[延修]) "Niding jiagongdinghuo guanlizanxingbanfacaoan qinghedinggongbu (拟定加工定货管理暂行办法草案请核定公布, Draft of Temporary Method of Processing Order Management for Approval and Publication)," January 6, 1953, from Shanghaishi gongshangju (上海市工商局) to Shanghaishi renminzhengfu (上海市人民政府), report

Part II
The Socialist Fiscal System and Shanghai

Chapter 5
Reform of the Fiscal and Taxation System

Abstract This chapter examines how Shanghai's taxation and local fiscal structure changed from the postwar period of the Republic of China (1945–1949) up to the early years of the People's Republic of China (1949–1956). The Chinese fiscal and taxation system experienced a series of dramatic changes before and after the establishment of the PRC, and therefore this chapter considers the changes in the fiscal structure and behavior of local governments due to the institutional transformation by tracing the historical development of the fiscal structure of Shanghai Municipality, carefully articulating the key differences between the fiscal and taxation systems of each period.

Keywords Fiscal and taxation system · Fiscal structure of Shanghai · Central-local fiscal relations · Division of central and local taxes

The fiscal system was the core of the socialist system in China because circulation of capital was carried out not through exchanges in financial markets but through governmental fiscal transfers based on a central economic plan. Most of the investment in industries, especially in heavy industries based on the Heavy-industry-priority Strategy, were carried out as fiscal expenditure by central and local governments. Consequently, the fiscal system was one of the most crucial aspects of managing the socialist system.

The following three chapters will explore the process through which the socialist fiscal system was implemented and how it functioned in Shanghai, with particular attention given to the central and local fiscal relationship. When discussing the fiscal system after 1949, it is necessary to keep in mind the historical context of the modernization of the fiscal system that had been ongoing since the late Qing period. As will be seen later, the late Qing and Republican central governments had long faced the problem of unifying and normalizing central-local fiscal relations in a context characterized by provincial devolution and significant local autonomy. In such a context, it is reasonable to ask how a socialist fiscal system, predicated on centralization, could have been implemented after 1949. Moreover, as raised in Chapter 1, how was the fiscal system informed by the locally decentralized character of the Chinese socialist system?

J. Kajima, *Shanghai under the Socialist System*, Studies in Economic History,
https://doi.org/10.1007/978-981-95-3225-4_5

As a first step toward answering these questions, this chapter undertakes an analysis of the changes in the taxation and fiscal structure of Shanghai Municipality from the postwar period of the Republic (1945–1949) up to the early years of the PRC (1949–1956).[1] The Chinese fiscal and taxation system experienced a series of dramatic changes before and after the establishment of the PRC in 1949. Previous research has shown how central governments during the Republican period carried out a fiscal and taxation policy known as "separation of national and local finances," which involved the clear separation of the central budget and sources of revenue from those of local government (Li 1929; Kaneko 1988). On the other hand, it is also clear that during the planned economy period, the central government commissioned local governments to collect central taxes, and its finances therefore depended on the remittances from local governments (Ishihara 1990; Tajima 2000).

While previous works are thus highly useful for understanding the fiscal and taxation system of each period, however, they have neglected to examine the influence of institutional change before and after 1949 (Jia 1962; Yang 1985; Guojia shuiwuzongju 2001; Fujimoto 1971; Hsiao 1987; Zuo and Song 1988; Liu 1988; Nambu 1991). These scholars took for granted the notion that the change engendered by the revolution was all-encompassing, and they were consequently not sensitive to the specific differences between the institutions of each period.[2] Although many studies on the fiscal system of the PRC begin by surveying that of the previous era as a prologue, they tend to consider fiscal system continuity only in the case of areas under CCP control before 1949. However, when analyzing the influence of institutional change it is imperative to examine how the fiscal structure and behavior of local governments changed due to that transformation by focusing on an area which had not previously experienced the policies of the CCP.

Some researchers have already considered the public finances of Shanghai, notable examples being Mōri (1990), Wang (1995) and Shanghai caizhengshuiwuzhi bianzuanweiyuanhui (1999). While these studies have provided much in the way of data and general remarks, they have neglected to conceptualize the change of fiscal structure over the course of the two periods in question. This chapter, therefore, applies a historical approach to changes in the fiscal structure of Shanghai Municipality, carefully articulating the key differences between the fiscal and taxation system of each period.

---

[1] This chapter is based on Kajima (2007) with additions and revisions.

[2] Zhao (2002, pp. 154–155) mainly examines the fiscal and taxation reform in 1994, which clearly separated central taxes from local taxes (分税制改革), and surveys changes in the fiscal and taxation policy system from the republican era to the present. It is interesting that he situates the fiscal system of the National Government period (1927–1949) in the same category as the system after 1994.

5.1 Reform of the Fiscal and Taxation System Before and After 1949

As previously discussed, in the wake of the change of power in 1949, the new government promptly started to change the former institutions in the name of revolution. Particularly in the case of the fiscal and taxation system, a great number of changes were conducted on the basis of not only the fiscal policy principles of the new government but also the objective circumstances of the early years of the PRC. This section will outline both the basic fiscal system of the postwar period of the Republic and that of the early years of the PRC, focusing in particular on fiscal management policy and the allocation of sources of revenue between the center and local government.

5.1.1 The Postwar Period of the Republic of China

The fiscal and taxation system of the postwar years of the Republican period should be understood as having essentially succeeded that of the prewar period. The National Government, founded in 1928, carried out a fiscal policy that was predicated on a clear separation of the central budget and sources of revenue from those of local government. This was done for the purpose of securing stable central revenue while giving local governments their own sources of revenue. It is well known that the revenue of the central government at that time depended upon three indirect taxes—namely the customs, salt tax, and consolidated tax (a consumption tax imposed on industrial products like cigarettes, cotton yarn, and matches when they left the factories) (Kubo 1983). Additionally, the government encouraged and promoted the introduction of direct taxes based on Western taxation principles, such as income tax, inheritance tax, and stamp tax in order to promote the modernization of the taxation system and secure central revenue (Lin 2005). The central government also established several taxation organs under the direct control of the central Ministry of Finance in various locations for the purpose of ensuring safe collection of the central taxes (Guojia shuiwuzongju 2001, pp. 136–140, 182–184, 211–212), but in practice the main source of tax revenue remained certain specific cities like Shanghai. Consequently, the revenue of the central government basically depended on taxes from those cities.

On the other hand, the National Government abolished local customs that had been an important source of revenue for local powers since the late Qing Dynasty, and in exchange allocated the revenue from the land tax and the newly-implemented business tax to the local level. The government also defined the allocation standards of sources of revenue to three levels—central, province (including special municipalities under the direct control of the Executive Yuan, and county (including county-level cities)—on the basis of the "Fiscal Revenue and Expenditure System Law" (财政收支系统法) issued in 1935. Finally, it also obligated local governments to submit a rough estimate in advance, and to make a local budget to be approved by the central

Table 5.1 Division of central and local taxes of China in July 1946

Central taxes	Local taxes
Customs	Deed tax
Salt tax	House tax
Commodity tax (renamed from consolidated tax)	Slaughter tax
Mining tax	Business license tax
Income tax	Vehicle and vessel license tax
Stamp tax	Party tax
Special business tax	Amusement tax
	Land tax
	Business tax
	Inheritance tax

Notes (1) Division based on "Fiscal Revenue and Expenditure System Law" modified and issued in July 1946. (2) Special business tax implemented in May 1947
Source Jiangsusheng zhonghuaminguo gongshangshuishoushi bianxiezu and Zhongguo dierlishidanganguan (1996, pp. 806–824)

government, while it offered to provide financial assistance to local governments when they encountered financial difficulties. These policies did not always produce satisfactory results. For example, Uchida (1984) suggests that Shanxi and Suiyuan provinces never produced a single local budget, and in all likelihood the central tax collected in the area had actually been approved as a central subsidy to them during the early 1930s. From this perspective, it is possible to see how the institutionalization of local finance was conducted as part of a campaign of nation-building under the National Government in the 1930s.[3]

After the outbreak of the Second Sino-Japanese War in 1937, the government introduced an excess profits tax and allocated both the land tax and the business tax to central revenue in order to secure central finances and manage the increasing expenditures that accompanied wartime. The fiscal system of the entire state was also changed from a three-level apparatus (central-province-county, as mentioned above) to a two-level one (national-local) for the sake of centralizing finances (Cui 2004; Hou 2000; Lin 2005). This highly centralized fiscal policy, however, was gradually removed after the war. The three-level fiscal system was then restored on the basis of the "Fiscal Revenue and Expenditure System Law," modified and issued in July 1946,[4] and the allocation of central and local taxes was defined as shown in Table 5.1.

The key point to note here is that some of the taxes that were central-level taxes in wartime—land tax, business tax, and inheritance tax—were once again allocated

[3] Jiangsusheng zhonghuaminguo gongshangshuishoushi bianxiezu and Zhongguo dierlishidanganguan (1996, pp. 760–764, 770–790, 2519–2565).

[4] Jiangsusheng zhonghuaminguo gongshangshuishoushi bianxiezu and Zhongguo dierlishidanganguan (1996, pp. 806–824).

to the local level, while special business tax was newly added to central taxes.[5] This illustrates how the fiscal and taxation policy of the postwar period of the Republic, despite a brief interruption by centralization brought on by wartime, was essentially continuous with that of the prewar era.

Table 5.2 indicates central revenue in the pre and postwar periods. It is a simple matter to see that revenue increased rapidly in 1946 and 1947 because of inflation,[6] and that the bonds and loans revenue for postwar rehabilitation amounted to an enormous sum.[7] However, also evident is a slight increase in the proportion of direct taxes (income tax, stamp tax, etc.) while the customs, salt tax and commodity tax all took a significant part as in the prewar era. This was the result of the promotion of direct taxes in wartime, and the composition of central revenue reveals the ongoing process of the National Government's modernization of the taxation system.

As mentioned above, in the postwar era the National Government retained a fiscal and taxation policy based on the separation of central and local finances, indicating a continuity from the prewar era that was briefly interrupted by wartime centralization. While its attempts were short-lived due to the civil war and hyperinflation, it is nevertheless important to take note of the National Government's guiding principles of fiscal and taxation policy.

---

[5] In the case of land tax in special cities under the direct control of the Executive Yuan, 60% of the collected amount was allocated to local revenue and the rest to central revenue; in provinces 70% went to local revenue (20% to the province, and 50% to the counties and cities below the provincial level). As for business tax, in special cities 70% went to local revenue (later changed to 100% in 1948), while in provinces the entire amount went to local revenue (50% to the province, and 50% to the counties and cities). Finally, in the case of inheritance tax in special cities, 15% went to local revenue, while in the provinces 30% did, although in 1947 the ratio was altered so that in special cities it was 30%, and in counties and cities it was 70% (Guojia shuiwuzongju 2001, pp. 424, 460–462). Special business tax was implemented as a central tax in May 1947, which was imposed on businesses involved in banking, trust, insurance, trading posts, export and import trade, and traffic, as well as on state-owned enterprises engaged to some degree in competition, and on commercial enterprises jointly managed by the central government and private entities. This tax competed with business tax as a source of local revenue, and resulted in discord between the central and local governments (Guojia shuiwuzongju 2001, p. 464; Pei et al. 1999, p. 44).

[6] It is essential to take into consideration the hyperinflation from 1948 to 1950 when discussing fiscal and taxation policy at that time. The wholesale price index in Shanghai was as follows: 1946: 2.64, 1947: 24.92, Jan.–Jul. 1948: 500.04, Aug.–Dec. 1948: 14.93, Jan.–May 1949: 2,454,115.38 (Jan. 1946 = 1.00), Jun.–Dec. 1949: 5.29, 1950: 21.79, 1951: 28.75, 1952: 29.04, 1953: 28.60, 1954: 28.71, 1955: 28.81, 1956: 28.73 (Jun. 1949 = 1.00) (Zhongguokexueyuan shanghaijingjiyanjiusuo and Shanghaishehuikexueyuan jingjiyanjiusuo 1958, pp. 173, 448–453).

[7] According to Jia (1962, p. 47), almost all of the "Bonds and Loans" revenue in 1946 consisted of bank loans (5,513.6 billion Yuan).

Table 5.2 Central government revenue of China, 1936, 1946, and 1947 (Unit: 1936: million Chinese Yuan, 1946 and 1947: 100 million Gold Yuan)

Year	1936			1946			1947		
	Amount	Percentage of tax revenue	Percentage of Total	Amount	Percentage of tax revenue	Percentage of total	Amount	Percentage of tax revenue (%)	Percentage of total
Tax revenue	761	100.0%	66.6%	12,992	100.0%	18.4%	104,680	100.0%	28.3%
Customs	408	53.6%	35.7%	3,351	25.8%	4.7%	23,166	22.1%	6.3%
Salt tax	170	22.4%	14.9%	2,100	16.2%	3.0%	19,087	18.2%	5.2%
Land tax	-	-	-	510	3.9%	0.7%	66	0.1%	*
Commodity tax	146	19.2%	12.8%	4,987	38.4%	7.0%	44,823	42.8%	12.1%
Income tax	7	1.0%	0.6%	539	4.1%	0.8%	7,582	7.2%	2.0%
Excess profit tax	-	-	-	273	2.1%	0.4%	2,129	2.0%	0.6%
Business tax	-	-	-	560	4.3%	0.8%	223	0.2%	0.1%
Special business tax	-	-	-	2	*	*	1,380	1.3%	0.4%
Inheritance tax	-	-	-	31	0.2%	*	365	0.3%	0.1%
Stamp tax	9	1.1%	0.8%	502	3.9%	0.7%	4,777	4.6%	1.3%
Mining tax	5	0.7%	0.4%	137	1.1%	0.2%	1,081	1.0%	0.3%
Bank tax	*	*	*	-	-	-	-	-	-
Tobacco and wine tax	14	1.9%	1.2%	-	-	-	-	-	-
Marketplace tax	*	*	*	-	-	-	-	-	-
Fines and fees	42		3.7%	2,181		3.1%	3,495		0.9%
Public business revenue	9		0.8%	311		0.4%	954		0.3%
Bonds and loans	330		28.9%	55,281		78.1%	260,935		70.5%

(continued)

Table 5.2 (continued)

Year	1936			1946			1947		
	Amount	Percentage of tax revenue	Percentage of Total	Amount	Percentage of tax revenue	Percentage of total	Amount	Percentage of tax revenue (%)	Percentage of total
Other revenue	-		-	4		0.0%	15		0.0%
Total	1,143		100.0%	70,771		100.0%	370,078		100.0%

Notes (1) "-" in the table indicates that the amount (or percentage) is zero, while "*" means the amount (or percentage) is not a significant figure after rounding off. This applies to all subsequent tables as well. (2) "Fines and fees" represents the combined total of "Fines and compensation," "Fees," "Sale of property and goods," "Contributions and donations," "Collection and borrowing in kind," and "Property interest" in the original table. (3) "Public business revenue" represents the combined total of "Public business interest revenue," "Public business revenue," and "Foundation and withdrawal of investments" in the original table. (4) The 1936 fiscal year was from 1st July 1936 to 30th June 1937, and the 1946 and 1947 fiscal years were from 1st January to 31st December each year. (5) In the original table the total revenue for 1936 is "1,195,403.50," but this table adopted the total amount of each item

Source Jiangsusheng zhonghuaminguo gongshangshuishoushi bianxiezu and Zhongguo dierlishidanganguan (1996, pp. 3019–3020, 3034–3040, 3077). The original data is from "Settlement Archives of the Budget Bureau, the National Government" in the Second Historical Archives of China

5.1.2 The Early Years of the People's Republic of China

In contrast to the system described above, the fiscal and taxation system after 1949 was vastly different from that of the Republic.[8] Immediately after the establishment of the PRC, the new government centralized the fiscal system in March 1950. It abolished local budgets and concentrated all revenue at the center (Caizhengbu zonghejihuasi 1982, pp. 31–36). The primary purpose of this policy was to control hyperinflation. At the same time, the government unified the various independent local budgets formed before 1949, in order to balance the central budget and limit the issuing of paper money. However, this radical centralization was just a temporary policy. After the currency was stabilized and the fiscal system unified, the central government moved to gradually disassemble the center-focused system. In 1951, it also established a system of budgetary administration consisting of three levels—the central government, greater administrative regions, and provinces. Two years later, in the wake of the abolishment of the greater administrative regions, the government adopted a second three-level system—this time consisting of the central government, provinces, and counties—which was closer to that of the National Government period (Caizhengbu zonghejihuasi 1982, pp. 45–48, 64–67).

The fiscal relationship between the center and the periphery after 1951 is usually referred to as embodying a policy of "centralized leadership and separate level management." Although the allocation of sources of revenue was often adjusted slightly, it can be summarized as shown in Table 5.3.

The key point to note here in comparison with the Republican period is the allocation standard of Central-local Shared Revenue and Central Subsidiary Revenue, including some important taxes. This standard was decided by the central government annually on the basis of the fiscal condition of the local governments, and as a result the number of fixed items of local revenue became substantially fewer than had been the case in the postwar period.[9]

---

[8] Fiscal and taxation system policy in CCP areas prior to 1949 took several unique forms in each area because CCP-controlled areas were dispersed, and each managed its fiscal policy by itself (Nambu 1991, pp. 4–8, 113–117). The main source of revenue in CCP areas was an agricultural tax called Gongliang that was collected in kind, although it varied somewhat by place and time. Li (1959, p. 58) refers to the fact that this agricultural tax accounted for 80% of the fiscal revenue of CCP areas during the Second Sino-Japanese War, and Tsukase (2001) points out that the main revenue for the northeast CCP areas was not industrial and commercial tax but rather agricultural tax and the profit from exporting crops to the Soviet Union and North Korea.

[9] See Caizhengbu zonghejihuasi (1982, pp. 47–48, 57–58, 66, 69, 81) and Wang (1995, pp. 62–63). Concretely, the "Rules for Central–Local Sharing of Revenue and Expenditure in the East China Greater Administrative Region for the 1954 Fiscal Year" (华东区1954年度财政收支分成办法), enacted by the East China Finance Bureau of the Central Ministry of Finance (财政部华东财政管理局) on December 17, 1953 provided for the allocation of Central-Local Shared Revenue and Central Subsidiary Revenue as follows: "(III) Central–Local Shared Revenue: (1) Agricultural tax: 55% is to be allocated to local governments in Shandong, Jiangsu and Zhejiang provinces [...] 100% to the central government in Shanghai. (2) Industrial and commercial taxes [...] 5% of the business tax is to be allocated to local government and 95% to the central government, and 100% of the income tax is to be allocated to the central government in Shanghai. (IV) Central Subsidiary

Table 5.3 Central taxes and local taxes of China in 1951

Central government revenue	Central-local shared revenue and central subsidiary revenue	Local government revenue
Customs	Agricultural tax	Transaction tax
Salt tax	Commodity tax	Slaughter tax
Central government Enterprise Revenue	Industrial and commercial taxes	Special consumption tax
	Cotton yarn tax	House tax
	Stamp tax	Real estate tax
	Commodity circulation tax	Vehicle and vessel license tax
	Interest income tax	Local government Enterprise Revenue

Notes (based on Caizhengbu zonghejihuasi 1982, pp. 64–67): (1) Industrial and commercial taxes was consisting of business tax and income tax. (2) Cotton yarn tax was imposed on selling cotton yarn, established in 1951. (3) Stamp tax and interest income tax were allocated to local revenue in 1953. (4) Commodity circulation tax was an amalgamation of the commodity tax, business tax, and stamp tax on specified goods, established in 1953. (5) Special consumption tax was imposed on parties, amusements, cold food, and hotels
Source Caizhengbu zonghejihuasi (1982, pp. 45–48, 56–58, 64–71, 79–85)

On the other hand, as for the taxation organization, in January 1950 the central government abolished existing tax offices under central control, and instead established new tax offices under local governmental control. The central government adopted a tax policy that commissioned local tax offices to collect all taxes—that is, both central and local taxes—in a given area (Caizhengbu shuiwuzongju 1987, pp. 49–53). In short, it is clear that the central government left the responsibility for taxation collection to local tax offices, from which it then siphoned the tax revenue. Moreover, the "Temporary Regulation of Budget and Settlement" (预算决算暂行条例), issued in August 1951, stipulated that local governments form their own budgets on the basis of the revenue and expenditure index decided beforehand by the central government (Zhongyangrenminzhengfu fazhiweiyuanhui 1953, pp. 124–130; Wang 1995, pp. 241–242). For example, the Shanghai Municipal Government calculated the amount of remittance to the central government (Central Remittance Expenditure, apart from central taxes) from its budgetary revenue on the basis of the rates in the revenue and expenditure index (ex. revenue: expenditure = 10:8).[10] In short, the size of the local budget and the amount of remittance to higher levels were decided

Revenue: [...] the allocation of commodity tax and commodity circulation tax to local governments is provided as follows: 76% is to be allocated to the central government and 24% to the local government in Shandong [...] 100% to the central government in Shanghai." The author of the present study has not seen the original text of this statute, and therefore the foregoing quotation is taken from Shanghai caizhengshuiwuzhi bianzuanweiyuanhui (1999, p. 166).

[10] Shanghai caizhengshuiwuzhi bianzuanweiyuanhui (1999, pp. 228–229). Local revenue in the PRC was separated into "budgetary revenue" and "extra-budgetary revenue." The remittance to the central government was calculated on the basis of "budgetary revenue," and the rest (subtracting the remittance to the central government from "budgetary revenue") then constituted "local shared

on the basis of the revenue and expenditure index produced by the central government, and it is evident that a key feature of the fiscal system consisted of the central government reducing items of local fixed revenue in order to place local budgets under its own direct control.[11]

Certainly this fiscal and taxation system was significantly different from the highly centralized system that had been established immediately after the 1949 revolution, but it was also far removed from the Republican system that had operated according to the separation of central and local finances. Naturally, there were other factors behind the introduction of this fiscal and taxation system, one of which was clearly the influence of the socialist fiscal policy of the Soviet Union. The Soviet Union at the time had adopted a fiscal system based on the principle of "democratic centralism." The Soviet fiscal system took the budget of the Soviet Union as the central budget and combined it with the budgets of the 15 Soviet Socialist Republics to form the "Soviet Union National Budget;" the government of the Soviet Union had the final authority to decide the extent of the sources of revenue of each level of government in order to match the national budget and economic plan (Kiga 1964, pp. 189–201; Satō 1965, pp. 116–117). It is likely that the fiscal and taxation policy of the PRC had its origin in this Soviet fiscal policy.

On the other hand, there was another, more pragmatic reason for the introduction of the new fiscal system. The National Defense Expenditure ("Expenditure on Armaments" in the accounting of 1950) had increased since the PRC's entry into the Korean War in 1950, and after the war the Economic Construction Expenditure correspondingly increased. The National Defense Expenditure was entirely borne by the central government, and the percentage it represented of the total national expenditure[12] reached 38.19% in 1950, and 41.64% in 1951.[13] Moreover, as Izutani (2001, pp. 147–148) mentions, since 1951 the national policy had changed to the pursuit of both military strength and economic construction. The Economic Construction Expenditure, 80% of which was borne by the central government, reached 30.34% of total expenditure in the national budget, while the central government's total expenditures also increased (Fujimoto 1971, pp. 50–51). Although the National Defense Expenditure had remained stable at around 25% of the total national budget since 1952, the Economic Construction Expenditure continued to increase through the course of the First Five Year Plan. From these observations, it is evident that the

revenue." Finally, the actual local revenue consisted of "local shared revenue" plus "extra-budgetary revenue" (Wang 1995, pp. 69–68).

[11] The meaning of "local" here includes all levels of government, such as greater administrative regions, provinces (including special cities) and counties (including county-level cities), and the same center-local relationships also existed within each "local" level: for example, a greater administrative region and the provinces in said region, or a province and the counties within said province (Zhongyangrenminzhengfu fazhiweiyuanhui 1953, pp. 124–130).

[12] By which is meant the total expenditure of all levels of government, namely the central government, greater administrative regions, provinces, and counties, as in the fiscal system of the Soviet Union.

[13] Zhongguoshehuikexueyuan and Zhongyangdanganguan (1995, pp. 660–662, 1210–1211) and Fujimoto (1971, p. 44).

increase in central expenditures during the early years of the PRC led to the introduction of a highly centralized fiscal and taxation system based on the socialist fiscal policy of the Soviet Union.[14]

Table 5.4 shows the national revenue (including central and local government revenues) during the early years of the PRC. Because of the difference between "central" and "national" revenue, it is not surprising that the customs ratio decreased from that of the postwar period indicated in Table 5.1, but it is likely that the decrease in the absolute amount of customs revenue after 1951 was mainly due to the embargo on Chinese exports by the US. On the other hand, the sum of the commodity taxes (including the cotton yarn tax in 1951–52 and the commodity circulation tax after 1953), the industrial and commercial tax, and the stamp tax consistently accounted for 25–30% of the national fiscal revenue and 50–60% of tax revenue, and in particular the ratio of the industrial and commercial tax, which had previously included the business tax, was quite large. It is clear that these constituted the primary revenue for the central government because the government could essentially control them as Central-local Shared Revenue, which explains why the government moved the business tax from local fixed revenue to Central-local Shared Revenue.

Another noteworthy point represented by Table 5.4 is the steady increase in State-owned Enterprise Revenue (profit and depreciation reserves from state-owned enterprises, except for tax). State-owned Enterprise Revenue accounted for 45% of the national revenue in 1956 and supported half of the national finances as tax revenue. While the amount of State-owned Enterprise Revenue shown in Table 5.4 is the sum of the profit of both central and local government enterprises, the ratio of the two of these is important for understanding the relationship between central and local government, as will be seen momentarily.

As shown by the comparison above, there were significant differences in the fiscal and taxation policy of the two periods, especially with regard to the policy on the relationship between central and local government. In sum, the fiscal and taxation policy system of the National Government after the war was based on the clear separation of the finances and sources of revenue of the central government from those of local government. On the other hand, the Communist government in the early years of the PRC implemented a new fiscal policy that reduced the sources of tax revenues of local government, while the central government itself took direct control of the local fiscal balance. The focus point of the change in fiscal and taxation policy was the distribution of the tax revenue and the profits of state-owned enterprises between the central and local governments. The next section will pursue this point through examining how these developments impacted Shanghai Municipality.

[14] At present, due to limited historical sources, it is not possible to know the specifics pertaining to the arguments and decision-making among the central CCP leaders at the time concerning fiscal and taxation policy.

Table 5.4 National revenue of China, 1951–1956 (Unit: 10 million new RMB yuan)

Year	1951			1952			1953		
	Amount	Percentage of tax revenue	Percentage of total	Amount	Percentage of tax revenue	Percentage of total	Amount	Percentage of tax revenue	Percentage of total
Tax revenue	714	100.0	49.4	930	100.0	46.6	1,197	100.0	46.0
Customs	69	9.7	4.8	48	5.2	2.4	50	4.2	1.9
Salt tax	34	4.8	2.3	40	4.3	2.0	46	3.9	1.8
Agricultural taxes	177	24.7	12.2	221	23.8	11.1	275	23.0	10.6
Commodity tax	161	22.6	11.2	202	21.7	10.1	132	11.0	5.1
Commodity circulation tax	-	-	-	-	-	-	271	22.6	10.4
Cotton yarn tax	13	1.9	0.9	17	1.8	0.9	-	-	-
Industrial and commercial taxes	188	26.4	13.1	270	29.0	13.5	341	28.5	13.1
Interest income tax	1	0.1	0.1	1	0.1	0.1	1	0.1	*
Stamp tax	21	3.0	1.5	33	3.5	1.6	13	1.1	0.5
Local taxes	-	-	-	81	8.7	4.0	-	-	-
Transaction tax	14	1.9	0.9	-	-	-	13	1.1	0.5
Slaughter tax	16	2.3	1.1	-	-	-	34	2.9	1.3
House tax	11	1.6	0.8	-	-	-	16	1.3	0.6

(continued)

Table 5.4 (continued)

Year	1951			1952			1953		
	Amount	Percentage of tax revenue	Percentage of total	Amount	Percentage of tax revenue	Percentage of total	Amount	Percentage of tax revenue	Percentage of total
Special consumption tax	3	0.4	0.2	-	-	-	3	0.2	0.1
Vehicle and vessel license tax	2	0.3	0.1	-	-	-	3	0.2	0.1
Land registration tax	3	0.4	0.2	-	-	-	-	-	-
Other taxes	-	-	-	17	1.9	0.9	-	-	-
State-owned Enterprise Revenue	321		22.3	532		26.6	767		29.5
Bank and insurance revenue	-		-	16		0.8	49		1.9
Bonds and loans	47		3.3	17		0.8	-		-
Other revenue	133		9.3	166		8.3	163		6.3
Balance brought forward	124		8.6	335		16.8	423		16.3
Seigniorage	104		7.2	-		-	-		-

(continued)

Table 5.4 (continued)

Year	1951			1952			1953		
	Amount	Percentage of tax revenue	Percentage of total	Amount	Percentage of tax revenue	Percentage of total	Amount	Percentage of tax revenue	Percentage of total
Total	1,443		100.0	1,997		100.0	2,600		100.0
Year	1954			1955			1956		
	Amount	Percentage of tax revenue	Percentage of total	Amount	Percentage of tax revenue	Percentage of total	Amount	Percentage of tax revenue	Percentage of total
Tax revenue	1,322	100.0	43.0	1,287	100.0	42.2	1,416	100.0	47.5
Customs	41	3.1	1.3	47	3.6	1.5	54	3.8	1.8
Salt tax	52	3.9	1.7	48	3.7	1.6	48	3.4	1.6
Agricultural taxes	331	25.1	10.8	307	23.9	10.1	297	20.9	9.9
Commodity tax	142	10.8	4.6	172	13.4	5.7	204	14.4	6.8
Commodity circulation tax	295	22.3	9.6	309	24.0	10.2	358	25.3	12.0
Cotton yarn tax	-	-	-	-	-	-	-	-	-
Industrial and commercial taxes	374	28.3	12.2	321	24.9	10.5	374	26.4	12.5
Interest income tax	1	0.1	*	1	0.1	*	1	0.1	*
Stamp tax	13	1.0	0.4	15	1.2	0.5	16	1.1	0.5

(continued)

Table 5.4 (continued)

Year	1954			1955			1956		
	Amount	Percentage of tax revenue	Percentage of total	Amount	Percentage of tax revenue	Percentage of total	Amount	Percentage of tax revenue	Percentage of total
Local taxes	-	-	-	-	-	-	-	-	-
Transaction tax	9	0.7	0.3	6	0.5	0.2	3	0.2	0.1
Slaughter tax	41	3.1	1.3	38	2.9	1.2	39	2.8	1.3
House tax	16	1.2	0.5	17	1.3	0.6	16	1.1	0.5
Special consumption tax	3	0.2	0.1	2	0.2	0.1	2	0.1	0.1
Vehicle and vessel license tax	3	0.2	0.1	3	0.2	0.1	3	0.2	0.1
Land registration tax	-	-	-	-	-	-	-	-	-
Other taxes	-	-	-	-	-	-	-	-	-
State-owned Enterprise Revenue	996		32.4	1,119		36.7	1,343		45.0
Bank and insurance revenue	179		5.8	236		7.7	72		2.4
Bonds and loans	-		-	-		-	-		-

(continued)

Table 5.4 (continued)

Year	1954			1955			1956		
	Amount	Percentage of tax revenue	Percentage of total	Amount	Percentage of tax revenue	Percentage of total	Amount	Percentage of tax revenue	Percentage of total
Other revenue	126		4.1	90		3.0	50		1.7
Balance brought forward	451		14.7	315		10.3	101		3.4
Seigniorage	-		-	-		-	-		-
Total	3,074		100.0	3,048		100.0	2,982		100.0

Notes (1) All the items indicated in old RMB in the original table were converted into new RMB (the central government implemented a change in the denominations of monetary units in March 1955, where the ratio of new RMB to old RMB was 1 to 10,000). The same applies to the subsequent tables. (2) “Agricultural taxes” represents the combined total of “Agricultural tax,” “Deed tax,” and “Special product tax” in the original table. (3) This table adopts the total amount of each item as “Total” for 1953–56, and they differ from the amounts indicated in the original table

Sources 1951–52: Zhongguoshehuikexueyuan and Zhongyangdanganguan (1995, pp. 1208–1209, 1216–1218); 1953–56: Zhongguoshehuikexueyuan and Zhongyangdanganguan (2000, pp. 222–223, 271–273, 279, 289, 291–293, 309, 836–837, 872)

5.2 Tax Collection and the Fiscal Revenue of Shanghai

Until the Second Sino-Japanese War, the fiscal and taxation system of Shanghai had been divided among the International Settlement, the French Concession, and the Chinese section, each managed by their own governments. As touched upon in the previous section, the Settlement and Concession were requisitioned and organized into the unified Shanghai Special Municipality by the Wang Jingwei regime (汪精卫政权) under Japanese military occupation after the outbreak of the Pacific War. Based on this wartime unification, the new Shanghai Municipality was finally established as a single Chinese fiscal administrative unit after the war (Qian 1946, pp. 104–114).

Many scholars have already examined taxation on commerce and industry during the Republican period, and their research indicates that the relationships between government and merchants at the time were complex; for example, tax collection was sometimes conducted by trade associations, through contracts or petitions, on behalf of the government (Coble 1980; Tomizawa 1991; Kaneko 2000). It is therefore natural that change in the taxation process through the postwar period of the Republic and the early years of the PRC is a highly significant research subject,[15] but due to space constraints this chapter can only discuss taxation organs and the amount of tax collection.[16] After discussing changes in tax collection, it will examine the influence of these changes on the fiscal revenue of Shanghai, while placing this analysis in the context of the changes in national fiscal and taxation policy discussed in the previous section.

5.2.1 *Tax Collection in Shanghai*

First, a brief outline of the economic conditions in Shanghai pertinent to taxation during the two periods in question is required. Although the postwar economy in general has usually been described as characterized by hyperinflation, it was in fact undergoing recovery in Shanghai because of the increasing demand for light

[15] Studies of taxation in cities during the early years of the PRC have developed during the 2000s; for example, Wang (2001) examines the case of Wuhan, and Chen (2005) discusses that of Tianjin and Shanghai. On balance, Wang indicates an improvement in taxation ability through "institutionalization" in the early years of the PRC, while Chen stresses instead the CCP's ability to organize taxpayers by means of the political mobilization of class conflict beyond the concept of "institutionalization." The author fundamentally concurs with their approach in considering taxation in cities, but the current study's perspective lies closer to that of Chen's than of Wang's. In any case, it is essential to address the following question: how and why was the CCP able to organize taxpayers and construct a minute taxation system?

[16] It is important to clearly distinguish the "amount of tax collection" from "tax revenue." The former refers to the actual amount of taxes collected in a given area, while the latter refers to the fiscal revenue of the central or local government derived from taxes. This distinction is necessary because the amount of taxes collected by a taxation organ at a given governmental level did not always belong to the revenue of the government.

industry products after the war.[17] Similarly, after the founding of the PRC in 1949 and the stabilization of prices in the first half of 1950, there was an almost continuous increase in the production output of the main industries in Shanghai, due to increased demand resulting from several factors: specifically, rehabilitation after the civil war, China's entrance into the Korean War in October 1950, and the start of the First Five Year Plan in 1953 (Shanghaishi tongjiju 1992, p. 37). The output of electric power generation directly connected with industrial production also clearly indicates these business upturns in both periods (Shanghaishi dianligongyeju shizhibianzuanweiyuanhui 1994, pp. 42–43). In light of the evidence, it can safely be concluded that the two periods represent an economic recovery, with an interregnum of confusion during the revolution between 1949 and 1950.

Figure 5.1 shows the changes in taxation organs in Shanghai from 1945 to 1962. It portrays how the Direct Tax Bureau and the Commodity Tax Bureau of the Central Ministry of Finance were established in October 1945 as the central tax collection organs, while local taxes were collected by the Shanghai Municipal Bureau of Finance (上海市财政局) in its own right. This indicates that there was a systematic division of tax collection duties between the central and local governments during the postwar stage of the Republican period, in accordance with the principle of separating local and national finances discussed above. This division of labor, however, was abolished after the founding of the PRC, and the Direct Tax Bureau, the Commodity Tax Bureau, and the taxation section of the Shanghai Municipal Bureau of Finance were integrated into the new Shanghai Municipal Bureau of Tax (上海市税务局) established in March 1950. This new organ was granted the authority to govern all tax collection tasks in Shanghai Municipality, including collection of the central taxes.

The same development occurred with taxation organs below the municipal level. In 1946, the Direct Tax Bureau had its own ten offices and four tax collection stations, the Commodity Tax Bureau had its own eight administrative districts and three inspection stations, and the Shanghai Municipal Bureau of Finance had its own local tax collection stations in seven sections of the city. In short, there were tax collection organs (of each of these three bureaucracies) below the municipal level in each area during the postwar Republican period. On the other hand, the government of the PRC established a three-level taxation system in the city, consisting of the Shanghai Municipal Bureau of Tax, Section Branch Offices (numbering 20 sections in urban areas and 10 sections in suburban areas), and Tax Collection Teams. These institutions were then given the authority to govern all taxation in a given area. Under this system, 33 Tax Collection Teams for each industry, 121 Tax Collection Teams for each section, 32 Commodity Tax Collection Teams, 20 Tax Collection Teams for peddlers, and 17 Tax Collection Teams for vendors were established one after another in 1952. Additionally, as indicated in Fig. 5.1, the size of the Shanghai Municipal Bureau of Tax's staff increased considerably from 1950 to 1952. From these observations one can surmise that the government in the early years of the PRC

---

[17] Jin (2006, pp. 93–97) and Shanghaishi gongshangxingzhengguanliju and Shanghaishi xiangjiaogongyegongsi shiliaogongzuozu (1979, p. 56).

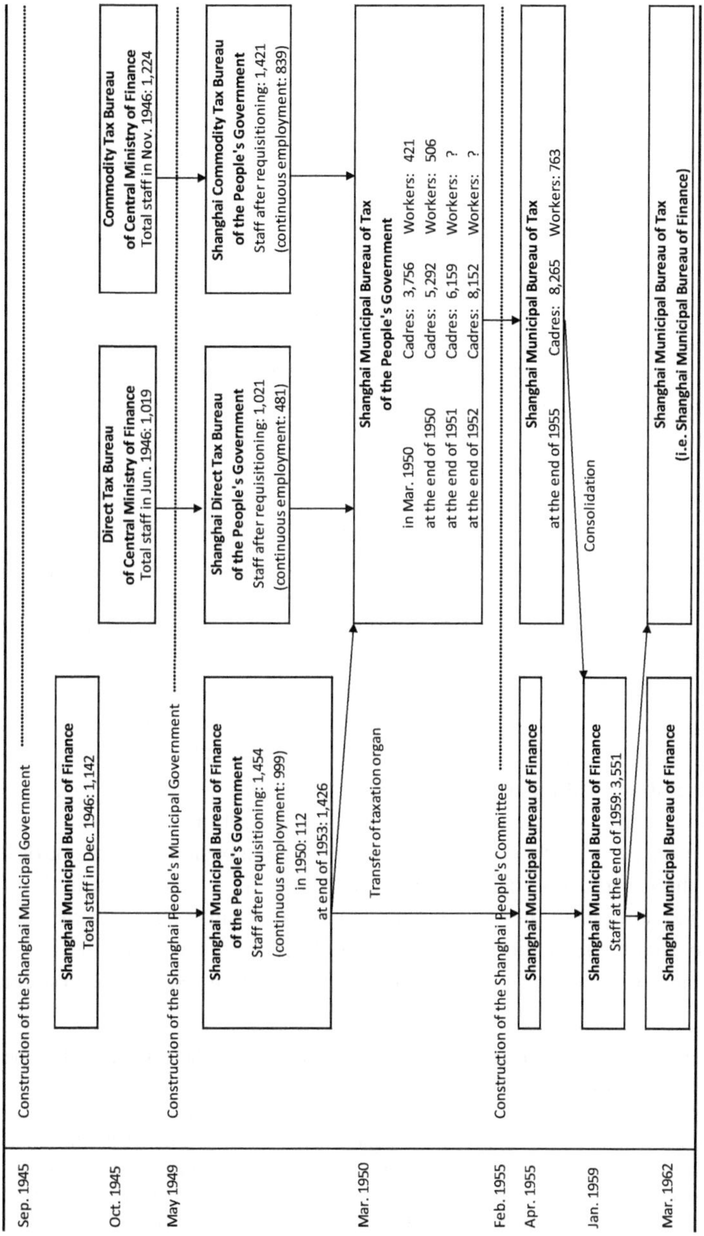

Fig. 5.1 Transition of fiscal and taxation organs and staff of Shanghai Municipality, 1945–1962. *Sources* Wang (1995, pp. 25–35, 711–713) and Zhonggongshanghaishiwei zuzhibu et al. (1991, pp. 96–97)

had constructed a much more substantial taxation system than that of its Republican predecessor (Wang 1995, pp. 695–710).

Building on this brief survey of the economic condition of Shanghai and the reorganization of the taxation organs, it is now possible to proceed to examine how the actual amount of tax collection in Shanghai changed during both periods, as shown in Table 5.5.[18] The first point clearly conveyed by Table 5.5 is that the commodity taxes accounted for a large percentage of the total amount of tax collection through both periods. The commodity taxes accounted for over 60% of the total amount in Shanghai during the postwar period of the Republic, and although this percentage fell to around 45% once after 1949, it rose again to 55–65% after the commodity circulation tax was introduced in 1953. The actual amount collected also increased steadily, especially during the early years of the PRC. It is therefore evident that this group of commodity taxes was one of the most important sources of tax income in Shanghai.[19]

On the other hand, one should note that the amount of income tax and business tax (including special business tax) collection was also intermittently increasing. These increases are clearly evident in Table 5.5, especially during 1946–1947 and 1950–1953. As for the proportion of income tax to the total amount of tax collection in Shanghai, it accounted for a little over 11% in 1947, steadily increasing to 12% in 1951, and then up to 18% in 1954. In 1952 it even briefly jumped to around 30% of the total. This indicates to what extent direct taxes, such as income tax and business tax, introduced in the 1930s and promoted by the National Government (particularly in wartime), had taken hold from the postwar period through to the early years of the PRC. Business tax had also accounted for around 13% since the postwar years of the Republic, and reached the 20–30% range during the early years of the PRC due to the steady increase in the amount of tax collection.

Several reasons for this increase in income tax and business tax can be determined, namely the broad economic recovery after 1949, the improvement in the economic monitoring abilities of the government due to the expansion of the state (i.e., public) economy, and the formation of a strict tax collection system through mass mobilization and an increase in tax organs and staff.[20] Gu Zhun (顾准), the first chief of the

---

[18] This tendency can also be seen reflected in the amount of tax collection deflated by the Shanghai wholesale price index given below.

[19] It is interesting to note that the proportion of commodity taxes (as a group) collected in Shanghai to the national commodity tax total changed significantly before and after 1949. Based on Tables 5.1 and 5.2, the proportion reached 53% in 1946 and 49% in 1947, but decreased to around 20% after 1951. Considering that the amount of commodity tax collection had been increasing steadily during this period, clearly the concentration of commodity tax-paying enterprises in Shanghai had gradually been weakening since 1949.

[20] Of course the tax rate was an important factor in the increase and decrease of the amount of tax collection, but for lack of space it can only be observed here that the business tax rate for financial and brokerage businesses in the early years of the PRC (1.5–15%) was higher than that of the postwar years of the Republican period (1.5–4%), and that the deduction rate of income tax for the manufacturing industry in the PRC (10–40%) was higher than that of the Republic (10%) (Guojia shuiwuzongju 2001, pp. 436–437, 441–443, 462–463; Liu 1988, Vol.2, pp. 13–28, 107–112, 413–420).

Table 5.5 Amount of tax collection in Shanghai, 1946–1956

Year	Commodity tax	Inheritance tax	Special business tax	Business tax	Income tax	Interest income tax	Stamp tax	Local taxes	Others	Total
Amount of tax collection (1946–Jul. 1948: 100 million Chinese Yuan, Aug. 1948–May 1949: 10 million Gold Yuan)										
1946	2,643	*	-	208	150	23	246	526	1	3,798
1947	21,950	18	2,191	2,105	3,870	293	167	2,415	4	33,013
Jan.–Jul., 1948	177,861	224	8,165	12,185	23,913	1,834	13,681	23,631	7	261,501
Aug.–Dec., 1948	21	*	*	1	3	*	2	4	*	31
Jan.–May, 1949	119,332	3	207	52,746	811	166	10,654	204,589	*	388,508
Percentage of total										
1946	69.6%	*	-	5.5%	3.9%	0.6%	6.5%	13.9%	*	100.0%
1947	66.5%	0.1%	6.6%	6.4%	11.7%	0.9%	0.5%	7.3%	*	100.0%
Jan.–Jul., 1948	68.0%	0.1%	3.1%	4.7%	9.1%	0.7%	5.2%	9.0%	*	100.0%
Aug.–Dec., 1948	67.6%	*	0.4%	2.1%	9.2%	0.9%	6.6%	13.4%	*	100.0%
Jan.–May, 1949	30.7%	*	0.1%	13.6%	0.2%	*	2.7%	52.7%	*	100.0%

(continued)

Table 5.5 (continued)

Amount of tax collection (10 thousand new RMB Yuan)										
	Commodity tax	Cotton yarn tax	Commodity circulation tax	Business tax	Income tax	Interest income tax	Stamp tax	Local taxes	Others	Total
Jun.–Dec., 1949	1,632	-	-	304	0	1	233	352	-	2,522
1950	21,529	-	-	14,211	2,206	229	2,725	-	6,416	47,317
1951	34,453	4,332	-	22,562	15,068	302	3,820	6,056	-	86,593
1952	39,427	6,440	-	23,526	33,676	288	4,558	6,353	-	114,267
1953	24,082	-	61,477	42,306	19,190	-	-	9,171	-	156,226
1954	25,235	-	67,908	40,133	31,795	-	-	9,307	-	174,378
1955	29,864	-	69,596	34,948	9,038	-	-	8,128	-	151,574
1956	36,028	-	82,993	41,448	10,811	-	-	7,650	-	178,931
Percentage of total										
Jun.–Dec., 1949	64.7%	-	-	12.1%	*	*	9.2%	14.0%	-	100.0%
1950	45.5%	-	-	30.0%	4.7%	0.5%	5.8%	-	13.6%	100.0%
1951	39.8%	5.0%	-	26.1%	17.4%	0.3%	4.4%	7.0%	-	100.0%
1952	34.5%	5.6%	-	20.6%	29.5%	0.3%	4.0%	5.6%	-	100.0%
1953	15.4%	-	39.4%	27.1%	12.3%	-	-	5.9%	-	100.0%

(continued)

Table 5.5 (continued)

Amount of tax collection (10 thousand new RMB Yuan)										
	Commodity tax	Cotton yarn tax	Commodity circulation tax	Business tax	Income tax	Interest income tax	Stamp tax	Local taxes	Others	Total
1954	14.5%	-	38.9%	23.0%	18.2%	-	-	5.3%	-	100.0%
1955	19.7%	-	45.9%	23.1%	6.0%	-	-	5.4%	-	100.0%
1956	20.1%	-	46.4%	23.2%	6.0%	-	-	4.3%	-	100.0%

Notes (1) "Percentage of total" is calculated on the basis of the original data. The same applies to the subsequent tables. (2) "Income tax" 1946–May 1949 represents the combined total of "Profit-making business income tax," "Wage income tax," and "Excess profits tax" in the original table. (3) "Local taxes" 1946–May 1949 is calculated by taking the "Tax revenue (except surtax)" of Shanghai of the item in question and subtracting the "Business tax" that said item required in the original table. (4) "Others" 1946–May 1949 represents the combined total of "Property sale income tax," "Property rent income tax," "Temporary income tax," "Fine," and so forth in the original table. (5) The amounts for "Business tax" and "Inheritance tax" in 1947 were inverted for each item in the original table, but this is an obvious error judging from other items in the original table, the amount of "Business Tax" in Table 5.6, Wang (1995, p. 499), and so forth. Therefore this table switched the amounts in question with each other. (6) "Business tax" in 1950 represents the combined total of "State-owned enterprise business tax," "Store business tax," "Peddling business tax," "Street stall business License Tax," and "Fixed Amount Industrial and Commercial Tax" of the original table; that of 1951–1952 is the combined total of "Periodic and Fixed Amount Industrial and commercial tax," "Peddling business tax," and "Street stall business license tax" in the original table. (7) "Others" in 1950 represents the combined total of "Slaughter tax," "House tax," "Real estate tax," "Vehicle and vessel license tax," and "Special consumption tax" in the original table. (8) "Local taxes" Jun.–Dec. 1949 represents the combined total of "Land prices tax," "Land tax," "Land value-added tax," "Deed tax," "House tax," "Slaughter tax," "Party tax," "Amusement tax," "Hotel tax," "Wharf tax," "Vehicle license tax," and "Vessel license tax" in the original table. For the breakdown of 1950–1956, see Table 5.6

Sources 1946–May, 1949: B97-1-340, pp. 232–235, 240–249; Jun. 1949–1956: B97-1-338, pp. 15, 17; B97-1-342, pp. 1, 46, 60; B97-1-343, p. 20; B97-1-344, pp. 3, 21; B97-1-345, pp. 1–2; B97-1-346, pp. 1, 3; B97-1-347, pp. 1, 3; B97-1-348, p. 1

Table 5.6 Fiscal Revenue of Shanghai, 1946–1956

Amount of revenue
(1946–Jul. 1948: 100 million Chinese Yuan, Aug. 1948–May 1949: 10 million Gold Yuan)

Year	Tax revenue							Financial assistance from central government	Public business revenue	Other revenue	City construction tax	Total
	Land taxes	Business tax	Slaughter tax	House tax	Party taxes	Other taxes	Total tax					
1946	32	1	43	19	398	34	527	103	-	75	77	782
1947	366	2,103	263	38	1,608	139	4,518	1,690	1	1,252	1,586	9,046
Jan.–Jul., 1948	754	12,185	1,757	132	10,201	1,103	26,132	3,646	18	5,963	9,684	45,443
Aug.–Dec., 1948	*	1	1	*	2	*	4	*	*	1	1	6
Jan.–May, 1949	1,907	52,746	49,768	126,783	25,530	600	257,334	-	7	38,892	59,539	355,772
Percentage of total												
1946	4.1%	0.1%	5.5%	2.4%	50.9%	4.4%	67.4%	13.2%	-	9.6%	9.9%	100.0%
1947	4.0%	23.2%	2.9%	0.4%	17.8%	1.5%	49.9%	18.7%	*	13.8%	17.5%	100.0%
Jan.–Jul., 1948	1.7%	26.8%	3.9%	0.3%	22.4%	2.4%	57.5%	8.0%	*	13.1%	21.3%	100.0%
Aug.–Dec., 1948	1.3%	11.4%	12.8%	8.0%	33.0%	0.7%	67.2%	0.9%	*	16.0%	16.0%	100.0%
Jan.–May, 1949	0.5%	14.8%	14.0%	35.6%	7.2%	0.2%	72.3%	-	*	10.9%	16.7%	100.0%

(continued)

Table 5.6 (continued)

Amount of revenue (10 thousand new RMB Yuan)												
	Tax revenue								Enterprise Revenue	Other revenue	Surtax	Total
	Stamp tax	Interest income tax	Slaughter tax	House taxes	Special consumption tax	Vehicle and vessel license tax	Central-local shared tax	Total tax				
Jun.–Dec., 1949	-	-	53	167	78	51	150	498	-	314	-	812
1950	-	-	516	4,800	625	475	-	6,416	105	3,842	606	10,969
1951	-	-	646	3,755	775	378	-	5,554	633	5,540	2,795	14,521
1952	-	-	938	3,812	603	287	18	5,657	1,513	9,245	9,303	25,718
1953	1,542	254	2,070	4,651	488	367	-	9,372	4,330	6,359	-	20,060
1954	1,248	283	2,738	4,299	449	374	2,007	11,397	7,243	6,891	1,683	27,214
1955	1,365	284	1,825	3,973	386	337	-	8,170	10,723	4,965	1,588	25,446
1956	1,703	219	2,031	3,083	303	312	-	7,650	16,382	4,775	1,763	30,571
Percentage of total												
Jun.–Dec., 1949	-	-	6.5%	20.5%	9.6%	6.3%	18.4%	61.3%	-	38.7%	-	100.0%
1950	-	-	4.7%	43.8%	5.7%	4.3%	-	58.5%	1.0%	35.0%	5.5%	100.0%
1951	-	-	4.5%	25.9%	5.3%	2.6%	-	38.2%	4.4%	38.1%	19.2%	100.0%
1952	-	-	3.6%	14.8%	2.3%	1.1%	0.1%	22.0%	5.9%	35.9%	36.2%	100.0%

(continued)

Table 5.6 (continued)

Amount of revenue (10 thousand new RMB Yuan)

	Tax revenue								Enterprise Revenue	Other revenue	Surtax	Total
	Stamp tax	Interest income tax	Slaughter tax	House taxes	Special consumption tax	Vehicle and vessel license tax	Central-local shared tax	Total tax				
1953	7.7%	1.3%	10.3%	23.2%	2.4%	1.8%	-	46.7%	21.6%	31.7%	-	100.0%
1954	4.6%	1.0%	10.1%	15.8%	1.7%	1.4%	7.4%	41.9%	26.6%	25.3%	6.2%	100.0%
1955	5.4%	1.1%	7.2%	15.6%	1.5%	1.3%	-	32.1%	42.1%	19.5%	6.2%	100.0%
1956	5.6%	0.7%	6.6%	10.1%	1.0%	1.0%	-	25.0%	53.6%	15.6%	5.8%	100.0%

Notes (1) This table does not include balances brought forward from the previous account. (2) "Land taxes" represents the combined total of "Land tax," "Deed tax," "Land value-added tax," and "Land prices tax" in the original table. (3) "Party taxes" represents the combined total of "Party tax," "Amusement tax," and "Hotel tax" in the original table. (4) "Other taxes" represents the combined total of "Business license tax," "Vehicle and vessel license tax," and "Wharf tax" in the original table. (5) "City construction tax" represents the combined total of "City construction tax," "City construction surtax on public utilities revenue," "City construction surtax on vehicle license tax," and "City construction surtax on house tax" in the original table. (6) "Financial assistance from central government" represents the combined total of "Financial assistance from the central government," "Central subsidy for local public business," "Surplus of operating and extraordinary expenses," "Charges for custody," "Charges for proxy collection," "Loans," "Collection of temporal payments" and so forth in the original table. (7) "Other revenue" 1946-May 1949 represents the combined total of "Fines and confiscations," "Fees," "Public property and rights," "Public construction charge," and "Others" in the original table. (8) Some figures from Jan.-Jul. 1948 and Aug.-Dec. 1948 were converted based on the ratio of 3 million Chinese Yuan to 1 Gold Yuan. (9) "Other revenue" in Jun. 1949–1956 represents the combined total of "Fees," "Fines and confiscations," "Public property," "Miscellaneous," "Surtax on public utilities" and so forth in the original table. (10) "House taxes" represents the combined total of "House tax," "Real estate tax," and "Deed tax" in the original table. (11) The core of "Central–local shared tax" consisted of "Business tax" in Jun.-Dec. 1949 and 1954, and "Agricultural tax" in 1952. (12) Some figures of tax revenue and totals from Jun 1949 to 1956 were different from those given in Table 5.5, but this table has adopted the original data. (13) "Surtax" represents the combined total of "Surtax on industrial and commercial tax," "Surtax on agricultural tax," and "Surtax on real estate tax" in the original table. (14) There is no data for "Financial assistance from central government" for Jan.-May 1949

Sources 1946–May 1949: B97-1-340, pp. 247–249. Jun. 1949–1956: B104-1-273, p. 2. In particular, "Financial assistance from the central government" in 1946–1948 and "Other revenue" in 1947 were based on the following materials: 1946: Q1-9-29, "Shanghaishi difang caizheng shouru shiji yu yusuan bijiaobiao 35 niandu shangbanniandu;" 1947: Q1-18-247, Table 5 "Shanghaishi 36 niandu caizheng shiji shouru;" 1948: Q1-18-174, pp. 167–168

Shanghai Municipal Bureau of Tax from March 1950 to February 1952, noted in his memoirs that an increased amount of tax (i.e., income tax and so forth) could be collected in March 1951 because of the establishment of collection organs below the municipal level (such as Tax Collection Teams), and the allocation of staff for each taxpayer, in September and October of the previous year.[21] From these observations it is clear that the amount of tax collection in Shanghai increased substantially during the early years of the PRC, but also that the tax collection system was based on a foundation that had been erected during the postwar period of the Republic.

5.2.2 Tax Revenue and Shanghai's Fiscal Structure

This raises another question: how did the fiscal structure of Shanghai change before and after 1949, in light of the change in tax collection discussed above? Table 5.6 shows the breakdown of the total revenue of Shanghai each year from 1946 to 1956.[22] At a glance, one can see the large proportion represented by tax revenue during the postwar Republican period. Tax revenue accounted for 50–60% of the total revenue each year from 1946 to 1949, meaning that the public finances of Shanghai were mainly supported by tax revenue in that period. Additionally, financial assistance from the central government was considerably important, followed by City Construction Tax and "Other Revenue."

With regard to the breakdown of tax revenue, the percentages represented by party tax, amusement tax, and hotel tax were all exceedingly large in 1946, but business tax accounted for around 25% and became the single largest item in 1947, when it was allocated to the local tax level. Although the percentage decreased after the latter half of 1948 due to hyperinflation and economic confusion, it is nevertheless fair to state that business tax was likely the main tax comprising Shanghai's revenue during the postwar years of the Republic.

On the other hand, it is important to note that although the tax revenue had occupied a certain proportion of Shanghai's total revenue during the early years of the PRC, it decreased to less than 50% in 1951 and finally dropped to around 25% in 1956. There were two main reasons for this decrease in the proportion of tax revenue. One is that the amount of tax revenue itself was in a state of stagnation. It stopped rising from 1950 to 1952, and then started decreasing from 1955 (although it rose once in 1953 as a result of the stamp tax and interest income tax being allocated to the

[21] See Gu (2002, pp. 161–163). Wang (2001, pp. 247–249) and Chen (2005, pp. 148–164) also note the improvement in tax collection ability below the municipal level in Wuhan, Shanghai, and Tianjin Municipalities.

[22] Normally it would be necessary to consider the role of local bonds in public finance, but there was no local bond revenue in Shanghai for both periods as far as the author can verify. Certainly the public finances of Shanghai had been supported by the issuing of local bonds before and during the Second Sino-Japanese War, but there appear to have been no such issues in the postwar period. On the other hand, in the early years of the PRC the task of floating national bonds, such as Victory Bonds in 1950, were often assigned to Shanghai (Qian 1946, pp. 104–114; Wang 1995, pp. 141–146).

local tax level, while the slaughter tax was on the rise). Recalling the breakdown of tax revenue during the postwar Republican period, it is likely that the reason for this decline in tax revenue was the removal of the business tax from the local tax level after 1949. In the early years of the PRC, the industrial and commercial tax, mainly consisting of business tax and income tax, was sometimes allocated specifically to Shanghai revenue as Central-local Shared Tax. This represented a substantial amount of financial support from the central government, but it could not constitute continuous, primary revenue for the public finances of Shanghai.

On the other hand, as Fig. 5.2 shows, the amount of business tax collection had been increasing until 1953, and is notable in that it was not only far larger than the total tax revenue, but moreover was also larger than the entire revenue of Shanghai almost every year. If business tax had been allocated to the local tax level continuously even after 1949, the proportion of tax revenue would have been far larger than it was. In short, although the Shanghai Municipal Government successfully increased the amount of business tax collection in the city, it failed to obtain the fruits of this endeavor as a result of the national reform of the fiscal and taxation system after 1949. The same can be said regarding the total amount of tax collection. As Table 5.5 indicates, the proportion that local tax (including business tax after 1947) collection constituted of Shanghai's total amount of tax collection amounted to a steady 13% during the postwar Republican period, but decreased to 4–7% after 1951.

The second reason for the decrease in the proportion of tax revenue was the increase in revenues other than tax. In 1950–52, "Other Revenue" (e.g., fees, fines and confiscations, public property revenue, miscellaneous revenue, surtax on public

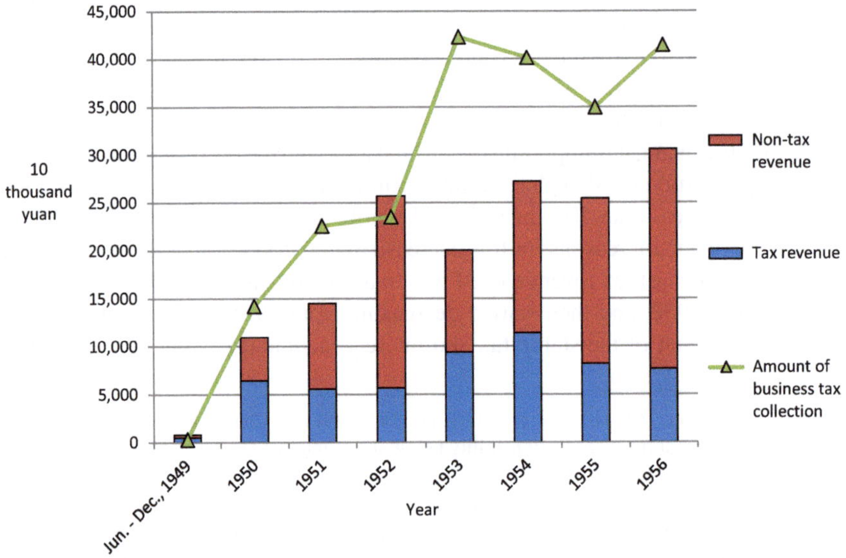

Fig. 5.2 Amounts of business tax collection, tax revenue, and non-tax revenue of Shanghai, June 1949–1956. *Sources* Tables 5.5 and 5.6

utilities revenue, and so on) and surtaxes (added to industrial and commercial tax, agricultural tax, and house tax) occupied an important place in the total revenue of Shanghai. The spectacularly rapid increase of "Other Revenue" in 1952 was mainly due to the influx of fines and confiscations from capitalists, such as those resulting from the aforementioned "Three Anti" and "Five Anti" campaigns that had begun from the end of 1951.[23]

Surtaxes mainly consisted of additions to industrial and commercial tax. The amount collected reached 17.29 million Yuan in 1951 (11.9% of Shanghai's total revenue that year) and 83.22 million Yuan in 1952 (32.4%) as the additional rate (imposed by the surtax) rose from the original 10% in 1951 to 15% in 1952 (Wang 1995, pp. 133–135). Collection of the surtax was stopped temporarily in 1953, and it was then formally allocated to Shanghai's local revenue as "Local Extra-budgetary Revenue" after 1954.[24] However, the rate was reduced to less than 5%, and the proportion of Shanghai's total revenue that it represented also correspondingly decreased.

It should be clear from the evidence presented thus far that the public finances of Shanghai were forced to depend on such extraordinary revenues as "Other Revenue" and surtax revenue for several years right after the foundation of the PRC, rather than receiving the fruits of its own increase in tax collection. In other words, these extraordinary revenues were necessary in order to compensate for the stagnation of tax revenue and the reduction of financial assistance from the central government. This change in the fiscal revenue structure—tax was no longer the primary source of revenue—was the first major impact of the post-1949 reform of the fiscal and taxation system on Shanghai. At the same time, it is also important to note that Enterprise Revenue had steadily increased since 1950, and that this brought about a structural change in the fiscal revenue of Shanghai after 1953, a point which will be taken up in the next chapter.

[23] On the "Three Anti" and "Five Anti" campaigns, see Chapter 3. According to Wang (1995, pp. 128–129), the percentage of fines and confiscations comprising "Other Revenue" in 1952 reached 37.7% (34.87 million yuan), and this amount accounted for 13.6% of the total revenue of Shanghai that year.

[24] "Local Extra-budgetary Revenue" was established as a formal item of revenue in Shanghai in 1954, based on the following instruction by the Central Government Administration Council: "It is permitted for provincial and city governments to collect in their own right a 2–6% surtax on the amount of industrial and commercial tax collection as the need arises, for the purpose of meeting the needs of local construction and solving problems outside the regular budget, on the principle that it must be of people's own accord and must not add to the burden of the people" (B1-1-1361). This local extra-budgetary revenue was mainly spent on city construction, such as the Sino-Soviet Friendship Building and People's Square Avenue in 1954 (B104-1-175). It is also the origin of the local extra-budgetary revenues that still exist in contemporary China.

References

English Language

Coble, Parks M. 1980. *The Shanghai Capitalists and the Nationalist Government 1927–1937*. Cambridge, Massachusetts: Council on East Asian Studies, Harvard University Press

Hsiao, Katharine Huang. 1987. *The Government Budget and Fiscal Policy in Mainland China*. Taipei: Chung-Hua Institution for Economic Research

Wang, Shaoguang. 2001. The Construction of State Extractive Capacity: Wuhan 1949–1953. *Modern China*. 27 (2): 229–261. https://doi.org/10.1177/009770040102700203

Chinese Language

Caizhengbu zonghejihuasi, ed. 1982. *Zhonghuarenmingongheguo caizheng shiliao diyiji: caizhengguanlitizhi, 1950–1980* (中华人民共和国财政史料 第1辑:财政管理体制1950–1980, Historical Materials of Public Finance of the People's Republic of China, Volume 1: Financial Management System 1950–1980). Beijing: Zhongguo caizhengjingji chubanshe

Caizhengbu shuiwuzongju, ed. 1987. *Zhonghuarenmingongheguo caizheng shiliao disiji: gongshangshuishou* (中华人民共和国财政史料 第4辑: 工商税收, Historical Materials of Public Financial of the People's Republic of China, Volume 4: Industrial and Commercial Tax Revenue). Beijing: Zhongguo caizhengjingji chubanshe

Chen, Yongfa. 2005. Zhonggong jianguochuqi de gongshangshuishou: yi tianjin he shanghai wei zhongxin (中共建国初期的工商税收:以天津和上海为中心, Industrial and Commercial Tax Revenue in the Early Years of the Founding of the People's Republic of China: Centered on Tianjin and Shanghai). *Zhongyangyanjiuyuan jindaishiyanjiusuo jikan* (中央研究院近代史研究所集刊, Journal of the Institute of Modern History, Academia Sinica) 48: 137–187. https://doi.org/10.6353/BIMHAS.200506.0137

Cui, Guohua, ed. 2004. *Kangrizhanzhengshiqi guominzhengfu caizhengjinrongzhengce* (抗日战争时期国民政府财政金融政策, Financial and Monetary Policies of the National Government during the Anti-Japanese War). Taipei: Taiwan Commercial Press. 1st edition: Cui, Guohua, ed. 1995. Xinan caizheng daxue chubanshe

Gu, Zhun. 2002. *Guzhun zishu* (顾准自述, Gu Zhun's Autobiography). Beijing: Zhongguo qingnian chubanshe

Guojia shuiwuzongju, ed. 2001. Zhonghuaminguo gongshangshuishou shigang (中华民国工商税收史纲, Outline of the History of Industrial and Commercial Tax Revenue during the Republic of China). Beijing: Zhongguo caizhengjingji chubanshe

Hou, Kunhong. 2000. *Kangzhanshiqi de zhongyang caizheng yu difangcaizheng* (抗战时期的中央财政與地方财政, The financial arrangements between the central and local governments during the Sino-Japanese War, 1937–1945). Taipei: Guoshiguan

Jia, Shiyi, ed. 1962. *Minguo caizhengshi sanbian* (民国财政史三编, The Financial History of Republic of China, Volume Three), Volumes 1 & 2. Taipei: Taiwan Commercial Press.

Jiangsusheng zhonghuaminguo gongshangshuishoushi bianxiezu and Zhongguo dierlishidanganguan, eds. 1996. *Zhonghuaminguo gongshangshuishou shiliaoxuanbian* (中华民国工商税收史料选编 第1辑:总合类, Selected Materials of Industrial and Commercial Tax Collection in the Republic of China, Volume 1: Comprehensive) Nanjing: Nanjing University Press

Jin, Zhihuan. 2006. *Zhongguo fangzhijianshegongsi yanjiu* (中国纺织建设公司研究(1945–1950), Research on China Textile Construction Company, 1945–1950). Shanghai: Fudan University Press

Li, Chengrui. 1959. Zhonghuarenmingongheguo nongyeshui shigao (中华人民共和国农业税史稿, A Draft History of the Agricultural Tax in the People's Republic of China). Beijing: Zhongguo caizhengjingji chubanshe

Li, Quanshi. 1929. *Guodi caizheng huafen wenti* (国地财政划分问题, The Problem of Central and local Public Finance Division). Shanghai: Shanghai shijie shuju

Lin, Meili. 2005. *Xiyangshuizhi zai jindaizhongguo de fazhan* (西洋税制在近代中国的发展, The Development of Western Taxation System in Modern China). Taipei: Institute of Modern History, Academia Sinica

Liu, Zhicheng, ed. 1988. *Zhonghuarenmingongheguo gongshangshuishoushi changbian* (中华人民共和国工商税收史长编, A Draft of History of Industrial and Commercial Taxation in the People's Republic of China), Volumes 1–3, Beijing: Zhongguo caizhengjingji chubanshe

Pei, Fei (Nataniel Peffer) and Wei Muting (Martin Wilbur) interviewed, Wu Xiuyuan translated, Gao Yunpeng proofread, Ma Jun annotated. 1999. *Cong shanghai shizhang dao "taiwan shengzhuxi": wu guozhen koushu huiyi* (从上海市长到"台湾省主席"(1946–1953年): 吴国桢口述回忆, From Mayor of Shanghai to 'President of Taiwan Province,' 1946–1953: Oral Memoirs of Wu Guozhen). Shanghai: Shanghai renmin chubanshe

Qian, Jianfu. 1946. Shiwunianlai shanghaishi caizheng ji qipipan (十五年来上海市财政及其批判, Fifteen Years of Shanghai Municipal Public Finance and the Criticism on it). *Caizheng pinglun* (财政评论, Financial Review), Vol. 15, No. 4

Shanghai caizhengshuiwuzhi bianzuanweiyuanhui, ed. 1999. *Shanghai caizhengshuiwuzhi ziliaochangbian* (上海财政税务誌资料长编, Draft and Materials of the History of Shanghai Public Finance and Taxation), Volumes I and II. Shanghai: Shanghai caizhengju and shanghai shuiwuju

Shanghaishi dianligongyeju shizhibianzuanweiyuanhui, ed. 1994. *Shanghai dianligongyezhi* (上海电力工业志, Shanghai Power Industry Chronicle). Shanghai: Shanghai shehuikexueyuan chubanshe

Shanghaishi gongshangxingzhengguanliju and Shanghaishi xiangjiaogongyegongsi shiliaogongzuozu, eds. 1979. *Shanghai minzu xiangjiao gongye* (上海民族橡胶工业, Shanghai Native Rubber Industry). Beijing: Zhonghua shuju

Shanghaishi tongjiju, ed. 1992. *Xinshanghai gongyetongjiziliao: 1949–1990* (新上海工业统计资料 (1949–1990), New Shanghai Industrial Statistical Data: 1949–1990). Beijing: Zhongguo tongjichubanshe

Wang, Weiquan, ed. 1995. *Shanghai caizhengshuiwuzhi* (上海财政税务志, Shanghai Fiscal and Taxation Chronicle). Shanghai: Shanghai shehuikexueyuan chubanshe

Yang, Yinpu. 1985. *Minguo caizhengshi* (民国财政史, History of the Republic of China's Public Finance). Beijing: Zhongguo caizhengjingji chubanshe

Zhao, Menghan. 2002. *Xinzhongguo caizhengshuishoushilungang* (新中国财政税收史论纲, Outline of the History of New China's Public Finance and Tax Revenue). Beijing: Jingjikexue chubanshe

Zhonggongshanghaishiwei zuzhibu, Zhonggongshanghaishiwei dangshiziliaozhengjiweiyuanhui, Zhonggongshanghaishiwei dangshiyanjiushi, and Shanghaishidanganguan. 1991. *Shanghaishi zhengquan xitong, difangjunshi xitong, tongyizhanzhanxian xitong, qunzhongtuanti xitong zuzhishi ziliao: 1949.5–1987.10* (上海市政权系统、地方军事系统、统一战线系统、群众团体系统组织史资料 (1949.5–1987.10), Historical Materials of Organizations of the Shanghai Municipal Government System, the Local Military System, the United Front System, the Mass Organization System: 1949.5–1987.10). Shanghai: Shanghai renmin chubanshe

Zhongguokexueyuan shanghaijingjiyanjiusuo, and Shanghaishehuikexueyuan jingjiyanjiusuo, eds. 1958. *Shanghai jiefangqianhou wujiaziliaohuibian: 1921 nian–1957 nian* (上海解放前后物价资料汇编 (1921年-1957年), Compilation of Price Data Before and After the Liberation of Shanghai: 1921–1957). Shanghai: Shanghai renmin chubanshe

Zhongguoshehuikexueyuan and Zhongyangdanganguan, eds. 1995. *Zhonghuarenmingongheguo jingjidanganziliaoxuanbian 1949–1952: Caizheng juan* (中华人民共和国经济档案资料选

编1949–1952 (财政卷), Selected Economic Archive Materials of the People's Republic of China 1949–1952: Financial Volume). Beijing: Jingjiguanli chubanshe

Zhongguoshehuikexueyuan and Zhongyangdanganguan, eds. 2000. *Zhonghuarenmingongheguo jingjidanganziliaoxuanbian 1953–1957: Caizheng juan* (中华人民共和国经济档案资料选编1953–1957 (财政卷), Selected Economic Archive Materials of the People's Republic of China 1953–1957: Financial Volume). Beijing: Zhongguo wujia chubanshe

Zhongyangrenminzhengfu fazhiweiyuanhui, ed. 1953. *Zhongyangrenminzhengfu falinghuibian: 1951* (中央人民政府法令汇编 (1951), Compilation of Laws and Regulations of the Central People's Government: 1951). Beijing: Renmin chubanshe

Zuo, Chuntai, and Song Xinzhong, eds. 1988. *Zhongguo shehuizhuyicaizheng jianshi* (中国社会主义财政简史, A Brief History of China's Socialist Public Finance). Beijing: Zhongguo caizhengjingji chubanshe

Japanese Language

Fujimoto, Akira. 1971. *Shinchūgoku no kokkazaisei no kenkyū* (新中国の国家財政の研究, Study on the Public Finance of New China). Tokyo: Yūhikaku

Ishihara, Kyōichi. 1990. 1970 nendai madeno chūgokukeizaikanri: shisutemu to jittai (1970年代までの中国経済管理——システムと実態, Chinese Economic Management up to the 1970s: System and Reality). In *Mōtakutōjidai no chūgoku: Gendaichūgokuron 1* (毛沢東時代の中国<現代中国論1>, China in the Mao Zedong Era: Discussions on Contemporary China No.1), ed. Mōri Kazuko, 146–185. Tokyo: Japan Institute of International Affairs

Izutani, Yōko. 2001. Chūgoku no shakaishugika to chōsensensō: taishū undō wo tekotoshita sōdōintaisei no kōchiku (中国の社会主義化と朝鮮戦争——大衆運動を梃子とした総動員態勢の構築, China's Socialization and the Korean War: Construction of a Total Mobilization System Using Mass Movements as a Lever). *Rekishigaku kenkyū* (歴史学研究, Journal of Historical Studies) 755 (Special Issue): 145–153

Kajima, Jun. 2007. "Seikenkoutai to shanghaishi zaiseikōzō no hendō: 1945–1956" (政権交代と上海市財政構造の変動 (1945–1956), The Chinese Communist Revolution and Changes in the Fiscal Structure of Shanghai Municipality: 1945–1956). *Ajia keizai* (アジア経済, Asian Economy) 48(7): 2–32. https://doi.org/10.24765/ajiakeizai.48.7_2

Kaneko, Hajime. 1988. Chūgoku no tōitsuka to zaiseimondai: 'kokuchi zaisei kakubun mondai wo chūshinni (中国の統一化と財政問題——『国地財政劃分』問題を中心に, China's Unification and Fiscal Issues: Focusing on the 'Central and Local Financial Division' Issue). *Shigaku kenkyū* (史学研究 (広島大学), Review of Historical Studies, Hiroshima University) 179: 19–39

Kaneko, Hajime. 2000. Shinmatsu minsho niokeru kōsoshō no nin'en seido (清末民初における江蘇省の認捐制度, The Lijin Tax-Farming System in Jiangsu in the Late-Qing and Early-Republican China). *Tōyōshi kenkyū* (東洋史研究, Journal of Oriental Researches) 59(2): 296–325. https://doi.org/10.14989/155342

Kiga, Kenzō, ed. 1964. *Sorenkeizai no ryūtsū zaisei kinyū seido* (ソ連経済の流通・財政・金融制度, Distribution, Finance, and Monetary System of the Soviet Economy), Seimeikai Series II. Tokyo: Seimeikai

Kubo, Tōru. 1983. Kokuminseihu no zaisei to kanzeishūnyū 1928–1937 (国民政府の財政と関税収入,1928–1937, National Government's Finance and Tariff Revenue: 1928–1937). In *Chūgokushi ni okeru shakai to minshū* (中国史における社会と民衆, Society and People in Chinese History), ed. Masubuchi Tatsuo sensei taikankinenronshu kankoukai, 213–232. Tokyo: Kyūko shoin

Mōri, Kazuko. 1990. 1970 nendai madeno chūō to chihō: Shanghaishi no kēsu (1970年代末までの中央と地方——上海市のケース, The Relationship between Central and Local Government until the Late 1970s: The Case of Shanghai). In *Mōtakutō jidai no chūgoku: Gendai chūgokuron 1*

(毛沢東時代の中国<現代中国論1>, China in the Mao Zedong Era), ed. Mōri Kazuko, 87–112. Tokyo: Japan Institute of International Affairs

Nambu, Minoru. 1991. *Gendai chūgoku no zaiseikinyūseisaku* (現代中国の財政金融政策, Fiscal and Financial Policies of Contemporary China). Tokyo: Taga shuppan

Satō, Hiroshi. 1965. *Soviet zaiseiron* (ソビエト財政論, Study on the Public Finance of the Soviet Union). Tokyo: Miraisha

Tajima, Toshio. 2000. Chūgoku no zaiseikinyū seidokaikaku: Zokuchiteki keizai shisutemu no keisei to henyō (中国の財政金融制度改革——属地的経済システムの形成と変容, Reform of China's Fiscal and Financial System: Formation and Transformation of Territorial Economic System). In *Gendai chūgoku no kōzōhendō 2 keizai: Kōzōhendō to shijōka* (現代中国の構造変動2 経済——構造変動と市場化, Structural Changes in Contemporary China, Volume 2, Economy: Structural Changes and Marketization), ed. Nakagane Katsuji, 73–106. Tokyo: University of Tokyo Press

Tomizawa, Yoshia. 1991. Mensatouzei no dōnyū wo meguru nicchubōshokushihon (綿紗統税の導入をめぐる日中紡織資本, The Countermeasures of Japanese and Chinese Cotton Textile Enterprises against the Enactment of the Cotton Yarn Conslidated Tax). *Shigaku kenkyū* (史学研究 (広島大学), Review of Historical Studies, Hiroshima University) 193: 29–52

Tsukase, Susumu. 2001. Kokkyō naisenki tōhokukaihōku niokeru chūgokukyōsantō no zaiseikeizaiseisaku (国共内戦期,東北解放区における中国共産党の財政経済政策, The Finance-Economy Policy of the Chinese Communist Party in the Liberated Districts of Northesat China during the Civil War Period). *Bulletin of Nagano University* (長野大学紀要) 23(3): 61–74. https://shinshu.repo.nii.ac.jp/records/3784

Uchida, Tomoyuki. 1984. 1930 nendai niokeru enshakuzanseiken no zaiseiseisaku (1930年代における閻錫山政権の財政政策, Fiscal Policies of the Yan Xishan Government in the 1930s). *Ajia keizai* (アジア経済, Asian Economy) 25(7): 11–39

Unpublished Primary Sources

B1, Shanghaishi renminzhengfu dangan (上海市人民政府档案, Shanghai People's Government Archives)

B1-1-1361, "Wei niju shanghaishi difangzichoujingfeifangan baoqinghebeiyou" (为拟具上海市地方自筹经费方案报请核备由, For the proposed Shanghai Municipal Self-Raised Funds Plan for approval), Shanghai People's Government to East China Administrative Committee, cc: East China Finance Committee (2), Shanghai Municipal Finance Committee and East China Financial Management Bureau, report (54), Hu Fu Mi Cai (沪府密财) No. 656, drafted on March 26, 1954, issued on April 1, 1954

B97, Shanghaishi shuiwuju dangan (上海市税务局档案, Shanghai Municipal Bureau of Tax Archives)

B97-1-338, "Shanghaishi shuiwutongji 1949 nian 6 yue zhi 12 yue" (上海市税务统计 1949年6月至12月, Shanghai Tax Statistics: June to December 1949), date of creation unknown

B97-1-340, "Shanghaishi shuiwutongji 1950 nian 4 yue zhi 6 yue" (上海市税务统计 1950年4月至6月, Shanghai Tax Statistics: April to June 1950), October 1950

B97-1-342, "Shanghaishi shuiwutongji 1950 nian 10 yue zhi 12 yue" (上海市税务统计 1950年10月至12月, Shanghai Tax Statistics: October to December 1950), June 1951

B97-1-343, "Shanghaishi shuiwutongji 1951 niandu" (上海市税务统计 1951年度, Shanghai Tax Statistics: 1951), August 1952

B97-1-344, "Shanghaishi shuiwutongji 1952 niandu" (上海市税务统计1952年度, Shanghai Tax Statistics: 1952), March 1953

B97-1-345, "Shanghaishi shuiwutongji 1953 niandu" (上海市税务统计 1953年度, Shanghai Tax Statistics: 1953), September 1954

B97-1-346, “Shanghaishi shuiwutongji 1954 niandu” (上海市税务统计 1954年度, Shanghai Tax Statistics: 1954), July 1955
B97-1-347, “Shanghaishi shuiwutongji 1955 niandu” (上海市税务统计 1955年度, Shanghai Tax Statistics: 1955), March 1956
B97-1-348, “Shanghaishi shuiwutongji 1956 niandu” (上海市税务统计 1956年度, Shanghai Tax Statistics: 1956), March 1957
B104, Shanghaishi caizhengju dangan (上海市财政局档案, Shanghai Municipal Bureau of Finance Archives)
B104-1-175, “1954 nian gongzuo zongjie” (1954年工作总结, Summary of Work in 1954), date of creation unknown
B104-1-273, Shanghaishi caizhengju (上海市财政局) ed. “Shanghaishi 1949 nian 1956 niandu caizhengshouzhi tongjibiao ji jibenjianshezhichu tongjibiao: baokuo difangzichou bufen” (上海市1949年-1956年度财政收支统计表及基本建设支出统计表 (包括地方自筹部分), Shanghai 1949–1956 Financial Revenue and Expenditure Statistics and Basic Construction Expenditure Statistics: including local self-raised part), October 1957
Q1, Shanghaishi zhengfu dangan (上海市政府档案, Shanghai Municipal Government Archives)
Q1–9–29, Shanghai caizhengju tongjishi (上海市财政局统计室) ed. “Shanghaishi difangcaizheng tongjiziliao di 3 hao baokuo 34 nian 9 yue zhi 36 niandu gexiang difangcaizheng shouzhi zhi tongjifenxishuzi” (上海市地方财政统计资料 第3号 (包括34年9月至36年度各项地方财政收支之统计分析数字), Shanghai Municipal Local Public Financial Statistics No. 3 Including the Statistical Analysis of Local Public Financial Revenues and Expenditures from September 1934 to 1936), October 1947
Q1–18–174, “Shanghaishi zhengfu 37 niandu tongjizongbaogao sifa jiatong dizheng deng zongjie” (上海市政府37年度统计总报告司法交通地政等总结, Summary on Shanghai Municipal Government Annual Statistical Report of 1937 by Ministries of Judiciary, Transportation, Land Administration, etc.), date of creation unknown
Q1–18–247, Shanghaishi caizhengju tongjishi (上海市财政局统计室) ed. “Shanghaishi difangcaizheng tongji zongbaogao 36 niandu” (上海市地方财政统计总报告 36年度, Shanghai Municipal Local Finance Statistical Annual Report of 1936), date of creation unknown

Chapter 6
Local Government and Local Enterprises

Abstract This chapter discusses the relationships between Shanghai's local public finance and the local enterprises that belonged to the Shanghai Municipal Government, paying particular attention to the category of "Enterprise Revenue" in the fiscal revenue and the fiscal expenditure of Shanghai for local enterprises, most especially Economic Construction Expenditure. A careful analysis based on the fiscal statistics of Shanghai here helps shed light on the dramatic changes that occurred in the municipality's fiscal structure in terms of the relationship between the Shanghai Municipal Government and the local state-owned and public-private jointly-owned enterprises after the socialist transformation in 1956 and, beyond that, in the wake of the decentralization policy in 1958.

Keywords Socialist transformation · Fiscal structure of Shanghai · Enterprise Revenue · Economic Construction Expenditure · Local enterprises

The previous chapter explored the impact of the fiscal and taxation reform before and after 1949 on Shanghai's local public finance, focusing in particular on the revenue structure. One of the key points was the transition in the Shanghai Municipal Government's main source of revenue, which moved from depending primarily on tax to other sources of income. Although the amount of tax collection in Shanghai had essentially increased during the first half of the 1950s, institutional changes in the fiscal and taxation system required Shanghai's local public finance to depend on less formal sources of revenue, like "other revenue" and surtaxes. Above all, "Enterprise Revenue," which had increased rapidly, became a vital revenue source for Shanghai's public finances.

This chapter builds on this to discuss the relationships between Shanghai's local public finance and the local enterprises that belonged to the Shanghai Municipal Government, paying particular attention to the category of "Enterprise Revenue" and the fiscal expenditure of Shanghai for local enterprises, most especially Economic Construction Expenditure.[1] The analysis here helps shed light on the dramatic change

[1] This chapter is based on Kajima (2007) with additions and revisions.

J. Kajima, *Shanghai under the Socialist System*, Studies in Economic History,
https://doi.org/10.1007/978-981-95-3225-4_6

undergone by Shanghai's fiscal structure after the socialist transformation in 1956 and, beyond that, in the wake of the decentralized policy in 1958.

6.1 The Socialist Transformation and Enterprise Revenue

First of all, it is important to clarify the concept of "Enterprise Revenue" as it existed within the socialist fiscal system of the time. "Enterprise Revenue," as an item of fiscal revenue in the PRC, referred to the total of the profits and depreciation reserves of enterprises owned by the government or owned jointly by public and private entities (Wang 1995, pp. 112–122). Thus, as a fiscal revenue item of central government it meant the total of profits and depreciation reserves from central state-owned and jointly-owned enterprises, whereas the same revenue item for the Shanghai Municipal Government encompassed the total from Shanghai's own local state-owned and jointly-owned enterprises. One should note that Enterprise Revenue was distinguished from the tax revenue collected from these enterprises.

The Central Government Administration Council had already anticipated that this Enterprise Revenue would become a key source of revenue for cities. This was because in 1951 the "Decision Concerning Further Adjustment of Local Public Finances of Cities" (关于进一步整理城市地方财政的决定) was issued, stating that "city governments must gradually develop their own enterprises and make the profits from these enterprises a reliable revenue item of their public finances" (Caizhengbu zonghejihuasi 1982, pp. 53–55). In fact, as Table 5.6 shows, the Enterprise Revenue of Shanghai had increased steadily since 1950, and proceeded to exceed the Tax Revenue, coming to account for half of the Total Revenue in 1955. This development represented a change of major proportions in the fiscal structure of Shanghai, because there had been almost no Public Business Revenue during the postwar period of the Republic.[2] Of course, some government-owned enterprises existed in Shanghai during the Republican period, such as China Textile Industries, Inc., which consisted of former Japanese-owned cotton mills requisitioned by the National Government after the war, and which was a gigantic company in scale. However, it was a central government-owned enterprise with branches and factories scattered across the country, and therefore neither its finances nor its management were matters related to the Shanghai Municipal Government (Jin 2006, pp. 47–59).

To understand what factors were involved in the increase in Enterprise Revenue, consider the breakdown provided in Table 6.1 for the post-1949 era. It is clear that until 1955, the primary elements comprising Enterprise Revenue were the City Public Utilities (e.g., waterworks, gasworks, streetcars, and buses) and Local Industry, followed by Construction, Commerce, and Fisheries. On the other hand, one should

[2] The public businesses managed by the Shanghai Municipal Government during the postwar period of the Republic consisted of only a few buses on regular routes, a gas company, some ferryboats, and two companies reopened after the war—namely the Bank of Shanghai City and a trust company. Additionally, the breakdown of revenue from these businesses was not open to the public (Qian 1946, p. 121).

also note the rapid increase in revenue from local jointly-owned (public-private) enterprises. The amount increased by a factor of 15 in the course of merely a year, skyrocketing from only 4.32 million Yuan in 1955 to 66.04 million Yuan in 1956, which naturally contributed to the substantial increase in total Enterprise Revenue for 1956.[3]

The most substantial reason for this rapid increase in the revenue from local jointly-owned enterprises was none other than the socialist transformation of private enterprises, which had been proceeding at the same time. It is clear from Table 4.2, which indicated the number of enterprises in the industrial sector of Shanghai by type of ownership, that the socialist transformation converted far more private enterprises into local jointly-owned enterprises than it did into central ones. Consequently, the increase in the number of local jointly-owned enterprises through the socialist transformation was the primary cause of the definitive change in the revenue structure of Shanghai.

Another significant factor behind the rapid increase in the revenue of local jointly-owned enterprises was a substantial change in the system of profit distribution of said enterprises. Previously, since 1949 jointly-owned enterprises had followed the same system as that of private enterprises, whereby the Enterprise Revenue obtained by the public finances of Shanghai had consisted only of the dividend paid by the ratio of public stock in those enterprises.[4] However, after the socialist transformation of all

[3] It should be noted that the Shanghai Municipal Government had already made an attempt to expand its own enterprises before 1955, as illustrated by the constant increase in the "local industry" revenue item during the early years of the PRC. The enterprises originally owned by the National Government in Shanghai initially belonged to the government of the East China Greater Administrative Region at the time of the military occupation and requisition in May 1949, but after a while seven or eight jointly-owned textile factories were allocated to the Shanghai Municipal Government. Additionally, the Local Industry Division of the Shanghai Municipal Financial and Economic Committee was established from June to July 1951, and it purchased, or changed some factories into, various jointly-owned enterprises prior to 1952: for example, Xinyu No.1 Cotton Mill, Guangzhong Dyeing and Weaving Factory, Yongxin Chemical Factory, Tianshan Chemical Factory, Guanleming Fountain Pen Factory (William K. Rockman, Inc.), and Xiechang Sewing Machine Factory (Gu 2002, pp. 185–190).

[4] The method of profit distribution for private enterprises was prescribed in Art. 25 of the "Temporary Regulation of Private Enterprises" (私营企业暂行条例) issued in December 1950: the profit after a settlement was firstly subjected to income tax, and the amount for supplying the deficiency and the legal reserves (over 10%). Secondly, fixed annual interest (Guxi, under 8%) was allocated to the stockholders based on the amount of each investment. Thirdly, the remaining income was distributed in four parts: (1) dividends to the stockholders and rewards for members of the Board (over 60%); (2) a fund for security and sanitation facilities (over 15% in industry and mining); (3) a fund for the welfare of workers and staff, bonuses and so forth (over 15%); and finally (4) others (Zhonggong zhongyang wenxianyanjiushi 1992, pp. 516–523). After a few years, the Government Administration Council Finance and Economic Committee implemented a new system known as "Sima fenfei" (四马分肥, sharing profits among four areas, lit. "dividing profits to four horses") in October 1953, which stipulated that the profit of private enterprises should be distributed among legal reserves, income tax, dividends to the stockholders (including rewards for members of the Board), and the fund for the welfare of workers and staff; in principle, moreover, it was forbidden for dividends to the stockholders to exceed 25% of the total profit (Shanghai shehuikexueyuan jingjiyanjiusuo 1980, p. 160).

Table 6.1 Breakdown of Enterprise Revenue of Shanghai, 1949–1956

Amount of enterprise revenue (10 thousand new RMB Yuan)	Construction	Local industry	City public utilities	Local jointly-owned	Commerce	Fisheries	Others	Total
Jun.–Dec., 1949	-	-	-	-	-	-	-	-
1950	20	16	36	-	19	-	15	105
1951	253	104	132	-	59	-	85	633
1952	88	573	369	55	201	-	226	1,513
1953	416	1,210	1,684	36	-	310	674	4,330
1954	1,009	2,218	1,904	75	-	978	1,059	7,243
1955	721	3,106	3,099	432	-	1,156	2,210	10,723
1956	307	4,398	3,255	6,604	-	-	1,818	16,382
Percentage of Total								
Jun.–Dec., 1949	-	-	-	-	-	-	-	-
1950	18.6%	15.0%	34.5%	-	17.9%	-	14.0%	100.0%
1951	40.0%	16.4%	20.9%	-	9.3%	-	13.4%	100.0%
1952	5.8%	37.9%	24.4%	3.7%	13.3%	-	15.0%	100.0%
1953	9.6%	27.9%	38.9%	0.8%	-	7.2%	15.6%	100.0%
1954	13.9%	30.6%	26.3%	1.0%	-	13.5%	14.6%	100.0%
1955	6.7%	29.0%	28.9%	4.0%	-	10.8%	20.6%	100.0%
1956	1.9%	26.8%	19.9%	40.3%	-	-	11.1%	100.0%

Notes (1) It is unknown what types of industry were included in "Local jointly-owned." (2) "Others" represents the combined total of "Agriculture," "Irrigation," "Transportation," "Posts and telecommunications," "Culture, education, and health," "Others," and "Public business" in the original table
Source "Shanghaishi 1949–1956 nian caizheng shouru tongjibiao" in B104-1-273

industries was completed in 1956, this system was replaced with a fixed-rate interest system. This new method of profit distribution stipulated that private stock holders were only to be paid fixed-rate (generally 5%) interest based on the amount of their investment at the time of the socialist transformation, irrespective of the actual profits of the enterprises.[5]

As a result, after the deduction of fixed-rate interest the remaining income from jointly-owned enterprises was counted as profit in the public finances of Shanghai. Some scholars have regarded this process as nothing other than the "extinction of capitalism" because of the complete separation between the actual enterprise profit and the dividends paid to private stock holders.[6] To some extent this is a reasonable assertion, but on the other hand, one should consider that this also meant that the primary stakeholder in the management, as well as the profits and losses, of the enterprises was now the government to which those enterprises belonged.

As mentioned above, the public finances of Shanghai Municipality were forced to depend on extraordinary revenues, such as fines and surtaxes, after 1949 due to the reduction of some fixed local tax revenues on the one hand and a decrease in Central Subsidiary Revenue on the other. Under these conditions, the increase in Enterprise Revenue as a result of the socialist transformation markedly reconfigured the revenue structure of Shanghai. This change can also be described as a process whereby the fiscal structure of Shanghai was changed from one mainly dependent on the tax revenue from various economic units in the city, as was the case during the postwar Republican period, into one dependent instead on the enterprise profit revenue from local state-owned and jointly-owned enterprises belonging to the Municipal Government, which was the situation after 1949.

6.2 The Fiscal Relationship Between the Shanghai Municipal Government and Local Enterprises

A detailed examination of the whole fiscal structure, including expenditures, makes it possible to more clearly understand the relationship between the public finances of Shanghai and the municipality's own local enterprises that was articulated above.

Table 6.2 indicates the expenditures of Shanghai during both periods. Firstly, it is surprising that the proportion of Livelihood Assistance for Government Employees was especially large during the postwar period of the Republic. This item consisted of

[5] See "Notice by CCP Shanghai Committee Socialist Transformation Team Concerning Implementation of the Fixed-rate Interest System for Jointly-owned Enterprises" (中共上海市委对资改造十人小组关于公私合营企业定股发息工作的通知) on 27th July 1956 in Zhonggongshanghaishiwei tongzhanbu et al. (1993, pp. 787–788) and Shanghai shehuikexueyuan jingjiyanjiusuo (1980, pp. 284–288).

[6] Shanghai shehuikexueyuan jingjiyanjiusuo (1980, pp. 284–288) and Gui (2006, pp. 230–233).

a subsidy to staff of the municipal government for the purpose of offsetting the hyperinflation of the time. It increased year after year, reaching 80% of total expenditures in January-August 1948.

It is also notable that the percentage represented by Economic Construction consistently remained over 20% until 1947, although it fell rapidly after 1948. This indicates that the Shanghai Municipal Government allocated a certain amount of funds for economic reconstruction expenses immediately after the war, but was gradually forced by the advancing civil war and hyperinflation to instead expend most of its revenue on Administration (including Livelihood Assistance for Government Employees). Nevertheless, it is important to note that Economic Construction at the time was not a profitable short-term investment, because there was almost no income from Public Business Revenue during the postwar years of the Republic (as shown in Table 5.6).

On the other hand, the expenditure structure during the early years of the PRC could be essentially characterized as a competition between the (1) Economic Construction, (2) Administration, and (3) Culture, education, and health items, with each comprising around 30% of expenditures. Further, it is particularly important to note the increase in the Central Remittance Expenditure, which was made to the central government from the local budget on the basis of the revenue and expenditure index decided beforehand by the central government. This remittance rose sharply from 12.13 million Yuan in 1954 to 72.17 million Yuan in 1955, when it came to account for 27.7% of Shanghai's total expenditures. This rapid increase was clearly connected to the increase in Enterprise Revenue at that time.

When one takes into account both the Central Remittance Expenditure and the rescinding of fixed local taxes discussed above, it becomes clear to what extent the central government siphoned off the public finances of Shanghai, as stressed by Lardy (1978, pp. 134–135) and Mōri (1990, pp. 97–102). In fact, there were complaints about the Central Remittance Expenditure from within the Shanghai Municipal Government shortly after its implementation, although ultimately such complaints themselves came under fire for reflecting a "self-centered way of thinking" in the "Three Anti" campaign in 1952.[7]

While keeping in mind these strict fiscal controls by the central government, it is important to consider in some detail the breakdown of Economic Construction Expenditure given in Table 6.3. At a glance, one readily observes that the expenditure on city public utilities occupied a major part of the total expenditures until

[7] Part of a "self-criticism document" produced by the Shanghai Municipal Bureau of Finance clearly illustrates the delicate position of Shanghai at that time: "... We recognized that the new fiscal policy concerning the fiscal separation between the central and local governments issued in 1951 can foster positive attitudes of local governments, but at the same time we also grasped the fiscal relationship between the national and local finances unclearly, and fostered our own self-centered way of thinking based on the old notion of the fiscal separation between central and local finances. For example, we were not sufficiently resolute in accomplishing our duty of Central Remittance Expenditure, and we had some complaints about not only having no subsidy from the central government for Shanghai, but also being required to remit over 7 million Yuan from our budget in 1951. At last we thought to resist, and tried to delay our duties (finally all was accomplished in March 1952)" (B104-1-116).

Table 6.2 Fiscal expenditure of Shanghai, 1946–1956

Amount of expenditure (1946–Jul. 1948: 100 million Chinese Yuan, Aug. 1948–May 1949: 10 million Gold Yuan)													
Year	Economic construction	Administration	Livelihood assistance for government employees	Culture, education, and health	Other expenditures	Total							
1946	172	127	421	79	7	806							
1947	1,477	860	3,398	719	439	6,892							
Jan.–Aug., 1948	4,379	6,365	70,292	5,302	273	86,612							
Sep.–Dec., 1948	*	5	-	*	*	5							
Jan.–Apr., 1949	163	7,975	-	225	28	8,390							
Percentage of total													
1946	21.4%	15.7%	52.3%	9.8%	0.8%	100.0%							
1947	21.4%	12.5%	49.3%	10.4%	6.4%	100.0%							
Jan.–Aug., 1948	5.1%	7.3%	81.2%	6.1%	0.3%	100.0%							
Sep.–Dec., 1948	9.0%	89.3%	-	*	1.7%	100.0%							
Jan.–Apr., 1949	1.9%	95.0%	-	2.7%	0.3%	100.0%							

(continued)

Table 6.2 (continued)

Amount of expenditure (10 thousand million new RMB Yuan)						
	Economic Construction	Administration	Culture, education, and health	Central Remittance Expenditure	Other expenditures	Total
Jun.–Dec., 1949	160	316	261	-	-	736
1950	1,532	3,426	2,952	-	77	7,988
1951	4,756	5,693	3,879	783	348	15,459
1952	8,698	5,679	6,485	3,290	184	24,335
1953	7,218	5,958	5,327	500	154	19,157
1954	7,924	6,566	7,129	1,213	1,807	24,639
1955	4,124	6,925	6,759	7,217	1,016	26,040
1956	10,293	7,304	10,465	6,491	395	34,948
Percentage of total						
Jun.–Dec., 1949	21.7%	42.9%	35.5%	-	-	100.0%
1950	19.2%	42.9%	37.0%	-	1.0%	100.0%
1951	30.8%	36.8%	25.1%	5.1%	2.2%	100.0%
1952	35.7%	23.3%	26.6%	13.5%	0.8%	100.0%
1953	37.7%	31.1%	27.8%	2.6%	0.8%	100.0%

(continued)

Table 6.2 (continued)

Amount of expenditure (10 thousand million new RMB Yuan)

	Economic Construction	Administration	Culture, education, and health	Central Remittance Expenditure	Other expenditures	Total
1954	32.2%	26.6%	28.9%	4.9%	7.3%	100.0%
1955	15.8%	26.6%	26.0%	27.7%	3.9%	100.0%
1956	29.5%	20.9%	29.9%	18.6%	1.1%	100.0%

Notes (1) "-" in the table indicates that the amount (or percentage) is zero, while "*" means the amount (or percentage) is not a significant figure after rounding off. This applies to all subsequent tables as well. (2) The breakdown of each item in the original tables is as follows: Aug. 1948–1946: Economic Construction: "Economy and construction" and "Land administration." Administration: "Exercise of political power," "Administration," "Society and relief," "Public security," "Financial affairs" and "Civil affairs and autonomy." Culture, education, and health: "Culture and education" and "Health;" Sep. 1948–Apr. 1949: Unknown; Jun. 1949–1956: Economic Construction: "Construction," "Local industry," "Reclamation for cultivation," "Agriculture," "Fisheries," "Irrigation," "Transportation," "Posts and telecommunications," "Commerce," "Culture, education, and health," "Investment in jointly-owned enterprises," "Other enterprises," "Other economic constructions," and "City public utilities." Administration: "Administration," "Judicature," "Prosecution," "Public security," "Political affairs," "Foreign affairs" and "Subsidy for democratic parties and people's groups." Culture, education, and health: "Culture," "Higher education," "Education," "Training of cadres," "Communication and broadcast," "Physical training," "Health," "Hospitality" and "Social relief and welfare." (3) The amount for Jan.–Aug. 1948 only included from Jan. 1 to Aug. 20. (4) The "Livelihood assistance for government employees" for Sep. 1948–Apr. 1949 was integrated into Administration. (5) There is no data for May 1949

Sources 1946–Apr. 1949: Wang (1995, pp. 153–156), and the breakdown of each item is based on the following materials: 1946: Q1-18-172, p. 172; 1947: Q1-18-247, Table 6, "Shanghaishi 36 niandu caizheng shiji zhichu (kemubie);" Jan.-Aug. 1948: Q432-2-196, p. 139; Q432-3-409, p. 7; Jun. 1949–1956: B104-1-273, p. 7

1953. On the other hand, it is more important to note that the expenditure on Local Jointly-owned Enterprises started increasing in 1953, and eventually exceeded the expenditure on city public utilities in 1956. Likewise one must consider the expenditure on Local Industry, which accounted for 26.7% of total Economic Construction Expenditure in 1951. Together, these observations serve to explain how in the early years of the PRC the Shanghai Municipal Government directly invested not only in public works, but also in local state-owned industrial enterprises and several types of jointly-owned enterprises.

It is important to note that these direct investments in local enterprises on the part of the public finances of Shanghai were conducted separately from the contemporaneous central investments in economic construction. To give but one example, no Shanghai-related project was present among the 156 national economic construction projects (of which 150 were actually implemented) that served as symbols of the First Five Year Plan (Dong and Wu 2004, pp. 413–416). In short, Shanghai was left out of the central investment plans that prioritized development in the interior, and as a result it invested in its local enterprises in its own right.

To advance this argument further, it is necessary to examine the profits and losses of the "Local Industry," "City Public Utilities," and "Local Jointly-owned Enterprises" items in the public finances of Shanghai, provided in Fig. 6.1. Each value in Fig. 6.1 was calculated by taking the enterprise profit of the item in question and subtracting the Economic Construction Expenditure that said item required. Analyzing the data given by Fig. 6.1 results in the following observations: "City Public Utilities" had almost balanced income and expenditure in 1955, although it had previously seen large deficits until 1954; "Local Industry" had steadily produced profits since 1953; "Local Jointly-owned Enterprises" became profitable in 1956; and the total profits and losses of local enterprises had been in the black since 1955. From these observations, it is clear that the public finances of Shanghai started to see substantial profits from 1955, through a cycle of (1) expending public finances on local enterprises, (2) producing added value in local enterprises, and (3) returning that added value to public finances in the form of Enterprise Revenue.

Moreover, this structure, having initially taken form by 1956, became more firmly established after the Great Leap Forward period (1958–1960). Figure 6.2 indicates the revenue and expenditure of Shanghai during 1952–1978, and shows that Enterprise Revenue increased by leaps and bounds, with the revenue exceeding by far the expenditure after 1959. This was the result of the large-scale decentralization of central enterprises to local governments, implemented in 1958 at the insistence of Mao (Caizhengbu zonghejihuasi 1982, p. 7). At first glance, it appears that there was a large amount of excess revenue over expenditures, but in fact the Central Remittance Expenditure was also correspondingly increased. In short, the central government siphoned off the profit from enterprises committed to Shanghai, while simultaneously holding down the city's revenue and expenditure index. This decentralization of central enterprises served to further expand the extent of the union between the Shanghai Municipal Government and local enterprises, and this configuration then remained the primary economic unit during the planned economy period, although it

Table 6.3 Breakdown of Economic Construction Expenditure of Shanghai, 1949–1956

Amount of expenditure (10 thousand new RMB Yuan)								
Year	Construction	Local industry	City public utilities	Local jointly-owned	Agriculture	Transportation	Others	Total
Jun.–Dec., 1949	1	9	131	-	-	-	18	160
1950	15	7	1,417	-	-	4	88	1,532
1951	118	1,268	3,113	-	5	125	127	4,756
1952	54	884	6,914	243	8	168	427	8,698
1953	238	200	6,301	63	43	32	343	7,218
1954	148	372	4,519	1,991	125	184	586	7,924
1955	74	166	2,584	638	241	48	372	4,124
1956	241	819	3,248	4,327	920	435	304	10,293
Percentage of total								
Jun.–Dec., 1949	0.6%	5.8%	82.3%	-	-	-	11.3%	100.0%
1950	1.0%	0.5%	92.5%	-	-	0.3%	5.7%	100.0%
1951	2.5%	26.7%	65.5%	-	0.1%	2.6%	2.7%	100.0%
1952	0.6%	10.2%	79.5%	2.8%	0.1%	1.9%	4.9%	100.0%
1953	3.3%	2.8%	87.3%	0.9%	0.6%	0.4%	4.7%	100.0%
1954	1.9%	4.7%	57.0%	25.1%	1.6%	2.3%	7.4%	100.0%
1955	1.8%	4.0%	62.7%	15.5%	5.9%	1.2%	9.0%	100.0%
1956	2.3%	8.0%	31.6%	42.0%	8.9%	4.2%	2.9%	100.0%

Notes (1) It is unknown what types of industry were included in "Local jointly-owned." (2) "Others" represents the combined total of "Fisheries," "Irrigation," "Posts and telecommunications," "Commerce," "Culture, education, and health," "Others," and "Other economic construction" in the original table. (3) "Agriculture" includes "Reclamation for cultivation" in the original table

Source B104-1-273, p. 7

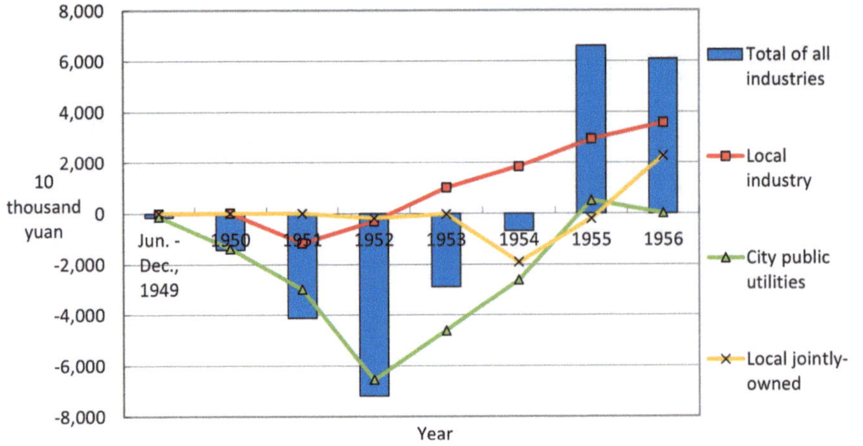

Fig. 6.1 Balances of local Enterprise Revenue and Economic Construction Expenditures in each category of Shanghai, 1949–1956. *Sources* Tables 6.1 and 6.3

was downsized temporarily due to the restoration of central enterprises as a backlash against the Great Leap Forward in the early 1960s.

Simultaneously, the investment from Shanghai's public finance to local enterprises also expanded. Figure 6.3 indicates the amount of central and local Construction Investment in Shanghai along with the ratio of local investment. Construction Investment here includes not only investment in enterprises but also several kinds of

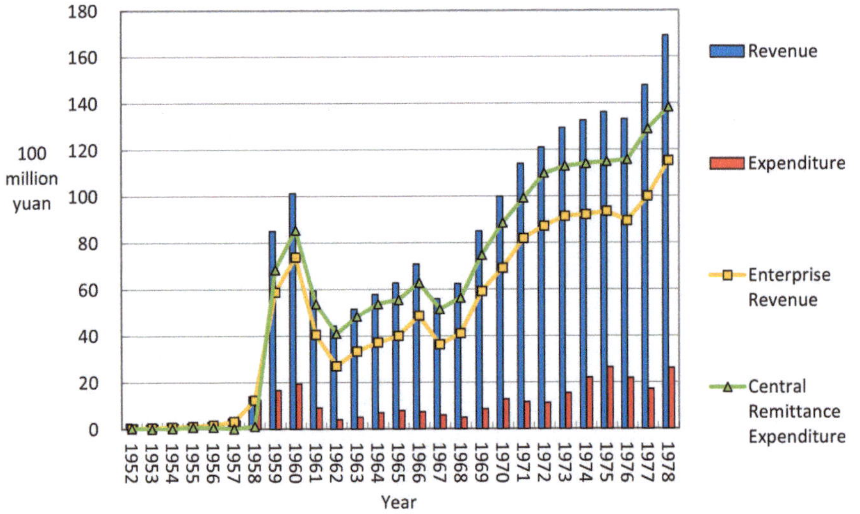

Fig. 6.2 Revenue, Expenditure, Enterprise Revenue and Central Remittance Expenditure of Shanghai, 1952–1978. *Notes* "Expenditure" in this figure does not include "Central Remittance Expenditure". *Source* Wang (1995), pp. 69–70, 102, 155–156

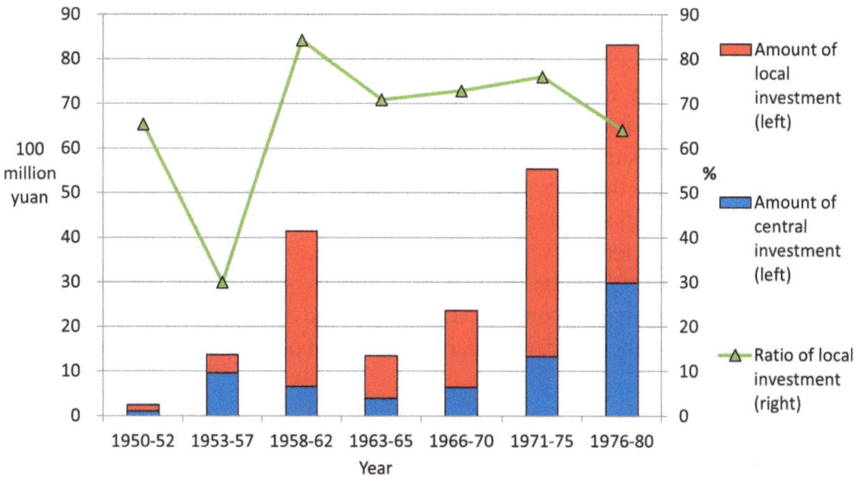

Fig. 6.3 Central and local construction investment in Shanghai, 1950–1980. *Notes* (1) According to the original table, the data is from Shanghaishi caizhengju, ed. *Shanghai caizheng tongji 1949–1987* (上海财政统计 1949–1987, Shanghai Fiscal Statistics), publisher unknown, p. 31. (2) "Local investment" includes "Local self-raising fund" in the original table. *Source* Wang (1995, pp. 168–169)

investment for fixed asset formation in Shanghai (e.g., bridges and parks). That being said, it also partly represents the scale of the amount of investment for enterprises, because the ratio of industrial investment to the total of Construction Investment was 30–50% in the first half of the 1950s and 50–70% from 1958 to the 1970s (Shanghaishi tongjiju 1992, p. 71).

Overall, the amount of local investment had increased during the planned economy period, particularly experiencing an enormous expansion in 1958–62 (which included but transcended the Great Leap Forward period), while central investment stagnated until at least 1975. As a result, the ratio of local investment remained high at 60–85%, except for a sharp decrease to 30% from 1953 to 1957 due to the expansion of central investment for the First Five Year Plan. To sum up, the Shanghai Municipal Government became the main entity of investment in Shanghai, especially after 1958, and alongside this the amount of investment itself also increased.

As shown above, the close relationship between public finance and local enterprise represented an enormous departure from previous practices, being essentially formed from whole cloth after 1949.[8] It is also crucial to keep in mind the significant background context to this change, namely that the profit from local enterprises

[8] On the other hand, the expansion of financial management duties of jointly-owned enterprises was an urgent problem for the Shanghai Municipal Government. One official document states: "We lack an independent attitude toward the financial management work of jointly-owned enterprises. Shanghai is the most concentrated city of private enterprises, and the socialist transformation of these was one of the main duties of our city. From this year the jointly-owned enterprises have largely increased, but we have never conducted an independent inquiry into their financial management work. If we only wait for direction from the central government, we cannot strengthen our

had become indispensable revenue, both for sustaining the public finances and for enabling the remittance to the central government in an environment of strict fiscal control from the center. It was therefore vital for the Shanghai Municipal Government to enable local enterprises to generate steady profits. To this end, the government was motivated to make positive investments in these enterprises and develop autonomous economic activities in the areas under its control.

This fiscal and taxation system—which was formally and theoretically centralized with strict control of local revenue and expenditure, but in practice left the actual processes of revenue collection to local governments—was one of the most significant factors governing the economic activities of the Shanghai Municipal Government, and served, furthermore, to sustain the finances of the state under the socialist economic system.[9]

References

English Language

Lardy, Nicholas R. 1978. *Economic Growth and Distribution in China.* Cambridge: Cambridge University Press

Chinese Language

Caizhengbu zonghejihuasi, ed. 1982. *Zhonghuarenmingongheguo caizheng shiliao diyiji: caizhengguanlitizhi, 1950–1980* (中华人民共和国财政史料 第1辑:财政管理体制1950–1980, Historical Materials of Public Finance of the People's Republic of China, Volume 1: Financial Management System 1950–1980). Beijing: Zhongguo caizhengjingji chubanshe

Dong, Zhikai and Wu Jiang. 2004. *Xin zhongguo gongye de dianjishi: 156 xiang jianshe yanjiu, 1950–2000* (新中国工业的奠基石:156项建设研究 (1950–2000), The Cornerstone of New China's Industry: A Study of 156 Projects, 1950–2000). Guangzhou: Guangdong jingji chubanshe

Gu, Zhun. 2002. *Guzhun zishu* (顾准自述, Gu Zhun's Autobiography). Beijing: Zhongguo qingnian chubanshe

Gui, Yong. 2006. *Siyou chanquan de shehui jichu: chengshi qiye chanquan de zhengzhi chonggou: 1949–1956* (私有产权的社会基础:城市企业产权的政治重构 (1949–1956), The Social Foundation of Private Property Rights: The Political Reconstruction of Urban Enterprise Property Rights (1949–1956). Shanghai: Lixin kuaiji chubanshe

Jin, Zhihuan. 2006. *Zhongguo fangzhijianshegongsi yanjiu* (中国纺织建设公司研究(1945–1950), Research on China Textile Construction Company, 1945–1950). Shanghai: Fudan University Press

---

ability to financially manage jointly-owned enterprises in sync with the advance of the socialist transformation" (B104-1-175).

[9] Tajima (1994, p. 6) characterized this fiscal and taxation system as "a centralized system based on decentralization."

Qian, Jianfu. 1946. Shiwunianlai shanghaishi caizheng ji qipipan (十五年来上海市财政及其批判, Fifteen Years of Shanghai Municipal Public Finance and the Criticism on it). *Caizheng pinglun* (财政评论, Financial Review), Vol. 15, No. 4

Shanghai shehuikexueyuan jingjisuo. 1980. *Shanghai zibenzhuyi gongshangye de shehuizhuyigaizao* (上海资本主义工商业的社会主义改造, The Socialist Transformation of Shanghai's Capitalist Industry and Commerce). Shanghai: Shanghai renmin chubanshe

Shanghaishi tongjiju, ed. 1992. *Xinshanghai gongyetongjiziliao: 1949–1990* (新上海工业统计资料 (1949–1990), New Shanghai Industrial Statistical Data: 1949–1990). Beijing: Zhongguo tongjichubanshe

Wang, Weiquan, ed. 1995. *Shanghai caizhengshuiwuzhi* (上海财政税务志, Shanghai Fiscal and Taxation Chronicle). Shanghai: Shanghai shehuikexueyuan chubanshe

Zhonggongshanghaishiwei tongzhanbu, Zhonggongshanghaishi dangshiyanjiushi, and Shanghaishidanganguan. 1993. *Zhongguo zibenzhuyigongshangye de shehuizhuyigaizao: Shanghai juan* (中国资本主义工商业的社会主义改造 (上海卷), The Socialist Transformation of China's Capitalist Industry and Commerce: Shanghai Volume), Volume I & II. Beijing: Zhonggong dangshi chubanshe

Zhonggong zhongyang wenxianyanjiushi, ed. 1992. *Jianguoyilai zhongyaowenxianxuanbian: di 1 ce* (建国以来重要文献选编 (第1册), Selection of Important Documents Since the Founding of the People's Republic of China: Volume 1). Beijing: Zhongyang wenxian chubanshe

Japanese Language

Kajima, Jun. 2007. "Seikenkoutai to shanghaishi zaiseikōzō no hendō: 1945–1956" (政権交代と上海市財政構造の変動 (1945–1956), The Chinese Communist Revolution and Changes in the Fiscal Structure of Shanghai Municipality: 1945–1956). *Ajia keizai* (アジア経済, Asian Economy) 48(7): 2–32. https://doi.org/10.24765/ajiakeizai.48.7_2

Mōri, Kazuko. 1990. 1970 nendai madeno chūō to chihō: Shanghaishi no kēsu (1970年代末までの中央と地方——上海市のケース, The Relationship between Central and Local Government until the Late 1970s: The Case of Shanghai). In *Mōtakutō jidai no chūgoku: Gendai chūgokuron 1* (毛沢東時代の中国<現代中国論1>, China in the Mao Zedong Era), ed. Mōri Kazuko, 87–112. Tokyo: Japan Institute of International Affairs

Tajima, Toshio. 1994. Chūgoku no kokuyūkigyōkaikaku to seihukan zaiseikankei (中国の国有企業改革と政府間財政関係, Reform of State-owned Enterprises and Inter-governmental Fiscal Relations in China). *Chūgoku kenkyū geppō* (中国研究月報, Monthly Journal of Chinese Affairs) 48(4): 2–31

Unpublished Primary Sources

B104, Shanghaishi caizhengju dangan (上海市财政局档案, Shanghai Municipal Bureau of Finance Archives)

B104-1-116, "Jiantao baogao" (检讨报告, Review Report), from Shanghai Municipal People's Government Finance Bureau to East China Finance Department, report, issued on June 2, 1952, Shi cai mi zi (市财秘字) No. 177, Attachment for "Wei baogaogongzuojiantao qingshenheyou" (为报告工作检讨请审核由, Request for examining the review report)

B104-1-175, "1954 nian gongzuo zongjie" (1954年工作总结, Summary of Work in 1954), date of creation unknown

B104-1-273, Shanghaishi caizhengju (上海市财政局), ed. "Shanghaishi 1949 nian 1956 niandu caizhengshouzhi tongjibiao ji jibenjianshezhichu tongjibiao: baokuo difangzichou bufen" (上海市1949年-1956年度财政收支统计表及基本建设支出统计表 (包括地方自筹部分), Shanghai 1949–1956 Financial Revenue and Expenditure Statistics and Basic Construction Expenditure Statistics: including local self-raised part), October 1957

Q1, Shanghaishi zhengfu dangan (上海市政府档案, Shanghai Municipal Government Archives)

Q1–18–172, "35 niandu tongji zongbaogao digao" (35年度统计总报告底稿, 1935 Annual Statistical Report Draft), date of creation unknown

Q1–18–247, Shanghaishi caizhengju tongjishi (上海市财政局统计室), ed. "Shanghaishi difangcaizheng tongji zongbaogao 36 niandu" (上海市地方财政统计总报告 36年度, Shanghai Municipal Local Finance Statistical Annual Report of 1936), date of creation unknown

Q432 Shanghaishi caizhengju dangan (上海市财政局档案, Shanghai Municipal Bureau of Finance Archives)

Q432-2-196, "Shanghaishi caizhengju guanyu canyihui dui tisong shizhenggongzuobaogao jueyian benju jiang zunbanqingxingbaohe" (上海市财政局关于参议会对提送施政工作报告决议案本局将遵办情形报核, Shanghai Municipal Bureau of Finance's Report on the Implementation of the Shanghai Municipal Representative Council's Resolution on the Administrative Work Report), date of creation unknown

Q432-3-409, "Shanghaishi caizhengju chengsong canhui caizhengbufen shizhengbaogao de chengwen ji dahui youguan caizhengbufen jueyian zhixing qingxingbiao deng" (上海市财政局呈送参会财政部分施政报告的呈文及大会有关财政部分决议案、执行情形表等, Shanghai Municipal Bureau of Finance's Submission of the Financial Part of the Administrative Report and the Shanghai Municipal Representative Council's Resolutions on the Financial Part, Implementation Status Table, etc.), date of creation unknown

Chapter 7
Interregional Comparison of Provincial-Level Local Public Finances

Abstract This chapter provides a regional comparison by utilizing the author's database of provincial-level local public finance during the planned economy period in order to clarify Shanghai's position within China as a whole. The database created by the author is a reconstruction of provincial, municipal, and autonomous region-level fiscal data recorded in local gazettes from 1949 to 1978, and presents comprehensive statistics on the fiscal revenue and expenditure of each area, as well as Central Subsidy Revenue, Central Remittance Expenditure, and the total revenue and total expenditure incorporating these intergovernmental transfers between the central government and local governments. The analysis focuses on the relative size of each local finance unit and the contribution of each local government to central public finance, as well as the relationship between each local fiscal structure and the regional economy (especially local enterprises), which reveals in what ways Shanghai's local fiscal model, discussed in Chapters 5 and 6, possessed distinct characteristics, and conversely in what ways it reflected general tendencies.

Keywords Provincial-level local public finances · Central Subsidy Revenue · Central Remittance Expenditure · Intergovernmental transfers between central and local governments · Local enterprises · Enterprise Revenue

As was set out in Chapters 5 and 6, the structure of local public finance in Shanghai underwent a series of major changes in the context of the institutional reforms of the 1950s. To put it simply, on the revenue side, Shanghai experienced a shift from being centered on tax revenue during the postwar Republican period to being focused instead on Local Enterprise Revenue; meanwhile, on the expenditure side, it saw a shift from being centered primarily on administrative expenses, including government employee living allowances, to instead being orientated around the Economic Construction Expenditure (excluding Central Remittance Expenditure). This chapter will now put these developments in broader context by examining how the structure of local public finance that formed in Shanghai in the 1950s compared to the situation in other regions in China.

J. Kajima, *Shanghai under the Socialist System*, Studies in Economic History,
https://doi.org/10.1007/978-981-95-3225-4_7

7.1 Perspectives and Methodology of the Interregional Comparison

It is pertinent to begin by reviewing the previous studies on the central-local fiscal relations and local fiscal structure during the planned economic period. Although many studies have already contributed to the growth of knowledge in this field, there are competing viewpoints based on varying perspectives.[1] Regarding the central-local fiscal relations during the planned economy period, it is known that there were cycles of centralization and decentralization. Relatively centralized policies were implemented from the early years of the 1950s until 1957 and in the early 1960s, whereas significant decentralization policies were adopted in 1958–60 during the Great Leap Forward and in the early 1970s (Caizhengbu zonghejihuasi 1982; Ishihara 1990). Lardy (1978) focused on the decentralization policy during the Great Leap Forward period, and argued that despite the central government's decentralization policy, there was no significant difference in the economic performance of each province, city, and autonomous region, suggesting that the central government's role of redistribution through finance was still intact, and that, moreover, the centralized elements essentially remained. On this point, Jin et al. (2005), quantitatively analyzing the relationship between local fiscal decentralization and regional economic development in China mainly in the 1980–1990s, pointed out that this redistribution function of the central government was relatively strong in the 1970s. Mori (1990) too, analyzing local public finance through focusing on Shanghai's case, emphasized the centralization aspect, noting that during the planned economy period there existed consistent control by the central government over Shanghai (mainly in the form of restrictions on fiscal autonomy and large remittances from Shanghai to the center).

On the other hand, Tajima (1994; 2000) highlighted China's historical fiscal structure of "central governments being dependent on local governments," by pointing to the high ratio of local revenue to the total (that is, central plus local) fiscal revenue during the planned economy period, and argued that fiscal management at the time was actually multi-layered (what he termed "graded management") and locally decentralized under a broader centralized institutional framework. Similarly, Chō (2001), starting from the view that the proportion of central-local government in total revenue represented the degree of centralization-decentralization, and that, moreover, the proportion of central-local government in the total expenditure served as marking the degree of concentration-deconcentration, identified the period of

[1] In mainland China, comprehensive reviews of the financial system during the planned economy period have been conducted by Caizhengbu zonghejihuasi (1982), Dangdai zhongguo congshu bianjibu (1988), Zuo and Song (1988), upon which groundwork subsequent studies such as those of Song (1997) and Zhao (2002) then built. In terms of scholarship outside of China, Donnithorne (1967), Miyashita (1967), Fujimoto (1971), Lardy (1978), Hsiao (1987), Ishihara (1990), Mori (1990), Nambu (1991), Tajima (1994; 2000, and a series of studies), and Chō (2001) are among the significant works that discuss the public finances of the planned economy period.

1952–56 as the prototype of the centralization-concentration model, and that of 1957–84 as the prototype of the decentralization-concentration model.

These discussions of China's central-local fiscal relations are valuable assets in building a foundation for understanding the fiscal system during the planned economy period. However, at the same time they share several common problems, the most important of which can be summarized as (1) the lack of a perspective that captures the regional diversity of local fiscal structures, and (2) the lack of accurate information that clarifies the actual situation of intergovernmental fiscal transfers.

Regarding the first of these two points, there are limits to what can be achieved in terms of assessing the centralized-decentralized nature of the entire fiscal system by focusing on individual cases as shown in the case of Mori (1990). On the other hand, it is also difficult to capture the diversity of local finances by analyzing national fiscal systems and utilizing national statistics that aggregate local fiscal statistics. In reality, the relationship between central and local finance varied greatly depending on the region and period, and the problem is that there is a distinct lack of methods available to accurately grasp such regional differences and time-series changes in an overview. In this sense, the method employed by Lardy (1978), which compared the changes in the fiscal structure of each province, city, and autonomous region before and after the decentralization policy of 1958, is instructive. However, due to the limited target period, said study has the drawback of not being able to capture the diachronic changes from 1949 to 1978.

As for the second of the two points, conventional research has with few exceptions discussed intergovernmental fiscal transfers based on aggregated national fiscal statistics, predicated on a dichotomy of central and local, while the actual amounts of vertical fiscal transfers between the central government and each local government were not indicated, which is to say, how much each region made to the center in terms of remittances and how much it received in terms of subsidies has been left unexplored. As will be mentioned later, this is also a problem that relates to the availability of statistical materials. In this sense, it is notable that Mori (1990) and Ishihara (1990) both mentioned the scale of central remittances to local finances using Shanghai and Tianjin as examples, but that their data was fragmentary. To fully understand China's central-local public finances during the planned economy period, it is essential to accurately grasp the amounts of fiscal transfer between the central government and each local government, which can then serve in turn as the basis for discussions on the central-local fiscal relationship.

Taking these problems into account, this chapter will conduct a comparative analysis of regional fiscal structures based on the "Chinese Provincial, Municipal, and Autonomous Region Local Fiscal Statistics Database, 1949–1978" compiled by the author and published as Kajima (2012).[2] This database is a reconstruction of provincial, municipal, and autonomous region-level fiscal data recorded in the local gazettes of each province, municipal city, and autonomous region (excluding Taiwan, which was never effectively controlled) from 1949 to 1978, such gazettes including for example Wang (1995) *Shanghai caizhengshuiwuzhi* (上海财政税务志, Shanghai Fiscal and Taxation Chronicle).

The major features of this database are: (1) it adopts a more detailed classification of local fiscal revenue and expenditure than existing fiscal statistical materials covering the planned economy period, and (2) it systematically records the Central Subsidy Revenue and Central Remittance Expenditure of each province, city, and autonomous region. Although some existing fiscal statistical resources, for example the Guojia tongjiju zonghesi (1990) *Quanguo gesheng, zizhiqu, zhixiashi lishitongji ziliaohuibian* (全国各省、自治区、直辖市历史统计资料汇编, Compilation of Historical Statistical Data for All Provinces, Autonomous Regions, and Municipalities Directly Under the Central Government) and Guojia tongjiju guominjingjizonghetongjisi (1999) *Xinzhongguo wushinian tongjiziliao huibian* (新中国五十年统计资料汇编, Compilation of Statistical Data for Fifty Years of New China),[3] record the diachronic fiscal statistics of each province, city, and autonomous region during the planned economy period, they include only limited items of fiscal

[2] This work is available for download on the website of the Sinology Initiative, Institute of Social Science, University of Tokyo: https://sinology-initiative.com/research-resources/481/. Furthermore, the data on Tianjin City in Kajima (2012), specifically the "Central Remittance Expenditure" of Tianjin City (p. 22), drew on new data that had been made available and was closer to the actual situation due to subsequent surveys. As a result, the "Total Expenditure," "Central Assistance/Remittance Balance," "Total Balance of Payments" and related charts and tables on the same page have also been revised, but here only the revised figures of each year for "Central Remittance Expenditure" are as follows (unit: 100 million yuan): 1950: 0.62, 1951: 2.52, 1952: 2.85, 1953: 4.88, 1954: 4.49, 1955: 4.74, 1956: 5.82, 1957: 6.17, 1958: 11.13, 1959: 15.25, 1960: 16.38, 1961: 9.21, 1962: 7.14, 1963: 7.15, 1964: 9.89, 1965: 9.75, 1966: 12.18, 1967: 10.91, 1968: 10.51, 1969: 16.48, 1970: 21.02, 1971–75: unknown, 1976: 21.01, 1977: 19.42, 1978: 23.24. See Cui (2000, pp. 46–47, 49, 52, 57). With these revised figures, the "anomaly" (a trend significantly different from that of the other regions) of the figures for Tianjin City identified in Kajima (2012, p. 9), has been resolved, and it now shows almost the same trend as the other regions. The analysis in the current chapter is based on these revised figures.

[3] Guojia tongjiju zonghesi (1990) published local fiscal revenue and expenditure statistics for each province, city, and autonomous region from 1949 to 1989. Its breakdown of fiscal revenue included "Enterprise Revenue" (企业收入) and "Various Tax Revenues" (各项税收), while expenditures were divided into "Capital Construction Allocations" (基本建设拨款), "Support for Rural Production Expenditures" (支援农村生产支出), "Cultural, Educational, Scientific, and Health Business Expenses" (文教、科学、卫生事业费), and "Administrative Expenses" (行政管理费). This work is one of the main materials available for studying the planned economy period, since it also records historical statistics in various fields such as population and the price indices of each province, city, and autonomous region in addition to fiscal statistics. Guojia tongjiju guominjingjizonghetongjisi (1999) is also a statistical material collection that describes the fiscal revenue and expenditure of each province, city, and autonomous region from 1949 to 1978 in a similar manner. The breakdown of revenue it employs includes "Enterprise Revenue" (企业收入) and "Tax Revenue" (税收), while its breakdown of expenditures includes "Capital Construction Allocations" (基本建设拨款), "Enterprise Potential Transformation" (企业挖潜改造), "Support for Agricultural Production and Business" (支援农业生产和事业), "Cultural, Educational, Scientific, and Health Business" (文

revenue and expenditure and do not comprehensively cover the structure of local fiscal revenue and expenditure. Moreover, a more serious shortcoming is that they do not explicitly record either the Central Subsidy Revenue, which was a subsidy from the central government to local governments, or the Central Remittance Expenditure, which was a remittance from local governments to the central government, making it impossible with such resources alone to diachronically analyze the fiscal transfer relationship between the central government and each province, city, and autonomous region government.[4]

教科学卫生事业), and "Administrative Management" (行政管理), adopting a framework almost identical to that of Guojia tongjiju zonghesi (1990).

On the other hand, the successors to these works, Guojia tongjiju guominjingjizonghetongjisi (2005) and Guojia tongjiju guominjingjizonghetongjisi (2010), record the "Local Fiscal General Budget Revenue and Expenditure" (地方财政一般予算收支额) of each province, city, and autonomous region from 1949 to 1978. However, the breakdown of revenue and expenditure has been modified according to the standards of the Reform period, which are simply not suitable for understanding the local fiscal revenue and expenditure situation during the planned economy period. For example, the breakdown of revenue is classified into "Value-Added Tax" (增值税), "Business Tax" (营业税), and "Enterprise Income Tax" (企业所得税), and for the 1949–1978 period, almost all of the columns are thus correspondingly blank for each province, city, and autonomous region. As for expenditures, they are classified into "Agricultural Expenditures" (农业支出), "Cultural, Educational, Scientific, and Health Business Expenses" (文教科卫事业费), "Administrative Expenses" (行政管理费), and "Social Security Subsidy Expenditures" (社会保障补助支出), and there is another problem here in that important expenditure items during the planned economy period, such as "Economic Construction Expenses" (经济建设费), are simply missing. Instead, in this book, the data for what was originally Economic Construction Expenses is instead incorporated into the statistical table for "Total Social Fixed Asset Investment" (全社会固定资产投资), separated from local fiscal statistics. Furthermore, the most basic statistical yearbook on China's public finances, Zhongguo caizhengnianjian bianjiweiyuanhui (various years), covers detailed financial statistics for the relevant fiscal year while only showing national-level aggregated figures for chronological statistics since 1949. If a yearbook on finance such as this had been published every year since 1949, it would be possible to create chronological historical statistics for each province, city, and autonomous region by gathering and linking the data for each year, but the yearbook was first published in 1992 and so this is just not possible.

Subsequently, more detailed statistical materials such as Caizhengbu guokusi yusuansi (1990–2009) *Difang caizheng tongjiziliao* (地方财政统计资料, Statistics of Local Public Finance) and Caizhengbu guokusi yusuansi (1993–2009) *Quanguo dishixian caizheng tongjiziliao* (全国地市县财政统计资料, Statistics of Local Public Finance of Prefectural-level Cities and Counties), which cover statistics at the provincial, city, and autonomous region level for each year, and even provide data for the prefecture-level cities and counties, were published. However, these also mainly feature statistics for the relevant fiscal year, and do not include chronological statistics. In addition, many of the financial statistical materials edited during the Reform period only include historical statistics for the most recent few years. For example, Lou (2000) *Xinzhongguo wushinian caizhengtongji* (新中国50年财政统计, Statistics of Public Finance of the New China for 50 years) only includes the fiscal revenue and expenditure statistics for each province, city, and autonomous region for the years 1994–1998.

[4] The collections of local financial statistics record mentioned above generally only include fiscal revenue and expenditure, or alternatively include the Central Subsidy Revenue and the Central Remittance Expenditure in their revenue and expenditure amounts without explicitly explaining how or why. For example, the local financial statistics of the Guojia tongjiju zonghesi (1990) generally include "Central Subsidy Revenue" in revenue but do not include "Central Remittance

To address these issues with existing local fiscal statistics, the author's database relies on local gazetteers' fiscal records to present comprehensive statistics on the fiscal revenue and expenditure of each of these areas, as well as Central Subsidy Revenue, Central Remittance Expenditure, and the total revenue and total expenditure incorporating these intergovernmental transfers between the central government and local governments.[5] Local gazetteers' records provide more detailed revenue and expenditure items than do existing fiscal statistics, and fortunately, diachronic data on Central Subsidy Revenue and Central Remittance Expenditure are available for most provinces, cities, and autonomous regions. This allows for the analysis of the fiscal transfer relationship between the central government and each of these areas, as well as the actual revenue and expenditure structure of local governments, including the aforementioned revenue and expenditure specifics that were unclear in existing fiscal statistics.

This chapter focuses on four points as a basis for comparing local finances: (1) the local fiscal revenue, expenditure, and fiscal balance of each province, city, and autonomous region; (2) the total balance of revenue and expenditure, including Central Subsidy Revenue and Central Remittance Expenditure; (3) the proportion of Enterprise Revenue in local fiscal revenue; and finally (4) the proportion of Economic Construction Expenditure in local fiscal expenditure. The first two points speak to the relative size of each local finance unit and the contribution of each local government to central public finance, while the latter two points indicate the relationship between each local fiscal structure and the regional economy (especially local enterprises). The purpose for this interregional comparison is to reveal in what ways Shanghai's local fiscal model, discussed in Chapters 5 and 6, possessed distinct characteristics, and conversely in what ways it reflected general tendencies.

Expenditure" in expenditure, a situation revealed after one compares the data to the statistics from local gazetteers mentioned later.

[5] The "total revenue and total expenditure" mentioned here is a concept newly set for the analysis in this chapter, and it should be noted that despite sharing the same name it differs in meaning from the previous "total revenue and total expenditure" term that was used in practice at the time of the planned economy period. The term as defined at that time included Budget Revenue and Expenditure (预算收入、支出, a concept close to Fiscal Revenue and Expenditure in this chapter), Central Subsidy Revenue, Central Remittance Expenditure, and Carry-over Funds from the previous fiscal year. For example, Guizhousheng caizhengting zonghejihuachu (1986, pp. 7–8), summarizes the concepts of total income and total expenditure as follows:

Total revenue = Current fiscal year Budget Revenue + Central Subsidy Revenue + Other special funds + Other procured funds (调入其他资金) + Carry-over funds from the previous fiscal year (上年结余)

Total expenditure = Current fiscal year Budget Expenditure + Central Remittance Expenditure + Other special expenditures + Carryover funds for this fiscal year (年终滚存结余)

This database, apart from the definition above, regards the figures of Fiscal Revenue and Expenditure plus Central Subsidy Revenue and Central Remittance Expenditure shown in the local gazetteers of each province, city, and autonomous region, as constituting "total revenue and total expenditure" since data for items other than Central Subsidy Revenue and Central Remittance Expenditure on the right side of the above formula are not explicitly available.

7.2 Comparative Analysis of Local Public Finances in Provinces, Municipalities, and Autonomous Regions

7.2.1 Local Public Finances of Provinces, Municipalities, and Autonomous Regions

First, to understand the fiscal scale of each province, city, and autonomous region, it is necessary to start with looking at the trends in their fiscal revenue, expenditure, and balance. The following regional comparisons take five to six units as samples: namely Shanghai and Liaoning Province, which had prominent positions, and the top (1st), middle (6th, 16th), and bottom (26th) units in terms of the average annual value of the relevant item (total of the relevant item for each province, city, and autonomous region from 1949 to 1978 divided by the number of years for which data exists for the relevant item for each of the aforementioned areas) among the remaining 29 provinces, cities, and autonomous regions. For Central Subsidy Revenue and Central Remittance Expenditure, if there were provinces, cities, or autonomous regions for which data did not exist, the sample rankings for the top, middle, and bottom groups were adjusted to exclude these regions.

Looking at Fig. 7.1, which compares the fiscal revenues of each province, city, and autonomous region, the first thing that stands out is the exceptional revenue size of Shanghai since 1959. This is followed by Liaoning in second place, and Heilongjiang in sixth place. The rapid expansion of fiscal revenue in Shanghai in 1959–60 was the result of the transfer of large-scale centrally-owned enterprises within Shanghai to the Shanghai Municipal Government in 1958, as discussed in the previous chapter. Similar expansions of fiscal revenue can be seen in Liaoning and Heilongjiang, albeit on a different scale. Furthermore, the trend of sustained expansion since the late 1960s is essentially the same in Shanghai, Liaoning, and Heilongjiang, which had relatively large fiscal revenues. On the other hand, there was a significant difference in scale apparent when comparing Shaanxi, ranked 16th, and Xinjiang, ranked 26th, to the larger-sized provinces, cities, and autonomous regions mentioned above, although similar tendencies of expansion can still be observed to a lesser extent. As a result, it is clear that there existed significant diversity, and particularly a significant disparity between the top and middle-lower ranks in terms of fiscal revenue.

By contrast, the fiscal expenditures of provinces, cities, and autonomous regions shown in Fig. 7.2 are significantly different when it comes to the status of fiscal revenue. It is notable that the top and bottom ranks of fiscal expenditure were much closer in amount, and that the range was smaller than the fiscal revenue, while there were some standout provinces and cities in terms of fiscal revenue, such as Shanghai and Liaoning. In particular, Shanghai, which had overwhelmed other regions in terms of fiscal revenue, ranked 9th in fiscal expenditure. Moreover, the gap between Sichuan in 1st place and Guizhou in 26th in terms of fiscal expenditure was not particularly large compared to fiscal revenue.

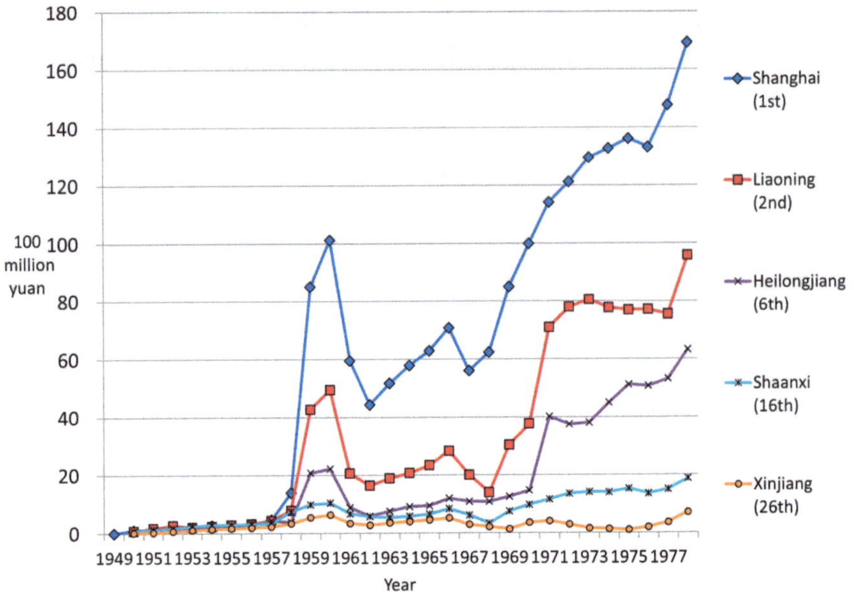

Fig. 7.1 Fiscal revenue of provincial-level local governments, 1949–1978. *Source* Kajima (2012)

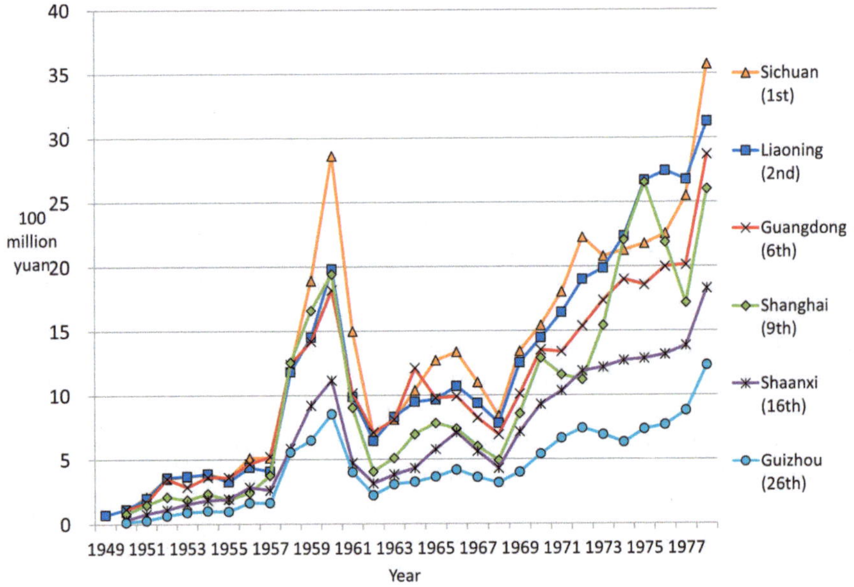

Fig. 7.2 Fiscal expenditure of provincial-level local governments, 1949–1978. *Source* Kajima (2012)

As for chronological changes in fiscal expenditure, the trend was similar to that of fiscal revenue in terms of undergoing a rapid increase in 1959–60 and then sustained expansion since the late 1960s. However, especially when comparing the maximum figure on the vertical axis of Fig. 7.2 (4 billion yuan) with that of Fig. 7.1 (18 billion yuan), it is clear that the scale of changes in the top ranks was smaller for fiscal expenditure than it was for fiscal revenue. Moreover, when calculating the difference between the highest and lowest annual averages of fiscal revenue and expenditure, the difference came out to 6.514 billion yuan for fiscal revenue, compared to just 1.261 billion yuan for fiscal expenditure.[6] From these observations, it is clear that the scale of fiscal expenditure in each province, city, and autonomous region was smaller in terms of regional differences compared to fiscal revenue.

The overall trend of local fiscal revenue and expenditure, which was characterized by the presence of prominent regions in fiscal revenue and the similarity among regions in fiscal expenditure, meant a substantial surplus in some regions from the perspective of local fiscal balance. Figure 7.3, which shows the fiscal balance (fiscal revenue minus fiscal expenditure) of each province, city, and autonomous region, has Shanghai ranking first, Liaoning second, and Beijing sixth, all with major fiscal surpluses recorded particularly since 1959. On the other hand, Gansu province, ranked 16th, and the Xizang (Tibet) Autonomous Region, ranked 26th, experienced periods of fiscal deficit, fluctuating around $\pm$ 0. Thus, as far as the local fiscal balance was concerned, there was a significant gap between the top and bottom structures of local finance.

7.2.2 *Fiscal Transfers Between Central and Local Government*

However, the image of regional disparities that emerges from examining the local fiscal balances does not necessarily reflect the reality. When considering the fiscal transfer relationship between the central and local governments, a somewhat different picture emerges. The situation can be better understood by examining the trends in Central Subsidy Revenue and Central Remittance Expenditure, which indicate the fiscal transfer between the central and local provincial-level governments, as well as by considering the total balance of revenue and expenditure of local public finance that emerges when they are combined with the fiscal balance.

Figure 7.4 shows the trend of Central Subsidy Revenue for each province, city, and autonomous region. Unfortunately, data could not be obtained for 12 provinces and cities, including Shanghai (as well as Beijing, Hebei, Shanxi, Anhui, Shandong, Hunan, Guangdong, Chongqing, Sichuan, Yunnan, and Shaanxi), and the average annual amount of the sample was adjusted to rank the 1st, 4th, 10th, and 16th places among the 19 provincial-level local governments. Notably, in all likelihood Shanghai had not received any central subsidies during the planned economy period since

[6] Calculated from the data for each province, city, and autonomous region in Kajima (2012).

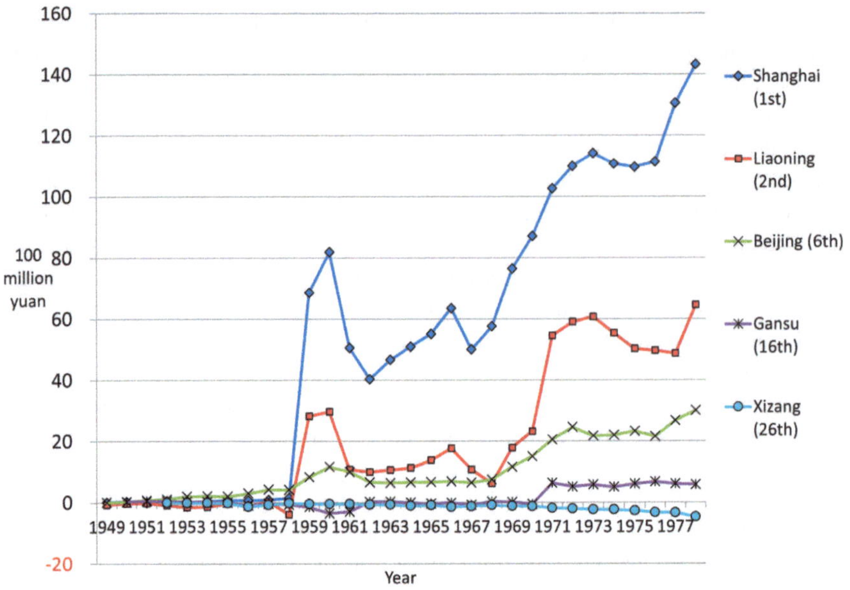

Fig. 7.3 Balance of revenue and expenditure of provincial-level local governments, 1949–1978. *Source* Kajima (2012)

the local gazetteers of Shanghai, Wang (1995) and Shanghai caizhengshuiwuzhi bianzuanweiyuanhui (1999), make no mention of Central Subsidy Revenue. As for other provinces and cities which lack Central Subsidy Revenue data, it is unclear whether this data was simply never made public or whether in fact there was no central subsidy to record.

Looking at Fig. 7.4, the sharp rise in Liaoning in 1958 and in Inner Mongolia and Xinjiang from the early 1970s is particularly striking. However, excluding these cases, there is little difference between the middle (Fujian in 9th place) and the bottom (Ningxia in 10th place), and all provinces, cities, and autonomous regions consistently remained at a level of around 400 million yuan or less. This indicates that the scale of subsidies from the central government enjoyed by each region amounted to about several hundred million yuan, except for specific periods and regions. This scale of subsidies from the central government likely played a significant role in effectively balancing the finances of middle- and lower-ranked provinces and autonomous regions that experienced a fiscal deficit (generally less than 500 million yuan) as shown in Fig. 7.3.

On the other hand, as shown in Fig. 7.5, there were significant differences in the Central Remittance Expenditure of each province, city, and autonomous region. Regarding the Central Remittance Expenditure, data could not be obtained for 7 provinces, cities, and autonomous regions (Anhui, Chongqing, Yunnan, Qinghai, Guangxi, Xizang, and Xinjiang), and for reasons of practicality this study focused

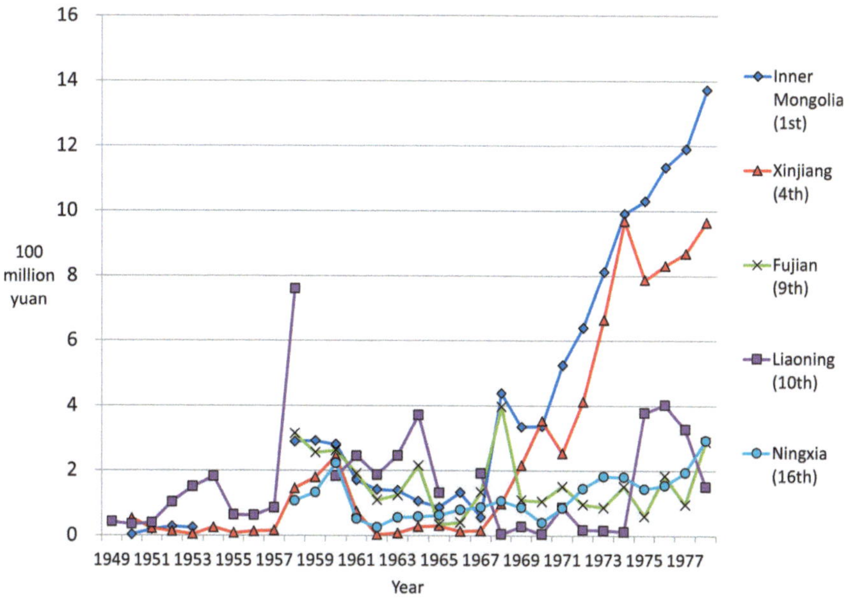

Fig. 7.4 Central Subsidy Revenue of provincial-level local governments, 1949–1978. *Source* Kajima (2012)

on Shanghai City (1st place), Liaoning Province (2nd place), and the 5th, 12th, and 20th places out of 23 provinces, cities, and autonomous regions.

In the case of Shanghai, which ranked first, the municipality had been increasing its Central Remittance Expenditure along with the increase in fiscal revenue since 1959 (as covered in the previous chapter), and Liaoning in 2nd and Heilongjiang in 5th place showed almost identical trends. This reveals that multiple provinces and cities that ranked high in fiscal revenue were making transfers to the central government according to their fiscal revenue scale, and, moreover, that the structure that developed in Shanghai in the 1950s was essentially one shared by other regions high in fiscal revenue. On the other hand, the Central Remittance Expenditure amounts of Hubei, in 12th place, and Shaanxi, at the bottom (ranking 20th) were only a few hundred million yuan (Shaanxi, in fact, recorded a slight minus in 1959, 1968, and 1978). These figures thus confirm that the amounts of Central Remittance Expenditure of the top provinces and cities were outstanding, just like their fiscal revenues and fiscal balances.

What should be noted here is the balance of total revenue and total expenditure in Fig. 7.6, which indicates the figures calculated as follows:

Balance of total revenue and total expenditure =

(Fiscal revenue + Central Subsidy Revenue)-(Fiscal expenditure + Central Remittance Expenditure)

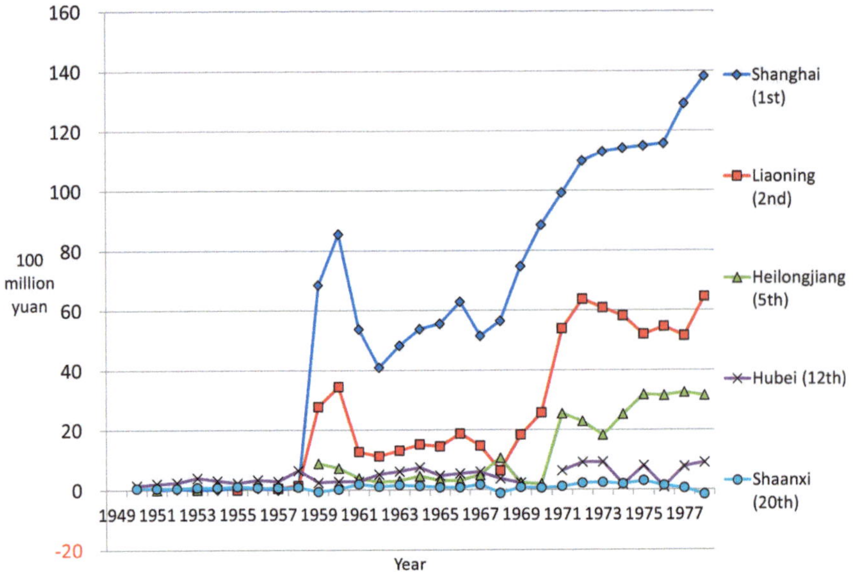

Fig. 7.5 Central Remittance Expenditure of provincial-level local governments, 1949–1978. *Source* Kajima (2012)

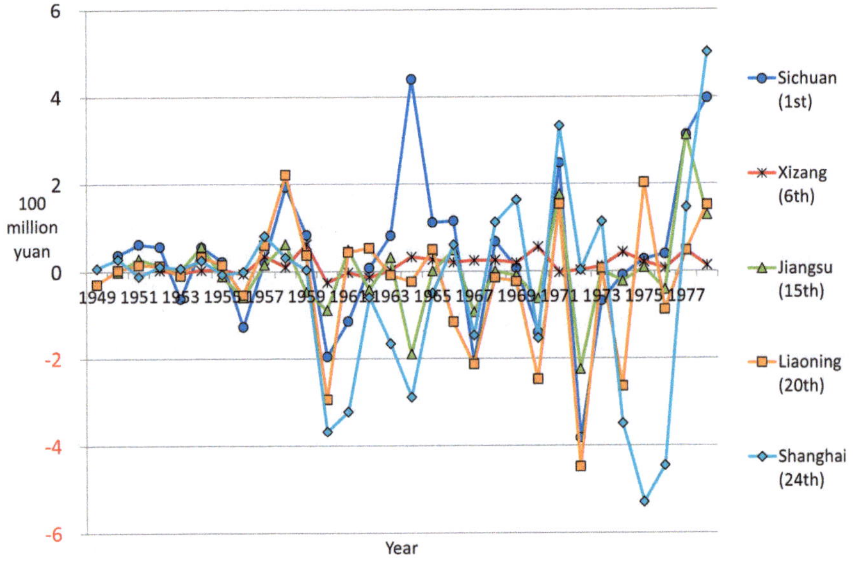

Fig. 7.6 Balance of total revenue and total expenditure of provincial-level local governments, 1949–1978. *Source* Kajima (2012)

Here, what is covered is part of the 28 provinces, cities, and autonomous regions, excluding Anhui, Chongqing, and Yunnan, where neither data on Central Subsidy Revenue nor Central Remittance Expenditure could be obtained. According to Fig. 7.6, unlike the fiscal balance shown in Fig. 7.3, the total balance of each year for all provinces, cities, and autonomous regions—including Sichuan, which ranked first, as well as Shanghai and Liaoning—was within ± 529 million yuan.[7] This means that the original disparities in the fiscal revenue and expenditure balance structure of each province, city, and autonomous region were adjusted to be at an almost constant level by fiscal transfers such as Central Subsidy Revenue and Central Remittance Expenditure.

However, as the fiscal balance before fiscal transfer with the central government in Fig. 7.3 shows, the fiscal surplus (excess revenue) of the top provinces and cities was extremely large, with an annual average of 5.55 billion yuan in Shanghai at the top spot and 1.043 billion yuan in Beijing in 6th place, while the deficit (excess expenditure) of the provinces and autonomous regions was relatively small, with an annual average of 137 million yuan in Xizang in 26th place, and even 312 million yuan in Inner Mongolia, the lowest among the 29 local provincial-level governments. From these figures, it is clear how the main thrust of fiscal transfer was the redirection of funds from the surplus provinces, cities, and autonomous regions to the central finances, while conversely the subsidies from the center to the deficit provinces, cities, and autonomous regions were relatively small.

Furthermore, turning to consider Fig. 7.7, which compares the annual average amount of net central remittances (Central Remittance Expenditures minus Central Subsidy Revenue) for each province, city, and autonomous region from 1949 to 1978 (excluding Anhui, Chongqing, and Yunnan, the same as in Fig. 7.6), reveals an important fact. Most provinces, cities, and autonomous regions, regardless of the particular amount, made net remittances to the central government (i.e., Central Remittance Expenditures minus Central Subsidy Revenue > 0), whereas only a few provinces (namely Fujian, Jiangxi, Qinghai, Guizhou) and autonomous regions had negative net central remittances. In other words, while industrial regions such as Shanghai and Liaoning made large central remittances, many other regions, excluding some provinces and autonomous regions, also accumulated central remittances according to their fiscal scale.

Examining the national-level public finance statistics helps to clarify the structure of fiscal transfers between the central and local provincial-level governments. Figure 7.8 and Fig. 7.9 show the amounts of central and local (aggregated) fiscal revenue and expenditure from 1953 to 1978, and the ratio of central revenue/expenditure to the total. Comparing these two figures, one can see how the central government's finances had been in a state of expenditure exceeding revenue since the late 1950s, while the national total (central plus local) public finance was almost balanced through the planned economy period. Notably, despite the ratio of central

[7] Even if the target regions were expanded to cover 29 provinces, cities, and autonomous regions, the figures for each year would still be within ± 1 billion yuan. Refer to Kajima (2012) data for each province, city, and autonomous region.

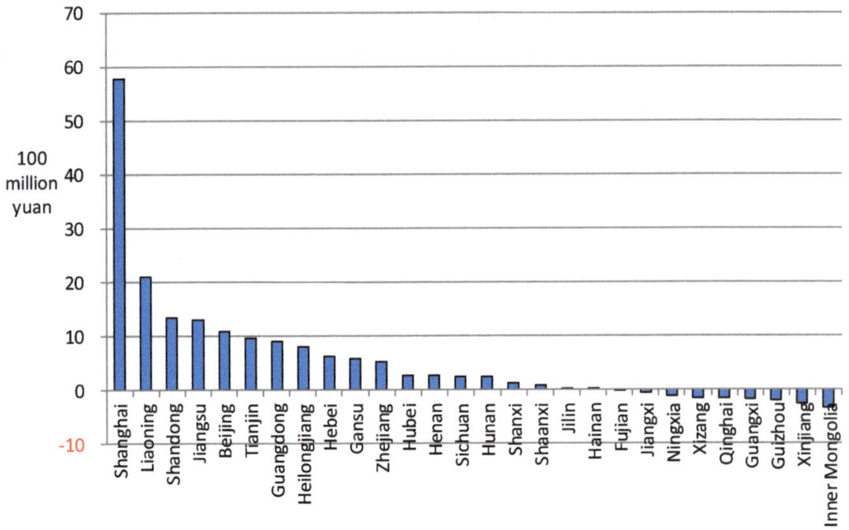

Fig. 7.7 Average net remittance from provincial levels to central government, 1949–1978. *Source* Kajima (2012)

fiscal revenue dropping sharply to between 11.8 and 35.2% after 1959, as shown in Fig. 7.8, the ratio of central fiscal expenditure recovered after a decline from 1958 to 1961, whereupon it stayed between 46.7 and 63.1%, as shown in Fig. 7.9.

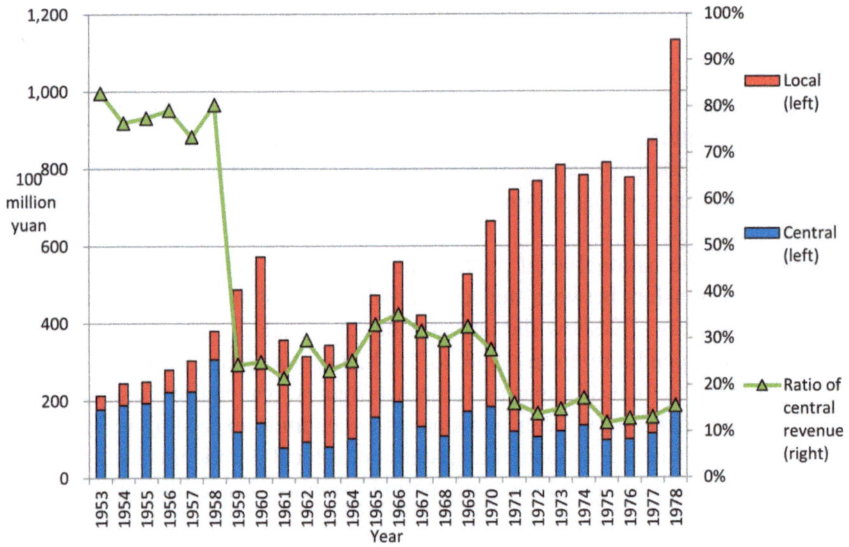

Fig. 7.8 Fiscal revenue of central and local governments, 1953–1978. *Sources* Kajima (2012); Lou (2000, pp. 25–26, 79–80, 157–159)

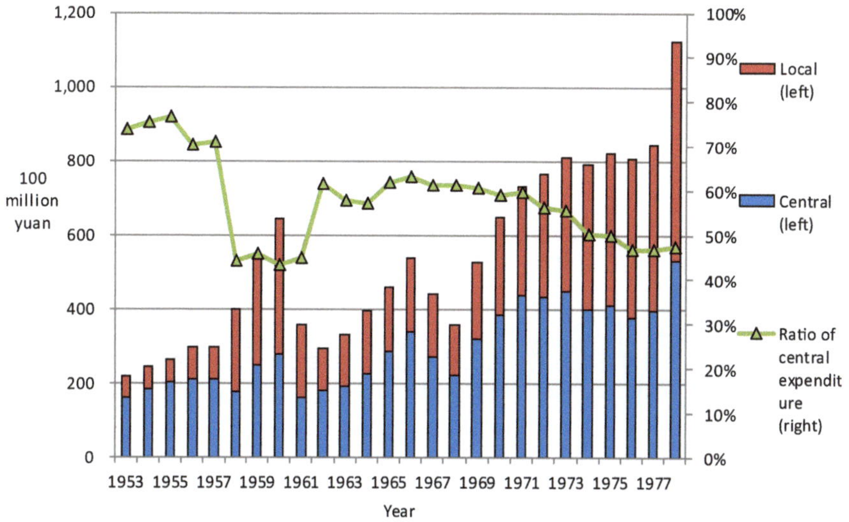

Fig. 7.9 Fiscal expenditure of central and local governments, 1953–1978. *Sources* Kajima (2012); Lou (2000, pp. 25-26, 79-80, 157–159)

This excess expenditure of the central government was mostly offset by the net Central Remittance Expenditure from each province, city, and autonomous region. Figure 7.10 compares the central government's annual excess expenditure (central fiscal expenditure minus central fiscal revenue) with the total annual net Central Remittance Expenditure (Central Remittance Expenditure minus Central Subsidy Revenue) of all provinces, cities, and autonomous regions calculated from the data in Fig. 7.4 and Fig. 7.5. Here, it is evident that the central government's annual excess expenditure and the total annual net Central Remittance Expenditure of all provincial-level local governments almost coincided from the 1960s onward, although there was a slight gap (total net remittances from each province, city, and autonomous region > excess part of central government expenditure) for the 1950s. In other words, the amount transferred to the central government as Central Remittance Expenditure from the regions roughly corresponded to the central government's fiscal deficit, further demonstrating the extent to which the finances of the central government during the planned economy period heavily depended on the transfer of fiscal revenue obtained by local governments.

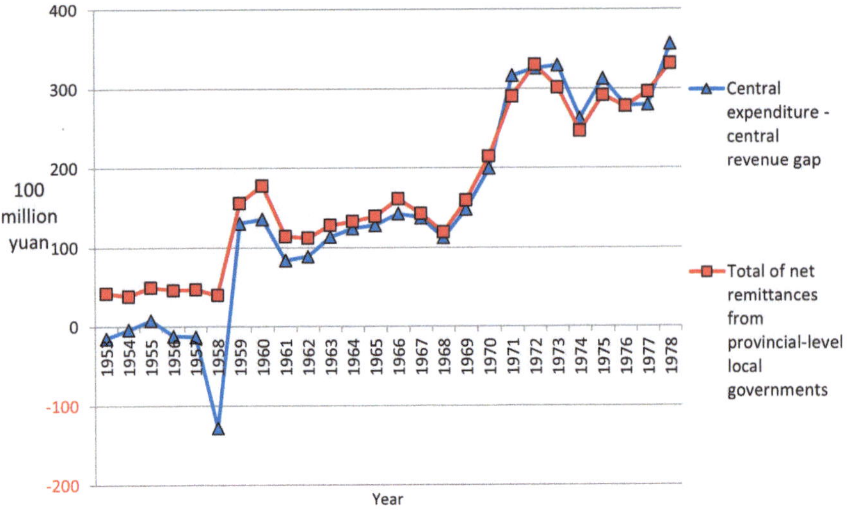

Fig. 7.10 Central government's revenue-expenditure gap and total of net remittances from provincial-level local governments to central government, 1953–1978. *Source* Kajima (2012)

7.2.3 Comparison of Local Fiscal Revenue and Expenditure Structure: The Ratio of Enterprise Revenue and Economic Construction Expenditure

Finally, it is important to consider the ratio of Enterprise Revenue to local fiscal revenue, which represents the relationship between local governments and the regional economy (mainly local enterprises), and the ratio of Economic Construction Expenditure to local fiscal expenditure. Note that the denominator for calculating the ratio here is not the total revenue/expenditure (including Central Subsidy Revenue and Central Remittance Expenditure) but rather the fiscal revenue/expenditure before governmental transfers with the central government.

Figure 7.11 shows the ratio of Enterprise Revenue to fiscal revenue for each province, city, and autonomous region. Looking at the trends, the ratios of Liaoning and Heilongjiang were relatively high at about 50% in the early 1950s. This is likely because there had already been a significant number of state-owned enterprises in northeastern China due to the requisition of old Japanese-owned enterprises from the Manchukuo period. On the other hand, by the mid-1950s, the Enterprise Revenue ratio in Shanghai, which had been a hub of private enterprise up to the Republican period, soared to nearly 90% due to the completion of socialist transformation, as covered in Chapter 4. Aside from that, after 1958, as already mentioned, the Enterprise Revenue ratio rose in many provinces, cities, and autonomous regions due to the transfer of centrally affiliated enterprises to local governments.

However, after 1961, while Shanghai consistently maintained a high level of about 60–70%, the ratio in many regions drastically decreased, and from that point onward

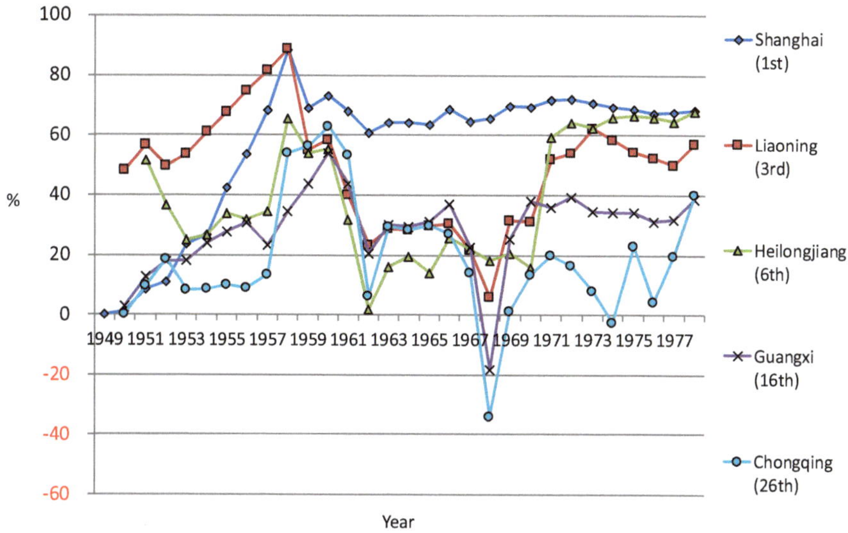

Fig. 7.11 Ratio of Enterprise Revenue to fiscal revenue of provincial-level local governments, 1949–1978. *Source* Kajima (2012)

it fluctuated sharply. In that sense, Enterprise Revenue was not necessarily a stable source of revenue for many provinces, cities, and autonomous regions, and Shanghai, which consistently relied on Enterprise Revenue, represented in this respect a special case. For example, there were cases like those of Chongqing and Guangxi in 1968, shown in Fig. 7.11, which recorded large deficits of Enterprise Revenue in a short period of time. Also, although not shown in the figure, there were cases where chronic Enterprise Revenue deficits put pressure on local finances, such as in Guizhou and Xinjiang.

On the other hand, the ratio of Economic Construction Expenditure of each province, city, and autonomous region to fiscal expenditure, as shown in Fig. 7.12, indicates that there was a relatively similar trend among provincial-level local governments compared to the Enterprise Revenue ratio. In the 1950s, the ratios of each province, city, and autonomous region were dispersed from anywhere between 0% and 70%, but during the Great Leap Forward period of 1958–60 the ratio rose all at once, converging to between 70 and 80%. Subsequently the ratio temporarily plummeted in 1962, but since then it experienced a continuous upward trend, and accounted for 50%–80% in all regions in the 1970s.

This shared trend in the ratio of Economic Construction Expenditure among provinces, cities, and autonomous regions since the late 1950s, and its continuous increase, was in essence the result of several industrial production promotion policies that the central government had ordered local governments to implement. These policies began with the Great Leap Forward, followed by the Third Front Construction in the 1960s, and finally the rural industrialization policy in the early 1970s. These policies were implemented by local governments under the command of the central

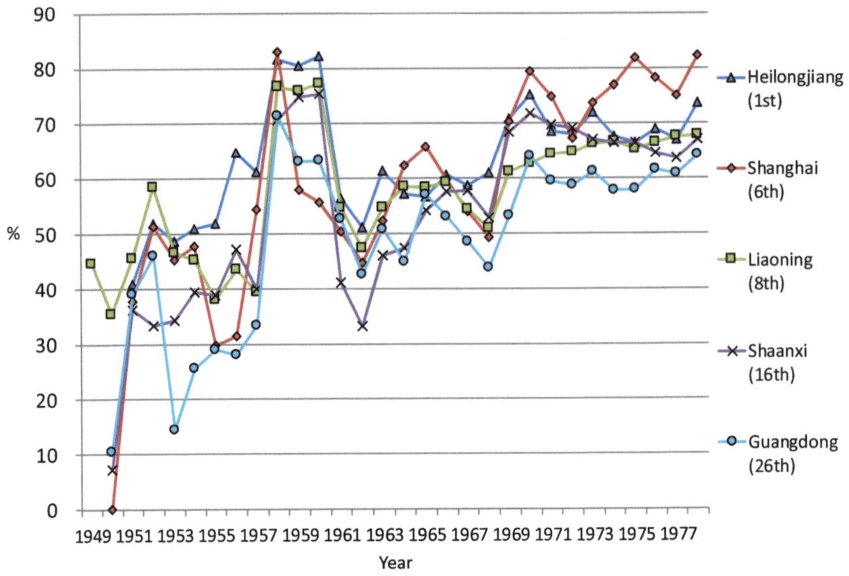

Fig. 7.12 Ratio of Economic Construction Expenditure to fiscal expenditure of provincial-level local Governments, 1949–1978. *Source* Kajima (2012)

government and aimed at increasing industrial production. For example, the Third Front Construction campaign was an inland economic development policy aimed at national defense, but while the central government led the "Big Third Front" (大三线), the "Small Third Front" (小三线) led by local governments was also carried out simultaneously. Under this policy, local governments were required to actively invest within their respective regions and contribute to forming a self-sufficient national defense system. The high ratio of Economic Construction Expenditure and the similar trend thereof among provincial-level local governments thus reflected the characteristics of the central government's policy implementation process, which depended on local governments.

This study so far has conducted a comparative analysis of the central-regional fiscal relations and local fiscal structure during the planned economy period, based on the "Chinese Provincial, Municipal, and Autonomous Region Local Fiscal Statistics Database, 1949–1978" at the provincial levels, while examining in what ways the local fiscal model of Shanghai, which was described in Chapters 5 and 6, was marked by both distinct characteristics that set it apart from other locales and elements that it had in common with them. This chapter's examination has revealed, moreover, the prominent position Shanghai's local public finance occupied within the country as a whole. Its abundant fiscal revenue, supported by Enterprise Revenue, and its large-scale Central Remittance Expenditure based on that fiscal revenue, were outstanding compared to those of other provinces, cities, and autonomous regions. In particular, the amount of Central Remittance Expenditure in Shanghai since 1959 reached 2.76

times the annual average of Liaoning, which was the second largest, and continued to be the most important foundation supporting central public finances during the planned economy period. On top of this, the consistently high proportion of Enterprise Revenue in fiscal revenue in Shanghai was unparalleled in other regions, and the local fiscal-local enterprise system analyzed in Chapter 6 was able to be stably established only in Shanghai, which possessed such a strong foundation of local enterprises in the first place. In this sense, it is no exaggeration to state that the local fiscal structure of Shanghai was on balance both unique in character and highly significant for China as a whole.

However, beyond this, the total balance of each province, city, and autonomous region, shown in Fig. 7.6, and the continuous net Central Remittance Expenditure from each over time, shown in Fig. 7.7, are also significant for comprehensively assessing the particular characteristics of the Shanghai model within the context of the socialist fiscal system. As Figs. 7.6 and 7.7 show, many other provinces and cities, including Liaoning, which boasted the second largest fiscal scale after Shanghai, had an excess of local fiscal revenue in some form even if they could not continuously rely on Enterprise Revenue like Shanghai. These locales produced Central Remittance Expenditures exceeding their Central Subsidy Revenue, while their fiscal expenditures after the central remittances were forced to be limited to a certain scale. In this sense, these provinces and cities, like Shanghai, operated under the common framework provided by the socialist fiscal system, which supported central finance through transfers from local fiscal revenue. Moreover, the high ratio of Economic Construction Expenditure to the fiscal expenditures of each province, city, and autonomous region is evidence of how each local government was being directed to actively commit to regional economic activities, in which regard Shanghai was no exception, as shown in Chapters 5 and 6. In sum, the local fiscal model of Shanghai, which has been the object of the analysis throughout the chapters that comprise Part II of the present study, was characterized by strong unique characteristics while nevertheless sharing some general elements with other locales due to the general frameworks and policies within which it had to operate.

References

English Language

Donnithorne, Audrey. 1967. *China's Economic System.* New York: F. A. Praeger

Hsiao, Katharine Huang. 1987. *The Government Budget and Fiscal Policy in Mainland China.* Taipei: Chung-Hua Institution for Economic Research

Jin, Hehui, Yingyi Qian, and Barry R. Weingast. 2005. Regional Decentralization and Fiscal Incentives: Federalism, Chinese Style. *Journal of Public Economics* 89(9): 1719–1742. https://doi.org/10.1016/j.jpubeco.2004.11.008

Lardy, Nicholas R. 1978. *Economic Growth and Distribution in China.* Cambridge: Cambridge University Press

Chinese Language

Caizhengbu guokusi yusuansi, ed. 1990–2009. *Difang caizheng tongjiziliao* (地方财政统计资料, Statistics of Local Public Finance). Beijing: Zhongguo caizhengjingji chubanshe

Caizhengbu guokusi yusuansi, ed. 1993–2009. *Quanguo dishixian caizheng tongjiziliao* (全国地市县财政统计资料, Statistics of Local Public Finance of Prefectural-level Cities and Counties). Beijing: Zhongguo caizhengjingji chubanshe

Caizhengbu zonghejihuasi, ed. 1982. *Zhonghuarenmingongheguo caizheng shiliao diyiji: caizhengguanlitizhi, 1950–1980* (中华人民共和国财政史料 第1辑:财政管理体制1950–1980, Historical Materials of Public Finance of the People's Republic of China, Volume 1: Financial Management System 1950–1980). Beijing: Zhongguo caizhengjingji chubanshe

Cui, Jindu, ed. 2000. *Tianjin caizheng wushinian: 1949–1999* (天津财政五十年 (1949–1999), Fifty Years of Public Finance of Tianjin: 1949–1999). Beijing: Zhongguo caizhengjingji chubanshe

Dangdai zhongguo congshu bianjibu, ed. 1988. *Dangdai zhongguo de caizheng* (当代中国的财政, Contemporary China's Finance), Volume I & II. Beijing: Zhongguo shehuikexue chubanshe

Guizhousheng caizhengting zonghejihuachu. 1986 *Guizhousheng caizhengshouzhi tongjiziliao 1950–1985* (贵州省财政收支统计资料1950–1985, Guizhou Provincial Finance Revenue and Expenditure Statistical Data 1950–1985). Guizhou: Guizhousheng caizhengting zonghejihuachu

Guojia tongjiju guominjingjizonghetongjisi, ed. 1999. *Xinzhongguo wushinian tongjiziliao huibian* (新中国五十年统计资料汇编, Compilation of Statistical Data for Fifty Years of New China). Beijing: Zhongguo tongji chubanshe

Guojia tongjiju guominjingjizonghetongjisi, ed. 2005. *Xinzhongguo wushiwunian tongjiziliao huibian* (新中国五十五年统计资料汇编, Compilation of Statistical Data for Fifty-Five Years of New China). Beijing: Zhongguo tongji chubanshe

Guojia tongjiju guominjingjizonghetongjisi, ed. 2010. *Xinzhongguo liushinian tongjiziliao huibian* (新中国六十年统计资料汇编, Compilation of Statistical Data for Sixty Years of New China). Beijing: Zhongguo tongji chubanshe

Guojia tongjiju zonghesi, ed. 1990. Quanguo gesheng, zizhiqu, zhixiashi lishitongji ziliaohuibian (全国各省、自治区、直辖市历史统计资料汇编, Compilation of Historical Statistical Data for All Provinces, Autonomous Regions, and Municipalities Directly Under the Central Government). Beijing: Zhongguo tongji chubanshe

Lou, Jiwei, ed. 2000. *Xinzhongguo wushinian caizhengtongji* (新中国50年财政统计, Statistics of Public Finance of the New China for 50 years). Beijing: Jingjikexue chubanshe

Shanghai caizhengshuiwuzhi bianzuanweiyuanhui, ed. 1999. *Shanghai caizhengshuiwuzhi ziliaochangbian* (上海财政税务誌资料长编, Draft and Materials of the History of Shanghai Public Finance and Taxation), Volumes I and II. Shanghai: Shanghai caizhengju and shanghai shuiwuju

Song, Xinzhong, ed. 1997. *Dangdai zhongguo caizhengshi* (当代中国财政史, The History of Contemporary China's Public Finance). Beijing: Zhongguo caizhengjingji chubanshe

Wang, Weiquan, ed. 1995. *Shanghai caizhengshuiwuzhi* (上海财政税务志, Shanghai Fiscal and Taxation Chronicle). Shanghai: Shanghai shehuikexueyuan chubanshe

Zhao, Menghan. 2002. *Xinzhongguo caizhengshuishoushilungang* (新中国财政税收史论纲, Outline of the History of New China's Public Finance and Tax Revenue). Beijing: Jingjikexue chubanshe

Zhongguo caizhengnianjian bianjiweiyuanhui, ed. Various years. *Zhongguo caizhengnianjian* (中国财政年鉴, China Fiscal Yearbook). Beijing: Zhongguo caizhengzazhishe

Zuo, Chuntai, and Song Xinzhong, eds. 1988. *Zhongguo shehuizhuyicaizheng jianshi* (中国社会主义财政简史, A Brief History of China's Socialist Public Finance). Beijing: Zhongguo caizhengjingji chubanshe

Japanese Language

Chō, Chūnin. 2001. Gendaichūgoku no seihukan zaiseikankei (現代中国の政府間財政関係, Intergovernmental Fiscal Relations of Contemporary China). Tokyo: Ochanomizu shobō

Fujimoto, Akira. 1971. *Shinchūgoku no kokkazaisei no kenkyū* (新中国の国家財政の研究, Study on the Public Finance of New China). Tokyo: Yūhikaku

Ishihara, Kyōichi. 1990. 1970 nendai madeno chūgokukeizaikanri: shisutemu to jittai (1970年代までの中国経済管理——システムと実態, Chinese Economic Management up to the 1970s: System and Reality). In *Mōtakutōjidai no chūgoku: Gendaichūgokuron 1* (毛沢東時代の中国<現代中国論1>, China in the Mao Zedong Era: Discussions on Contemporary China No.1), ed. Mōri Kazuko, 146–185. Tokyo: Japan Institute of International Affairs

Kajima, Jun. 2012. *Chūgoku keikakukeizaiki zaisei no kenkyū: Shō chokkatsushi jichiku tōkei kara* (中国計画経済期財政の研究——省・直轄市・自治区統計から, China's Fiscal System during the Planned Economy Era), University of Tokyo Institute of Social Science Contemporary Chinese Research Series No.10. Tokyo: Contemporary China Research Base, Institute of Social Science, The University of Tokyo

Miyashita, Tadao. 1967. *Shinchūgoku no tsūkaseisaku* (新中国の通貨政策, New China's Monetary Policy), Seimeikai Series V. Tokyo: Seimeikai

Mōri, Kazuko. 1990. 1970 nendai madeno chūō to chihō: Shanghaishi no kēsu (1970年代末までの中央と地方——上海市のケース, The Relationship between Central and Local Government until the Late 1970s: The Case of Shanghai). In *Mōtakutō jidai no chūgoku: Gendai chūgokuron 1* (毛沢東時代の中国<現代中国論1>, China in the Mao Zedong Era), ed. Mōri Kazuko, 87–112. Tokyo: Japan Institute of International Affairs

Nambu, Minoru. 1991. *Gendai chūgoku no zaiseikinyūseisaku* (現代中国の財政金融政策, Fiscal and Financial Policies of Contemporary China). Tokyo: Taga shuppan

Tajima, Toshio. 1994. Chūgoku no kokuyūkigyōkaikaku to seihukan zaiseikankei (中国の国有企業改革と政府間財政関係, Reform of State-owned Enterprises and Inter-governmental Fiscal Relations in China). *Chūgoku kenkyū geppō* (中国研究月報 , Monthly Journal of Chinese Affairs) 48(4): 2–31

Tajima, Toshio. 2000. Chūgoku no zaiseikinyū seidokaikaku: Zokuchiteki keizai shisutemu no keisei to henyō (中国の財政金融制度改革——属地的経済システムの形成と変容, Reform of China's Fiscal and Financial System: Formation and Transformation of Territorial Economic System). In *Gendai chūgoku no kōzōhendō 2 keizai: Kōzōhendō to shijōka* (現代中国の構造変動2経済——構造変動と市場化, Structural Changes in Contemporary China, Volume 2, Economy: Structural Changes and Marketization), ed. Nakagane Katsuji, 73–106. Tokyo: University of Tokyo Press

Part III
Industrial Development in Shanghai under the Socialist System

Chapter 8
The Impact of the Heavy-Industry-Priority Strategy: The Textile and Machinery Industries

Abstract This chapter examines the transition of the industrial structure of Shanghai through conducting a comparative analysis of the textile and machinery industries, which were the main industries in the municipality, based on the available statistical data. The textile industry was the core of the light industry that symbolized the development of Shanghai's modern industry up to the Republican period. On the other hand, the machinery industry, which likewise developed before the establishment of the PRC, was a sector of heavy industry that received focused investment and experienced substantial growth due to the government's "Heavy-industry-priority Strategy" during the planned economy period.

Keywords Industrial structure of Shanghai · Textile industry · Machinery Industry · Heavy-industry-priority Strategy · Enterprise Revenue · Profit-fixed assets ratio

As revealed in the first two parts, the formation of the socialist system in the 1950s gave rise to a structure in Shanghai where local governments and local enterprises were closely linked. The socialist transformation, which reached its completion in 1956, turned many existing private enterprises into local public-private jointly-owned enterprises, and incorporated them under the management of the Shanghai Municipal Government, just like the local state-owned enterprises. As a result, local state-owned and public-private jointly-owned enterprises belonging to the Shanghai Municipal Government formed a symbiotic relationship within the framework of the socialist financial system, wherein local enterprises contributed their profits to the municipal government's public finances in the form of Enterprise Revenue while investments to local enterprises were primarily made from government finances. Furthermore, the large-scale transfer of centrally-managed enterprises to local control in 1958 dramatically increased the number of enterprises managed by local governments, and the relationship between local governments and local enterprises in Shanghai in particular played a significant role within the financial structure of the central and local government system as a whole.

J. Kajima, *Shanghai under the Socialist System*, Studies in Economic History,
https://doi.org/10.1007/978-981-95-3225-4_8

The last part of this study will undertake an examination of the relationship between local governments and local enterprises under this socialist system by focusing on several specific industries as case studies. The formation of the socialist system in the 1950s covered all industries, but the structures of each industry, being the product of their own distinct historical trajectories of development, were necessarily diverse and the impacts of institutional changes on each industry were consequently also different. The focus in these chapters is on discussing the various aspects of the impact of the introduction of the socialist system in each industry, thereby clarifying the diversity of the development processes that occurred under the socialist system. This perspective will then enable a more nuanced and critical understanding of the reality of Shanghai's economy under the socialist system by situating it within the wider context of these transformative processes.

This chapter, by way of providing a preliminary frame of reference for the case studies of individual industries to follow, will examine the transition of the industrial structure of Shanghai and conduct a comparative analysis on the textile industry and machinery industry, which were the main industries of the municipality, based on the available statistical data. The textile industry, as mentioned in Part I, was the core of the light industry that symbolized the development of Shanghai's modern industry up to the Republican period. On the other hand, the machinery industry, which likewise developed before the establishment of the PRC, was a sector of heavy industry that received focused investment and experienced great growth during the planned economy period. The introduction and first chapter have already set the scene by drawing on macro statistics to outline the process of industrialization of both China as a whole and Shanghai in particular under the government's "Heavy-industry-priority Strategy," but the task of this chapter is to examine the process of change in the overall industrial structure in light of the reality of the core industries of light and heavy industry, and to moreover examine the impact of the promotion of industrialization on industrial development in Shanghai.

8.1 The Industrial Organization of Shanghai

It is necessary to begin by first surveying the transition of the overall industrial structure of Shanghai during the planned economy period. Table 8.1 and Fig. 8.1 show the output value of the main industries in Shanghai and the share that each made up of the total output value for the municipality. The first point to note is that, as already touched on in Chapter 3, the textile industry made up an overwhelming share (over 50%) in the early 1950s. Although its share gradually declined thereafter, it managed to maintain the second position among all industries almost without interruption after 1958, fluctuating around 20% (it slipped to third place only from 1966 to 1970). This data well illustrates how the textile industry remained one of the main pillars of Shanghai's industry throughout the planned economy period.

On the other hand, as the share of the textile industry declined, the heavy industry sectors such as the machinery, chemical, and metallurgy industries came to the fore. In

Table 8.1 Average annual output value of main industries in Shanghai, 1950–1980 (each term) (Unit: 100 million yuan)

Year (term)	1950–52	1953–57	1958–62	1963–65	1966–70	1971–75	1976–80
Textile	26.73	43.03	51.63	49.42	67.51	74.01	117.43
Machinery	6.71	20.16	72.19	50.31	96.68	129.62	180.29
Metallurgy	1.95	7.22	22.20	25.74	34.39	52.44	61.05
Chemical	4.70	12.76	28.87	38.29	70.90	54.10	72.36
Others	13.22	26.51	42.32	44.65	56.09	78.84	107.81
Total	53.31	109.68	217.20	208.40	325.58	389.01	538.94

Notes (1) Output value of 1950–57, 1958–70 and 1971–80 are calculated based on fixed prices of 1952, 1957 and 1970, respectively. (2) "Others" includes food, power, coal and coke, petroleum, construction materials, lumber, sewing, leather, papermaking, manufacturing for culture, education and art, and others (remainder after subtracting above-mentioned industries from total) in the original table

Source Shanghaishi tongjiju (1992, pp. 28–33)

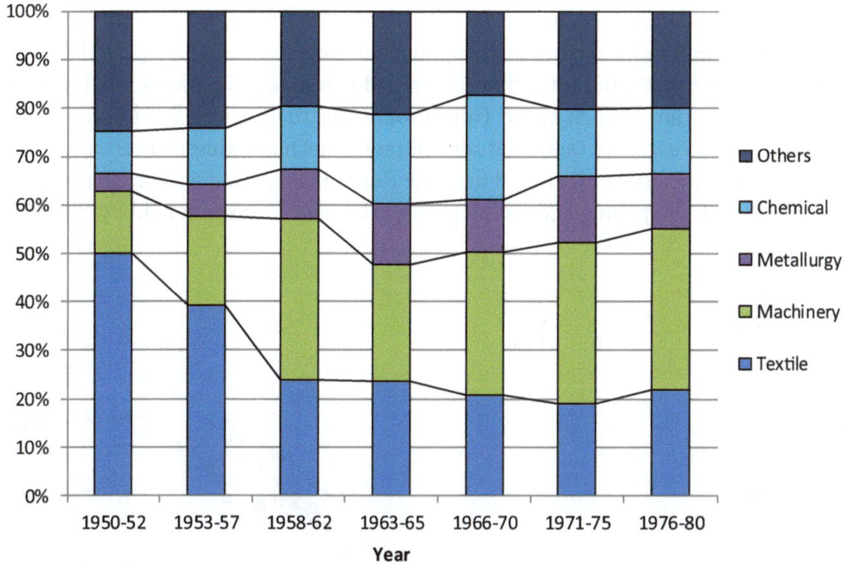

Fig. 8.1 Percentage of output value comprised by main industries in Shanghai, 1950–1980. *Source* Table 8.1

particular, the expansion of the machinery industry was remarkable, reaching a share of 33.2% in 1958–62, overtaking the textile industry and consistently maintaining the top position thereafter. Following this were the chemical and metallurgy industries, and together these three industries established a structure that came to account for 50–60% of the total share in the years after 1958. The change in industrial structure from light industry to heavy industry in Shanghai in the 1950s and 1960s, as shown in Table 2.2 in Chapter 2, was driven specifically by the surge in the machinery industry.

This reversal of shares between the light and heavy industries can be more clearly seen from Fig. 8.2, which shows the transition of the output value of major industries in index form. The output value of the textile industry increased about five times over the course of the 28 years from 1952 to 1980, which was below the average for all industries, while the output value of the machinery, metallurgy, and chemical industries reached 30–40 times. In other words, while these heavy industry sectors achieved remarkable production expansion, the production of the textile industry was relatively stagnant despite maintaining a significant presence in Shanghai's industrial makeup.

On the other hand, Table 8.2, which shows the position of Shanghai's textile and machinery industries in the context of national output during the planned economy period, indicates the textile industry was hovering around 20–30% of the national share during subsequent decades, while gradually reducing its share from the 34.7% it had represented in 1952. As for the machinery industry, it fluctuated from 25.3% in 1952, but consistently maintained over 20% until the end of the 1960s, whereupon it declined to the upper tens in the 1970s. The fact that the share of both industries in Shanghai declined trend-wise throughout the planned economy period is most likely due to the promotion of self-sufficient industrialization policies in all regions, including inland areas, such as the Third Front Construction (三线建设) campaign. As a result, the structure of industrial concentration that had endured in certain regions such as Shanghai and the Northeast until the Republican period was gradually transformed through the planned economy period. However, the share held by Shanghai

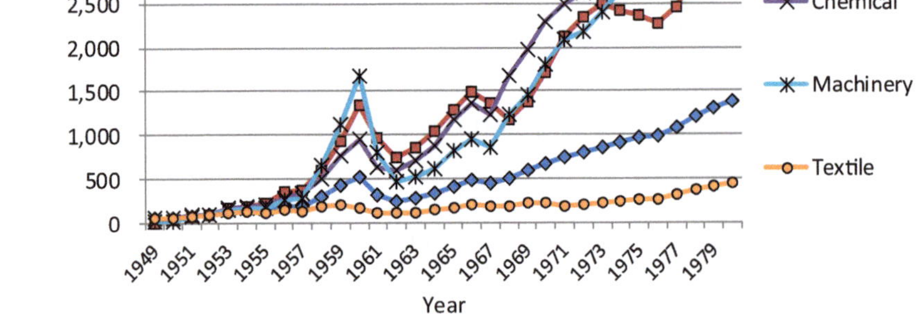

Fig. 8.2 Output value indices of main industries in Shanghai, 1949–1980. *Note* 1952 = 100. *Source* Shanghaishi tongjiju (1992, pp. 34–35)

Table 8.2 Average annual output value of textile and machinery industries in China and Shanghai, 1952–1980 (each term) (Unit: 100 million yuan)

Year (term)	Textile industry			Machinery industry		
	China	Shanghai	Shanghai's share in China (%)	China	Shanghai	Shanghai's share in China (%)
1952	94.3	32.7	34.7	39.0	9.9	25.3
1953–57	130.6	43.0	32.9	96.3	20.2	20.9
1958–62	182.7	51.6	28.3	299.3	72.2	24.1
1963–65	177.8	49.4	27.8	242.6	50.3	20.7
1966–70	250.2	67.5	27.0	417.0	96.7	23.2
1971–75	343.2	74.0	21.6	717.5	129.6	18.1
1976–80	542.5	117.4	21.6	1,121.7	180.3	16.1

Note Output values of 1950–57, 1958–70 and 1971–80 are calculated based on fixed prices of 1952, 1957, and 1970, respectively
Sources Guojia tongjiju gongyejiaotongwuzi tongjisi (1985, pp. 34–35) and Shanghaishi tongjiju (1992, pp. 28–33)

was generally around 20–30% in both industries, and there was no change in the fact that Shanghai remained one of the main industrial centers in China.

To sum up, the textile and machinery industries were both major industries in Shanghai and they also constituted a significant share of their respective sectors nationwide during the planned economy period, even as the trends in their output growth value diverged. This difference in output value trends was, clearly, the result of the government's Heavy-industry-priority Strategy, which utilized intensive government investment to promote the development of heavy industry. However, an issue worth considering here is how this strategy affected the course of the development of these two industries in Shanghai, each of which had a strong historical foundation dating back to the Republican period.

There is a vast amount of research on China's textile and machinery industries, especially on the cotton industry, which was the core of the textile industry.[1] However, research on either of these industries during the planned economy period is far less voluminous, and there have been almost no studies undertaken from the perspective of comparing the two industries. The following sections aim to alleviate this situation somewhat by examining the performances of the two industries under the socialist system, in the context of the trajectory of their historical development.

[1] Regarding the development of both industries during the planned economy period, outlines exist such as Dangdai zhongguo congshu bianjibu (1984, 1990). Additionally, Zhonghuarenmingongheguo guojiatongjiju gongyetongjisi (1958) and Onoe (1971) include statistical data and an overview of each industry. Ou (2009) and Kubo (2011) have discussed the continuity of technology that existed in the form of Japanese cotton spinning and weaving factories in China from the pre-1945 era up to the PRC. As for the textile industry before and after 1949, also see Brasó Broggi (2016), Cliver (2020), and Peng (2020).

8.2 The Development of the Textile and Machinery Industries

Before delving into a specific analysis of the two industries in question, it is necessary to clarify their definitions. "Textile industry" (纺织工业) in China at the time referred in the general sense to the industry that spun, wove, and dyed natural and synthetic fibers such as cotton, hemp, silk, and wool.[2] More specifically, however, the term as an industrial classification category during the planned economy period also included the manufacture of textile machinery and equipment, in addition to industries such as cotton spinning, weaving, dyeing, woolen fabrics, silk fabrics, hemp fabrics, knits, and synthetic fibers.[3]

On the other hand, "machinery industry" (机械工业) generally referred to those industries that manufactured general machinery (prime movers, industrial machinery, machine tools, etc.), electrical machinery, transportation machinery (automobiles, railway vehicles, ships, etc.), precision machinery, and arms. In China during the planned economy period, it was composed of civilian sectors on the one hand, encompassing such products as power generation equipment, construction machinery, instruments, automobiles, motorcycles, mining equipment, machine tools, and agricultural machinery under the jurisdiction of the central government's Ministry of First Machinery Industry (第一机械工业部), and on the other hand, the weapons industry and electronics industry, which were managed by separate ministries. The entire industry was, and is in the scholarship, also sometimes referred to as the "mechanical and electrical industry" (机电工业) (Kojima 1989, p. 41; Marukawa 2000b, p. 214).

The historical trajectories followed by these two industries in China differed significantly.[4] In the case of the textile industry, China had a long history of indigenous handicrafts in the cotton industry, supported by a vast domestic market, and in the silk industry, which had been a traditional export industry. However, modern mechanized factories did not appear in China until the late nineteenth century, and the Shanghai Machine Weaving Bureau, China's first mechanized cotton spinning

[2] Kojima (1989, p. 328). It should be noted that a major difference at the time between China's textile industry and Japan's textile industry was that China classified industries by raw materials such as cotton fabrics, woolen fabrics, and silk fabrics, whereas Japan mainly employed classification by manufacturing processes such as spinning, weaving, and knitting.

[3] Dangdai zhongguo congshu bianjibu (1984, p. 13). According to Kojima (1989, p. 328), the "textile industry" as a major classification of industry in China included the sewing industry until 1958 (when it was split off), and was then in 1965 combined with not only the sewing industry once more but the leather industry as well, becoming the "textile, sewing, and leather industry." Also, the textile machinery and equipment manufacturing industry was reclassified as the "industrial equipment [sector] of the machinery industry" in the 1980s. However, it is unclear how the textile machinery and equipment manufacturing industries were actually classified after the 1980s, since the various statistics in Shanghai fangzhigongyezhi bianzuanweiyuanhui (1998) refer to textile machinery and equipment as part of the textile industry up to the latest fiscal year covered by that work, 1995.

[4] The following historical outline is based on Kubo et al. (2016, pp. 21–39, 43–45, 58–63).

industry, was established in 1880 (and operations only commenced in 1890). After the Treaty of Shimonoseki in 1895, foreign companies rushed to enter the cotton spinning industry in Chinese treaty port cities, and Chinese capital companies themselves soon followed suit. In the twentieth century, the entry of Japanese capital cotton spinning and weaving factories (在华纺) into China, and the development of Chinese capital cotton industry companies due to the First World War, established Shanghai as a major center of mechanized cotton production in China.

As an indicator of the development of the cotton industry up to the Republican period, consider Fig. 8.3, which shows the self-sufficiency rate of machine-made cotton products in China. Note that the production volume in this figure also includes the production of foreign capital factories located in China, such as Japanese capital cotton spinning and weaving factories. Figure 8.3 reveals that China became essentially self-sufficient in cotton yarn in the 1910–1920s, exceeding 100% in 1930, and that cotton cloth also showed a steady increase in self-sufficiency rate during the 1920–1930s, reaching 86.5% in 1936. In other words, the cotton industry as a whole was almost self-sufficient before the outbreak of the Second Sino-Japanese War. After war broke out, the cotton industry underwent a complex development process, with the relocation of some factories to the inland area following the relocation of the National Government to Chongqing, the "prosperity of the solitary island" of factories remaining in coastal cities under Japanese occupation in wartime, and the takeover of private factories by the China Textile Construction Company after the conclusion of the war. Despite all this turbulence due to the years of conflict, China's cotton industry had achieved a significant level of development by 1949, and Shanghai remained firmly at its center.

As for the machinery industry, this too was introduced to China in the second half of the nineteenth century, and its development route can be broadly divided into two categories (Kubo et al. 2016, pp. 60–61). One was the ship repair yards for the Western trading ships, where foreign capital factories were first established, followed in turn by Chinese capital factories. The Dalong Iron Works (大隆铁厂), established in Shanghai in 1902, would later grow into China's largest private machinery factory. The other route of introduction was the arms industry. State-owned factories established in various places in the 1860s for the purpose of weapon manufacturing and shipbuilding were the forerunners here, such as the Jiangnan Manufacturing Bureau (江南制造局) which was established in Shanghai in 1865. The Bureau separated its weapons manufacturing and shipbuilding departments in 1905, and the shipbuilding department later became independent under the name Jiangnan Shipyard (江南造船所) in 1912.

Based on these early foundations, China's machinery industry made significant progress along with the growth of light industry. Particularly important was the development of the textile machinery and equipment manufacturing industry, which accompanied the development of the textile industry. These efforts began with the imitation production of various machine components, and by the end of the 1920s the industry was capable of producing full sets of main machinery and equipment such as spinning machines and power looms on its own. The machinery industry also succeeded in domesticating production of machinery and equipment for the

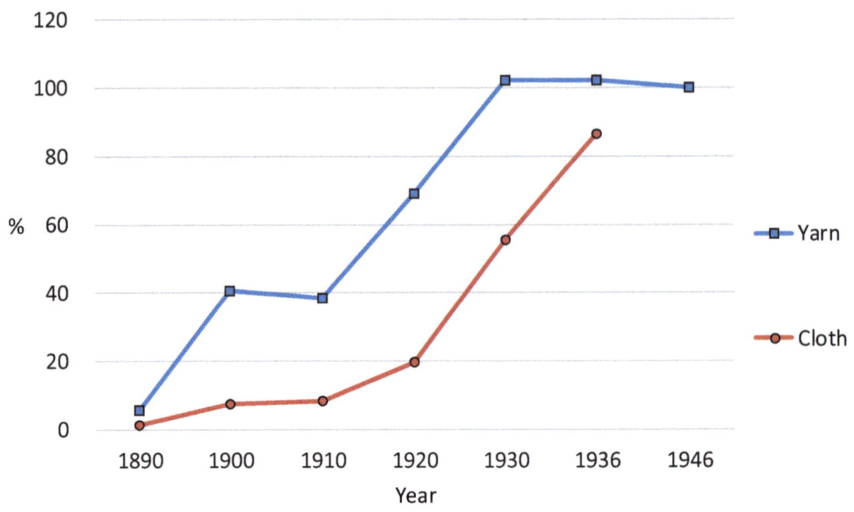

Fig. 8.3 China's self-sufficiency rate of machine-made cotton yarn and cloth, 1890–1946. *Notes* (1) "Self-sufficiency rate" is calculated as follows: (Amount of production) / (Amount of production + imports – exports). (2) The data in this table only covers cotton products made in modern factories. (3) Data for cloth in 1946 is not available. *Sources* Kubo et al. (2016, pp. 23–24) and Kajima (2022, p. 191)

food processing and match manufacturing industries, as well as various internal combustion engines, and large bridge piers.

However, a significant difference between the textile industry and the machinery industry was that machinery products were still heavily dependent on imports, while the textile industry had almost achieved self-sufficiency as of the 1930s. Despite the aforementioned development of the machinery industry, its self-sufficiency rate, as shown in Table 8.3, was at most 10–20% in 1931 (Kubo et al. 2016, p. 60). During the Second Sino-Japanese War, the machinery industry developed to a certain extent, especially in key industries for military production, but the self-sufficiency rate, including for civilian goods, remained at a fairly low level.

The difference in the progress of import substitution in the textile industry and that in the machinery industry became one of the important factors behind the launch of the Heavy-industry-priority Strategy after 1949. The restriction of trade with Western countries due to China's participation in the Korean War in 1950, and the deterioration of relations with the Soviet Union in the late 1950s, put pressure on the supply of imported machinery products in China. On the other hand, just as the supply dried up, domestic demand for machinery industry products was increasing, due to the very same Heavy-industry-priority Strategy. As a result, there was great pressure placed upon the machinery industry to rapidly achieve self-sufficiency, which was not a problem faced by the then already largely self-sufficient textile industry. In this situation, the machinery industry in Shanghai, which had already achieved a

Table 8.3 Production and imports of machinery products of China, 1931 (Unit: 10 thousand yuan)

Products	Amount of production	Output value (a)	Import value (b)	Self-sufficiency rate (%) (a)/((a) + (b))
Machinery for textile production	...	183.7	2,150.1	7.9
Pumps	127 pumps	1.8	144.6	1.2
Agricultural machinery	...	24.4	106.3	18.7
Motors	15k horsepower	75.0	883.5	7.8

Note "..." indicates no data available
Source Kubo et al. (2016, p. 61)

significant level of development in this area during the Republican period, as shown in Table 8.2, would play an important role.

8.3 Performances Under the Socialist System: Investments and Profits

The first section of this chapter covered the development of both industries in Shanghai during the planned economy period, and in particular the trends reflected in output value. This section will compare and analyze the performance of both industries during the same period in more detail by focusing on the accumulation of investment from government finance, which was the amount of fixed assets, and the profits that flowed back to government finance in the form of Enterprise Revenue.

The data used in this section is primarily drawn from so-called "specialized gazetteers" (专业志) among the local gazetteers of Shanghai, and specifically the works Shanghai fangzhigongyezhi bianzuanweiyuanhui (1998) and Shanghai jidiangongyezhi bianzuanweiyuanhui (1996). These gazetteers were comprehensive collections of documents edited by administrative organizations overseeing each industry formed during the planned economy period in Shanghai, such as the Shanghai Municipal Bureau of Textile Industry (上海纺织工业局) in the case of the textile industry, in order to summarize the history of their respective jurisdictions in the 1990s.

These specialized gazetteers have a significant advantage in that they provide data such as the fixed asset values and profits of each industry. However, they also share a drawback, in that the range they cover is defined by the jurisdiction of each administrative organization, and this range does not necessarily coincide with the textile industry or machinery industry that existed in Shanghai. Comparing the output value of each industry in Shanghaishi tongjiju (1992) with the output value listed in these gazetteers reveals that for the machinery industry, the figures given by Shanghai

Table 8.4 Average annual capital construction investment in main industries in Shanghai, 1950–1980 (each term) (Unit: 100 million yuan)

Year (term)	1950–52	1953–57	1958–62	1963–65	1966–70	1971–75	1976–80
Textile	0.03	0.12	0.24	0.14	0.07	0.82	0.73
Machinery	0.13	0.58	1.98	0.91	0.63	1.14	1.60
Metallurgy	0.02	0.05	1.00	0.38	0.51	0.84	3.71
Chemical	0.02	0.07	0.61	0.59	0.28	2.06	0.96
Others	0.04	0.30	1.57	0.73	1.44	2.36	2.81
Total	0.24	1.12	5.41	2.76	2.94	7.22	9.81

Note Breakdown of "Others" same as in Table 8.1
Source Shanghaishi tongjiju (1992, pp. 72–73)

jidiangongyezhi bianzuanweiyuanhui (1996) only constitute about 40–60% of those given in Shanghaishi tongjiju (1992), although in the case of the textile industry both sources are almost identical.[5] This indicates that the jurisdiction of the bureau responsible for the machinery industry, the Shanghai Municipal Bureau of First Mechanical and Electrical Industry (上海市第一机电工业局), covered only a part of the actual machinery industry that existed in Shanghai, and in that sense, the data from this specialized gazetteer cannot be regarded as accurately representing the entire machinery industry in Shanghai.

A further problem is that the data given in Shanghai fangzhigongyezhi bianzuanweiyuanhui (1998) includes not only the textile industry proper, but also the textile machinery and equipment manufacturing industry. This was due to the jurisdiction of the Shanghai Municipal Bureau of Textile Industry also including the manufacture of textile machinery and equipment. Consequently, although the manufacture of textile machinery was an important part of Shanghai's machinery industry, it is impractical to make adjustments such as separating the data pertaining to the textile machinery and equipment manufacturing industry from the figures given by the gazetteer in order to maintain consistency within the data set. According to the breakdown of profits in the textile industry listed in Shanghai jidiangongyezhi bianzuanweiyuanhui (1996, pp. 285–288), the textile machinery and equipment industry generally accounted for about 5% of the total textile industry profits, while the largest cotton spinning occupied about 15–40%.

First of all, to survey the overall investment situation in both industries it is necessary to consider the amount of Capital Construction Investment by industry in Shanghai, as shown in Table 8.4 and Fig. 8.4. The data given here is not derived from the aforementioned specialized gazetteers, but covers the entire industry, as was the case with Table 8.1 and Fig. 8.1.

Table 8.4 and Fig. 8.4 reveal the extremely high share of investment that the machinery industry received until the mid-1950s. In 1950–52 and 1953–57, it accounted for about 50% of the total Capital Construction Investment in Shanghai,

[5] Shanghaishi tongjiju (1992, pp. 28–36), Shanghai fangzhigongyezhi bianzuanweiyuanhui (1998, pp. 278–284), and Shanghai jidiangongyezhi bianzuanweiyuanhui (1996, pp. 10–14).

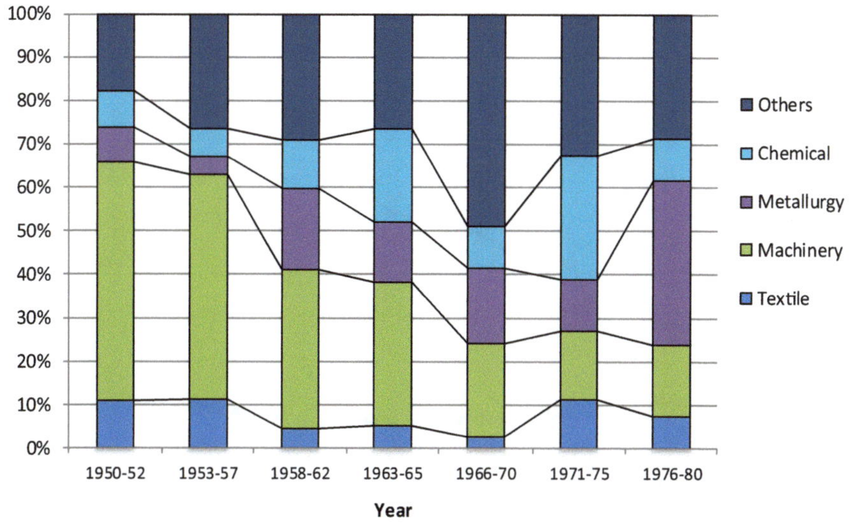

Fig. 8.4 Percentage by main industry of capital construction investments in Shanghai, 1950–1980. *Source* Table 8.4

illustrating just how much the government sought to advance the development of the machinery industry at the time. Subsequently, however, this ratio declined, and by the 1970s it was merely 15%. The main cause of this decline in the share accorded to the machinery industry was the rapid expansion of the "others" category from 1966 to 80, the chemical industry from 1971 to 75, and the metallurgy industry from 1976 to 80. The specific causes of the rapid expansion of "others" from 1966 to 80 are not known,[6] but the expansion of the chemical industry from 1971 to 75 was in all likelihood due to the establishment of the Shanghai Petrochemical General Plant (上海石油化工总厂) in 1972, while the expansion of the metallurgy industry from 1976 to 80 was due to construction starting on the Shanghai Baoshan Steel General Plant (上海宝山钢铁总厂) in 1978 (Wang 1995, pp. 161–162). In any event, if one considers the total of heavy industries such as the machinery, metallurgy, and chemical industries, they account for 48–71% of the total throughout the planned economy period. On the other hand, investment in the textile industry was at a very low level compared to its above-mentioned large share of output value, even in the years when it received a relatively high amount of investment, notably 1950–52, 1953–57, and 1971–75, at about 11%.

This emphasis on heavy industry in Capital Construction Investment by the government can also be seen in Fig. 8.5, which compares the trends in the fixed asset values (depreciated, same hereafter) of the textile and machinery industries based on the specialized gazetteers' data. Looking at the figures, the fixed asset

[6] The rapid expansion of this "other" category was due to an increase in unidentified items (the difference between the total in the original table and the sum of each item), and it is impossible to specify the details.

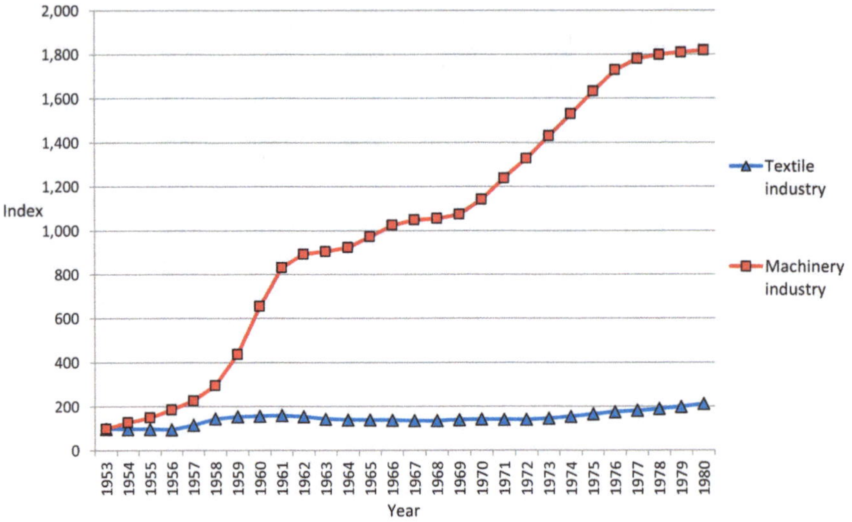

Fig. 8.5 Fixed asset values of Shanghai's textile and machinery industries, 1953–1980. *Notes* (1) 1953 = 100. (2) Fixed asset value here means net annual average value of fixed assets after depreciation. *Sources* Shanghai fangzhigongyezhi bianzuanweiyuanhui (1998, pp. 278–284); Shanghai jidiangongyezhi bianzuanweiyuanhui (1996, pp. 10–14)

value of the machinery industry grew by a factor of 18 from 1953 to 1980, while the textile industry only doubled. This trend in fixed asset values is consistent with the trend in output values of the machinery and textile industries shown in Fig. 8.2. In other words, throughout the planned economy period the production facilities of the machinery industry were expanded with active investment, while investment in the textile industry remained relatively low and the expansion of production facilities was restrained. From another point of view, the implication of these figures is that Shanghai's textile industry maintained its production through being largely dependent on the production facilities developed up through the Republican period, rather than as a result of the sort of government investment that was driving the machinery industry.

On the other hand, what about the profits generated by both industries and their contributions to Shanghai's local public finances? Table 8.5 and Fig. 8.6, based on the specialized gazetteers' data, show the profits of the textile and machinery industries from 1949 to 1980, and what percentage they comprised of the Enterprise Revenue item in the Shanghai Municipal government's fiscal revenue.[7] It should be noted that a certain amount of the profits of both industries was likely allocated to the internal reserves and employee welfare funds of each enterprise, and therefore the ratio of the profit to Shanghai's Enterprise Revenue cannot be considered analogous to a breakdown of Enterprise Revenue by industry in Shanghai. Further, the profits

[7] Unfortunately, it is impossible to compare the profit/production value ratio directly here, as the production value data at current prices is available for neither industry.

of the machinery industry here do not represent the entire machinery industry in Shanghai, due to the issues mentioned above. In that sense, the comparison of profits and Enterprise Revenue here is not intended to be comprehensive, but rather serves to illustrate their relative sizes.

Table 8.5 Enterprise Revenue in Shanghai's local public revenue, and profits of textile and machinery industries, 1950–1978 (Unit: 100 million yuan)

Year	Enterprise Revenue in Shanghai's local public revenue	Textile industry profit	Ratio to Enterprise Revenue (%)	Machinery industry profit	Ratio to Enterprise Revenue (%)
1950	0.01	0.40	3,809.5	0.10	952.4
1951	0.12	0.76	610.4	0.21	168.7
1952	0.28	1.42	510.6	0.38	136.6
1953	0.47	2.22	469.6	1.03	217.9
1954	0.72	2.61	360.3	1.15	158.8
1955	1.07	2.16	201.4	1.43	133.4
1956	1.64	3.04	185.6	1.44	87.9
1957	3.15	4.51	143.1	2.10	66.7
1958	12.34	8.22	66.6	6.25	50.6
1959	58.75	10.80	18.4	11.88	20.2
1960	73.83	9.05	12.3	20.41	27.6
1961	40.52	5.86	14.5	9.13	22.5
1962	27.01	5.54	20.5	4.25	15.7
1963	33.28	7.43	22.3	4.93	14.8
1964	37.10	8.28	22.3	5.72	15.4
1965	39.87	10.48	26.3	7.57	19.0
1966	48.60	11.75	24.2	10.04	20.7
1967	36.20	8.88	24.5	5.73	15.8
1968	40.98	10.66	26.0	6.83	16.7
1969	59.25	13.74	23.2	9.55	16.1
1970	69.12	14.16	20.5	12.24	17.7
1971	81.99	14.14	17.2	14.80	18.1
1972	87.24	15.64	17.9	15.66	17.9
1973	91.46	16.49	18.0	16.45	18.0
1974	92.13	16.20	17.6	16.64	18.1
1975	93.41	16.81	18.0	16.48	17.6
1976	89.48	16.78	18.8	14.62	16.3
1977	100.01	19.30	19.3	14.99	15.0
1978	115.31	22.06	19.1	17.04	14.8

Sources Wang (1995, p. 102), Shanghai fangzhigongyezhi bianzuanweiyuanhui (1998, pp. 278–284) and Shanghai jidiangongyezhi bianzuanweiyuanhui (1996, pp. 10–14)

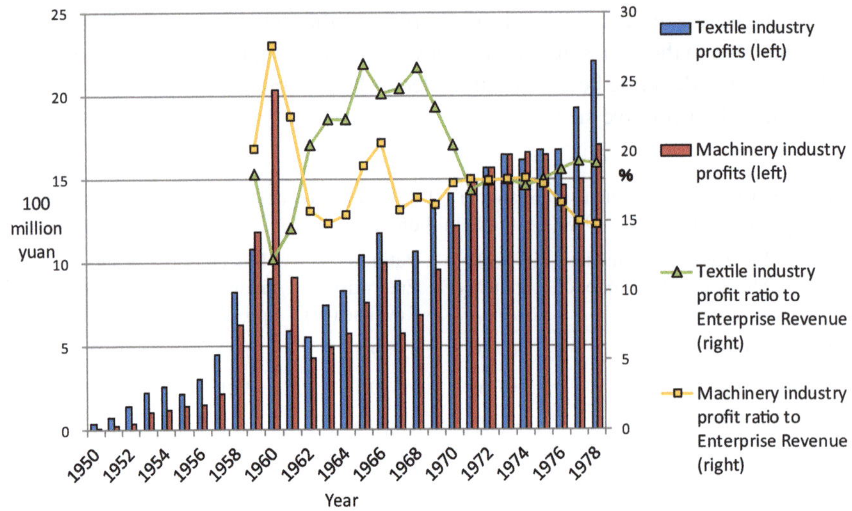

Fig. 8.6 Profits of textile and machinery industries, and ratio to Enterprise Revenue in Shanghai's local public revenue, 1950–1978. *Note* "Textile industry profit ratio to Enterprise Revenue" and "Machinery industry profit ratio to Enterprise Revenue" here only cover after 1959. *Source* Table 8.5

One more point, illustrated in Table 8.5, is that both industries had an extremely high ratio of profits to Enterprise Revenue in Shanghai's local public financial revenue until 1958. Specifically, this exceeded 100% in the textile industry until 1957, and in the machinery industry until 1955. This is because, as seen in Chapters 4 and 7, there were many large-scale state-owned and public-private jointly-owned enterprises affiliated with the central government in Shanghai, and the profits from these essentially belonged to the central government's finances, rather than to Shanghai's local public finances, until the policy of decentralizing central enterprises was implemented in 1958.[8] Conversely, the ratio of the profits of both industries to Shanghai's Enterprise Revenue decreased after 1958 since many central enterprises were "sent down" to Shanghai, which greatly expanded the scale of Shanghai's Enterprise Revenue. As discussed in Chapter 6, in light of the fact that the strong relationships between local governments and local enterprises, which characterized China's socialist system, were established by way of the 1958 policy of sending down central enterprises, the ratio of profits to Shanghai's Enterprise Revenue after 1959 needs to be seen as the actual contribution of both industries to Shanghai's local public finances during the planned economy period.

Considering these statistical issues helps clarify the trends in the profits of both industries and their ratio to Shanghai's Enterprise Revenue after 1959. First, looking at the absolute amount of profit, one notes the difference between the two industries

[8] Of course, it is likely that there existed portions of the profits from both industries that were incorporated into Shanghai's public finances as Enterprise Revenue before 1958. However, the amount and ratio of such are unknown.

falls within about 500 million yuan throughout the planned economy period, although the profit of the machinery industry surged in 1960, recording about twice that of the textile industry, and the gap between the two industries widened in the late 1970s when the textile industry rose. Of course, the machinery industry mentioned here only accounted for about 40–60% of the total output value of the entire machinery industry in Shanghai, and therefore the total profit of the entire machinery industry would be expected to exceed that of the textile industry. Indeed, if one estimates based on the coverage rate of the output value of the specialized gazetteers' data, and assumes a constant ratio of profit to output value, the total profit of the machinery industry can be estimated to have been about twice that of the textile industry.

As for the ratio of the profits of both industries to Shanghai's Enterprise Revenue after 1959, the ratio of the textile industry exceeded or was equal to that of the machinery industry except for the years of 1959–61, 1971, and 1974. However, looking at the upper and lower bounds of the ratio, the textile industry was 12.3–26.0% and the machinery industry 13.4–27.6%, which indicates that both were almost the same width. The total of both industries' ratios came to 33.9–45.3%, and if one assumes the aforementioned profit of the entire machinery industry, it generally came to about half or more of Shanghai's Enterprise Revenue. As already mentioned, the profit of these two industries does not directly indicate the breakdown of Shanghai's Enterprise Revenue, but it nevertheless makes it possible to estimate the rough scale of the contribution of both industries to Shanghai's local public finances.

Finally, Fig. 8.7 shows the ratio of profits to fixed assets for both industries by combining the profits data from Table 8.5 with the fixed asset data from Fig. 8.5. The profit-fixed asset ratio indicates how much profit each industry generated per unit of fixed assets, demonstrating the efficiency of fixed asset utilization. The first thing that stands out in Fig. 8.7 is the extremely high ratio of the machinery industry during the Great Leap Forward period of 1958–60. Looking back at Fig. 8.5, the amount of fixed assets in the machinery industry surged during the same period, but the increase in profits, shown in Fig. 8.6, was even more remarkable. However, the subsequent decline was also rapid, suggesting that this was a transient change associated with the increase in production quotas due to the Great Leap Forward policy. A similar trend can be seen in the textile industry during the same period.

What is more noteworthy is that the gap between the ratio of the two industries had been widening since the 1960s, as the ratio in the textile industry had been continually rising while that of the machinery industry fell stagnant. In the trend of fixed asset amounts for both industries, shown in Fig. 8.4, the textile industry showed a slight increase in the late 1970s, but no major changes, while the machinery industry continued to increase, particularly in the early 1970s. Considering these trends in fixed asset amounts of both industries, it is evident that the textile industry was generating profits by improving the utilization efficiency of existing facilities while simultaneously restraining the expansion of production facilities. By contrast, the machinery industry, while having its production facilities expanded through aggressive investment, saw no significant improvement in the efficiency of fixed asset utilization, and so remained at about the same level as it had been in the 1950s.

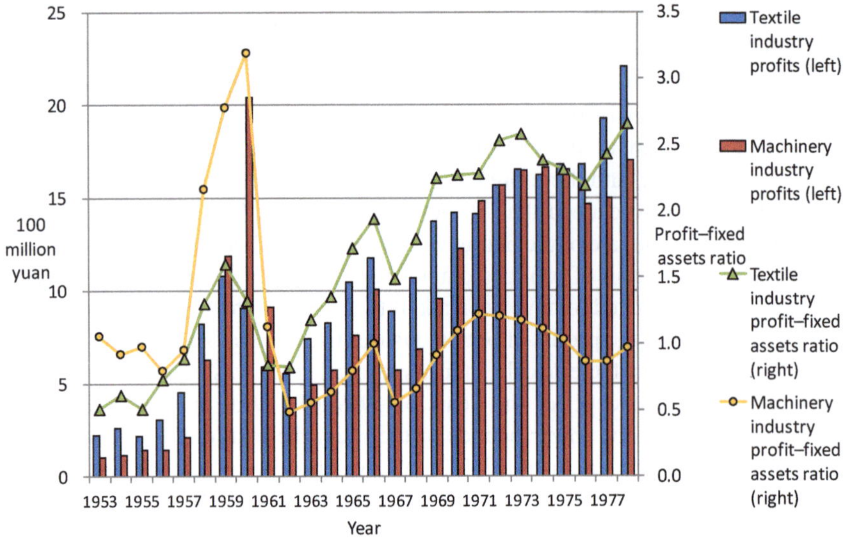

Fig. 8.7 Profits and profit-fixed assets ratio of textile and machinery industries in Shanghai, 1953–1978. *Note* Fixed assets are depreciated value and mid-term value, which is calculated to average the year-end value and the previous year-end value in the original data. *Sources* Shanghai fangzhigongyezhi bianzuanweiyuanhui (1998, pp. 278–284), Shanghai jidiangongyezhi bianzuanweiyuanhui (1996, pp. 10–14), and Kajima (2022, p. 197)

Regarding these trends in the capital efficiency of the textile and machinery industries in Shanghai, Marukawa (2000a)'s analysis of the capital-output ratio of the light and heavy industries based on national-level data suggests that this same tendency was occurring nationwide.[9] Marukawa points out that there was a trend of increasing the capital-output ratio (i.e., a decrease in capital efficiency) in the heavy industry, while at the same time there occurred a decrease (i.e., increasing capital efficiency) in the light industry. In the examination of the profit-fixed asset ratio of the textile and machinery industries in Shanghai in this section, the deterioration of efficiency in the machinery industry was not clearly discernible, but the improvement of efficiency in the textile industry was readily apparent. In particular, the improvement in performance in terms of profits, which directly contributed to the Shanghai Municipal Government's local public finances, indicates that the textile industry was a reliable industry that consistently provided returns with minimal investment for the government. In this sense, the significance of light industry, represented by the textile industry that had already been developing since the Republican period, should not be underestimated, even while at the time the government was emphasizing the development of heavy industry under the Heavy-industry-priority Strategy.

[9] Marukawa (2000a, pp. 19–23). Unfortunately, it was not possible to analyze the capital-output ratio of either industry in this section since the output value data at current prices is unavailable for either for the planned economy period.

This chapter has examined the development of the textile and machinery industries, which were central industries in Shanghai during the planned economy period, based on the trajectories of their historical development and through utilizing various bodies of available statistical data. These two industries were major industrial forces that all but monopolized the first- and second-rank positions in terms of output value share in Shanghai during the planned economy period, and their profits also represented major contributions, amounting to anywhere from 10% to nearly 30% of Shanghai's Enterprise Revenue from 1959 onward. However, the development of the two industries followed significantly different paths. The analysis in this chapter revealed how the machinery industry, which expanded its production scale and became a leading industry in Shanghai, was backed by abundant investment in the course of the transition from light to heavy industry, whereas the textile industry maintained production using existing facilities despite relatively limited investment by the government.

The trajectory of development of Shanghai's machinery industry embodied the industrialization of heavy industry under the socialist system. Under the overall policy of the Heavy-industry-priority Strategy, the demand for machinery products increased rapidly, while the import of foreign products was restricted due to changes in the international environment. The machinery industry in Shanghai, which had already established a significant foundation by the Republican period, took on the role of domestic manufacture of an increasing array of machinery products. The intensive investment in the machinery industry in Shanghai was understood as a means of bridging the gap between the state of development of China's machinery industry up until 1949 and the Heavy-industry-priority Strategy adopted afterward.

On the other hand, the textile industry consistently pursued a policy of saving new investment and utilizing its legacy of Republican-era development as much as possible. Under this policy, as shown by the analysis in this chapter, the textile industry was able to efficiently generate profit. This policy was based on the premise that China's textile industry, centered on Shanghai, had already basically achieved import substitution until 1949. In other words, there was the prospect that domestic demand could be met just by efficiently utilizing existing facilities without expanding the production scale with new investment. Moreover, even if the equipment degraded and the technology became obsolete internationally, it would not have been a major problem provided that the sales market was domestically focused and the government's supply monopoly was maintained under the socialist system.[10] The trajectory of development of the textile industry was thus significantly different from the style of development that it had pursued in the face of international competition through the Republican period. In that sense, despite the lack of investment the development of the textile industry was itself also strongly influenced by the introduction of the socialist system and the promotion of the Heavy-industry-priority Strategy.

---

[10] Cotton products were exported during the planned economy period, but they were produced separately from products for the domestic market. See Kubo (2011).

References

English Language

Brasó Broggi, Carles. 2016. *Trade and Technology Networks in the Chinese Textile Industry: Opening Up Before the Reform*. New York: Palgrave Macmillan US. https://doi.org/10.1057/9781137494054

Cliver, Robert. 2020. *Red Silk: Class, Gender, and Revolution in China's Yangzi Delta Silk Industry*. Cambridge, Massachusetts: Harvard University Asia Center. https://doi.org/10.1353/book.113528

Kajima, Jun. 2022. Light Industry: Socialist Industrialization and Textile Industry. In *Studies on the Chinese Economy During the Mao Era*, ed. Katsuji Nakagane, 187–204. Singapore: Springer, Singapore. https://doi.org/10.1007/978-981-19-5410-8_9

Peng, Juanjuan. 2020. *The Yudahua Business Group in China's Early Industrialization*. Lanham, Maryland: Lexington Books

Chinese Language

Dangdai zhongguo congshu bianjibu, ed. 1984. *Dangdai zhongguo de fangzhigongye* (当代中国的纺织工业, Contemporary China's Textile Industry). Beijing: Zhongguo shehuikexue chubanshe

Dangdai zhongguo congshu bianjibu, ed. 1990. *Dangdai zhongguo de jixiegongye* (当代中国的机械工业, Contemporary China's Machinery Industry), Volume I & II. Beijing: Zhongguo shehuikexue chubanshe

Guojia tongjiju gongyejiaotongwuzi tongjisi, ed. 1985. *Zhongguo gongyejingji tongjiziliao 1949–1984* (中国工业经济统计资料1949–1984, China Industrial Economic Statistical Data 1949–1984). Beijing: Zhongguo tongji chubanshe

Shanghai fangzhigongyezhi bianzuanweiyuanhui, ed. 1998. *Shanghai fangzhigongyezhi* (上海纺织工业志, Shanghai Textile Industry Chronicle). Shanghai: Shanghai shehuikexueyuan chubanshe

Shanghai jidiangongyezhi bianzuanweiyuanhui, ed. 1996. *Shanghai jidiangongyezhi* (上海机电工业志, Shanghai Machinery and Electrical Industry Chronicle). Shanghai: Shanghai shehuikexueyuan chubanshe

Shanghaishi tongjiju, ed. 1992. *Xinshanghai gongyetongjiziliao: 1949–1990* (新上海工业统计资料 (1949–1990), New Shanghai Industrial Statistical Data: 1949–1990). Beijing: Zhongguo tongjichubanshe

Wang, Weiquan, ed. 1995. *Shanghai caizhengshuiwuzhi* (上海财政税务志, Shanghai Fiscal and Taxation Chronicle). Shanghai: Shanghai shehuikexueyuan chubanshe

Zhonghuarenmingongheguo guojiatongjiju gongyetongjisi, ed. 1958. *Woguo gangtie dianli meitan jixie fangzhi zaozhi gongye de jinxi* (我国钢铁、电力、煤炭、机械、纺织、造纸工业的今昔, Past and Present of Our Country's Steel, Electricity, Coal, Machinery, Textile, and Paper Industries). Beijing: Tongji chubanshe

Japanese Language

Kojima, Reiitsu, ed. 1989. *Chūgoku keizaitōkei keizaihō kaisetsu* (中国経済統計・経済法解説, Explanation of Chinese Economic Statistics and Economic Law). Tokyo: Institute of Developing Economies

Kubo, Tōru. 2011. 1950 nendai no chūgoku mengyō to zaikabō gijutsu (1950年代の中国綿業と在華紡技術, China's Cotton Industry in the 1950s and the Technological legacy of Japanese Cotton Companies in China). In *Kindai chūgoku wo ikita nikkei kigyō* (近代中国を生きた日系企業, Japanese Companies in Modern China), eds. Tomizawa Yoshia, Kubo Tōru, Hagiwara Mitsuru, 93–115. Suita: Osaka University Press

Kubo, Tōru, Kajima Jun, Kigoshi Yoshinori. 2016. *Tōkei de miru chūgoku kingendai keizaishi* (統計でみる中国近現代経済史, Economic History of Modern China: An Approach Based on Statistical data). Tokyo: University of Tokyo Press

Marukawa, Tomoo, ed. 2000a. *Ikōki chūgoku no sangyōseisaku* (移行期中国の産業政策, China's Industrial Policy in Transition). Chiba: Institute of Developing Economies. http://hdl.handle.net/2344/00012460

Marukawa, Tomoo, ed. 2000b. *Chūgoku sangyō handobukku 2001–2002 nenban* (中国産業ハンドブック 2001-2002年版, China Industry Handbook 2001–2002 Edition). Machida: Sōsōsha

Onoe, Etsuzō. 1971. *Chūgoku no sangyō ricchi ni kansuru kenkyū* (中国の産業立地に関する研究, Study on Industrial Location in China). Tokyo: Institute of Developing Economies

Ou, Eilin. 2009. *Chūgoku bōshokukikaiseizougyō no kibankeisei: gijutsuiten to nishikawa akiji* (中国紡織機械製造業の基盤形成——技術移転と西川秋次, The Formation of China's Textile Machinery Manufacturing Industry: Technology Transfer and Akiji Nishikawa). Tokyo: Gakujutsu shuppankai

Chapter 9
The Restructuring of Industrial Organization: The Rubber Processing Industry

Abstract This chapter focuses on Shanghai's rubber processing industry in order to illustrate the change in industrial organization, which had originally been decentralized, before and after 1949, especially through examining the process of the socialist transformation. Shanghai's rubber processing industry prior to 1949 was characterized by a few large companies capable of producing automobile tires coexisting alongside countless small and medium-sized enterprises with simple facilities and small capital scales due to the comparatively low technical barriers to entry for products such as rubber shoes and other miscellaneous goods. Even after the reorganization following the Second World War and the Chinese Communist Party takeover in 1949, private enterprises continued to make up the core of the rubber processing industry, and there was no significant expansion of state-owned or public-private jointly-owned enterprises in this area. The chapter sheds light on how Shanghai's rubber processing industry was reorganized by changes in the international environment in the early 1950s, at precisely the same time that the socialist system was being established.

Keywords Industrial organization · Light industry · Rubber processing industry · Socialist transformation

The previous chapter dealt with the textile and machinery industries, which were the main industries in Shanghai during the planned economy period. This chapter, adopting a slightly different perspective, will turn to examine the restructuring of industrial organizations, by focusing on the case of the rubber processing industry, which had played a key role in the development of light industry during the Republican period.[1]

One of the main reasons for focusing on the rubber processing industry in this chapter is because of the insights that it can offer due to the characteristics of its market structure. Shanghai was known as the center of China's rubber processing industry, with numerous companies concentrated there. The industry generated a

[1] This chapter is based on Kajima (2005) and Jiadao (2007) with additions and revisions.

J. Kajima, *Shanghai under the Socialist System*, Studies in Economic History,
https://doi.org/10.1007/978-981-95-3225-4_9

wide range of products, including rubber shoes, tires and tubes for bicycles, rickshaws[2] and automobiles, and rubber belts. Among these, although the manufacture of automobile tires required a significantly high level of technology, the technical barriers to entry for other products, especially rubber shoes and other miscellaneous goods, were comparatively low, making the industry accessible to new entrants. Consequently, the industry became characterized by a few large companies capable of producing automobile tires coexisting alongside countless small and medium-sized enterprises with simple facilities and small capital scales, which were sensitive to market conditions and underwent a process of increases and decreases over time. Even after the reorganization following the Second World War and the CCP takeover in 1949, private enterprises made up the core of the rubber processing industry, and there was no significant expansion of state-owned or public-private jointly-owned enterprises. In this respect, the industry had markedly different characteristics from the textile industry, which had a portion of its production facilities nationalized or turned into state-owned (e.g., China Textile Construction Company) or public-private jointly-owned enterprises before and after 1949. However, at the same time the rubber processing industry's case was typical of Shanghai's light industries in at least one respect, namely the large number of small and medium-sized enterprises.[3]

Two other important factors to consider are the extent to which the Chinese rubber processing industry depended on overseas raw materials, and the value of rubber products as military supplies. In the first case, the raw material for the rubber processing industry, raw rubber itself (i.e., natural rubber), was not produced in China, and the industry therefore relied entirely on imports from Southeast Asia and other regions. Consequently, the rubber processing industry was enormously influenced by the import situation of raw rubber. This was strongly bound up with the developments following the outbreak of the Korean War in 1950, discussed in Chapter 4, leading to the implementation of material control. As for the second point, rubber products were also used as military supplies in the form of military shoes and raincoats, and the increase in military demand due to China's participation in the Korean War changed the supply system of the rubber processing industry. In these respects, the rubber processing industry was an industry that was profoundly affected by changes in the international environment in the early 1950s, at precisely the same time that the socialist system was being established. For all these reasons, the rubber processing industry can be an insightful case for shedding light on the development of industry in Shanghai and the context within which this occurred.

Regarding studies of the rubber processing industry in Shanghai, there are already specialized materials such as Shanghaishi gongshangxingzhengguanliju and Shanghaishi xiangjiaogongyegongsi shiliaogongzuozu (1979) and Shanghai xiangjiaogongyezhi bianzuanweiyuanhui (2000). Although such works provide a plethora

[2] The original Chinese term is "力车轮胎," which was something of a broad concept that included not only bicycles and rickshaws, but also tricycles and hand carts (Shanghai xiangjiaogongyezhi bianzuanweiyuanhui 2000, pp. 188–191).

[3] For example, on the prevalence of small and medium-sized enterprises in the chemical industry, including the rubber processing industry, see Kajima (2005).

of useful basic information, they pay little attention to the historical changes in industrial organization before and after 1949 since their primary concern is with focusing on the processes of state control, increases in production, and improvements in productivity pertaining to industrial development after the establishment of the PRC. Therefore, this chapter also aims to fill this lacuna by examining the historical changes in the industrial organization of the rubber processing industry, focusing on the characteristics outlined above.

9.1 The Rubber Processing Industry in Shanghai

9.1.1 The Birth and Development of Shanghai's Rubber Processing Industry

It is apt to begin this section with an overview of the process of development of Shanghai's rubber processing industry.[4] The first rubber processing company in Shanghai was the Chinese Manufacturing Rubber Co., Ltd. (中华製造橡皮有限公司), established by two overseas Chinese brothers in Japan, Rong Zhusan (容祝三) and Rong Ziguang (容子光), in 1919. Under the favorable market conditions of cheap raw rubber and high prices for rubber processed products, the Shanghai rubber processing industry entered a period of rapid development (1925–1931). In particular, the Shanghai Yichang Rubber Goods Manufacturing Factory (上海义昌橡皮物品製造厂), established by Liu Yongkang (刘永康) and Shi Zhishan (石芝珊) in 1927 (and later renamed the Zhengtai Xinji Rubber Factory [正泰信记橡胶厂], abbreviated as Zhengtai Rubber Factory [正泰橡胶厂], in 1934), became a major company famous for its "Warrior" (回力) brand of rubber shoes and tires. Then there was the Dazhonghua Rubber Factory (大中华橡胶厂), established by Yu Zhiqing (余芝卿), Xue Fujii (薛福基), and Wu Zhesheng (吴哲生) in 1928, which launched the "Double Coin" (双钱) brand and succeeded in manufacturing China's first automobile tires in 1934, becoming the largest rubber processing company in China. In addition to these two major companies, many small and medium-sized companies were established in Shanghai, and by 1933, Shanghai's rubber processing companies accounted for 48 out of 74 nationwide, making it a major hub for the industry (Chūshikensetsushiryō seibiiinkai 1940, pp. 38–39). The main market for these companies was domestic areas such as Jiangsu, Zhejiang, Hunan, Hubei, Jiangxi, and so on, with almost no exports. Rubber shoes in particular, as the main product of the industry, had a significant market in both cities and rural areas across China.

When tracing the development of Shanghai's rubber processing industry, it is impossible to ignore the relationship with its counterpart in Japan, for Japan's rubber processing industry had an important impact in various ways. Almost all

---

[4] The following overview is primarily based on the descriptions given in Shanghaishi gongshangxingzhengguanliju and Shanghaishi xiangjiaogongyegongsi shiliaogongzuozu (1979, pp. 1–40).

of the prominent managers of rubber processing companies in Shanghai were originally merchants called "Dongyangzhuang" (东洋庄), which specialized in importing Japanese products for sale in China. Having gained experience in importing rubber products from Japan, many of them began to invest in the rubber processing industry in Shanghai. Furthermore, many companies imported production equipment from Japan and hired Japanese technicians when setting up their rubber processing factories. On the other hand, China was also a major market for Japan's own rubber processing industry. According to 1936 statistics, Japanese products accounted for 45.3% of China's total 155,528 imported automobile tires (including tubes), 85.6% of its 1,141,415 bicycle and rickshaw tires, and 94.4% of its 5,592,150 pairs of rubber shoes (including rubber-soled shoes).[5] The situation for China's own industry worsened after 1932, as many Chinese small and medium-sized factories were forced to stop production or close due to intensified competition with Japanese products. Clearly, Japanese rubber products were the biggest rivals for Shanghai's rubber processing industry in the 1920s and 1930s, and large Chinese companies like Dazhonghua and Zhengtai worked to grow sustainably through competition with Japanese products.

With the outbreak of the Second Sino-Japanese War in July 1937 and the Japanese military occupation of Shanghai on August 13 of the same year, Japanese companies advanced into Shanghai's rubber processing industry, backed by military power, seizing and merging Chinese rubber processing factories. Some Chinese rubber processing factories continued to operate under the economic control of the Japanese army. For example, Zhengtai Rubber Factory tied up with a Japanese company, Aikelong Trading Company (爱克隆洋行), and was reorganized into the Aikelong Trading Company Rubber Department (爱克隆洋行橡胶部) to continue production.[6] Other Chinese companies evacuated inland, such as the fourth factory of Dazhonghua, which was relocated to Chongqing, the wartime capital of the National Government, via Wuhan.[7]

In this way, the Shanghai rubber processing industry, from its beginnings among pioneering rubber product import merchants, had achieved a considerable degree of development by 1945. The relationship with the Japanese rubber processing industry played a particularly important role in this process, and therefore, when the war concluded in 1945 and the Japanese rubber processing industry withdrew from China and East Asia as a whole, it heralded the beginning of a new era for the Shanghai rubber processing industry.

---

[5] Shanghaishi gongshangxingzhengguanliju and Shanghaishi xiangjiaogongyegongsi shiliaogongzuozu (1979, pp. 34, 115). It is notable that the amount of imports from Japan included products from British capital factories in Japan (Chūshikensetsushiryō seibiiinkai 1940, pp. 60–61).

[6] Subsequently, due to the reorganization of the Aikelong Trading Company (爱克隆洋行) into the Continental Trading Company (大陆洋行), it was renamed the Rubber Department of the Continental Trading Company (Shanghaishi gongshangxingzhengguanliju and Shanghaishi xiangjiaogongyegongsi shiliaogongzuozu 1979, pp. 51–52).

[7] As for the evacuation of factories in Shanghai inland during the Second Sino-Japanese War, refer to Sun (1991, pp. 52–60), and Wu (2001, pp. 5–25).

9.1.2 *The Shanghai Rubber Processing Industry in the Postwar Period*

On the eve of the end of the Second World War, there were 35 Chinese rubber processing factories in Shanghai (Shanghaishi gongshangxingzhengguanliju and Shanghaishi xiangjiaogongyegongsi shiliaogongzuozu 1979, p. 53). Alongside these, there were the former Japanese-owned rubber processing factories, which were confiscated by the Shanghai Municipal Government on October 24, 1945, based on the "Regulation on Handling Former Enemy Industries in Shanghai District" (上海区敌伪产业处理办法) promulgated by the National Government. In total 21 rubber processing factories were confiscated in Shanghai, but these were generally small in scale. Besides the Daito Rubber Industry Company (大東護謨工業株式会社) and the China Electric Industry Company (中華電気工業株式会社) being confiscated by the National Government, others such as the International Rubber Goods Machinery Factory (万国橡皮品机器厂), Shanghai Meiji Industrial Company (上海明治産業株式会社), and the Hankou Rubber Industry Shanghai Branch (漢口護謨工業所上海支店) were returned to their original owners, while the remaining 16 factories were put up for auction (Shanghaishi gongshangxingzhengguanliju and Shanghaishi xiangjiaogongyegongsi shiliaogongzuozu 1979, pp. 55, 57–58).

The auction of these former Japanese-owned factories became an opportunity for large Chinese companies such as Dazhonghua and Zhengtai to further expand the scale of their businesses. Dazhonghua Rubber Factory bought several factories and became the largest rubber processing company in the country by 1948, owning 6 manufacturing factories, 5 raw material processing factories, 1 machinery repair factory, 1 machinery repair workshop, and 1 packaging workshop. Zhengtai Rubber Factory founded the Shanghai Rubber Factory (上海橡胶厂), which was confiscated by the National Government's Ministry of Transportation's Automobile Equipment General Warehouse (国民政府交通部汽车器材总库), a second factory, and bought Tongyong Rubber Factory (通用橡胶厂) and Minfeng Paper Factory (民丰纸厂) to form a third factory and a calcium carbonate manufacturing facility, respectively (Shanghaishi gongshangxingzhengguanliju and Shanghaishi xiangjiaogongyegongsi shiliaogongzuozu 1979, p. 55). At the same time, both companies reorganized their sales offices and distribution centers (that is, their wholesale bases) formed before and during the war and expanded their sales networks nationwide. For example, Dazhonghua Rubber Factory rebuilt and newly established distribution centers in Nanjing, Wenzhou, Guangzhou, Hangzhou, Tianjin, and Taipei (Shuangqian xiongfeng bianweihui 1993, p. 34; Qian 1994, pp. 48–50). As a result, Dazhonghua's network expanded nationwide, as shown in Fig. 9.1.

Looking at the changes in the production volume of the main products of Dazhonghua Rubber Factory from 1928 to 1949 shown in Table 9.1 reveals that production increased significantly after the Second World War. The basic factor behind this increase in production was the postwar reconstruction demand. Previous studies have emphasized that the Shanghai rubber processing industry was hit by the

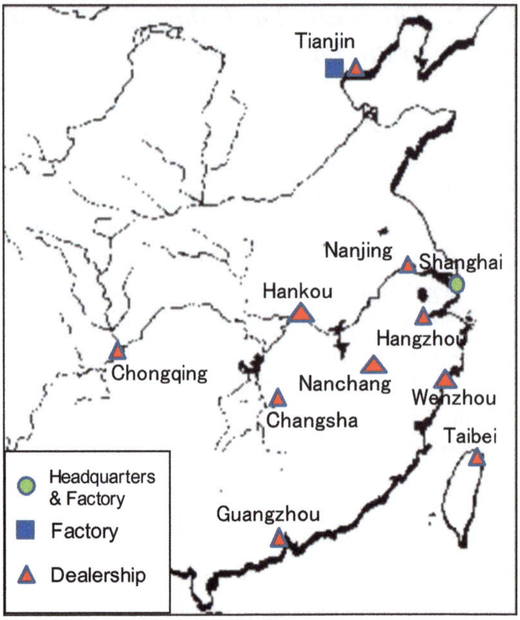

Fig. 9.1 Networks of Dazhonghua Rubber Factory, 1948. *Sources* Map created by author based on Shuangqian xiongfeng bianweihui (1993, p. 34)

massive import of automobile tires from the US after the war (Shanghaishi gongshangxingzhengguanliju and Shanghaishi xiangjiaogongyegongsi shiliaogongzuozu 1979, pp. 59–60). However, the impact of this would actually have been limited, since the production volume of automobile tires by Dazhonghua Rubber Factory, which was almost the only automobile tire manufacturer in Shanghai at that time, clearly exceeded its prewar peak level in 1947.[8] As for the increased production of main products such as bicycle and rickshaw tires and rubber shoes, one of the major factors at work there was the exit of Japanese products after the war, which presented Chinese companies with a vast market in contrast to the situation before the war when, as outlined above, rubber product imports from Japan were truly enormous in scale. At any rate, overall, Dazhonghua Rubber Factory significantly expanded its production scale compared to before the war.

On the other hand, this prosperity after the Second World War characterized not only large corporations like Dazhonghua, but also the rubber processing industry as a whole, as evidenced by the establishment of numerous small and medium-sized rubber processing factories one after another in the early postwar years. The proliferation of these small and medium-sized factories further increased the number of companies in the Shanghai rubber processing industry compared to the situation before the war. As of May 1949, there were 95 companies and 106 factories in the Shanghai rubber processing industry appearing in the statistics, a major increase from the 35 factories that had existed in 1945. Looking at the distribution of the number of rubber manufacturing mixers, the core unit of production equipment, out of a total

[8] Zhengtai Rubber Factory started producing automobile tires in 1947 (Qian 1994, pp. 40–43).

Table 9.1 Production of Dazhonghua Rubber Factory, 1928–1949

Year	Rubber shoes (10 thousands)	Tires and tubes for bicycles and rickshaws (10 thousands)		Tires and tubes for automobiles (10 thousands)	
		Tires	Tubes	Tires	Tubes
1928	5.63	-	-	-	-
1929	109.05	-	-	-	-
1930	300.00	-	-	-	-
1931	638.02	-	-	-	-
1932	604.55	-	-	-	-
1933	755.16	-	-	-	-
1934	666.17	0.95	-	-	-
1935	642.76	6.34	4.23	0.69	0.37
1936	874.63	19.40	14.64	1.47	1.17
1937	871.24	27.12	15.76	1.81	1.75
1938	818.16	24.95	30.51	0.73	0.69
1939	742.08	33.34	38.73	0.80	0.64
1940	559.13	40.30	32.84	0.75	0.67
1941	665.52	38.67	25.00	0.80	0.59
1942	117.21	16.87	13.12	0.03	0.01
1943	83.04	6.84	9.27	0.15	0.18
1944	17.15	5.72	5.63	0.66	0.70
1945	37.75	7.34	6.84	0.21	0.29
1946	605.27	34.00	28.82	1.37	1.05
1947	1,182.80	54.11	57.77	2.71	2.70
1948	1,132.26	48.62	57.19	2.29	2.43
1949	647.90	27.16	21.86	0.59	0.52

Source Shuangqian xiongfeng bianweihui (1993, pp. 270–273)

of 497 units in all factories, Dazhonghua Rubber Factory had 93 units, Zhengtai Rubber Factory 63 units, and Hongda Rubber Factory (宏大橡胶厂) 28 units. The rest were spread across 4 companies with 11–20 units, 15 companies with 6–10 units, and 73 companies with 1–5 units (Shanghaishi gongshangxingzhengguanliju and Shanghaishi xiangjiaogongyegongsi shiliaogongzuozu 1979, pp. 53, 73). While the large scale of the Dazhonghua and Zhengtai operations is immediately noticeable, what also should be noted is the large number of small-scale companies with 1–5 mixers.

Previous studies have viewed this proliferation of small and medium-sized enterprises as the product of blind and speculative development, emphasizing that this trend was a "fictitious prosperity" (Shanghaishi gongshangxingzhengguanliju and Shanghaishi xiangjiaogongyegongsi shiliaogongzuozu 1979, p. 54). Although the increase in these companies may have been fueled to some degree by speculation under the postwar inflation, the more important factor was companies responding to the aforementioned market expansion in the wake of the withdrawal of Japanese products after the war. Looking at the share of rubber shoe production in Shanghai from available sources, the share of the three major companies, Dazhonghua, Zhengtai, and Hongda, came to 37.68% of the total 18,854,571 pairs of rubber shoes produced in Shanghai from August to October 1947 (with the percentage for bicycle and rickshaw tires being 79.33%, and that for automobile tires being 100%), which is no doubt substantial (Shanghaishi gongshangxingzhengguanliju and Shanghaishi xiangjiaogongyegongsi shiliaogongzuozu 1979, p. 74). However, this means that other small and medium-sized enterprises produced the remaining 62.32%, and collectively were therefore significant producers in the rubber shoe market. In the context of the withdrawal of Japanese products and postwar reconstruction demand, there was a certain inevitability to the establishment of small and medium-sized enterprises, and it would not be accurate to simply view this as "fictitious prosperity."

To sum up, the Shanghai rubber processing industry after the war was expanding its production scale against the backdrop of postwar reconstruction demand, while the number of companies was greatly increasing due to the establishment of small and medium-sized enterprises.

9.2 The Influence of Governmental Economic Control in the Early 1950s

9.2.1 Governmental Control Over Raw Rubber Distribution

As already mentioned, the total number of companies in the Shanghai rubber processing industry was 95 (106 factories) at the time of the occupation of Shanghai by the People's Liberation Army in May 1949. Of these, the only rubber processing companies owned by the National Government were the Central Electric Equipment Factory Shanghai Manufacturing Factory under the Resource Committee (资源委员会中央电工器材厂上海制造厂) and the Central Processing Factory (中央加工厂), both of which were seized by the PRC government along with the rubber processing workshop of the Chinese Nationalist Party Navy Shanghai Factory (国民党海军上海工厂) (Shanghaishi gongshangxingzhengguanliju and Shanghaishi xiangjiaogongyegongsi shiliaogongzuozu 1979, p. 173). Subsequently, private rubber processing factories such as Dafu (大孚), Hongxing (红星), Zhenxin (振新), Shisheng (实生), Yuehua (越华), and Weili (威力) were either seized or purchased by the Shanghai Municipal Government, and became central or local state-owned enterprises (Shanghai xiangjiaogongyezhi bianzuanweiyuanhui 2000, pp. 50–51). However, in spite of these developments the proportion of state-owned enterprises in the Shanghai rubber processing industry remained relatively low in 1949, with the bulk of the industry still comprised of private enterprises.

As for the environment surrounding the rubber processing industry in Shanghai, the biggest change that occurred around the time of regime change from 1948 to 1950 was a reduction in the supply of raw rubber in the market. The surge in raw rubber prices in China had already begun in 1948, and subsequently, the market price of raw rubber rose significantly due to causes such as the naval blockade by the Chinese Nationalist Party in 1949, the outbreak of the Korean War in June 1950, and the US trade restrictions on China in December 1950. As shown in Fig. 4.1, the price of raw rubber in Shanghai began to soar rapidly from May 1950, and continued to rise at a pace far exceeding the general price index until November of that same year. This surge in raw rubber prices prompted a government response, and as discussed in Chapter 4, the Shanghai Military Control Committee and the Shanghai Municipal Government promulgated the "Temporary Measures for Strengthening Market Management and Cracking Down on Speculation" (关于加强市场管理取缔投机的暂行办法) on December 18 in 1950, and began to control prices and materials.[9] After that, rubber prices fell, then rose again, and then began to relatively stabilize from June 1951.

This stabilization of raw rubber prices was related to the governmental policy controlling raw rubber. Looking at Fig. 9.2, which shows the amount of raw rubber imported, it is clear that the volume of imports in 1950–51 reached 1–2 times that of the 1945–49 period when the rubber processing industry was booming, and even exceeded the import volume of Japan at that time. Although China's import volume declined in 1952 in the wake of the US embargo policy against China, it recovered in 1953, likely due mainly to the agreement between the Chinese government and the Ceylon government on the barter of rice and rubber in 1952, whereby the nations decided that China would exchange 270,000 tons of rice for 50,000 tons of raw rubber annually for five years from 1953 to 1957.[10] Considering that the annual import volume of raw rubber in the Republican period was generally around 20,000 tons (the highest point having been 38,900 tons in 1947), this 50,000 tons was a truly large number and essentially met the raw material demand of China's rubber processing industry at the time. Moreover, the sudden increase in China's raw rubber imports in 1956 was attributed to the fact that the British government, which had consistently argued that the US trade restriction policy against China was unreasonable, lifted the trade ban on the Federation of Malaya against China in May 1956 (Hibino 1956). These government-led developments involving the import of raw rubber since 1952 brought about the stabilization of raw rubber prices in China, while also contributing to governmental reinforcement of control over raw rubber distribution.

---

[9] "Temporary Measures for Strengthening Market Management and Cracking Down on Speculation" (关于加强市场管理取缔投机的暂行办法), Zhongguokexueyuan shanghaijingjiyanjiusuo and Shanghaishehuikexueyuan jingjiyanjiusuo (1958, pp. 574–575).

[10] "Five-year Trade Agreement between the Central People's Government of the People's Republic of China and the Government of Ceylon on Rubber and Rice" (中华人民共和国中央人民政府锡兰政府关于橡胶和大米的五年贸易协定), December 18, 1952, Zhongguoshehuikexueyuan and Zhongyangdanganguan (1994, pp. 557–560).

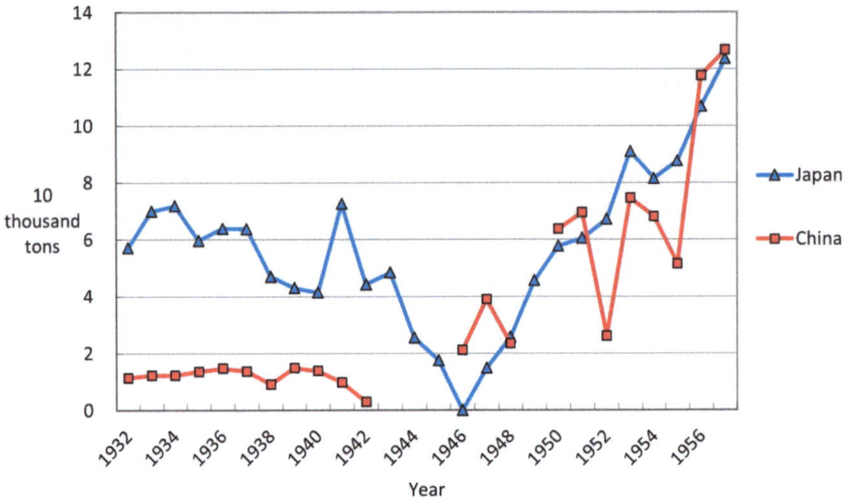

Fig. 9.2 Raw rubber imports of China and Japan, 1932–1957. *Notes* (1) China's rubber imports from 1940 to 1942 and from 1946 to 1948 include reclaimed rubber, old rubber, and other raw rubbers. (2) Data for China's imports from 1943 to 1945 and for 1949 is unavailable. (3) China's imports from 1932 to 1945 do not include the imports of Manchukuo. *Sources* China, 1932–1948: Shanghaishi gongshangxingzhengguanliju and Shanghaishi xiangjiaogongyegongsi shiliao-gongzuozu (1979, pp. 32–33, 44, 59). Original data from the "Chinese Maritime Customs Service, Shanghai;" China, 1950–1957: Zhongguo duiwaijingjimaoyinianjian bianjiweiyuanhui (1984), p. IV–115; Japan, 1932–1950: Nihon gomu kōgyōkai (1969), Appendix 1, p. 105. Original data from the "Annual Return of Foreign Trade of Japan;" Japan, 1951–1957: Nihon gomu kōgyōkai (1971), Appendix 1, p. 34. Original data from the "Annual Return of Foreign Trade of Japan" and the "Monthly Report on Foreign Trade of Japan."

9.2.2 Governmental Monopolization of Product Sales Channels

With the government controlling the raw rubber supply, the relationship between the Shanghai rubber processing industry and the government gradually became closer through the processing order policy discussed in Chapters 3 and 4. Table 9.2 tracks the changes in the production volume of the Shanghai rubber processing industry during the planned economy period. It illustrates how the production volume of major products increased in 1951, and despite experiencing occasional short-term decreases continued overall to increase until the late 1950s. The surge in tires and tubes for automobiles in 1951 is particularly remarkable.

The basic cause of this increase in production in the early 1950s can be attributed to the reconstruction demand following the civil war on the one hand, and the increase in military demand on the other. As seen in Chapter 4, rubber products such as tires, shoes, and raincoats were essential military supplies, and the participation of the Chinese Volunteer Army in the Korean War created an enormous demand for such products. In order to secure sufficient military supplies, the amount of processing

Table 9.2 Production of rubber processing industry in Shanghai, 1949–1978

Year	Rubber shoes (10 thousands)	Tires for bicycles and rickshaws (10 thousands)	Tires for automobiles (10 thousands)	Tubes for automobiles (10 thousands)
1949	2,302	60.0	0.8	0.6
1950	2,071	55.0	0.9	0.9
1951	3,199	64.3	7.2	7.5
1952	2,827	77.4	7.7	7.4
1953	4,470	116.8	7.5	7.0
1954	4,321	125.1	10.5	8.5
1955	4,909	123.5	8.7	7.4
1956	5,344	153.5	15.2	14.2
1957	6,627	206.8	16.0	15.7
1958	8,398	424.8	33.1	32.9
1959	6,101	380.8	49.3	45.0
1960	5,209	425.8	49.8	44.9
1961	3,459	377.6	38.8	31.7
1962	5,137	388.2	40.0	39.3
1963	5,258	425.2	55.7	53.1
1964	5,282	482.3	68.5	70.0
1965	5,234	452.0	75.1	80.4
1966	4,774	363.2	74.4	79.9
1967	3,411	318.7	61.0	65.0
1968	4,142	318.4	82.4	68.7
1969	5,137	485.1	100.5	100.3
1970	4,836	503.2	114.3	120.7
1971	4,906	536.3	114.5	120.2
1972	4,511	584.5	118.9	119.7
1973	5,004	632.5	126.4	130.0
1974	5,158	688.4	130.0	133.7
1975	5,335	705.2	136.0	133.7
1976	4,897	701.2	130.3	136.9
1977	5,402	711.9	140.2	140.9
1978	5,908	771.5	149.6	146.1

Note Production data except for "Rubber shoes" only includes production by enterprises belonging to Shanghai Municipal Bureau of Chemical Industry
Source "Rubber shoes" from Shanghaishi tongjiju (1992, p. 39); others from Shanghai huaxuegongyezhi bianzuanweiyuanhui (1997, pp. 450–451, 465–466)

orders made to private rubber processing factories of state-owned enterprises and state organizations (including military-related institutions) also increased. According to the company history of the Zhengtai Rubber Factory, the military rubber shoes produced in the factories of Dazhonghua, Zhengtai, and Yisheng (义生) in the second half of 1951 amounted to 12 million pairs (Qian 1994, p. 71). This accounted for 37.5% of Shanghai's total production of 31.99 million pairs, shown in Table 9.2, for the whole of 1951.

However, as shown in Chapters 3 and 4, many problems arose in the process of executing the expanded processing orders under wartime. Moreover, in the "Three Anti" and "Five Anti" movements that unfolded from the end of 1951 to 1952, the collusion among the personnel of state-owned enterprises, those of governmental organizations and private entrepreneurs that had occurred during wartime was criticized as an example of the "Three Evils" and "Five Poisons."[11] For instance, Zhengtai Rubber Factory was accused of tax evasion and other crimes during the "Five Anti" campaign, and was designated a serious violator (严重违法户), with a tax of 45.5 billion yuan (equivalent to 4.55 million new RMB) levied upon it. In April 1952, the manager, Yang Shaozhen (杨少振), was arrested, although he was released seven months later (Qian 1994, p. 72). Previous studies have emphasized the profit-seeking and speculative nature of capitalists as the cause of the problems that arose among state-owned enterprises, state organizations, and private enterprises (Shanghaishi gongshangxingzhengguanliju and Shanghaishi xiangjiaogongyegongsi shiliaogongzuozu 1979, pp. 178–181). However, it is clear from the previous analysis that the approach developed to manage production among the government and private enterprises as military demand surged suffered to some extent from structural problems.

As a result, after the "Five Anti" campaign, the government's control over private enterprises intensified, and the subcontracting and ordering by state organizations and state-owned enterprises came to occupy a large proportion of the production of the Shanghai rubber processing industry. At Zhengtai Rubber Factory, from May 1952 onward, all automobile tires were subcontracted from the Shanghai Municipal Bureau of Light Industry Management (上海市轻工业管理局), while bicycle and rickshaw tires and rubber shoes were ordered from the China Department Store (中国百货公司). Zhengtai finally adopted a production style of "determining production volume based on sales volume (sales-based production)" through processing orders from state-owned enterprises and state organizations (Qian 1994, p. 72). The production of the Dazhonghua Rubber Factory also came to consist entirely of processing orders from state-owned enterprises and state organizations from June 1952, with automobile tires subcontracted from the Electrical Appliances for Transportation Company (交通电器公司), bicycle and rickshaw tires and shoes ordered from the China Department Store, and gloves and ball tubes purchased from the

---

[11] Shanghaishi gongshangxingzhengguanliju and Shanghaishi xiangjiaogongyegongsi shiliaogongzuozu (1979, pp. 178–180). For the situation of the cotton spinning and weaving industry, refer to Izutani (2007, Chapter 3).

Trade Trust Company (贸易信托公司).[12] Looking at the rubber processing industry in Shanghai as a whole, 105 companies received processing order tasks from state-owned enterprises, state organizations, and cooperatives (with 8 subcontracting, 84 ordering, 2 unified purchasing and exclusive sales, and 11 purchasing and intermediary sales) out of 116 large-scale private rubber processing enterprises in 1953 (B31-1-125).

This government policy of processing orders for private rubber processing enterprises promoted the stabilization of rubber product sales channels and inevitably reduced transactions in the market. This shift was best reflected by the closure of the nationwide sales networks owned by large private enterprises. The Dazhonghua Rubber Factory lost its nationwide network of production and distribution, shown in Fig. 9.1, in 1952 (Shuangqian xiongfeng bianweihui 1993, p. 221), and Zhengtai Rubber Factory similarly, due to the start of unified purchasing from the China Department Store, had successively closed its sales offices in Shanghai and other regions by January 1953 (Qian 1994, p. 73). In other words, as the main purchasers of products shifted to state agencies and state-owned enterprises, the direct relationship between industrial companies and the market was divided, with distribution and industrial production clearly separated into two systems which were under the control of the related governmental organization. This represented one of the most significant changes that occurred in the process of the government expanding its economic control.

9.3 The Socialist Transformation and the Restructuring of Industrial Organization

9.3.1 "Prosperity" Under Economic Control

As seen in the previous section, the government's control over the distribution of raw rubber and rubber processed products was essentially established from 1952 to 1953. However, what needs to be noted is that despite this significant change, the structure within the rubber processing industry under this new regime of economic control did not necessarily move toward concentration in response to said control. This requires some explanation.

The number of Shanghai rubber processing companies from 1949 to 1956 showed a sharp increase, especially in small and medium-sized enterprises. As already noted, the number of rubber processing companies in Shanghai as of May 1949 was 95 (106 factories), but a report by the Shanghai Municipal Bureau of Second Light Industry (上海市第二轻工业局) pointed out the following:

[12] Shanghai Dazhonghua Rubber Factory "The Process of the Socialist Transformation of Dazhonghua Rubber Factory," Zhonggongshanghaishiwei tongzhanbu et al. (1993, p. 1337).

> [The number of companies] increased to 177 in 1950, and to 203 in 1951, due to the increase in military-related tasks and the rise in people's purchasing power. After the end [of the "Five Anti" campaign] in 1952, raw rubber was officially designated as a distributed material by the government, and processing orders began. Production gradually normalized, and by the end of the year the number of companies reached 224. The [number by the] end of 1953 was 255, and [by the end of] 1954 was 239. (B5-2-6)

Further, according to another source, the number had reached 536 at the time of the implementation of the socialist transformation from private companies to public-private jointly-owned ones across the entire industry in January 1956.[13] Thus, even in a situation where the government controlled raw rubber, many small and medium-sized enterprises emerged due to the aforementioned increase in reconstruction demand and military demand.

This increase in the number of companies, however, was not desirable from the perspective of the government's control over production and distribution in the industry, and as seen in Chapter 4, the government's management personnel were appealing for assistance with handling difficulties in management as well as voicing the need for the reorganization of industries.[14] However, in terms of the supply and demand of rubber processed products, the trend of an increasing number of companies indicates that the increase in demand at that time exceeded the production capacity of the existing rubber processing industry, and so additional production capacity was needed. In other words, the management difficulties highlighted by the government's management personnel embodied the contradiction between the supply–demand balance and management by the government at the time.

Thus, it was no easy task for the government to properly carry out production management due to the increase in the number of companies based on the expansion of demand, while at the same time a governmental control system was being established for the distribution of raw rubber and rubber products. In this context, as seen in Chapter 4, governmental management personnel began to conceive of a more direct management system, that is to say, the notion of transforming private companies into public-private jointly-owned ones.

[13] Shanghai xiangjiaogongyezhi bianzuanweiyuanhui (2000, pp. 50–51). However, Appendix Table 6.1 of the book, "Shanghai Rubber Industry 536 Household Name List at the Time of Public and Private Joint Management, 1956" in the same work includes many units such as "Industrial Society" and "Rubber Society" which hardly ever appeared in other previous industry directories. Therefore, it is not feasible to simply compare these figures with the previous statistics.

[14] On this point, refer to the following historical source, Song Jiwen (宋季文) "Talk on the Problem of Processing Orders" (关于加工订货问题的讲话), May 19, 1952, Zhonggongshanghaishiwei tongzhanbu et al. (1993, p. 143).

9.3.2 *Reorganization of the Rubber Industry Through the Socialist Transformation*

The socialist transformation implemented from 1954 to 1956 had a significant impact on the organization of the rubber processing industry. As already mentioned, prior to 1954 private enterprises had occupied the lion's share of Shanghai's rubber processing industry, and there were only a few local state-owned enterprises and no public-private jointly-owned ones (Shanghaishi gongshangxingzhengguanliju and Shanghaishi xiangjiaogongyegongsi shiliaogongzuozu 1979, p. 194). However, in 1954, the Zhengtai Rubber Factory (正泰橡胶厂) and Zhongnan Rubber Factory (中南橡胶厂) were transformed into the first public-private jointly-owned enterprises in the industry, to serve as models for the process. Dazhonghua Rubber Factory (大中华橡胶厂), Hongda Rubber Factory (宏大橡胶厂), Shuanglong Rubber Factory (双龙橡胶厂), Xinya Rubber Factory (新亚橡胶厂), and Qingong Rubber Factory (勤工橡胶厂) also applied to undergo the transformation to public-private jointly-owned enterprises in that same year. With these large companies becoming public-private jointly-owned ones, the socialist transformation of the core of Shanghai's rubber processing industry was essentially completed by the end of 1954. Then, in the fall of 1955, the Shanghai Rubber Industry Association, a trade association of the industry, applied to the government for the socialist transformation of the entire industry, and by January 20, 1956, all 536 companies making up Shanghai's rubber processing industry had become public-private jointly-owned enterprises.

The key changes brought about by the implementation of the socialist transformation in the Shanghai rubber processing industry were, firstly, the restructuring of organization, and secondly, the formation of a management system for the industry at the local level. The main point in the restructuring of organization was the integration of many small and medium-sized enterprises. In the rubber processing industry, the reorganization under the socialist transformation program was carried out based on the principles of "keep the main part unchanged, and adjust the minor parts" (大部不動，小部调整), and "the big lead the small, the advanced lead the backward" (以大带小，以先进带落后). As a result, the total number of companies (including state-owned and former jointly-owned) was reduced to 473 by the initial adjustment following the socialist transformation of the entire industry, and was reduced again to 244 by the first reorganization, which was carried out from 1956 to the second half of 1957. In addition, these 244 companies were divided into 62 independent factories, 26 central factories, and 156 satellite factories (Shanghaishi gongshangxingzhengguanliju and Shanghaishi xiangjiaogongyegongsi shiliaogongzuozu 1979, pp. 197–200). An independent factory was a large-scale factory that engaged in independent production, whereas a central factory was a factory with a relatively solid production base, which was expected to manage satellite factories that were of smaller scale and utilizing inferior equipment. On the other hand, of the 229 companies that were abolished after the initial adjustment, 10 were relocated to Shaanxi, Henan, Anhui, Nanjing, and other areas (Shanghai huaxuegongyezhi bianzuanweiyuanhui 1997, pp. 68–69). Moreover, the second reorganization, from the first half of 1958 to the end of 1959, reduced the number of companies still further, down to just 106 (of which 64 were independent factories, 15 central factories, and 27 satellite factories) (Shanghai xiangjiaogongyezhi bianzuanweiyuanhui 2000, pp. 344–346). Clearly, the purpose of this restructuring of organization was to increase the concentration of production in the Shanghai rubber processing industry and to form a system that could more smoothly adapt to the government's economic plan.

As for the management system for the rubber processing industry at the local level, the Shanghai Rubber Industry Company (上海市橡胶工业公司) was established in February 1956 to serve as a unit that could manage the whole rubber processing industry in Shanghai, with the Shanghai Municipal Bureau of Second Light Industry Rubber Industry Office (上海市第二轻工业局橡胶工业处) as its parent body (Shanghai xiangjiaogongyezhi bianzuanweiyuanhui 2000, pp. 51, 330–332). This company underwent a somewhat complex process of development, splitting into the Shanghai Tire and Rubber Shoes Industry Company (上海市轮胎胶鞋工业公司) and the Shanghai Rubber Miscellaneous Goods Industry Company (上海市橡胶杂品工业公司) in September 1956, both of which were then placed under the supervision of the Shanghai Municipal Bureau of Chemical Industry (上海市化学工业局) from May 1957, before merging once again in April 1958, even reclaiming its prior name as the Shanghai Rubber Industry Company. Through the course of this process, ultimately a three-level industrial management system was formed in Shanghai, consisting of government organizations (Shanghai Municipal Bureaus of Second Light Industry and Chemical Industry), specialized companies (Shanghai Rubber Industry Company, Shanghai Tire and Rubber Shoes Industry Company, and Shanghai Rubber Miscellaneous Goods Industry Company) and individual rubber processing companies.

It is important to note here that this restructuring of organizations and the formation of management systems at the local level completely divided the nationwide network of large companies formed during the Republican period. As already mentioned, the establishment of a governmental distribution system for rubber products had already fragmented the sales networks of large companies at the processing order stage. In addition to this, however, the large companies' ownership of their local factories in various places was now transformed into a public model in the wake of the socialist transformation, while their local factories were placed under the management of their respective local governments (depending on where a particular factory was located) as public-private jointly-owned enterprises. For example, after the implementation of the socialist transformation of the Dazhonghua Rubber Factory, the company's sixth factory, located in Tianjin, was separated from the Dazhonghua main body in Shanghai and instead became Tianjin Dazhonghua in October 1954 (Shuangqian xiongfeng bianweihui 1993, p. 53). In similar fashion the Wanli Xingji Rubber Factory (万里兴记橡胶厂) in Guangzhou, which had been acquired by the Zhengtai Rubber Factory in 1943 (then renamed Guangzhou Zhenglong Rubber Factory [广州正隆橡胶厂] in 1945 and Zhengtai Xinji Guangzhou Branch Factory [正泰信记广州分厂] in 1951), was separated from the Zhengtai Group on June 1, 1955, since the Guangzhou Municipal Government independently transformed the factory into a public-private jointly-owned enterprise and merged it with the Guangzhou Dahua Rubber Wheel Factory (广州大华胶轮厂) (Qian 1994, p. 36; A36-2-69).

Figure 9.3 shows the changes in the production of major products in the form of an index, and is helpful to assess the situation of the Shanghai rubber processing industry after the aforementioned organizational restructuring and the formation of the industrial management system at the local level. It is clear that the production of rubber shoes, which were the main products of traditional small and medium-sized rubber processing companies, aside from a temporary increase in 1958 remained at about the same level as 1956 from 1960 through to 1978. On the other hand, the production of automobile tires and tubes significantly increased and by the 1970s had reached 15 times the production volume of 1952, and by 1978 this had increased even further to about 20 times. Although it is necessary to take into account the difference in the scale of production volume at the base year of 1952, it is evident that this gap in production specialties between rubber shoes and automobile tires represents how the production of rubber shoes by small and medium-sized enterprises, which had long symbolized the Shanghai rubber processing industry before the socialist transformation, was quite restricted, while by contrast the production of automobile tires and tubes, which required a higher level of technological capacity, was promoted under the industrial management system. This was a major shift in the structure of the Shanghai rubber processing industry, which had previously been characterized by numerous small and medium-sized enterprises, wrought by the socialist transformation of 1956.

Based on the above discussion in this chapter, it is possible to summarize the process from the immediate postwar years to the socialist transformation of the

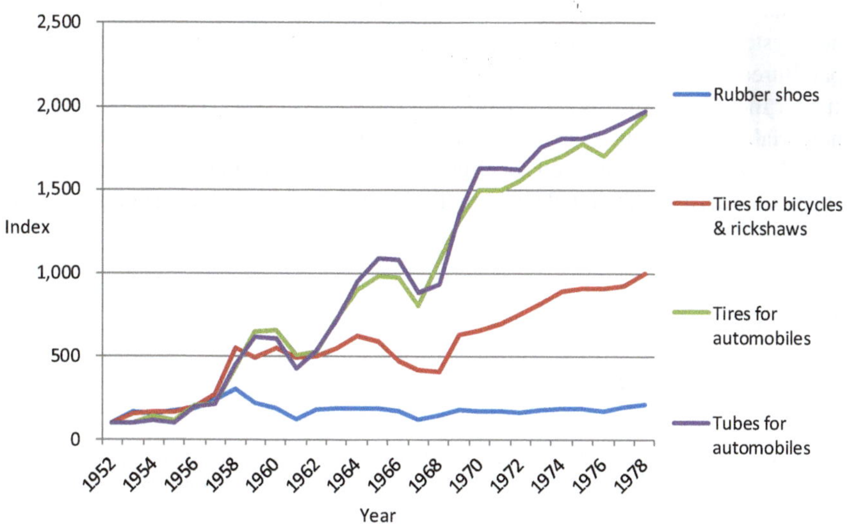

Fig. 9.3 Indices of production of rubber processing industry in Shanghai, 1952–1978. *Note* 1952 = 100. *Source* Table 9.2

Shanghai rubber processing industry as follows. After the war, the industry was booming due to factors such as postwar reconstruction demand and the withdrawal of Japanese products, and traditional, large companies such as Dazhonghua and Zhengtai expanded their scale. On the other hand, many small and medium-sized enterprises were established due to the favorable market conditions of the time, and the number of enterprises in the industry increased even more than before the war.

After the military occupation of Shanghai by the Chinese Communist Party in May 1949, the price of raw rubber soared due to factors such as the Nationalist Party's maritime blockade and the outbreak of the Korean War, and the government began to take control of the distribution of raw rubber. Moreover, the number of processing orders from state-owned enterprises and government organizations to private factories rose sharply due to the increase in military demand, and the government's control over the distribution of rubber products also intensified. However, at the same time, the number of small and medium-sized enterprises increased further due to the growth in demand, and the government recognized difficulties in production management involving private factories, especially the small and medium-sized ones.

In this context, the socialist transformation from 1954 to 1956 was nothing less than a process of cutting off the tradition of relatively low production concentration that had previously characterized the Shanghai rubber processing industry, and adapting it to a management system in line with the government's control. The Shanghai rubber processing companies were reorganized into independent factories, central factories, and satellite factories, while the large companies were deprived of their local factories in other regions, and small and medium-sized enterprises were merged or closed. As a result, the production organization of the Shanghai rubber processing industry was unified under a three-level local management system, consisting of local administrative organizations (e.g., Shanghai Municipal Bureau of Chemical Industry), local specialized companies (e.g., Shanghai Rubber Industry Company), and individual rubber processing companies. This local industrial management system, which evolved against the backdrop of the close financial relationship between local governments and local companies revealed in Chapter 6, was a significant element in the formation of the Chinese socialist system.

References

Chinese Language

Jiadao, Run (Kajima, Jun). 2007. Shanghai xiangjiaogongye de shichang he chanyezuzhi: 1946–1956 (上海橡膠工業的市場和産業組織:1946–1956, Market and Industrial Organization of Shanghai Rubber Industry: 1946–1956). In *Liangan sandi lishixue yanjiusheng yantaohui lunwenxuanji (2006)* (両岸三地歴史学研究生研討会論文選集 (2006), Selected Papers of Graduate Students in History Research in Mainland, Taiwan and Hong Kong, 2006), ed. Hu Chunhui and Tang Qihua, 443–453. Hong Kong: Centre for Asian Studies, Hong Kong Chu Hai College and Taipei: Department of History, National Chengchi University

Qian, Yiqing, ed. 1994. *Huili zhi lu: Zhengtai xiangjiaochang fazhanshi* (回力之路: 正泰橡胶厂发展史, The Road of Hui Li: The Development History of Zhengtai Rubber Factory). Beijing: Gaige chubanshe

Shanghai huaxuegongyezhi bianzuanweiyuanhui, ed. 1997. *Shanghai huaxuegongyezhi* (上海化学工业志, Shanghai Chemical Industry Chronicle). Shanghai: Shanghai shehuikexueyuan chubanshe

Shanghai xiangjiaogongyezhi bianzuanweiyuanhui, ed. 2000. *Shanghai xiangjiaogongye zhi* (上海橡胶工业志, Shanghai Rubber Industry Chronicle). Shanghai: Shanghai shehuikexueyuan chubanshe

Shanghaishi gongshangxingzhengguanliju and Shanghaishi xiangjiaogongyegongsi shiliao-gongzuozu, ed. 1979. *Shanghai minzu xiangjiao gongye* (上海民族橡胶工业, Shanghai Native Rubber Industry). Beijing: Zhonghua shuju

Shanghaishi tongjiju, ed. 1992. *Xinshanghai gongyetongjiziliao: 1949–1990* (新上海工业统计资料 (1949–1990), New Shanghai Industrial Statistical Data: 1949–1990). Beijing: Zhongguo tongjichubanshe

Shuangqian xiongfeng bianweihui, ed. 1993. *Shuangqian xiongfeng: dazhonghua xiangjiaochang fazhanshi, 1926–1992* (双钱雄风:大中华橡胶厂发展史 (1926–1992), Double Coin Heroic Wind: A Developmental History of the Dazhonghua Rubber Factory: 1926–1992). Beijing: Qiyeguanli chubanshe

Sun, Guoda. 1991. *Minzugongye daqianxi: Kangrizhanzhengshiqi minyinggongchang de neiqian* (民族工业大迁徙:抗日战争时期民营工厂的内迁, The Great Migration of Native Industries: The Inland Migration of Private Factories during the Anti-Japanese War). Beijing: Zhongguo wenshi chubanshe

Wu, Jingping et al. 2001 *Kangzhanshiqi de shanghai jingji* (抗战时期的上海经济, Shanghai's Economy during the Anti-Japanese War of Resistance). Shanghai: Shanghai renmin chubanshe

Zhonggongshanghaishiwei tongzhanbu, Zhonggongshanghaishi dangshiyanjiushi, and Shanghaishidanganguan. 1993. *Zhongguo zibenzhuyigongshangye de shehuizhuyigaizao: Shanghai juan* (中国资本主义工商业的社会主义改造 (上海卷), The Socialist Transformation of China's Capitalist Industry and Commerce: Shanghai Volume), Volume I & II. Beijing: Zhonggong dangshi chubanshe

Zhongguo duiwaijingjimaoyinianjian bianjiweiyuanhui, ed. 1984. *Zhongguo duiwaijingjimaoyinianjian 1984* (中国对外经济贸易年鉴1984, China Foreign Economic Trade Yearbook 1984). Beijing: Zhongguo duiwaijingjimaoyi chubanshe

Zhongguokexueyuan shanghaijingjiyanjiusuo, and Shanghaishehuikexueyuan jingjiyanjiusuo, eds. 1958. *Shanghai jiefangqianhou wujiaziliaohuibian: 1921 nian – 1957 nian* (上海解放前后物价资料汇编 (1921年-1957年), Compilation of Price Data Before and After the Liberation of Shanghai: 1921–1957). Shanghai: Shanghai renmin chubanshe

Zhongguoshehuikexueyuan and Zhongyangdanganguan, eds. 1994. *Zhonghuarenmingongheguo jingjidanganziliaoxuanbian 1949–1952: Duiwaimaoyi juan* (中华人民共和国经济档案资料选编1949–1952 (对外贸易卷), Selected Economic Archive Materials of the People's Republic of China 1949–1952: Foreign Trade Volume). Beijing: Jingjiguanli chubanshe

Japanese Language

Chūshikensetsushiryō seibiiinkai, trans and ed. 1940 *Gomukōgyō hōkokusho* (護謨工業報告書, Rubber Industry Report), Translation Compilation Report No. 21. Nanjing: Chūshikensetsushiryō seibijimusho henyakubu. Japanese translation of Quanguojingjiweiyuanhui. 1935. *Xianjiaogongye baogaoshu* (橡膠工業報告書). Publish place unknown

Hibino, Yoshio. 1956. Chincom list no kanwa: Eiseifu malei gomu no chūkyō muke kinyu kaijo (チンコムリストの緩和——英政府、マレイ・ゴムの中共向禁輸解除, Relaxation of the

CHINCOM List: British Government Lifts Ban on Malaysian Rubber Exports to China) *Sekai shūhō* (世界週報, World Weekly) 37 (20): 47–50

Izutani, Yōko. 2007. *Chūgoku kenkokushoki no seiji to keizai: Taishū undō to shakaishugitaisei* (中国建国初期の政治と経済—— 大衆運動と社会主義体制, Politics and Economy in the Early Years of the People's Republic of China: Mass Movements and the Socialist System). Tokyo: Ochanomizu shobō

Kajima, Jun. 2005. Sengo kara jinminkyōwakokushoki ni kaketeno shanghai kagakukōgyō saihen: Gomukōgyō wo chūshinni (戦後から人民共和国初期にかけての上海化学工業再編——ゴム工業を中心に, Reorganization of Shanghai Chemical Industry from the Postwar Period to the Early years of the People's Republic: Focusing on the Rubber Industry). In *20 seiki no chūgoku kagakukōgyō: Eiri kagaku tengen denka to sono jidai* (20世紀の中国化学工業——永利化学・天原電化とその時代, The Origins and Development of China's Chemical Industry), Institute of Social Science Research Series No.17, ed. Tajima Toshio, 81–98. Tokyo: Institute of Social Science, The University of Tokyo

Nihon gomu kōgyōkai. 1969. *Nihon gomu kōgyōshi dai 2 kan* (日本ゴム工業史 第二巻, History of Japan's Rubber Industry: Volume II). Tokyo: Tōyō keizai shinpōsha

Nihon gomu kōgyōkai. 1971. *Nihon gomu kōgyōshi dai 3 kan* (日本ゴム工業史 第三巻, History of Japan's Rubber Industry: Volume III). Tokyo: Tōyō keizai shinpōsha

Unpublished Primary Sources

A36, Zhonggong shanghaishiwei gongyezhengzhibu dangan (中共上海市委工业政治部档案, The Industrial Politics Department of the Shanghai Municipal Committee of the Chinese Communist Party Archives)

A36-2-69, "Zhengtai xiangjiaochang guangzhoufenchang niyou dangdi heying" (正泰橡胶厂广州分厂拟由当地合营, Zhengtai Rubber Factory Guangzhou Branch's plan to be transformed into a local joint public-private operation enterprise), January 1954, official letter (公函), sender: Zhou Ke (周克), Private Industry Department of Shanghai Municipal Committee of Chinese Communist Party (中共上海市委私营工业部), received document No. 7 (收文第7号). In "Benbu guanyu heyingwenti yu shiwei gongyeshengchanweiyuanhui zhi laiwanwenshu" (本部关于合营问题与市委工业生产委员会之来往文书, Our department's correspondence with the Industrial Production Committee of the Shanghai Municipal Committee on the issue of joint operation)

B5, Shanghaishi renminweiyuanhui qinggongyebangongshi dangan (上海市人民委员会轻工业办公室档案, Light Industry Office of the Shanghai People's Committee Archives)

B5-2-6, Shanghaishi dierqinggongyeju (上海市第二轻工业局, Shanghai Municipal Bureau of Second Light Industry) "Xiangjiao gongye wunianlai gongchanxiao qingkuang" (橡胶工业五年来供产销情况(初稿, 绝密), Rubber Industry's Supply, Production and Sales Situation in the Past Five Years: First Draft, Top Secret), May 12, 1955, Hu Ren Ban Shou Fen (沪人办收分) (55), No. 1152. In Shanghaishi renminweiyuanhui qinggongyebangongshi (上海市人民委员会轻工业办公室, Shanghai People's Committee Light Industry Office) "Shanghaishi qing fang gongye geju ji youguandanwei guanyu gongchanxiao qingkunag baogao" (上海市轻,纺工业各局及有关单位关于供产销情况报告, Report on Supply, Production and Sales Situation by the Shanghai Municipal Bureaus of Light Industry, Textile Industry and Related Units)

B31, Shanghaishi tongjiju dangan (上海市统计局档案, Shanghai Municipal Bureau of Statistics Archives)

B31-1-125, "1953 nian siyingdaxinggongyeqiye jieshoujiagongdinghuodengrenwu de qiyedanweishu ji zhigongrenshu" (1953年私营大型工业企业接受加工订货等任务的企业单位数及职工人数, The Number of Enterprises and Workers Accepting Processing Orders and Other Tasks in Large Private Industrial Enterprises in 1953), In "Shanghaishi daxingjiagongdinghuo fazhanzhuangkuang 1953 nian–1955 nian (上海市大型加工订货发展状况 (1953年-1955年), Status of Large Processing Orders in Shanghai: 1953–1955)," date of creation unknown

Chapter 10
The Material Distribution System: The Cement Industry

Abstract This chapter takes up the cement industry to examine the relationships between the central government's material distribution policy and the behavior of local enterprises, paying particular attention to the regional cement supply and demand relationship in Shanghai during the planned economy period. Shanghai, as the center of modern industry in China during the Republican period, had developed its cement industry to some extent before 1949 while simultaneously being a major consumer of cement. However, no large-scale cement factories were built in Shanghai after the establishment of the PRC since the central government adopted an inland-focused development strategy and did not mark Shanghai as a priority investment target. On the other hand, Shanghai experienced several surges in cement demand due to the central government's industrial production promotion policy, while at the same time the cement distribution from the central government was insufficient, making it a region that was forced to deal with a "vertical shortage" of cement. This chapter examines the behavior of each entity involved in material distribution in Shanghai under the socialist system.

Keywords Vertical shortage · Material distribution system · Cement industry · Regional supply and demand · Centralized control

Chapter 9 explored how a local-level industrial management system based on local governments and local specialized companies was formed through the socialist transformation of 1956, by analyzing the restructuring of the industrial organization of the rubber processing industry. This chapter will take the analysis in a new direction by demonstrating how this leadership role of local governments was not just limited to the level of production, but also extended to the distribution of production goods, by focusing on the example of the cement industry.[1]

Cement was long regarded as an important controlled material under the Chinese socialist system, and was classified as a state unified distribution material (国家统一分配物资), a top-class priority under the distribution system, in the first year of

[1] This chapter is based on Kajima (2010) with additions and revisions.

J. Kajima, *Shanghai under the Socialist System*, Studies in Economic History,
https://doi.org/10.1007/978-981-95-3225-4_10

the First Five Year Plan (1953–57). As a result, cement, along with other key materials steel and coal, was incorporated into the material distribution plan compiled by the State Planning Commission (国家计划委员会), a central government organization, and was placed in principle under the central government's control (Dangdai zhongguo congshu bianjibu 1993, pp. 6–10). In this material distribution system, local governments served as management units for material distribution in their respective regions, and therefore each local government was actively involved in the production and distribution of materials as well as the related supply–demand relationship in the region in question. This chapter takes up the case of the cement industry to highlight how this system functioned.

A centralized material distribution system in a socialist system is the institutional premise of what János Kornai termed a "shortage economy" (Kornai 1980). Kornai classified "shortages" into several types, with a "vertical shortage" being defined as a shortage that occurs based on a hierarchical relationship when the total demand of intermediate organizations and enterprises receiving allocations exceeds the disposable amount of the central organization, under a system wherein goods are managed vertically by said central organization. Considering the principles of a planned economy, the central organization, which ultimately formulates the industrial production plan that determines the total demand of intermediate organizations and companies for production goods, should not trigger a "vertical shortage" if the industrial production plan and the goods distribution plan are formulated and implemented without any contradictions. However, such "vertical shortages" were occurring daily in actual planned economies, suggesting that some kind of discrepancy was inevitably occurring in the process of formulating and implementing the plans.

When applying this concept of "vertical shortage" to the Chinese socialist system, it is important to note, as Ishihara points out, that the centrally controlled goods management system initially formed in China was greatly reduced after the 1970s due to the increase in goods controlled by local governments, the relaxation of planned management, and problems with the information processing capabilities of the central organization (Ishihara 1990). In other words, the premise of "vertical shortage," i.e., vertical goods management by the central organization, was undergoing change in China. Therefore, grasping what mechanism caused this trend toward decentralization of the goods management system and how it related to the "vertical shortage" of goods is essential.

The key point here is the behaviors of government organizations at all levels, and of state-owned enterprises, which were the main entities demanding the goods. Many former studies, including Ishihara (1990), have focused on the proportion of management authority between the central and local governments in China's material distribution system. However, equally important in the operation of the material distribution system was the fluctuation in local demand for materials. As will be discussed later, local demand for materials fluctuated greatly over time in conjunction with central policies in China, and therefore, local governments responded independently according to the gap between local demand for materials and the amount of said materials that were distributed by the central government.

This chapter pursues these points and examines the behavior of the Shanghai Municipal Government in relation to cement production and distribution, paying particular attention to the regional cement supply and demand relationship in Shanghai during the planned economy period. Shanghai, as the center of modern industry in China during the Republican period, had developed its cement industry to some extent before 1949 while also being a major consumer of cement. However, no large-scale cement factories were built in Shanghai after the establishment of the PRC since the central government adopted an inland-focused development strategy and did not mark Shanghai as a priority investment target. On the other hand, Shanghai experienced several surges in cement demand due to the central government's industrial production promotion policy, while at the same time the cement distribution from the central government was insufficient, making it a region that was forced to deal with a "vertical shortage" of cement.

Regarding works on the Chinese material distribution system during the planned economy period, there is a representative overview by Dangdai zhongguo congshu bianjibu (1993), as well as the detailed studies by the aforementioned Ishihara (1985, 1989, 1990). On the other hand, there are also specialized local gazetteers on the production and distribution of cement in Shanghai (Shanghai jianzhucailiaogongyezhi bianzuanweiyuanhui 1997; Shanghai wuziliutongzhi bianzuanweiyuanhui 2003). However, the problem is that the former works deal with the entire material distribution system, so the behavior of each entity, especially the local governments, are simply excluded from the analysis. As for the latter sources, their perspective is limited to each administrative division since these local works were edited by the regional governmental bureaus (specifically, of the Ministry of Construction Industry and the Bureau of Materials). The upshot of this situation is that in previous works it was not possible to capture the changes in demand and supply in a specific region in conjunction with each other, and the responses of each entity regarding the distribution of cement were not sufficiently examined. In light of these problems, this chapter seeks to examine the cement supply–demand relationship in Shanghai under the socialist system, and examine the behaviors of each entity involved in material distribution, especially the local government.

10.1 The Material Distribution System and Cement

10.1.1 The Material Distribution System

First of all, it is necessary to set out an overview of the material distribution system under the Chinese socialist system. One of the most important points to keep in mind is just what was meant by "materials" (物资). "Materials" under the socialist system were distinct from the inclusive meaning of materials in the general sense, and instead referred specifically to production goods and capital goods that circulate among state-owned enterprises.[2] This was a concept that formed a pair with "commodities" (商品), lied to a state-owned enterprise, it ds, agricultural products, and some production goods and capital goods that circulated among non-state-owned enterprises (e.g., between state-owned enterprises and collectively-owned enterprises, between collectively-owned enterprises, between state-owned enterprises and individuals, etc.), and these two conceptual units formed the two major systems of distribution under the socialist system.

The key point is that the "materials" and "commodities" categories were distinguished not by the nature of the items they encompassed but by the management system at work and the process of formulating supply plans. The very same item could be classed as either a "material" or a "commodity" depending on the management system and supply plan that was handling it. For example, in the case of cement, if the cement produced by a state-owned enterprise was supplied to a state-owned enterprise, it would be counted under "materials." However, if a state-owned enterprise instead supplied the cement to a collectively-owned enterprise, or if the cement in question was produced by a collectively-owned enterprise, it would instead be considered to fall under "commodities." In other words, "materials" within this system did not simply refer to all production goods and capital goods, but instead was a label affixed to those production goods and capital goods that circulated through a specific route, namely between state-owned enterprises.[3]

Moreover, as shown in Table 10.1, there were classifications from Class 1 to Class 3 according to the management level of the materials. Class 1 materials, managed by the State Planning Commission, and Class 2 materials, managed by various ministries of the State Council, both belonged to the management of central government organizations, and so broadly speaking they were collectively referred to as centrally-distributed materials.[4] Class 3 materials, on the other hand, included a significantly

[2] For the definition of "materials," refer to Ishihara (1985, pp. 37–41), Ishihara (1989), and Horii (2005, pp. 18–20).

[3] The "materials" mentioned subsequently all refer to "materials" in the context of the socialist system, and so no quotation marks are used.

[4] The balance sheet and distribution plan for each class of materials were established once a year, with the Class 1 materials being handled under the supervision of the State Planning Commission by the State Bureau of Material Management, the Class 2 materials by the State Council ministries, and the Class 3 materials by the provinces, municipalities, autonomous regions, special zones, provincial cities, and counties at each level of the material management bureau system. However, at the stage of the distribution plan, specific standards, and supply units of materials were not yet determined, and these were instead decided at the order meeting (订货会议) held at each level. The state order meeting was generally held twice a year (October–November of the year prior to the year being planned, and April–May of the plan year), with the production management department for the materials dealing with the supply side (key production enterprises incorporated in the state plan, etc.), and the material management department collecting the "order lists" (订货单) from the demand side (materials management departments of each province, autonomous region, municipality, and State Council departments, etc.). Then, after both parties jointly adjusted the supply and demand, the production enterprise and the entity making the demand would determine the specific variety, standard, quantity, supply point, and delivery date for the materials in question, and conclude a contract. See Ishihara (1989, p. 317) and Dangdai zhongguo congshu bianjibu (1993, pp. 113–116).

larger number of items, encompassing a variety of items other than what fell under the Class 1 and 2 materials headings.

It is important to note here that the number of items in each class of materials was also not consistent, and changed over time. Initially, when the material management system was introduced in 1950, only eight types of materials—steel, lumber, coal, cement, refined soda, copper, machine tools, and hemp bags—were designated as Class 1 controlled materials. The total number of centrally-distributed materials, including Class 1 and 2, increased significantly during the First Five Year Plan period from 1953 to 1957. However, the number of Class 1 materials decreased significantly in the early 1960s and the 1970s, in line with how the direct management of materials by the State Planning Commission declined due to the decentralization policies implemented during the same period. Along with the "downward shift" of central enterprises during this period, the central government shifted its material distribution policy from "unified planning and distribution" (统筹统支) to "regional balance, covering deficits" (地区平衡，差额调拨), and promoted the transfer of material management authority to the local governments (Dangdai zhongguo congshu bianjibu 1993, pp. 17–18).

There were also considerable fluctuations in the material management organization depending on the period. The initial central-level organization was the Material Distribution Office (物资分配处), established by the Planning Bureau of the Financial and Economic Committee of the Government Administration Council (政务院财政经济委员会计划局), which was then upgraded to the Material Distribution Bureau (物资分配局) in 1952. During the First Five Year Plan period, the General Bureau of Material Distribution (物资供应总局) was established at the central level, while various ministries of the State Council and the local governments of provinces, autonomous regions, and municipalities directly under the central government each established their own material distribution organizations, forming a multi-layered material management system. The State General Bureau of Material Management (国家物资管理总局), established in 1963 during the backlash from the decentralization of the Great Leap Forward, played a central role as a nationwide unified material management organization. The General Bureau was upgraded to the Ministry of Material Management (物资管理部) in the following year, and six general companies were established for handling metals, electromechanical materials (machinery and electrical products), building materials, wood, chemical products, and storage and transportation around the same time. However, this ministry was abolished during the decentralization of 1970, and an independent organization at the central level did not reappear until the establishment of the State General Bureau of Materials (国家物资总局) five years later in 1975 (Dangdai zhongguo congshu bianjibu 1993, pp. 3–30).

Thus, the material management system during the planned economy period was based on the principle of material distribution according to a clear, but evolving, plan, with the management of Class 1 and 2 materials by the central government as its backbone. However, as the existence of materials in the form of "commodities" outside of "materials" circulation among state-owned enterprises, and the transfer of material management authority to local governments due to decentralization policies,

Table 10.1 Management authority, main items and numbers thereof for each class of materials in China, 1950–1978

	Class 1 (State unified distribution materials)	Class 2	Class 3
Management authority	General Bureau of Material Management (物资总局) under supervision of State Planning Commission	Each ministry of State Council (central government)	Local government's Bureau of Materials (物资局) at provincial and lower levels
Main items	Pig iron, steel, cast iron pipes, scrap steel, copper, aluminum, lead, zinc, tin, raw coal, gasoline, electricity, cotton yarn, cotton cloth, jute bags, caustic soda, refined soda, rubber, timber, cement, steam boilers, electric motors, transformers, lathes, grinding machines, etc	Manganese steel, steel wire, cadmium, fire-resistant building materials, asbestos slate, magnesia clinker, rolling machines, keyway cutters, electric-powered hoists, conveyor belts, etc	Brick, tile, sand, stone and other materials produced and consumed at local levels
Year	Number of item		
1950	8		
1951	33		
1952	55		
1953	112	115	5,000
1954	121	140	
1955	162	139	
1956	234	151	
1957	231	301	
1958	93	336	
1959	67	218	
1960	75	342	
1961	87	416	
1962	153	345	
1963	256	260	
1964	370	222	
1965			5,929
1966	326	253	
1972	49	168	
1973	50	567	

(continued)

Table 10.1 (continued)

	Class 1 (State unified distribution materials)	Class 2	Class 3
1975	52	565	
1978	53	636	

Note "Main items" were largely main materials in the First Five Year Plan period, 1953–1957
Sources Ishihara (1985, p. 42), Ishihara (1990, p. 159), and Dangdai zhongguo congshu bianjibu (1993, pp. 8–10). Original data for "Class 1" and "Class 2" are from Yamagishi and Ii (1986, p. 120). For "Class 3," year 1953 is from Ma (1986, pp. 463–466), and year 1965 is from Zhou (1984, pp. 70–72)

indicate, it was not always the case that management by the central government was fully or consistently implemented.

10.1.2 Management of Cement Production and Distribution

What of the system for managing cement production and distribution specifically? Fig. 10.1 shows China's production and import/export of cement at the national level. The amount of cement produced in China during the planned economy period increased gradually from the 1950s, but decreased sharply in 1961–62 and 1967–68 (the causes most likely being the impact of the Great Leap Forward policy and the chaos caused by the Cultural Revolution, respectively), and showed a relatively stable increase after 1969. Despite several periods of stagnation, cement production increased significantly overall through the 1970s, and reached 65.24 million tons in 1978 (at the start of the Reform and Opening-up Policy), which was some five times what it had been a decade earlier in 1968. In other words, in terms of production volume, the increase in the last 10 years of the approximately 29 years of the planned economy period particularly stands out.

Also, looking at imports and exports, it may be somewhat surprising given the import situation during the Republican period (when Chinese cement imports were mainly from Japan and the US), but China during the planned economy period was a net exporter of cement (including specialized products such as white cement). While exports accounted for a significant proportion of production until the expansion of production in the late 1960s, imports consistently remained at several hundred thousand tons, and it was not until after 1979 that they overtook exports. This indicates that cement was prioritized for export under the managed trade system, and that the domestic cement supply during the planned economy period depended almost entirely on domestic production. This production and import/export situation was a significant underlying premise of the domestic material management system.

It was thus with this premise in mind that cement was placed under control by the government at a relatively early stage, and was designated as a Class 1 material

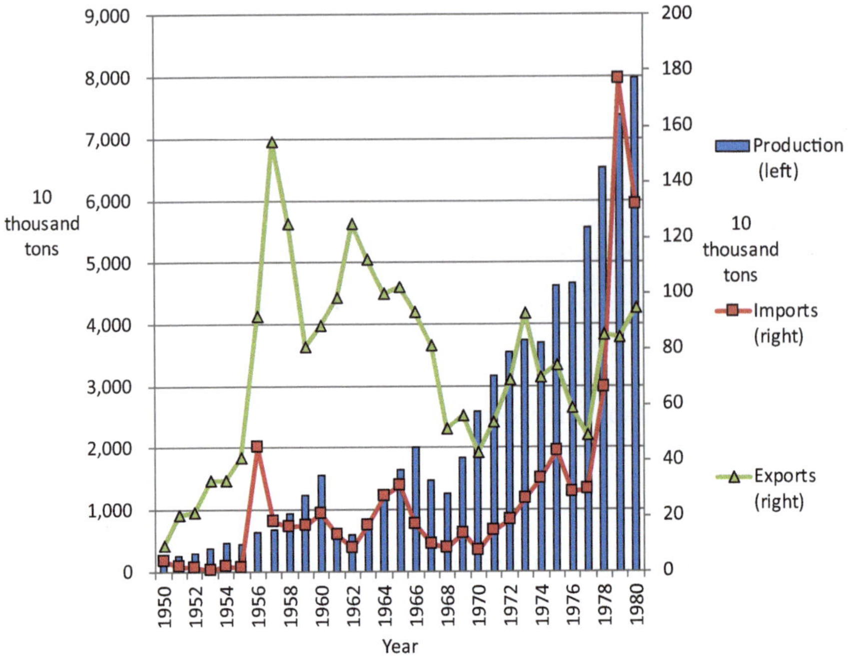

Fig. 10.1 China's cement production, imports and exports, 1950–1980. *Sources* Zhongguo shuinixiehui (2007, p. 604) and Zhongguo duiwaijingjimaoyinianjian bianjiweiyuanhui (1984, pp. IV-104, IV-114)

in 1953. Cement production and distribution were managed from two perspectives, namely the production sector and the material sector, just like other materials. The central institution for national cement production management was the Ministry of Construction Materials Industry (建筑材料工业部), established at the central level in 1956, while on the distribution side, the aforementioned State General Bureau of Material Management, and its subordinate organization, the China Construction Materials General Company (中国建筑材料总公司), played a central role. However, as seen in the previous section, the central institutions of the material management sector were fluid in their organization, and as the case of Shanghai below will further illustrate, the subordinate organizations established within each level of government were relatively independent in their behavior, operating under the strong influence of local governments while also being more generally under the control of the central government organizations.

Moreover, due to the high cost of transportation, cement was a material that was relatively suitable for the decentralization policy of material management authority discussed in the previous section. In 1960, the central government encouraged local self-sufficiency in cement through reforming the distribution methods of the material within its state plan.[5] This allowed local governments to reserve a certain portion of cement production within their respective regions as local resources. Although the plan ended up being abolished after merely a year due to management difficulties, it nevertheless had some impact in stimulating local government support for cement production. Then, in 1970, the "regional responsibility system" (地区包干制) that was implemented for all materials was also put into place for cement. Under the stated principle of "balancing [production] within the region under the unified plan of the state, converting the deficient aspects, adjusting the variety of products, and guaranteeing delivery to the superior institutions," all cement produced locally now belonged to local management, except for a certain amount to be delivered to the upper-level institutions. This policy too aroused enthusiasm for local production, and continued to function until it was abolished nationwide in 1978–79 (Dangdai zhongguo congshu bianjibu 1993, pp. 36–37, 43).

Regarding these decentralization policies, Dangdai zhongguo congshu bianjibu (1993) identifies various problems from the perspective of national unified material management, while offering the evaluation that "the material resources controlled by the localities significantly increased, arousing the enthusiasm of the localities and accelerating the development of local industries, especially the 'five small industries' (五小工业)."[6] Despite these problems, decentralization nevertheless progressed as a result of these policies. Ishihara (1985) compared the total national amount of cement production and the state unified distribution amount (国家统一分配量, the amount distributed by the central government based on the state plan) in 1965 and 1980, and stressed that, while the state unified distribution amount increased in absolute terms (11.6 million tons in 1965 to 23.22 million tons in 1980), its ratio to the total production (16.34 million tons in 1965 to 79.86 million tons in 1980) decreased from 71.0% to 29.1% (Ishihara 1985, pp. 42–48). In other words, in the latter half of the planned economy period, the bulk of cement production generally shifted to

[5] The decision on the central-local distribution of cement promulgated by the State Council in 1960 stipulated that the excess (over the planned amounts) production of cement factories under the State Council (10 factories) would be distributed at a ratio of 70% to the central government and 30% to the local government, while the excess production of key local cement factories (22 factories) would be distributed at a ratio of 30% to the central government and 70% to the local government. It also stipulated that 95% of the planned production of non-key local cement factories (9 factories) would be allocated to the central government and 5% to the local government, and that all excess production would be kept locally. Beyond this, it further stipulated that all production from small shaft kilns (立窑) and extended production facilities of large-scale factories by local investment would fall under local self-use (Dangdai zhongguo congshu bianjibu 1993, p. 272).

[6] Dangdai zhongguo congshu bianjibu (1993, p. 37). The specific problems mentioned were as follows: 1. Many enterprises' production and construction plans were still centrally allocated, but the material resources were controlled by the local governments, so the coordination between the two was severed; 2. The central and local governments had to negotiate the amount of material dispatch and import (exports and imports) every year, and it was difficult to coordinate them and reach an agreement; and 3. Some local governments reported that the central departments only imposed tasks on the decentralized former central enterprises under their jurisdiction without supplying raw materials, and "only moved the household registration without moving the food supply relationship," thereby increasing the burden on the local governments, while the central departments had different opinions on such matters.

the purview of local governments, and the increase in national production shown in Fig. 10.1 after 1969 was brought about by production outside of the state plan.

However, so far, it is not necessarily clear why the decentralization of material management authority stimulated local governments to produce more cement at the local level. The next section will clarify this trend through an analysis of the cement supply and demand relationship in the Shanghai cement industry under the mechanisms discussed above, i.e., the nationwide material management system and the cement production and distribution structure.

10.2 The Development of the Shanghai Cement Industry

This section will outline the basic structure of the cement industry in Shanghai, focusing on its historical background and the changes brought about by the introduction of the socialist system in the years following 1949.

10.2.1 Historical Background

The origins of Shanghai's cement industry can be traced back to the establishment of the Chinese Merchant Shanghai Cement Company (华商上海水泥股份有限公司, hereinafter "Shanghai Cement Company," 上海水泥公司) by businessmen Liu Hongsheng (刘鸿生) and others in 1920.[7] The company set up a factory on the banks of the Huangpu River in the southeastern part of Longhua Town (龍华镇), a suburb of Shanghai, and installed two German-made Polysius wet rotary kilns (with a daily production of about 200 tons), commencing production in August 1923. Aside from this, the only other cement factories established in Shanghai during the Republican period were the Tianxiang Industrial Company Cement Factory (天祥实业公司水泥厂), established in August 1941 during the Second Sino-Japanese War (production began in 1942, with an annual production capacity of 18,000 tons in 1945, see Wang 2005, p. 116); the Guanghua Cement Factory (光华水泥厂), which specialized in white cement and had a daily production of 8 tons; the Jianya Cement Factory (建亚水泥厂), with a daily production of 20 tons, and the Shunchang Company Cement Factory (顺昌公司水泥厂), with an annual production of 15,000 tons, the latter three being established in 1947, and all four operations being small in scale (Shanghai jianzhucailiaogongyezhi bianzuanweiyuanhui 1997, pp. 14–15, 56). Therefore, it is clear that the history of Shanghai's cement industry prior to the establishment of the PRC largely overlapped with the history of the Shanghai Cement Company.

[7] The company decided to change its name to Shanghai Cement Co., Ltd. (上海水泥股份有限公司) on June 29, 1946, after the Second World War (this was officially implemented on January 1, 1948). See Shanghai shuinichang (1990, p. 173).

The Shanghai Cement Company was one of the leading Chinese cement companies at the time, known for its "Elephant" brand, alongside the Qixin Cement Company (启新洋灰公司) in Hebei, the China Cement Company (中国水泥公司) in Nanjing, and the Guangdong Xicun Cement Factory (广东西村士敏土厂) in Guangdong.[8] Looking at its production volume during the Republican period, it generally ranged from 50,000 to 80,000 tons before the war, reaching a peak of 97,800 tons in 1936 (Shanghai shuinichang 1990, pp. 25, 32, 40). After the outbreak of the war it was occupied by the Japanese army and came under the management of Onoda Cement (小野田セメント), one of the leading Japanese cement companies. Due to the impact of the conflict, the factory was forced to halt production in 1938 and 1939, greatly reducing its production volume, but from 1940 onward it managed an annual output of from 40,000 to 70,000 tons. After the war, it struggled in the face of the influx of American-made cement, and was forced to halt production from September 1946 to July 1947. However, after resuming production, it recovered to about half of its prewar peak production volume in 1948, just before the occupation of Shanghai by the CCP in May 1949 (Shanghai shuinichang 1990, pp. 36–37).

One of the characteristics of Shanghai's cement industry was that it depended on other regions for its primary raw material, limestone, and its fuel, coal, despite being itself located in the suburbs of a major city. The transportation cost was therefore one of the major issues in the industry's management. The Shanghai Cement Company transported limestone from the Chenwanshan Mine (陈湾山矿山, developed by the company) in Huzhou (湖州), Zhejiang Province, to Longhua Town by ship (see Fig. 10.2), and by 1930 it owned 40 barges for such transportation (Shanghai shuinichang 1990, p. 17). As for coal, the company utilized coal scraps from the transport ships under Liu Hongsheng, who was selling coal from the Kai Luan Coal Mine (开滦煤矿) in Tangshan (唐山), Hebei Province, and the Jiawang Coal Mine (贾汪煤矿) in Xuzhou (徐州), Jiangsu Province, in the Yangtze River basin (Shanghai jianzhucailiaogongyezhi bianzuanweiyuanhui 1997, p. 60).

Although the main market for the Shanghai Cement Company during the Republican period was primarily Shanghai itself, the company's share in the Shanghai market was not necessarily dominant, due to the aforementioned problem of securing its raw material supply. In fact, the company's history, Shanghai shuinichang (1990), states that "before the outbreak of the [Second Sino-Japanese War], the sales volume of Elephant brand cement in Shanghai accounted for about 3/4 of the total sales volume of the factory and about 1/3 of the total sales volume of the Shanghai cement market" (Shanghai shuinichang 1990, p. 10). At that time, Shanghai was the largest city in China, with a strong demand for cement, and so both domestic and foreign cement companies were competing fiercely for the Shanghai market.[9] Compared to

[8] There are numerous studies on the Liu Hongsheng business group, including specifically Shanghai Cement Co., Ltd., but refer in particular to Chan (2006), Ro (2010), and Shu (2010).

[9] Observers at the time estimated the cement consumption in Shanghai in the mid-1930s to be 30% of the national total of 700,000 tons, so about 230,000 tons, and the shipment volume for the Shanghai market at that time was 90,000 tons for Shanghai Cement Company, 80,000 tons for the Qixin Cement Company (启新洋灰公司), and 70,000 tons for the China Cement Company (中国水泥公司). Considering the annual cement import volume of Shanghai Port at that time, which

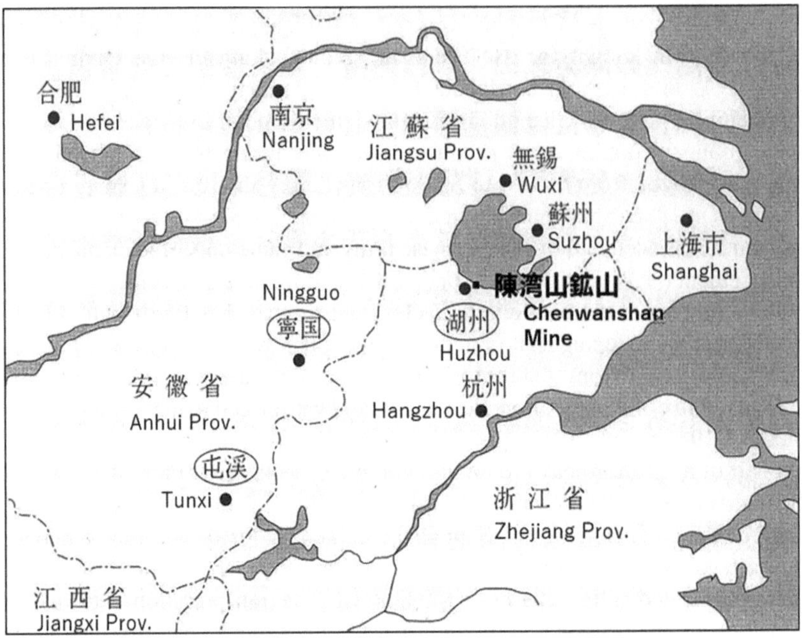

Fig. 10.2 Map of Shanghai and East China. *Source* Created by author

the scale of this enormous market, Shanghai's own cement industry was still relatively small, and the city's demand was thus met by the influx of cement from other regions.

10.2.2 The Socialist System and the Shanghai Cement Industry

The takeover of power by the CCP in 1949 and the subsequent introduction of a socialist system greatly changed the situation surrounding the Shanghai cement industry. Like other industries, the cement industry gradually took on the form of a non-market planned economy and public ownership of the means of production in the 1950s. The former was promoted by the material control policy after 1950, while the latter was brought about by the socialist transformation completed in 1956.

As for the material control policy, the government had already been placing orders (订货) for cement from the Shanghai Cement Company since late April 1950. Subsequently, cement orders from government and military agencies such as the East

was about 10,000–40,000 tons, the share of Shanghai Cement Company would come to about 30–40%. See Nihon portland cement dōgyōkai chōsabu and Kobayashi (1936, p. 29), Zongshuiwusishu tongjike (various years).

China Industrial Department (华东工业部), Shanghai Municipal Industrial Relief Committee (上海市工赈委员会), Zhejiang Water Conservancy Bureau (浙江水利局), Hangzhou Construction Bureau (杭州建设局), East China Supporting Front Highway Committee (华东支前公路委员会), Jiangxi Military Region Command (江西军区司令部), and the East China Air Force Agency (华东空军机关, responsible for airport repair and construction) increased rapidly, ultimately accounting for 90% of the factory's annual sales volume that year. Since November 1950, the production and sales of the Shanghai Cement Company were incorporated into the state plan, with all of the company's products being purchased and sold uniformly by the East China Industrial Department.[10] As for the selling price, it tended to be fixed from the late 1950s. The factory delivery price (brand unknown, ordinary Portland cement 500, paper bag packaging) fluctuated from between 56 and 74 yuan per ton from 1950 to 1957, but was fixed at 52 yuan from 1958 and maintained this price until 1977. The wholesale price (Elephant brand, ordinary Portland cement 400, paper bag packaging) was in similar fashion set at 73 yuan from 1956, and remained fixed until it rose to 80 yuan in the 1970s (Shanghai jiagezhi bianzuanweiyuanhui 1998, pp. 470–472; Zhongguokexueyuan shanghaijingjiyanjiusuo, and Shanghaishehuikexueyuan jingjiyanjiusuo 1958, pp. 510–511).

Furthermore, with its incorporation into the national production and sales plan, the Shanghai Cement Company was subject to the unified distribution of raw materials and fuel by the state. For coal, after 1950 the supply mainly shifted to the Datong (大同) and Yangquan (阳泉) coal mines in Shanxi Province, and the Huainan (淮南) and Huaibei (淮北) coal mines in Anhui Province. On the other hand, for limestone, in 1957 the Shanghai Cement Company had to transfer the Chenwanshan Mine in Huzhou, Zhejiang Province, as well as the own ships needed for limestone transportation, to the local government upon request. After that, although it received supplies from limestone mines in Zhejiang, Jiangsu, and Anhui provinces, the company continued to face difficulties in production as a result of limestone shortages (Shanghai jianzhucailiaogongyezhi bianzuanweiyuanhui 1997, p. 60; Shanghai shuinichang 1990, pp. 64–66). This territorial control by local governments, associated with the public ownership of these resources and property rights, was a defining characteristic of the Chinese socialist system (Tajima 2000).

[10] Shanghai shuinichang (1990, pp. 53–54, 57). As for the ordering relationship with the East China Industrial Department, the order contract was divided into semi-annual periods, and the annual cement production volume and purchase price were determined after central review based on mutual discussions. At the time of sale, the East China Industrial Department distributed what were called receipt certificates (提货单) to each purchasing unit, which then received the product from the Shanghai Cement Company based on these. Payments were made in two installments, the first and second halves of each month, based on the settlement between the Shanghai Cement Factory and the East China Industrial Department. From January 1953 onward, the supervisory organization of the Shanghai Cement Company changed from the East China Industrial Department to the East China Chemical Industry Bureau (华东化工局) and the Shanghai Office of the Central Ministry of Heavy Industry (中央重工业部上海办事处). The procedures for sales were simplified through this change. The purchasing units contracted directly with the Shanghai Cement Company based on the notification certificates issued by the bureau, and then made payments and deliveries.

Against the backdrop of these reorganizations in both production and sales, the Shanghai Cement Company signed an agreement to undergo transformation into a public-private jointly-owned enterprise with the Shanghai Municipal Bureau of Heavy Industry Management (上海市重工业管理局) on June 21, 1954, and consequently became the public-private jointly-owned Shanghai Cement Factory (上海水泥厂) in 1955. On January 1, 1956, moreover, it merged with the Tianxiang Industrial Company Cement Factory (天祥实业公司水泥厂) in Shanghai, and became a central enterprise belonging to the Central Ministry of Heavy Industry's Bureau of Construction Materials Industry (中央重工业部建筑材料工业局) (Shanghai shuinichang 1990, pp. 62–63). According to the list of central government-affiliated cement factories nationwide as of 1956, the production capacity of the Shanghai Cement Factory at that time was 190,000 tons per year, ranking 16th overall, while the top position was occupied by the public-private jointly-owned Qixin Cement Factory, which had an annual production of 580,000 tons (Wang 2005, pp. 134–135). However, in July 1958, the affiliation of the Shanghai Cement Company was transferred from the Central Ministry of Heavy Industry to the Shanghai Municipal Government due to the implementation of the "downward" (下放) policy of central enterprises discussed above (Shanghai shuinichang 1990, p. 70).

Figure 10.3 summarizes the cement production and distribution management organizations at both the central and Shanghai levels during the planned economy period. In response to the management of production and distribution at the central level being divided into the construction materials industry system and the materials management system (including the China Construction Materials General Company (中国建筑材料总公司), a corresponding system was developed in Shanghai consisting of the Bureau of Construction Engineering (建筑工程局), the Construction Materials Industry Company (建筑材料工业公司), and production units such as the Shanghai Cement Factory as the production system, with the Shanghai Municipal Bureau of Material Management (上海市物资局) and the Shanghai Branch of the China Construction Materials Company (中国建筑材料公司上海市公司) as the distribution system. In other words, there coexisted a vertical management system for production and distribution at the central level, from which the central authorities managed Shanghai, and a territorial management system in Shanghai, and these two systems shifted in influence over the industry according to the central government's policy at the time.

Thus, the major change under the socialist system was that cement production and distribution were each incorporated into the state plan and reorganized accordingly. In a sense, this meant the clear separation of the two functions of production and sales that formerly private cement companies had themselves managed. As a result, production units were engaged only in production by order of the production management system, and subsequent distribution was entrusted to the materials management system. However, another key point to note here is that the management mechanisms of both systems were not necessarily centralized nationwide, and while cement production enterprises were vertically subordinate to the central government's corresponding agencies, they also operated under the framework of the local administrative control of Shanghai.

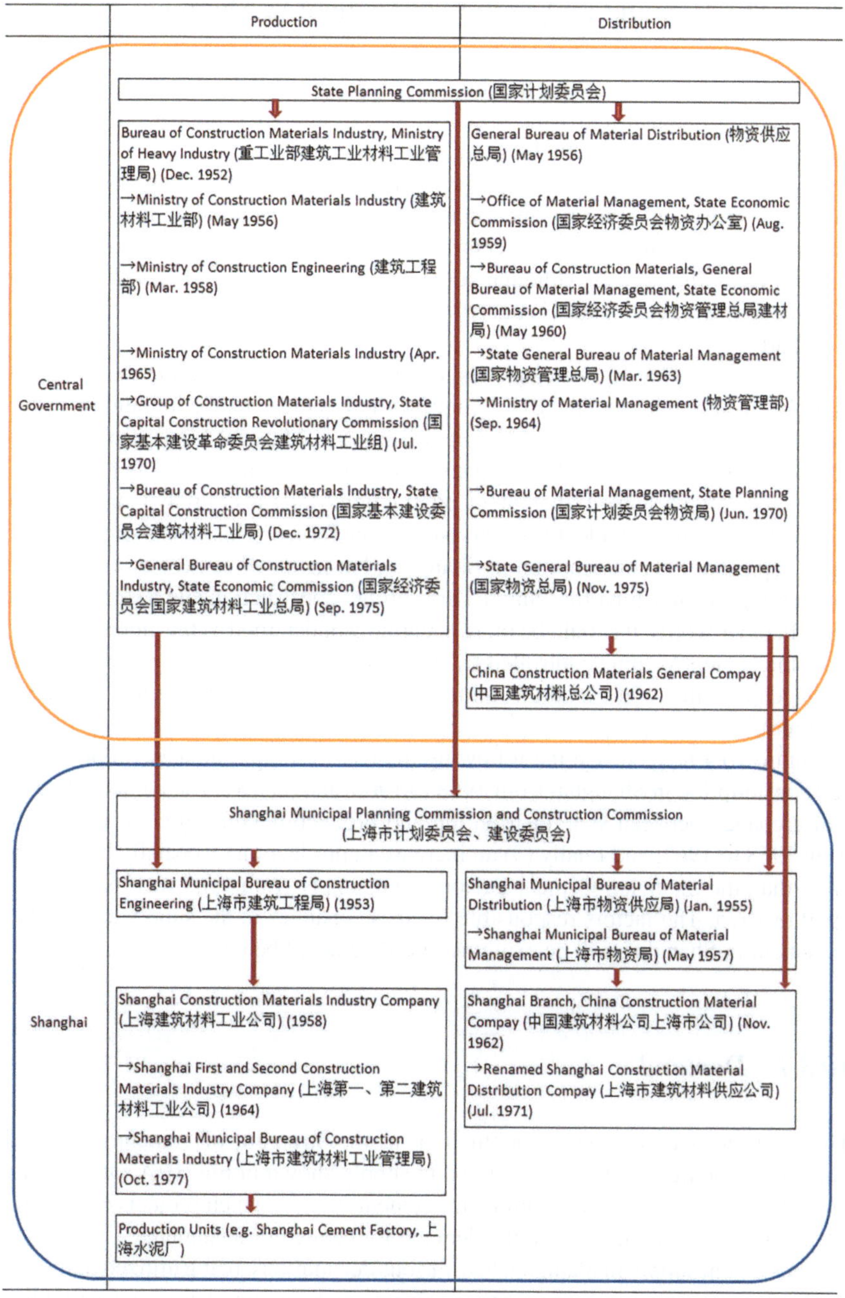

Fig. 10.3 Management organizations for cement production and distribution in the Central Government and Shanghai, 1949–1978. *Note* Figures in parentheses indicate year and month of establishment of organization. Down arrows indicate supervisory relationship. *Sources* Chō (1995, pp. 93–98), Wang (2005, p. 167), Dangdai zhongguo congshu bianjibu (1990, p. 657), and Dangdai zhongguo congshu bianjibu (1993, pp. 27–29, 271–274, 676–677)

10.3 The Demand and Supply of Cement in Shanghai

This section will examine what the relations between supply and demand for cement were like in Shanghai under the socialist system, and what the data reveals about how each entity responded to the situation.

Figure 10.4 shows the trends in cement production (including the Shanghai Cement Factory and other production units), supply, consumption, and state distribution (i.e., distribution from the central plan to Shanghai) in Shanghai during the planned economy period. Although some items are inevitably somewhat fragmentary due to the lack of data, it is nevertheless possible to grasp the basic trends from this chart.

Before embarking upon an analysis, it is necessary to first explain the concept of "supply" as it applies to Fig. 10.4. "Supply" here represents the amount of cement supplied through the Shanghai Municipal Bureau of Material Management and the China Construction Materials Company, Shanghai Branch (中国建筑材料公司上海市公司) (later renamed Shanghai Construction Materials Supply Company after 1971), the latter being under the supervision of the former. This supply did not necessarily represent the consumption in Shanghai, but included cement as a type of aid to other regions in China for "Small Third Front" construction and to foreign countries. In other words, it should be more accurately understood as the amount released from the cement volume controlled by the Shanghai Municipal Bureau of Material Management (this was called the cement "resource volume" in the terminology of the time).

Figure 10.4 helps reveal the following trends: (1) a rapid increase in production and consumption in Shanghai from 1958 to 1960, and then a subsequent decline; (2) a discrepancy between state distribution and production/consumption in Shanghai from 1958 to 1962; and finally (3) an increase in production (especially by factories other than the Shanghai Cement Factory) and supply from 1963 to 1966 and from 1969 to 1975. The factors responsible for these changes in the supply and demand of cement in Shanghai will be examined in more detail below.

10.3.1 Demand

This section takes a more in-depth look at the structure of cement demand in Shanghai. The trends of consumption and supply shown in Fig. 10.4 and the information pertaining to the destinations for cement (that is, which projects cement was supplied to) offer some clues to the demand for cement in Shanghai.

The cement supply in Shanghai had various destinations, being utilized mainly for production, repair, capital construction, private use, agricultural use, civil air defense, foreign aid (such as for Vietnam), disaster relief, and use by central enterprises in Shanghai. In particular, the most significant destinations were capital construction, repair, and agriculture, with annual supplies in the 1960s totaling 120,000–220,000

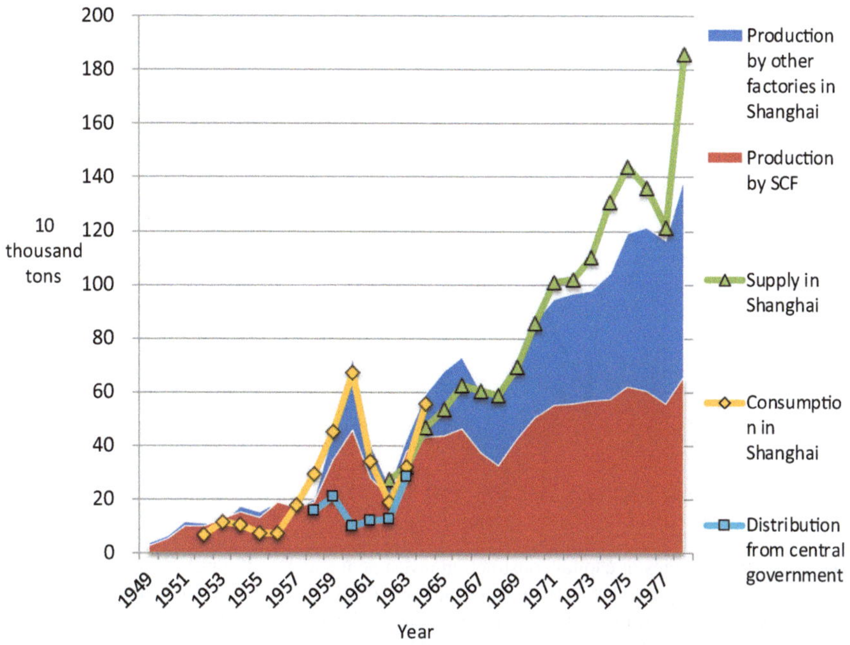

Fig. 10.4 Shanghai's cement production, supply, consumption and distribution from central government, 1949–1978. *Notes* (1) "Supply in Shanghai" likely includes the amount of self-sufficient production and supply of Hongqi Cement Factory, which belonged to the Shanghai Municipal Bureau of Real Estate, supply for the central government's organizations and enterprises in Shanghai, "Small Third Front Construction" (小三线) and foreign countries for aid. (2) "Consumption in Shanghai" includes the amount of consumption by self-sufficient units. *Sources* Total production in Shanghai: Shanghai jianzhucailiaogongyezhi bianzuanweiyuanhui (1997, p. 54); Production by SCF: Shanghai shuinichang (1990, p. 190); Supply in Shanghai: Shanghai wuziliutongzhi bianzuanweiyuanhui (2003, pp. 242–243); Consumption in Shanghai: "Difangxitong zhuyaowuzi xiaofeiliang ji bizhong: 1957–1962 nian" (地方系统主要物资消费量及比重 1957–1962年, Main Commodity Consumption and Proportion of Local Systems: 1957–1962) in B31-1-230 and "Zhuyaowuzi xiaofeiliang" (主要物資消費量, Main Commodity Consumption) in B31-1-232; Distribution from the central government: "Difangxitong zhuyaowuzi xiaofeiliang ji bizhong: 1957–1962 nian" in B31-1-230 and "Zhuyaowuzi fendiqudaohuoliang" (主要物资分地区到货量, Main Commodity Arrival Volume by Region) in B31-1-232

tons for capital construction (25.2–45.7% of the total supply), 70,000–130,000 tons for repair, and 21,600–149,500 tons for agriculture (Shanghai wuziliutongzhi bianzuanweiyuanhui 2003, pp. 236–240).

While there were, naturally, various factors determining increases or decreases in demand, it is to be expected that there was a correlation between the supply for capital construction, which accounted for the largest proportion of the supply, and the amount of capital construction investment in Shanghai. Looking at the time-series changes from Fig. 10.5, which shows the year-on-year growth rates of Shanghai's capital construction investment and cement consumption/supply since 1953, it is clear

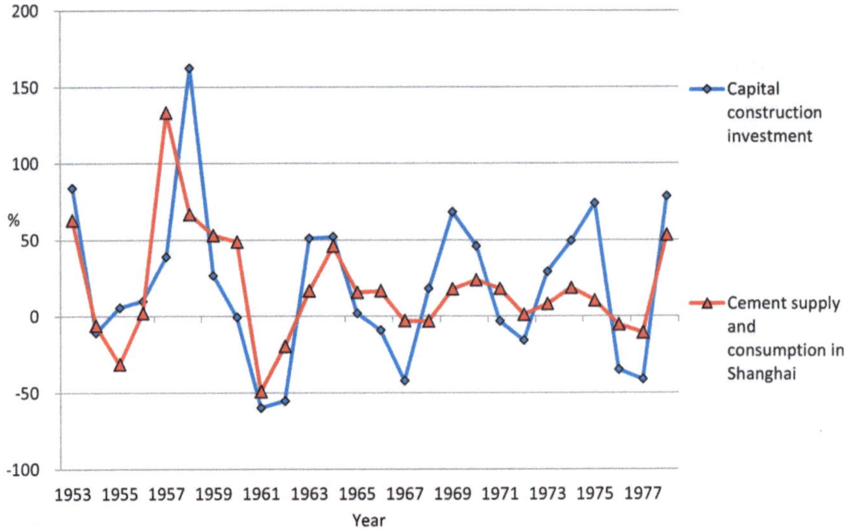

Fig. 10.5 Growth rates of capital construction investment and growth rates of cement supply and consumption in Shanghai, 1953–1978. *Note* Data for "Cement Supply and Consumption in Shanghai" in 1952–1961 is from "Consumption in Shanghai," and that in 1962–1978 is from "Supply in Shanghai." Sources: Shanghaishi tongjiju (1992, p. 71) and Shanghai wuziliutongzhi bianzuanweiyuanhui (2003, pp. 242–243); "Difangxitong zhuyaowuzi xiaofeiliang ji bizhong: 1957–1962 nian" (地方系统主要物资消费量及比重 (1957–1962年), Main Commodity Consumption and Proportion of Local Systems: 1957–1962) in B31-1-230, and "Zhuyaowuzi xiaofeiliang" (主要物资消费量, Main Commodity Consumption) in B31-1-232

that the years when the basic construction investment growth rate was relatively high (above the average for 1953–78) were 1953, 1957–60, 1963–64, 1969–70, 1973–75, and 1978, while years that saw high cement supply growth rate were 1953, 1957–60, 1964, 1970, 1974, and 1978. Although there is a degree of discrepancy, these periods almost coincide (correlation coefficient is 0.622; the cause of the sudden increase in cement consumption in 1957 is unknown). This makes it possible to infer that changes in the amount of capital construction investment were one of the major factors influencing Shanghai's cement demand.

Looking more closely at the causes of the increases in capital construction investment and cement consumption/supply—with the periods of increase being 1953, 1957–60, 1964, 1970, 1974, and 1978—one can find a correlation between increases in capital construction investment and various projects and policies: the start of the First Five Year Plan in 1953, the Great Leap Forward from 1958 to 1960, the "Small Third Front" construction project in 1964, the local industrialization policy in 1970,[11] the construction of the Shanghai Petrochemical General Factory (上海石油化工总厂) in 1974, and the construction of the Baoshan Steel General Factory (宝山钢铁总厂) in 1978.

[11] On the local industrialization policy in the early 1970s, refer to Tajima (1990).

The increase in cement consumption due to the start of the First Five Year Plan in 1953 is relatively easy to understand. As for the increase in 1957–60, the source Shanghai shuinichang (1990) states,

> In 1958, the national capital construction project was massively expanded. Shanghai's capital construction task was very heavy, and the demand for cement also increased dramatically. At that time, the cement needed by Shanghai was more than 800,000 tons per year, but the Shanghai area could only produce 170,000 tons of ordinary Portland cement per year at the Shanghai Cement Factory (Longhua Factory), which was far from satisfying the demand. (Shanghai shuinichang 1990, p. 70)

This suggests that the demand for capital construction projects surged due to the Great Leap Forward, and the cement supply could not keep up.

The demand spurred by the construction efforts as part of the "Small Third Front" in 1964 will be discussed later along with the corresponding supply issues. As for the local industrialization policy of 1970–71, which mainly focused on rural industrialization at the county level, this was based on the expansion of the administrative districts of Shanghai Municipality in 1958, which were discussed in Chapter 2. The promotion of rural industrialization at the county level around 1970 resulted in increased demand for cement in the suburb counties of Shanghai. In response, construction materials companies (建筑材料公司) were established in the suburbs of each county in Shanghai in 1972, and under the principle of "mainly depending on horizontal relationships, in combination with vertical and horizontal relationships," the distribution of construction materials needed for agriculture, forestry, livestock, side jobs, fishing, and urban industrial construction within each county was organized (Shanghai wuziliutongzhi bianzuanweiyuanhui 2003, p. 239).

The construction of the Shanghai Petrochemical General Factory was the largest capital construction project in Shanghai after the establishment of the PRC, and the Shanghai Construction Materials Company issued the "Regulations on the Supply of Construction Materials Needed for the Petrochemical General Factory Project" (石油化工总厂工程需用建筑材料的供应办法), supplying 664,600 tons of cement for the first phase of construction alone. When it came to the construction of the Baoshan Steel General Factory four years later in 1978, a total of 2.525 million tons of cement was supplied in the first and second phases of construction. These massive construction projects caused a great demand for cement in Shanghai (Shanghai wuziliutongzhi bianzuanweiyuanhui 2003, p. 238).

Considering these factors behind the rapid increase in demand for cement, it can be said that they all had their origin in the implementation of the central government's policies to promote industrial production. Industrial policies or industrial development campaigns such as the First Five Year Plan, the Great Leap Forward, the "Small Third Front," and the local industrialization policy, were all called for nationwide as part of the overall central government policy, even if they were implemented in practice on a local basis for each local area. The construction of the Shanghai Petrochemical General Factory and the Baoshan Steel General Factory was a slightly different matter from the above policies, but both of these were introduced as enormous projects planned at the central level. In other words, the demand fluctuations in Shanghai were mainly caused by policies led by the central government. The problem for Shanghai was then how to respond to this greatly fluctuating demand situation in a planned economy where there existed almost no route to procure cement from the market.

10.3.2 Supply I: State Distribution

It is therefore apt to move on to the consideration of supply. The first point to note is state unified distribution (国家统一分配). One of the main sources of supply in Shanghai, this referred to cement allocated to Shanghai from the state (central) plan. As already mentioned, cement was a Class 1 material, and therefore it was basically distributed based on the state plan decided by the central government. However, in the case of Shanghai, cement was not physically transported from other regions except in emergencies, as will be mentioned later. The Shanghai Cement Factory, the core production unit in Shanghai, had been incorporated into the state plan, and the state unified distribution amount in Shanghai, therefore, meant the amount of cement transferred to the Shanghai Municipal Government's management from the factory's production. Conversely, even if the cement was produced in Shanghai, it did not automatically fall under Shanghai's management so long as it was incorporated into the state plan.

The problem at the local level was to what extent this state unified distribution amount actually met the demand for cement in Shanghai. Although only partial data is available for investigating this issue, the situation during 1958–63 can be clarified by looking back at Fig. 10.4. As pointed out above, consumption exceeded the state unified distribution amount in every year except 1963, and especially in 1960, consumption grew rapidly and the gap between the two became significantly larger. On this point, Shanghai wuziliutongzhi bianzuanweiyuanhui (2003) states that "in the 1960s, the cement that the state distributed to Shanghai was 125,000–250,000 tons per year, accounting for 45.1–53.6% of the total city demand," suggesting that such a situation existed throughout the 1960s (Shanghai wuziliutongzhi bianzuanweiyuanhui 2003, p. 232). The upshot of all this was that the state unified distribution was unable to fully meet the cement demand in Shanghai from at least the late 1950s to the 1960s.

However, it is important to recognize that, as seen in the previous section on the material distribution system, the distribution system based on the state plan was not necessarily fixed, but rather operated in a relatively flexible manner depending on the period. The decentralization policy of the late 1950s to the early 1960s, and then in renewed fashion in 1970, loosened the vertical line of "state unified distribution" in cement management to a certain extent, allowing autonomous cement procurement activities by local governments. Especially in the case of Shanghai, the "regional responsibility system" for cement was implemented in 1967, which was earlier than in other regions, and as a result, the Shanghai Municipal Government was able to place all of the cement produced by the Shanghai Cement Factory—a "unified distribution" factory incorporated into the state plan—under its (the municipal government's) management, except for the supply committed to central enterprises in Shanghai (Shanghai wuziliutongzhi bianzuanweiyuanhui 2003, p. 232).

In addition to this decentralization policy, the Shanghai Branch of the China Construction Materials Company, a material management agency in Shanghai mentioned above, had requested that its supervising organization permit an increase in the distribution of cement to Shanghai, drawing from the increased production of Shanghai's producers. Consequently, in 1963, the State Construction Materials Industry Bureau (国家建材工业局) agreed to increase the distribution to Shanghai by 77,000 tons, using Shanghai's increased cement production (Shanghai wuziliutongzhi bianzuanweiyuanhui 2003, p. 232). Thus, although the state unified distribution amount through the regular route was not by itself sufficient, the central government had given discretion to local governments in procuring cement by allowing flexibility in the operation of the material distribution system. This was also a significant premise underlying the cement procurement actions of the Shanghai Municipal Government itself, which will be considered next.

10.3.3 Supply II: Self-Procurement by Shanghai

This section will examine the cement self-procurement activities of the Shanghai Municipal Government, by classifying them into three types: the expansion of the production facilities of the Shanghai Cement Factory, the construction of new factories, and imports from other regions.

a. Expansion of Production Facilities of Shanghai Cement Factory

The first type was the expansion of the production facilities of the Shanghai Cement Factory, via investment by the Shanghai Municipal Government. As can be seen in Fig. 10.4, the production volume of the Shanghai Cement Factory had been gradually increasing overall, despite several sudden increases and decreases. This was partly due to the proactive stance of the Shanghai Municipal Government toward the expansion of the company's facilities. As already mentioned, the Shanghai Cement Factory was transferred to the local government's management in 1958 due to the "downward" policy for central enterprises. This led to the Shanghai Municipal Planning Commission and Construction Commission becoming actively involved in the expansion of the facilities of the Shanghai Cement Factory in order to alleviate Shanghai's cement supply shortage (Shanghai shuinichang 1990, p. 70).

This is demonstrated by Table 10.2, which lists the expansion of the facilities of the Shanghai Cement Factory and the main bodies of investment expenditure during the planned economy period. The direct expansion of production capacity listed in the table includes the strengthening of facilities and the construction of new factories for the No.1 and No.2 kiln systems in 1958–59, as well as the addition of the No. 6 kiln and related facility updates in 1971–74. Looking at the investment expenditure institutions for these two projects, the former was funded by investment from the Shanghai

Municipal Government.[12] Regarding the latter, although the construction of the No.6 kiln was carried out with investment from the State Construction Commission as a national basic construction project, the technical, large-scale renovation of the kiln was fueled by investment from the Shanghai Finance Bureau, which amounted to 5.31 million yuan, greatly exceeding the state investment of 1.283 million yuan. In addition, many of the investments related to improving productivity and safety were made at the Shanghai Municipal level, while investments from the central level were mainly for tests to promote the introduction of new technologies, such as preheater testing and the introduction of bulk cement. These particulars demonstrate how the Shanghai Municipal Government was actively involved in the expansion and maintenance of the production capacity of the Shanghai Cement Factory.

b. Construction of New Factories

In terms of increasing the production capacity of the Shanghai cement industry, the construction of new cement factories by the Shanghai Municipal Government and its subordinate units contributed more significantly than did the expansion of the existing facilities of the Shanghai Cement Factory. As Fig. 10.4 shows, the production volume of the Shanghai Cement Factory accounted for almost all of Shanghai's cement production until 1958, while that of other production units little. However, during the Great Leap Forward period of 1959–60, cement production by other production units rose sharply for a brief interval, and then expanded again after 1964, before experiencing continuously increases after 1970.

This structural change in the cement production in Shanghai coincides with the establishment years of each cement factory in the city during the planned economy period shown in Table 10.3. Most factories, except for the Shanghai Cement Factory, were established in a concentrated burst in 1958–59, and then after 1970, which was clearly in response to the rapidly increasing cement demand during those periods. If one compares the annual average production volumes of 1965–69, the total production of the four factories of Hongqi (红旗), Wusong (吴淞), Yangjing (洋泾), and Jinshan (金山) (excluding Shanghai White Cement Factory (上海白水泥厂), which specialized in the production of special products such as white cement) established in 1958–59 amounted to 234,000 tons, which was only about half of the 406,000 tons produced by the Shanghai Cement Factory. Furthermore, since the 1970s, small cement factories came to be newly built and renovated in various counties in the suburbs of Shanghai in order to satisfy the demand resulting from the county-level local industrialization policy.

A particularly interesting case among these new cement factories established by the Shanghai Municipal Government was the Shanghai Shengli Cement Factory

---

[12] The "Shanghai 1959 National Economic Plan Report" (上海市1959年国民经济计划报告) stated, "The investment in capital construction by the local government in 1959 was 560 million yuan, […] industrial investment in the local government's capital construction was 380 million yuan, […] [and] important projects related to the increase in raw material production included the new construction of the Wujing Chemical Factory (吴泾化工厂) and the Wujing Coking Factory (吴泾煉焦厂), as well as the expansion of the Shanghai Cement Factory" (Shanghaishi jihuaweiyuanhui 1998, p. 42).

Table 10.2 Investments in expansion of production facilities of Shanghai Cement Factory, 1949–1978

Year and month	Investment details	Organizations initiating/ leading investment	Organizations expending investment	Investment amount
1956–63	Trial installation of preheater	Technical Section, State MCM	State MCM	50,000 yuan (installation of equipment and trial) 69,380 yuan (trial)
1958–59	Expansion of facilities of No.1 and No.2 kilns and construction of new factory for No.5 kiln (Term 1 and 2 from Jul. 1958, Term 3 from Nov. 1958)	Shanghai PC Shanghai BCEI	Shanghai Municipality	Term 1: over 460,400 yuan Term 2: 5,059,200 yuan (Equipment: 3,102,200 yuan Construction: 1,957,000 yuan) Term 3: 14,358,500 yuan
1961	Technical reform of cooling, dustproofing, etc. of No.1 and No.2 kilns (completed in Feb. 1962)	Shanghai BCEI	Shanghai PC	2,500,000 yuan
Aug. 1965	Installation of high-performance dust chambers in No.1 -4 kilns (completed in 1968)	Shanghai BCEI	Shanghai PC State EC and Ministry of Finance	500,000 yuan (Shanghai PC) 700,000 yuan (State EC and Ministry of Finance)
Jan. 1966	Reinforcement of transportation, packing, drying over fire and dustproofing of pulverized coal ash	Shanghai PC Shanghai IPC	Shanghai BF	500,000 yuan (technical reform)
1966	Expansion of cylindrical body of No.5 kiln (completed in Sep. 1968)	Shanghai BCEI	Shanghai PC	254,800 yuan
Jan. 1966	Expansion of facilities for bulk cement carrier trucks	State EC	State EC	400,000 yuan
1971	Construction of No.6 kiln (wet rotary kiln) (production started in 1974)	Shanghai RC of BCEI	State CC	1,283,000 yuan

(continued)

Table 10.2 (continued)

Year and month	Investment details	Organizations initiating/leading investment	Organizations expending investment	Investment amount
1973–74	Updating No.6 kiln facilities to increase production ability	Industry and Transportation Group, Shanghai RC	Shanghai BF	1,850,000 yuan (technical reform) 3,460,000 yuan (additional investment and Shanghai major reform)
1978	Technical reform and major repair of No.1,3,5 kilns (completed in Sep. 1982)	Shanghai Municipality	Shanghai Municipality	650,000 yuan
Apr. 1978	Repair of No.6 kiln	State General BCMI	State General BCMI	3,100,000 yuan
Jul. 1978	Master plan for acceleration of development of bulk cement	State MCM	State MCM	2,580,000 yuan
1978	Reform and update of No.1 workshop (production officially started in 1984)	Shanghai BCMI	State PC, EC and Shanghai Municipality	State: Converting equipment of Baoshan Cement Factory (宝山水泥厂), equivalent to approximately 9,930,000 yuan, to SCF Shanghai: Self-financing the sum remaining after subtracting state investment Total investment in Apr. 1983, when project officially approved: 76,237,500 yuan

Notes PC = Planning Commission (计划委员会), BCEI = Bureau of Construction Engineering Industry (建筑工程局), IPC = Industrial Production Commission (工业生产委员会), RC = Revolutionary Commission (革命委员会), EC = Economic Commission (经济委员会), CC = Construction Commission (建设委员会), MCM = Ministry of Construction Materials (建筑材料工业部), BCMI=Bureau of Construction Materials Industry (建筑材料工业局), BF = Bureau of Finance (财政局). In original source, "Technical section, Ministry of Construction Materials Engineering" (建筑材料工程部技术司) is probably a misprint for "Technical section, Ministry of Construction Materials Industry" (建筑材料工业部技术司)

Source Shanghai shuinichang (1990, pp. 60, 70–75, 83–86, 91–92, 96–98, 104–105, 109, 182)

Table 10.3 Cement factories in Shanghai, 1949–1978

Name	Year of establishment	Location	Annual average production, 1965–1969	Notes
Shanghai Cement Factory	1920	Longhua Town (龍华镇)	40.6	Production started in 1923
Shanghai Hongqi Cement Factory	1958	Jiading County (嘉定县)	4.0	Belonged to Shanghai Municipal Bureau of Real Estate
Shanghai Yangjing Cement Factory	1958	Pudong Yangjing Town (浦东洋涇镇)	5.4	Belonged to Shanghai Municipal Bureau of Textile Industry when established
Shanghai Wusong Cement Factory	1958	Near Wenzaobang (蕰藻浜)	10.7	
Shanghai Jinshan Cement Factory	1959	Zhujing Town, Jinshan County (金山县朱涇镇)	3.3	Established as Jinshan Steel Factory, Jinshan county (金山县金山钢铁厂) in 1958
Shanghai White Cement Factory	1962	Wujing Industrial Area (吴涇工业区)	1.8	Established as part of Unified Factory belonged to No.4 Engineering Company, Shanghai Municipal Bureau of Construction Materials Industry (上海市建材工业局第四工程公司附属联合工厂) in 1959
Shanghai Pujiang Cement Factory	1970		-	
Shanghai Shengli Cement Factory	1970	Ningguo County, Anhui Province	-	Established as Huizhou Zhuanqu Shengli Cement Factory (徽州专区胜利水泥厂) in 1970, and renamed Shanghai Shengli Cement Factory in January 1974. Converted to Anhui province in 1985 and renamed Shengli Branch, Ningguo Cement Factory (宁国水泥厂胜利分厂)

(continued)

Table 10.3 (continued)

Name	Year of establishment	Location	Annual average production, 1965–1969	Notes
Shanghai Pudong Cement Factory	1971	Pudong	-	Established as Chuansha Refining Factory, Chuansha County Bureau of Agricultural Machinery (川沙县农机局川沙冶炼厂) in 1971. Dry rotary kiln installed in 1976. Renamed Shanghai Chuansha Cement Factory (上海川沙水泥厂) in 1981
Shanghai Songjiang Cement Factory	1971	Songjiang Town (松江镇)	-	Annual production of 10,000 tons when established
Shanghai Fengxian Cement Factory	1971	Northern part of Fengxian County (奉贤县)	-	
Nanhui Cement Factory	1973	Nanhui County (南汇县)	-	
Qingpu Cement Factory	1975	Qingpu County (青浦县)	-	
Chongming Cement Factory	1976	Chongming County (崇明县)	-	Production started in May 1979

Notes (1) Cement factories in the above table only cover ones listed in sources, not necessarily all factories in Shanghai during planned economy period. (2) "Annual average production" of Shanghai White Cement Factory is not for 1965–1969, but 1965–67 due to lack of data
Sources Shanghai jianzhucailiaogongyezhi bianzuanweiyuanhui (1997, pp. 10–45, 61–64), Shanghai shuinichang (1990, pp. 93–96), and B109-3-71

(上海胜利水泥厂), which started production in 1970. This factory was built in Ningguo County (宁国县), Anhui Province (see Fig. 10.2), with investment from the Shanghai Municipal Government, and its origin lay in the "Small Third Front" construction movement mentioned above, itself a component of the "Third Front Construction" that was rolled out nationwide from 1964.[13] The "Small Third Front" construction initiative aimed to build rear industrial bases in inland mountainous areas in preparation for an impending war with the US and the Soviet Union, and

[13] On the Third Front Construction and the Small Third Front, refer to Marukawa (1993), and Go (2002).

Shanghai's "Small Third Front" was set up in the Huizhou Special Division (徽州专区) in southern Anhui Province. This project triggered a large demand for cement for capital construction in the area, and so the Shanghai Economic Planning Commission (上海市经济计画委员会) and the Shanghai Municipal Bureau of Construction Engineering (上海建筑工程局) instructed the Shanghai Cement Factory to build a cement factory in the area in light of the high cost of transporting cement from Shanghai to Huizhou (Shanghai shuinichang 1990, p. 81).

Initially, the Tunxi Cement Factory (屯溪水泥厂), which was built as a primitive or backyard-style (土法) factory in Tunxi (屯溪), Anhui Province during the Great Leap Forward period, was renovated with investment and personnel from Shanghai. However, due to the relocation of the capital construction target area and quality issues at the Tunxi Cement Factory, it was decided to build a new factory, Shanghai Shengli Cement Factory in Ningguo County, Anhui Province in 1967 (the Tunxi Cement Factory was transferred to the Huizhou Special District government free of charge in 1968). The cement produced by the Shanghai Shengli Cement Factory was incorporated into the state's unified distribution materials and mainly put to use meeting the needs of Shanghai's "Small Third Front" construction as well as the Shanghai area itself. This factory continued to support Shanghai's cement supply until it was transferred to the local government of Ningguo in 1985 (Shanghai wuziliutongzhi bianzuanweiyuanhui 2003, p. 233).

In a similar fashion to the new cement factory construction undertaken in other regions, it should be noted that the Shanghai Municipal Government also worked to develop raw material resources for Shanghai. The Shanghai Construction Materials Company (上海建筑材料公司), from April 1971 onward, developed two limestone mines in Jurong County (句容县) and Dantu County (丹徒县) in Jiangsu Province, with a prepayment of 1.31 million yuan and equipment provision, and charged them with providing an annual output of 300,000 tons to the Shanghai Municipal Bureau of Metallurgical Industry (上海市冶金局). In 1972, the Shanghai Municipal Government developed limestone mines in Longxi (龍溪), Wuxing County (吴兴县) and Qingshan (青山), Changxing County (长兴县) in Zhejiang Province, and Linshan (林山), Dantu County, in Jiangsu Province, yielding an annual output of 1 million tons of limestone. In 1973, it also developed nine more limestone mines, including in Huanglongdong (黄龍洞), Wuxing County and Meixi (梅溪), Anji County (安吉县) in Zhejiang Province, and the annual output of these mines, which amounted to some 300,000 to 400,000 tons, was, except for a portion needed for local use, supplied to Shanghai (Shanghai wuziliutongzhi bianzuanweiyuanhui 2003, p. 235). Clearly, the government put considerable effort into securing limestone in response to the rapid increase in cement demand in Shanghai from the 1970s.

c. Imports from Other Regions

Aside from expanding existing facilities and establishing new ones, the authorities also imported cement from other regions, both domestically and abroad. One method adopted was essentially a form of barter exchange called "cooperative exchange" (协作串换). Such "cooperative exchange" began in 1972, and the cement that the

Shanghai Construction Materials Company obtained from other regions reached 2,500–4,796 tons per year in 1972–74.

There were also cases where cement was imported from abroad to cope with the sudden increase in demand. The Shanghai Construction Materials Company applied for a foreign exchange amount totaling 74.42 million US dollars from the Shanghai Planning Committee (上海市计划委员会), and imported 1.5832 million tons of cement and cement-related materials from 1972 onward (it is unclear until when, but in light of the descriptions of the materials in question it likely continued into the late 1980s).[14]

This analysis of the structure of cement demand and supply in Shanghai has revealed the following: (1) the increase in cement demand in Shanghai was primarily due to central government-led industrial production promotion policies; (2) there was a low level of state unified distribution through regular routes, and the material management system operated in practice in a flexible manner; and (3) the Shanghai Municipal Government undertook autonomous procurement activities in order to respond to the increase in cement demand, through utilizing non-market methods such as the expansion of production facilities, the construction of new factories, and finally barter exchanges and imports from abroad. In other words, while the central government advocated the principle of a planned economy characterized by the centralized management of materials, in practice it had to deal with supply–demand gaps caused by its own industrial policy, which it did by delegating the solution of supply shortages to local governments. This structure determined the process of development of the cement industry in Shanghai during the planned economy period, with small cement factories, as part of the "five small industries," scattered alongside the state unified distribution factory, the Shanghai Cement Factory.

What about the cement supply and demand situation in Shanghai after 1978? Generally speaking, the Reform and Opening-up Policy began in 1978. However, the "shortage economy" that had been developed over a long period did not disappear overnight, and supply shortages similar to those of the planned economy period were seen even in the early 1980s. In terms of cement, demand surged due to the implementation of successive construction projects, and the trend of supply shortages thus intensified.

Reflective of this reality, the procurement of cement in the form of barter exchanges, such as the "cooperative exchange" seen in the planned economy period, continued to exist after 1978. In the "Notice on Arranging the Main Material Plan Required for Material Cooperation in 1982" (关于安排1982年物资协作所需主要

[14] Shanghai wuziliutongzhi bianzuanweiyuanhui (2003, pp. 234–236). The original paper that this chapter was based on stated that "The Shanghai Building Materials Company applied to the Shanghai Planning Commission for a foreign exchange amount of 74.42 million yuan, and imported 1.5832 million tons of cement based on this in 1972" (Kajima 2010, p. 162). However, this was technically inaccurate in that the cement import volume was not for 1972 alone but instead the cumulative amount since 1972; moreover, the unit of foreign exchange was US dollar, and the items imported using the foreign exchange included not only cement but also glass plates and diamond raw materials. The author would like to express his gratitude to Professor Zhang Xinyuan for pointing out this error and enabling its correction.

物资计画的通知) issued by the Shanghai Planning Commission in February 1982, cement and other construction materials were considered important materials to be cooperatively import[ed] (协进, i.e., to be procured in cooperation with other regions and institutions) while bicycles, sewing machines, washing machines, color TVs, tobacco, beer, chemical industrial products, cars, housing, and so on were designated cooperative export (协出) materials, which were to provide the compensation for the cooperative import materials. In 1986, 91 cars and 4996 square meters of housing were cooperatively exported, while more than 70,000 tons of cement were cooperatively imported (Shanghai wuziliutongzhi bianzuanweiyuanhui 2003, pp. 234–235).

What significantly changed this situation was the increase in cement procurement through the market. With the recovery of market functions after 1978, the relative role of state unified distribution declined, and,

> From 1979 to 1984, the cement distributed by the state to Shanghai was 620,000 to 1.02 million tons, more than three times the amount before the implementation of the 'regional responsibility system,' but the proportion of the state unified distribution to Shanghai's total demand decreased from about 50% to about 34%... […] ...after 1984, the varieties and quantities of construction materials distributed by the state to Shanghai gradually decreased. (Shanghai wuziliutongzhi bianzuanweiyuanhui 2003, p. 232)

In Shanghai, it was not until the late 1980s that cement procurement through the market began to cover most of the demand, whereupon the long-running problem of cement shortages was basically resolved.

In conclusion, this chapter has examined the relationship between the material distribution system and local supply and demand in Shanghai, using the cement industry as a case study. The implications derived from this can be summarized under three main headings, as follows:

(1) The Structure of the "Vertical Shortage" in Cement

During the planned economy period, cement was primarily under the control of the State Planning Commission as a Class 1 material, and the distribution was not through the market but instead based on the central plan. This meant that the central government had the authority to vertically control the overall supply of cement. At the same time, the central government, in principle, should have been able to control the supply and demand of cement in each region, and for every unit, while distributing cement accordingly, since it wielded the decision-making authority for industrial planning, a policy that strongly influenced cement demand.

However, in reality, the central government did not (or could not) distribute cement in accordance with the cement demand caused by its own industrial production promotion policies. As shown, the various surges in cement demand in Shanghai were primarily triggered by policies initiated by the central government itself, but the state unified distribution of cement from the central government to Shanghai was insufficient to meet these needs from at least the late 1950s to the 1960s. This was a problem resulting from the central government's inability to grasp demand and carry out distribution efficiently, as well as a structural problem caused by pushing for an overly ambitious industrial production promotion policy nationwide relative to the existing cement supply capacity.

(2) The Central Government's Attitude toward "Vertical Shortages"

The attitude of the central government toward the "vertical shortage" of cement at the local level was to introduce flexibility into the material distribution system itself. The adjustment of the cement distribution ratio in 1960 and the introduction of the "regional responsibility system" in 1970 (in 1967 in the case of Shanghai) were measures to relax the vertical control of materials by the central government, a fundamental premise of the planned economy, by delegating material management authority to the local governments. Through these relaxation adjustments, the central government prompted local governments to address the shortages of cement in their respective regions through exercising a degree of discretionary power, instead of distributing cement from the central government in accordance with demand at the local level.

(3) The Response of Local Governments to "Vertical Shortages"

Under such circumstances, the Shanghai Municipal Government carried out various autonomous initiatives to secure the supply of cement in Shanghai. However, procurement through the market was restricted under the planned economy, and so the government's cement procurement activities had to rely on measures such as the expansion of existing production facilities, the establishment of new factories, and bartering with other domestic regions and/or arranging imports. The small cement factories that emerged one after another in Shanghai in the 1970s, the so-called "five small industries," first emerged within this context, and the expansion of local cement industry production outside the state plan, seen nationwide during the same period, was a phenomenon that can clearly be attributed to the material distribution system of the planned economy period and the central government's industrial production promotion policies, in a similar vein to the case of Shanghai examined in this chapter.

To summarize from the above case study on cement in Shanghai, the material distribution system during the planned economy period can be described as a system that, while based on the institutional premise of planned material distribution by the central government, in reality, took on the form it did only through local governments being permitted to resolve the "vertical shortages" that arose when the central government could not fully control the supply–demand gap. Of course, it is not possible to simply generalize the case of cement in Shanghai, since it was unique in that there existed, first, a considerable degree of cement production capacity in the initial stage; second, a potentially high cement demand as an industrial city; and third, the financial and human resources of the Shanghai government, which made it possible to procure cement through autonomous activities to a certain extent. Moreover, it should be noted that such a system was not "planned" by the central government from the beginning, but instead gradually developed through the process of the central government tacitly approving structures that arose in the course of implementing its original plan. In any case, this structure of dealing with the "vertical shortage" of cement through autonomous actions led by local governments disappeared only in the late

1980s, when the function of the market was restored, and the "shortage economy" was resolved.

References

English Language

Chan, Kai Yiu. 2006. *Business Expansion and Structural Change in Pre-war China: Liu Hongsheng and His Enterprises, 1920–1937*. Hong Kong: Hong Kong University Press

Kornai, János. 1980. *Economics of Shortage*. Amsterdam; New York; Oxford: North-Holland Publishing Company

Chinese Language

Dangdai zhongguo congshu bianjibu, ed. 1990. *Dangdai zhongguo de jianzhucailiaogongye* (当代中国的建筑材料工业, Contemporary China's Building Materials Industry). Beijing: Zhongguo shehuikexue chubanshe

Dangdai zhongguo congshu bianjibu, ed. 1993. *Dangdai zhongguo wuziliutong* (当代中国物资流通, Contemporary China's Material Circulation). Beijing: Dangdai zhongguo chubenshe

Ma, Hong, ed. 1986. *Zhongguo jingji yu guanli rumen* (中国经济与管理入门, Introduction to Chinese Economy and Management). Kunming: Yunnan renmin chubanshe

Shanghai jiagezhi bianzuanweiyuanhui, ed. 1998. *Shanghai jiagezhi* (上海价格志, Shanghai Price Chronicle). Shanghai: Shanghai shehuikexueyuan chubanshe

Shanghai jianzhucailiaogongyezhi bianzuanweiyuanhui, ed. 1997. *Shanghai jianzhucailiao-gongyezhi* (上海建筑材料工业志, Shanghai Building Materials Industry Chronicle). Shanghai: Shanghai shehuikexueyuan chubanshe

Shanghaishi jihuaweiyuanhui, ed. 1998. *Shanghaishi jihuabaogaoji* (上海市计划报告集(1949–1998), Shanghai Planning Report Collection: 1949–1998). Publisher unknown

Shanghaishi tongjiju, ed. 1992. *Xinshanghai gongyetongjiziliao: 1949–1990* (新上海工业统计资料 (1949–1990), New Shanghai Industrial Statistical Data: 1949–1990). Beijing: Zhongguo tongjichubanshe

Shanghai shuinichang, ed. 1990. *Shanghai shuinichang qishinian: 1920–1980* (上海水泥厂七十年 (1920–1980), Seventy Years of Shanghai Cement Factory: 1920–1980). Shanghai: Tongji University Press

Shanghai wuziliutongzhi bianzuanweiyuanhui, ed. 2003. *Shanghai wuziliutong zhi* (上海物资流通志, Shanghai Material Circulation Chronicle). Shanghai: Shanghai shehuikexueyuan chubanshe

Wang, Yanmou, ed. 2005. *Zhongguo shuinifazhanshi* (中国水泥发展史, History of China's Cement Development). Beijing: Zhongguo jiancaigongye chubanshe

Zhongguo duiwaijingjimaoyinianjian bianjiweiyuanhui, ed. 1984. *Zhongguo duiwaijingjimaoyini-anjian 1984* (中国对外经济贸易年鉴 1984, China Foreign Economic Trade Yearbook 1984). Beijing: Zhongguo duiwaijingjimaoyi chubanshe

Zhongguokexueyuan shanghaijingjiyanjiusuo, and Shanghaishehuikexueyuan jingjiyanjiusuo, eds. 1958. *Shanghai jiefangqianhou wujiaziliaohuibian: 1921 nian – 1957 nian* (上海解放前后物价资料汇编 (1921年-1957年), Compilation of Price Data Before and After the Liberation of Shanghai: 1921–1957). Shanghai: Shanghai renmin chubanshe

Zhongguo shuinixiehui, ed. 2007. *Zhongguo shuini nianjian: 2001–2005* (中国水泥年鉴(2001–2005), China Cement Yearbook: 2001–2005) Changchun: Jilin jiaoyu chubanshe

Zhou, Taihe, ed. 1984. *Dangdai zhongguo de jingjitizhigaige* (当代中国的经济体制改革, Economic System Reform in Contemporary China). Beijing: Zhongguo shehuikexue chubanshe
Zongshuiwusishu tongjike, ed. Various years. *Haiguanzhongwaimaoyi tongjiniankan* (海关中外贸易统计年刊, Customs Foreign Trade Statistical Yearbook). In *Zhongguo jiuhaiguanshiliao* (中国旧海关史料, China Old Customs Historical Materials), ed. 2001. Zhongguo jiuhaiguanshiliao bianjiweiyuanhui. Beijing: Jinghua chubanshe

Japanese Language

Chō, Zenryō. 1995. Chūgoku niokeru cement ryūtsūtaisei (中国におけるセメント流通体制, Cement Distribution System in China). In *Chūgoku ni okeru seisanzairyūtsū: Shōhin to kikō* (中国における生産財流通——商品と機構, Circulation Systems of Production Materials in China), ASEDP No.29, ed. Harada Tadao, 93–98. Tokyo: Institute of Developing Economies
Go, Gyōrin. 2002. *Mōtakutō jidai no kōgyōkasenryaku: Sansenkensetsu no seijikeizaigaku* (毛沢東時代の工業化戦略——三線建設の政治経済学, The Industrialization Strategy during the Mao Zedong Era: The Political Economy of the Third Front Construction). Tokyo: Ochanomizu shobō
Horii, Nobuhiro. 2005. Sekitan kyōkyūtaisei no hensen: Keikakukeizaiki no senryakubusshi shijōkeizaika niokeru henyō (石炭供給体制の変遷——計画経済期の戦略物資,市場経済化における変容, Transition of Coal Supply System: Strategic Materials in the Planned Economy Period, Transformation in Market Economy). *Gendai chūgoku kenkyū* (現代中国研究, Modern and Contemporary China Studies) (17): 17–35
Ishihara, Kyōichi. 1985. Keikakuka to kakaku (計画化と価格, Planning and Pricing). In *Tenki ni tatsu chūgokukeizai: Shinkeizaiseisaku no shosō to sonohaikei* (転機に立つ中国経済——新経済政策の諸様相とその背景, Chinese Economy at a Turning Point: Various Aspects of the New Economic Policy and Its Background), ed. Maruyama Nobuo, 37–86. Tokyo: Institute of Developing Economies
Ishihara, Kyōichi. 1989. Busshi (物資: 物資,国営企業間で流通する生産財・資本財, Materials: Materials, production goods and capital goods circulating among state-owned enterprises), In *Chūgokukeizaitōkei keizaihō kaisetsu* (中国経済統計・経済法解説, Explanation of Chinese Economic Statistics and Economic Law), ed. Kojima Reiitsu, 315–322. Tokyo: Institute of Developing Economies
Ishihara, Kyōichi. 1990. 1970 nendai madeno chūgokukeizaikanri: shisutemu to jittai (1970年代までの中国経済管理——システムと実態, Chinese Economic Management up to the 1970s: System and Reality). In *Mōtakutōjidai no chūgoku: Gendaichūgokuron 1* (毛沢東時代の中国<現代中国論1>, China in the Mao Zedong Era: Discussions on Contemporary China No.1), ed. Mōri Kazuko, 146–185. Tokyo: Japan Institute of International Affairs
Kajima, Jun. 2010. Keikakukeizaiki no cement jukyū to busshikanriseido (計画経済期上海のセメント需給と物資管理制度, Cement Supply and Demand and the Material Management System in Shanghai during the Planned Economy Period). In Chūgoku cement sangyō no hatten: Sangyōsoshiki to kōzōhenka (中国セメント産業の発展——産業組織と構造変化, Development of China's Cement Industry: Industrial Organization and Structural Change), eds. Tajima Toshio, Shu Inki, Kajima Jun, 137–165. Tokyo: Ochanomizu shobō
Marukawa, Tomoo. 1993. Chūgoku no 'sansen kensetsu' (中国の『三線建設』, The 'Third Front' of China) *Asia keizai* (アジア経済, Asian Economy) 34(2): 61–80 and 34(3): 76–88
Nihon portland cement dōgyōkai chōsabu, and Kobayashi Yukio, eds. 1936. *Shina cement kōgyō gaikan* (支那セメント工業概観, Overview of China's Cement Industry), Chōsa shiryō No. 3. Osaka: Nihon portland cement dōgyōkai
Ro, Chōryō. 2010. Kindai chūgoku cement sangyō to shijō kyōsō carutelu mondai (近代中国セメント産業と市場競争・カルテル問題, Modern Chinese Cement Industry: Market Competition and Cartel Issues). In *Chūgoku cement sangyō no hatten: sangyōsoshiki to kōzōhenka* (中国

セメント産業の発展——産業組織と構造変化, Development of Chinese Cement Industry: Industrial Organization and Structural Change), eds. Tajima Toshio, Shu Inki, Kajima Jun, 33–53. Tokyo: Ochanomizu shobō

Shu, Inki. 2010. Kindai chūgoku cement sangyō to shikinchōtatsu: Liu kōsei kigyō shūdan to shanghai kashō cement kōshi (近代中国セメント産業と資金調達——劉鴻生企業集団と上海華商水泥公司, Modern Chinese Cement Industry and Fundraising: Liu Hongsheng Business Group and Shanghai Cement Company). In *Chūgoku cement sangyō no hatten: sangyōsoshiki to kōzōhenka* (中国セメント産業の発展——産業組織と構造変化, Development of Chinese Cement Industry: Industrial Organization and Structural Change), eds. Tajima Toshio, Shu Inki, Kajima Jun, 55–75. Tokyo: Ochanomizu shobō

Tajima, Toshio. 1990. Chūgoku no keizaihendō: Daiyakushin shōyakushin to keizaikaikaku (中国の経済変動——大躍進・小躍進と経済改革, Economic Fluctuations in China: Great Leap Forward, Small Leap Forward and Economic Reform). *Ajia keizai* (アジア経済, Asian Economy) 31(4): 41–60. http://hdl.handle.net/2261/7480

Tajima, Toshio. 2000. Chūgoku no zaiseikinyū seidokaikaku: Zokuchiteki keizai shisutemu no keisei to henyō (中国の財政金融制度改革——属地的経済システムの形成と変容, Reform of China's Fiscal and Financial System: Formation and Transformation of Territorial Economic System). In *Gendai chūgoku no kōzōhendō 2 keizai: Kōzōhendō to shijōka* (現代中国の構造変動2 経済——構造変動と市場化, Structural Changes in Contemporary China, Volume 2, Economy: Structural Changes and Marketization), ed. Nakagane Katsuji, 73–106. Tokyo: University of Tokyo Press

Yamagishi, Takeshi and Ii Kenichiro, trans (author unknown). 1986. *Chūgoku shakaishugi busshikanritaisei shiryaku* (中国社会主義・物資管理体制史略, Brief History of Chinese Socialism and Material Management System). Tokyo: Japan External Trade Organization

Unpublished Primary Sources

B31, Shanghaishi tongjiju dangan (上海市统计局档案, Shanghai Municipal Bureau of Statistics Archives)

B31-1-230, Shanghaishi tongjiju (上海市统计局). "1958–1962 nian Shanghaishi guominjingji tongjiziliao: wuzi" (1958–1962年上海市国民经济统计资料(物资), Shanghai National Economic Statistics Data: Commodities, 1958–1962), December 1963

B31-1-232, Shanghaishi tongjiju. "1963 nian wuzitongji ziliaohuibian" (1963年物资统计资料汇编, Compilation of Commodity Statistics in 1963, (unpublished) handwritten copy, date of creation unknown

B109, Shanghai wuziju dangan (上海市物资局档案, Shanghai Municipal Bureau of Material Management Archives)

B109-3-71, "1965 nian 1969 nian shuiniziyuan gongying kucun qingkuangbiao" (1965年-1969年水泥资源,供应,库存情况表, Cement Resources, Supply, and Inventory Status Table, 1965–1969). In Shanghaishi wuziju gemingweiyuanhui yewugongzuozu (上海市物资局革命委员会业务工作组) "1965 nian 1969 nian zhuyao wuzi tongjiziliao neibuziliao" (1965–1969年主要物资统计资料 (内部资料), Main Materials Statistical Data 1965–1969: Internal Material), Confidential, February 1970

Chapter 11
Regional Integration and Interregional Network: The Power Industry

Abstract This chapter analyzes the formation of an interregional network under the socialist system, focusing on the case of the Shanghai power industry from the immediate postwar period to the planned economy period. Since before the Second Sino-Japanese War, the Shanghai power industry possessed a rich electricity generation capacity fueled by foreign companies, and was structurally independent from neighboring regions. However, after the establishment of the PRC and the outbreak of the Korean War, the industry was reorganized under the control of the Chinese government and was connected to an interregional power network, the East China Power Grid. As a result, Shanghai became an importer of electricity from other provinces within the grid without itself carrying out large-scale power source development. The upshot of this process is that within a government-led interregional network like what had been established in the PRC, the characteristics of the Shanghai power industry that had developed during the Republican period had no choice but to undergo a dramatic transformation.

Keywords Regional integration · Interregional networks · Power industry · Shanghai Power Company · East China Power Grid

As has been seen in the case studies of industries in Chapters 9 and 10, local governments played a significant role in economic behavior under the socialist system. However, this was not necessarily the case for all industries. What needs to be emphasized is that the autonomy of local governments highlighted thus far was a phenomenon that only developed within the framework of the socialist system, predicated on a centralized structure and a leading role being accorded the central government atop the vertical line. The electric power industry, which is the focus of the current chapter, was an industry where the management of the central government was relatively strong, and therefore its historical development in Shanghai presents a different trajectory from that of the rubber processing industry and the cement industry discussed previously.[1] However, this does not contradict the discussions in

[1] This chapter is based on Kajima (2006, 2008) with additions and revisions.

J. Kajima, *Shanghai under the Socialist System*, Studies in Economic History,
https://doi.org/10.1007/978-981-95-3225-4_11

the previous two chapters, but rather returns the focus to another major aspect of the Chinese socialist system, namely the leading role of the central government.

Another point to note in the case of Shanghai's power industry is that a major part, if not the bulk, of its process of historical development was carried out by foreign companies. Many studies have pointed out that foreign capital played an important role in China's economic development since the late nineteenth century.[2] The power industry was one field in which this was particularly the case. From the late Qing Dynasty through the Republican period, the power industry in China developed intensively in two regions: the Northeast, where power development was actively promoted by Japanese companies under the Manchukuo regime established in 1932, and the eastern coastal region, where development was led by Western companies. Particularly in Shanghai, the Shanghai Municipal Council Electricity Department (公共租界工部局电气处), established in 1893, followed by the Shanghai Power Company (上海电力公司), an American company established in 1929 by acquiring the aforementioned department, grew alongside the French Company of Tramways and Electricity (法商电车电灯公司), and several Chinese power companies that developed in Chinese residential areas, as the entire industry developed in step with the growth of modern industry in Shanghai.[3] The power generation capacity of Shanghai in 1935 reached 251,000 kW, which accounted for 42.9% of the total power generation capacity of 585,000 kW nationwide (excluding the Northeast region), and so in this industry too Shanghai had a central role: it was a major component of the nation's power industry (Zhongyangdangbu guominjingjijihuaweiyuanhui 1937, pp. 9–10).

On the other hand, an interregional power transmission network connecting Shanghai and the neighboring provinces, such as Jiangsu and Zhejiang, remained essentially undeveloped throughout the Republican period. In light of the development process of the power industry in Japan, which established the concentrated "Five Major Power Companies" (五大电力) system through interregional power price competition in the 1920s, one might imagine that in a similar fashion the foreign power companies possessing abundant power generation capacity in Shanghai, such as the Shanghai Power Company, would expand high-voltage power lines to neighboring provinces in search of markets, and form monopolies through price competition (Hashimoto 1977–1978). However, this was not the case. Foreign power companies in Shanghai were unable to expand their businesses outside of Shanghai due to laws restricting the entry of foreign companies into public services outside their settlement and concession; consequently, these companies, for all their capacity, were largely limited to the role of supplying the rapidly-developing modern industries within Shanghai itself. Although the National Government Construction Committee (国民政府建设委员会) promoted the integration of small-scale power plants in Jiangsu Province to some extent in the 1930s, the outbreak of the Second Sino-Japanese War prevented the power industry in Shanghai and surrounding areas from

[2] On the development process of China's power industry, refer to Tajima (2008).

[3] On the power industry in Manchukuo and Shanghai, refer to Hori (1987), and Kanemaru (1993).

being connected by an interregional transmission network.[4] Moreover, even within Shanghai, there was a complex situation in that multiple power companies held their own exclusive business rights (专营权) within specific areas within the city.

This situation, where multiple power companies coexisted within Shanghai, ended after the establishment of the PRC since—in the wake of the Shanghai Power Company having attempted, but failed, to integrate Shanghai's power companies during the postwar Republican period—each power company became a state-owned or public and private jointly-owned enterprise and placed under the unified management system of the Shanghai Municipal Bureau of Electric Industry Management (上海市电业管理局) in the mid-1950s. After the government-initiated integration in the mid-1950s, an interregional power transmission network was finally put into place. Known as the East China Power Grid (华东电网), it connected Shanghai and Jiangsu, Zhejiang, and Anhui Provinces, in line with the government's industrial development strategy.

The main purpose of this chapter is to examine the development of regional integration and the formation of an interregional distribution network under the socialist system, by focusing on the case of Shanghai's power industry from the postwar period through to the establishment of the PRC and the completion of the socialist transformation. Although there have been previous studies investigating the development of Shanghai's power industry, there has been little on its transition before and after 1949. Li Daigeng's pioneering work on the history of China's power industry mainly focuses on the evaluation of production, such as power generation facilities after 1949, and the studies of Kanemaru Yuichi, Wang Shuhuai, and Lin Meili mainly target the period up to the Second Sino-Japanese War, and do not discuss the postwar period (Li 1983, 1984; Kanemaru 1992, 1993; Jinwan 1999; Wang 1991; Lin 1990). Specialized publications such as Shanghaishi dianligongyeju shizhibianzuanweiyuanhui (1994) in the Shanghai local gazetteer (地方志) series, as well as Shanghaishi dianligongyeshi bianweihui (2003), Shanghai dianwangdiaodushi bianweihui (2004), and Huadong dianwangdiaodushi bianweihui (2004), mention post-1949 developments in general terms, but do not sufficiently discuss the structural changes from the Republican period to the planned economy period after 1949.

Therefore, this chapter begins with an examination of the historical process of the integration of the Shanghai power industry, from the postwar period to the early years of the PRC. It then explores the structural changes in Shanghai's power industry

---

[4] For the integration process of the power industry in Jiangsu Province in the 1930s, refer to Kanemaru (1994, pp. 189–192). According to Kanemaru, the main Chinese power companies which promoted integrating small-scale power plants since the mid-1930s were the Capital Power Plant (首都电厂) in Nanjing City and the Qishuyan Power Plant (戚墅堰电厂) in Wujin County (武进县) belonging to the National Government Construction Committee (国民政府建设委员会), the privately-owned Suzhou Power Plant (苏州电厂) in Suzhou, and the Chinese Merchant Electric Company (华商电气公司), Zhabei Hydroelectric Company (闸北水电公司), and Pudong Electric Company (浦东电气公司) in Shanghai. However, looking at Table 1 of Kanemaru (1994), the three companies in Shanghai merged only small-scale power plants in the suburbs of Shanghai, and therefore their range of integration was relatively limited at this stage.

under the socialist system by analyzing the changes in the status of Shanghai within both the national and East China power grids during the planned economy period.

11.1 The Power Industry in Shanghai

11.1.1 The Postwar Period

After the Second World War, state-owned enterprises had a significant share in the Chinese power industry since the National Government Resources Committee (国民政府资源委员会) confiscated and nationalized as "enemy property" the former Japanese power companies that had been established in China. The total power generation of the power companies under the Resources Committee in 1947 reached 54.9% of China's overall total power generation by virtue of the Committee controlling almost all of the power facilities in the Northeast region, including the former Manchuria Electric Co., Ltd. (満洲電業株式会社) (Zheng et al. 1991, pp. 152, 188).

The situation in Shanghai at the time, however, was quite different, despite the city serving as another major hub of the Chinese power industry. As already mentioned, the power industry in Shanghai was made up of several power companies coexisting within the city before the onset of the Second Sino-Japanese War, including the American-funded Shanghai Power Company, the Sino-American joint venture West Shanghai Power Company (沪西电力公司, essentially a subsidiary of the Shanghai Power Company), the French Company of Tramways and Electricity, and the Chinese Merchant Electric Company (华商电气公司), Zhabei Hydroelectric Company (闸北水电公司), and Pudong Electric Company (浦东电气公司). This fragmented power supply situation was temporarily unified when the Japanese-funded Central China Hydroelectric Corporation (華中水電株式会社, a subsidiary of the China Development Corporation, 中支那振興株式会社), established in June 1938 after the outbreak of the war, took over the Chinese Merchant Electric Company, Zhabei Hydroelectric Company, and Pudong Electric Company, and then further confiscated the Shanghai Power Company and West Shanghai Power Company after the outbreak of the Pacific War.[5]

However, on September 17, 1945, after the end of the war, when the Shanghai Municipal Bureau of Public Utilities (上海市公用局) took over the Central China Hydroelectric Corporation under a special envoy of the National Government's Ministry of Economic Affairs (国民政府经济部特派员), the five companies were returned to their original owners, and each also recovered the exclusive business rights that they had agreed upon (with the Shanghai Municipal Government or the Settlement and Concession authorities) to recognize their exclusive business management in each area before the war. For example, the Shanghai Power Company had signed a contract with the Shanghai Municipal Council of the International Settlement (上

[5] For the establishment of the Central China Hydroelectric Company and its survey activities, refer to Kanemaru (2002); (2005).

海公共租界工部局), upon acquiring the council's Electricity Department in 1929, for exclusive business management in the International Settlement for 40 years. The West Shanghai Power Company, when it was established in 1935, had similarly signed a contract with the Shanghai Municipal Government, under the supervision of the National Government, for exclusive business rights for 30 years.[6] Thus, the situation immediately after the Second World War saw Shanghai's power supply environment return to its prewar state with various companies coexisting.

Looking at the situation of the Shanghai power industry in 1946 shown in Tables 11.1 and 11.2, the total electricity generation capacity was 223,000 kW, which accounted for 17.5% of the national total of 1,281,000 kW.[7] As for the breakdown by company, the Shanghai Power Company produced 78.9% of the city's total capacity, overwhelming the others as same just as was the case before the war, while the electricity generation facilities of the Chinese Merchant Electric Company and the Pudong Electric Company had not yet been restored in 1946. Total electricity generation in Shanghai at the time amounted to 783 million kWh, which was 21.6% of the national total of 3.63 billion kWh, and the Shanghai Power Company itself thus contributed a significant share of the national total. Other companies purchased electricity from the Shanghai Power Company, which remained dominant since the Chinese Merchant Electric Company and the Pudong Electric Company were unable to generate power and Zhabei Hydroelectric Company, while producing power, was not back up to its prewar level. As for the sales market of the Shanghai power companies, industrial use accounted for more than 60%, excluding the French Company of Tramways and Electricity, which was mainly focused on household use (Shanghaishizhengfu tongjichu 1947, category 11, p. 16). Most of the electricity generated in Shanghai was consumed within Shanghai, and this consumption was strongly tied to the industrial power demand in Shanghai as before the war.

When turning to look at power generation fuel (raw material consumption), it is notable that both the Shanghai Power Company and the French Company of Tramways and Electricity used petroleum. The petroleum consumption of the former increased to 353,000 tons in 1947 after most of its boilers were converted for petroleum use in response to the petroleum urgently provided by the US military after the war, while the coal consumption was reduced to 226,000 tons (Shanghaishi dianligongyeju shizhibianzuanweiyuanhui 1994, p. 48). As a result, the city's total petroleum consumption reached 378,000 tons, exceeding its coal consumption of 322,000 tons (Shanghaishizhengfu tongjichu, publication year unknown, category 10, pp. 16–17). Generally, especially when considering that the heat generated by

[6] Zaishanghai chūgokutsūshinsha chōsabu (1937, pp. 13–14, 37–39). In the exclusive business rights contract between the Shanghai Power Company and the Shanghai Municipal Council, 5% of the electricity and power fee income was paid to the Shanghai Municipal Council every six months, and if there was a profit exceeding 10% of the capital, half of the excess amount was reserved as a special fund for reducing electricity charges; moreover, if there was a dividend of more than 100%, half of it was used to reduce electricity charges. However, according to the analysis given in Zaishanghai chūgokutsūshinsha chōsabu (1937), it seems that this provision was not necessarily fulfilled.

[7] For the figures of the national total, refer to Li (1983, pp. 27–28).

Table 11.1 Power companies in Shanghai, December 1946

Name	Ownership	Year of establishment	Amount of capital (thousand yuan)	Supply area	Electricity generation facility		
					Type of motor	Number	Electricity generation capacity (10 thousand kW)
Shanghai Power Company (上海电力公司)	US	1929	56,502	Former International Settlement	Steam turbine	14	17.6
West Shanghai Power Company (沪西电力公司)	US-Chinese jointly-owned	1935	3,000	West Shanghai extra-settlement roads district	-	-	-
French Company of Tramways and Electricity (法商电车电灯公司)	French	1902	125,000	Former French Concession	Diesel engine	4	1.2
Zhabei Hydroelectric Company (闸北水电公司)	Public (Shanghai Municipality)	1911	9,000	Zhabei district	Steam turbine	4	3.5
Chinese Merchant Electric Company (华商电气公司)	Chinese private	1904	6,000	Southern City (南市) district	-	-	-
Pudong Electric Company (浦东电气公司)	Chinese private	1919	1,500	Pudong district	-	-	-
Total						22	22.3

Notes (1) Unit of "Amount of capital" for French Company of Tramways and Electricity is thousand francs. (2) "Electricity generation facility" of Shanghai Power Company and Zhabei Hydroelectric Company include facilities under repair and out of order, while that of French Company of Tramways and Electricity does not include facilities of Dongjiadu Waterwork Factory (董家渡水厂)

Sources Shanghaishizhengfu tongjichu (1947, category 11, p. 12). "Year of establishment" corrected based on Kanemaru (1993, p. 60)

Table 11.2 Electricity generation, sales and raw material consumption of power companies in Shanghai, 1946

Name	Electricity generation and purchasing (100 million kWh)			Sales (100 million kWh)			Raw material consumption (10 thousand tons)	
	Electricity Generation	Purchased	Total	Sales in Shanghai	Wholesale	Total	Petroleum	Coal
Shanghai Power Company (上海电力公司)	7.07	-	7.07	3.77	2.59	6.37	21.4	30.4
West Shanghai Power Company (沪西电力公司)	-	1.37	1.37	1.16	0.13	1.3	-	-
French Company of Tramways and Electricity (法商电车电灯公司)	0.64	0.13	0.77	0.67	-	0.67	1.7	-
Zhabei Hydroelectric Company (闸北水电公司)	0.12	0.59	0.71	0.53	0.04	0.57	-	1.7
Chinese Merchant Electric Company (华商电气公司)	-	0.38	0.38	0.31	-	0.31	-	-
Pudong Electric Company (浦东电气公司)	-	0.25	0.25	0.15	0.05	0.2	-	-
Total	7.83	2.73	10.57	6.61	2.81	9.42	23.1	32.1

Notes (1) "Purchased" means electricity purchased from other power companies. (2) "Total" is not necessarily equal to total of each item but original source as is. "Wholesale" includes wholesale to outside of Shanghai

Source Shanghaishizhengfu tongjichu (1947, category 11, pp. 22, 26)

petroleum is about six times that of the same amount of coal, it is clear that petroleum was the main source of power generation fuel in Shanghai after the war. At that time, China's petroleum self-sufficiency rate was about 10–20%, mainly imported from the three oil major companies—Standard Oil, the Asiatic Petroleum Company, and Texaco—and the fuel oil used by the Shanghai Power Company was able to be imported at a low price by agreement (Kubo et al., 2016, pp. 99–100; Zheng et al., 1991, p. 183).

These particulars all speak to the unique structure of the postwar Shanghai power industry, which possessed about 17% of the national electricity generation capacity, but depended on imports from overseas for its power generation fuel. Moreover, almost the entirety of the city's power generation and consumption occurred within the city itself, and the interrelationship with neighboring regions was relatively weak in terms of the market and power generation fuel supply. This structure had come about in the first place as a result of the city's special political and economic situation as a treaty port since the late Qing Dynasty, and continued to exert influence on the industry even after the war when the International Settlement and the Concessions disappeared.

11.1.2 The Plan to Establish the United Power Company

In light of the above, it would be no exaggeration to say that electricity generation in postwar Shanghai was almost entirely dependent on the Shanghai Power Company. However, as the power demand increased due to postwar reconstruction, the company was unable to fully cope, worsening the power shortage situation in Shanghai (Shanghaishi dianligongsi 1946, pp. 1–2). To solve this problem, a plan to establish the United Power Company (联合电力公司) was proposed, mainly by the Shanghai Power Company itself.

The details of the plan can be seen in the promotional materials published by the Shanghai Power Company at the time. One of these states,

> Each power company in Shanghai has been supplying specific areas since its establishment, and each company has a legal monopoly only within a part of the city's business area. Each company is an independent organization, and their funds, power generation capacity, number of customers, power usage load, and other major matters are all different. [...] However, they are currently facing a common problem of not being able to meet the city's power demand due to damage to facilities incurred during the war. The plan for "United Power" is to solve this problem by building a central power station.[8]

The promotional material goes on to list the advantages of a central power station, which were as follows: (1) It could reduce the necessary funds; (2) The equipment had a large capacity, and the power generation cost would be economical; (3) It could supply the basic load from the most efficient power generation facilities, while

[8] This quotation and subsequent references are from Shanghai Power Company, *A Plan for Relieving Shanghai's Electric Power Shortage: The "United Power" Plan*, May 1947, Q5-3-5469.

relatively old and inefficient equipment would be used only briefly at peak load, which was economical; (4) It could reduce the equipment at each company and minimize unproductive investment; and (5) It could gradually eliminate the differences in power supply costs and power prices of each company.

Furthermore, it states that "Currently, there is a shortage of 60,000 kW of power generation capacity in Shanghai," and that this supply shortage was becoming more serious day by day. It asserts that this "shortage of power generation capacity will reach at least 100,000–150,000 kW," and estimated that the power generation capacity that the new "United Power Company" would need to install within 15 years would be 500,000 kW. As a first step, what was proposed was the installation of a 100,000 kW power generation facility along the Huangpu River and the construction of a 132,000 V high-voltage ring line connecting the power stations of the existing power companies. Considering that the total power generation capacity of the entire city of Shanghai was 223,000 kW as of 1946, this was a very long-term and large-scale construction plan, anticipating a significant future increase in power demand in the city.

In response to this plan put forward by the Shanghai Power Company, the Shanghai Municipal Government and the Shanghai Municipal Representative Council (上海市参议会), which was the representative body of the people of Shanghai established after the Second World War, generally expressed agreement. The Shanghai Municipal Bureau of Public Utilities originally intended to uniformly control all power companies in Shanghai, and in April 1947, it appointed a technical committee to examine the plan to establish the United Power Company (Shanghaishi dianligongyeju shizhibianzuanweiyuanhui 1994, p. 467). The Shanghai Municipal Representative Council also adopted the United Power Company plan in March 1947, having considered the serious power shortage the city was facing at the time. On the other hand, there was also a degree of opposition among other Chinese power companies in Shanghai, but they had little choice but to agree with the plan in the face of pressure from the municipal government and foreign capital.[9]

The focus in realizing the plan for establishing the United Power Company was the exclusive business rights contract that had to be newly concluded between the Shanghai Municipal Government and the United Power Company. On this point, a syndicate consisting of Du Yuesheng (杜月笙, Chairman of the Chinese Merchant Electric Company), Qian Xinzhi (钱新之, Chairman of the Zhabei Hydroelectric Company), Tong Shiheng (童世亨, General Manager of the Pudong Electric Company), P.S. Hopkins (President of the Shanghai Power Company), and Li Ming

[9] For example, the Zhabei Hydroelectric Company secretly established the Far East Electric Co., Ltd. (远东电气股份有限公司), which specialized in business investment and company acquisitions, to counter the expansion of the Shanghai Power Company. They purchased all or most of the shares of small power companies located outside the business area of Zhabei Hydroelectric, such as in Xianghua (翔华), Dayao (大耀), Shengming (生明), Huangdu (黄渡), Huaxingyong (华兴永), and Zhenru (真如). The company also dispatched Qian Xinzhi (钱新之) as the plenipotentiary representative of the United Power Company, while Wang Jianshi (王兼士) was the leader of the Far East Company (Shanghaishi dianligongyeju shizhibianzuanweiyuanhui 1994, p. 448). These particular activities by Chinese power companies at the time are a worthy topic of future research.

(李铭, Advisor to the Shanghai Power Company) was formed in July 1947, and drew up a contract draft which it then revised repeatedly at six meetings held from September 4 to 16, 1947.[10] This exclusive business rights contract draft was finally passed at the 95th municipal meeting of the Shanghai Municipal Government, thereby concluding preparations for the establishment of the United Power Company in Shanghai.

However, things rapidly ran into trouble when the time came to put the plan into action. In December 1947, Wu Guozhen (吴国桢), the Mayor of Shanghai, applied to the Executive Yuan of the National Government and the Ministry of Economic Affairs to purchase 2–3 units, with a total capacity of 50,000 kW, of used Japanese machinery and equipment, in order to establish the United Power Company. However, ultimately he was unable to gain approval from the National Government. The reasoning behind the National Government's refusal to grant him permission can be inferred from the response of the Ministries of Economic Affairs, Finance, Foreign Affairs, and Land Administration of the Executive Yuan and the National Economic Committee and Resources Committee following their deliberation on the United Power Company plan, which was sent to Shanghai on March 1, 1948 (Q1-14-456b).

The response stated that,

> [While] we generally agree with Shanghai's plan to establish the United Power Company to solve the power shortage and promote industrial production, even if it involves borrowing foreign capital or the participation of foreign investors [...] the form of the draft is no different from the various exclusive business rights contracts of the public utilities managed by foreigners in the former concessions and the West Shanghai Power Company, and such methods should not be used again now that the unequal treaties have been abolished. [...] In the draft, the United Power Company can sell and transmit electricity outside the boundaries of the Shanghai jurisdiction area, which will expand the business scope of foreign capital companies. [...] The draft claims to be established based on our country's laws, but when a dispute arises between the two parties, it grants the right to appoint an arbitrator to the president of the British Electrical Engineers Association, and the decision made by the arbitration is final and not bound by our country's laws. The provisions regarding the obligation to perform the contract of the participating companies and the United Power Company are unilateral, which is nothing but a revival of the unequal treaties. [...] Taking into account all the above points, the original contract draft is in conflict with the current law in both form and content, and its establishment is difficult to permit.

This response from the National government brings to mind a case in 1930, years before the Second Sino-Japanese War, in which a supervisory organ of the National government expressed disapproval of concluding contracts with foreign-owned power plants when the Zhabei Hydroelectric Company tried to renew its power purchase contract with the Shanghai Power Company (Zaishanghai chūgokutsūshinsha chōsabu 1937, pp. 57–58). The continuity in how it responded to these cases may suggest that the National government had a strong and consistent awareness of sovereignty infringement from before the war years to afterward. Of course, such emphasis on sovereignty infringement should not be seen merely as a simple expression of nationalist ideology, but should also be examined from

[10] For the draft contract, refer to Q1-14-456a.

the perspective of the interests related to the central government's power industry integration policy after the war.[11]

In any event, attempts to integrate the Shanghai power industry, mainly led by foreign companies after the war, despite having gained the approval of the Shanghai Municipal Government and the Shanghai Municipal Representative Council, ultimately failed since they could not gain the approval of the National government, which had issues with the exclusive business rights contracts used by foreign companies.

11.2 Regional Integration in the Early Years of the PRC

11.2.1 The Outbreak of the Korean War and the Onset of Military Control

As covered in Chapter 3, when Shanghai was militarily occupied by the People's Liberation Army on May 27, 1949, the Shanghai Military Control Committee was organized to serve as the highest authority during the military control period, and the takeover and management of Shanghai's government organizations and state-owned enterprises began in earnest. Further, the basic policy of the CCP at that time regarding the takeover of state-owned and public enterprises was basically one of maintaining the status quo ("keep it as it is," 原封不動), and all private enterprises and their property were to be protected and not violated.[12] As for foreign-owned enterprises, the instructions of the CCP Central Committee issued on January 14, 1949, restrained speech and behavior about hasty prohibitions and confiscations of the economic privileges, commerce and industry, and investments of all capitalist countries' governments and individuals in China for the time being, although no formal decisions were offered.[13]

Under this policy principle, the response to the foreign companies that comprised much of Shanghai's power industry was extremely cautious. The Shanghai Municipal

[11] At present, the author does not have specific information on the detailed plans for the integration of the power industry in Shanghai and Jiangsu Province by the National Government after the war. However, recalling the integration process of the power industry in Jiangsu Province by the National Government Construction Committee in the 1930s, as pointed out by Kanemaru (1994), it is possible to imagine that the National Government was exploring a long-term plan for the integration of the power industry in the region, including Shanghai, after the war.

[12] Central Committee of the CCP, "Instructions on Taking Over the Cities in South of the Yangtze River to the East China Bureau" (关于接管江南都市给华东局的指示), April 25, 1949, and the East China Bureau (华东局), "Instructions on Taking Over the Work of the Cities in South of the Yangtze River (Excerpt)," (关于接管江南城市工作的指示 (节录)), April 1, 1949, Zhongyangjuanbianjibu (1992, pp. 30–33).

[13] Central [Committee of the CCP], "Instructions on Diplomatic Work" (关于外交工作的指示), January 19, 1949, Zhongyang danganguan (1992, pp. 44–49).

Bureau of Public Utilities (上海市公用局) summarized its policy toward foreign public utility companies for three months after the military occupation, stating,

> Our policy towards public utility companies run by foreign capital is generally carried out very carefully and cautiously, following the Shanghai Municipal Committee of the Chinese Communist Party's instructions and consulting with the Foreign Residents Affairs Office (外侨事务处) closely whenever something happens, while firmly grasping the instructions of Political Commissioner Rao Shushi (饶漱石).... Under the condition that foreign capital strictly adheres to government laws and regulations, it must be protected, destruction from all sides must be controlled, and assistance must be given during difficulties. Under this policy, reforms are gradually implemented. (B1-2-389)

Furthermore, regarding the exclusive business rights of foreign companies, the report encapsulated the stance of maintaining the status quo:

> After we liberated Shanghai, we neither acknowledged nor denied these contract issues. However, in fact, these contracts continue to be effective, and foreigners generally exercise their rights and fulfill their obligations according to the contracts... Based on our own subjective power (technology and financial power), we recover and manage what we can manage by ourselves. For those things that we do not have the power to manage by ourselves, we re-contract with them based on the policy that foreigners will manage them for a while. However, it is still too early, and the conditions are not ripe, so we can only make plans and prepare. (B1-2-389)

As for the situation of Shanghai's power industry on the ground in 1949, the power generation was significantly fluctuating. It was 104 million kWh in January for the whole city, but dropped to 36 million kWh in April, then recovered to 59 million kWh in May, and continued on a recovery streak for the rest of the year. Ultimately it managed to maintain a level slightly below that of 1946 at 932 million kWh for 1949 as a whole (Shanghaishi renminzhengfu mishuchu 1949, publication year unknown, category "Public services," p. 183).

However, the environment surrounding Shanghai's power industry was gradually changing, particularly in terms of petroleum usage. As shown in Fig. 11.1, petroleum imports plummeted from June 1949 due to the Nationalist Party's naval blockade, and supply was severely strained.[14] In response to this situation, the CCP's Central Committee concentrated on supplying coal to Shanghai, and, as a result, the main source of power generation fuel, which had been petroleum during the postwar years of the Republican period, was transformed to coal (Zhongguo gongyejingjiyanjiusuo, 1949).

Moreover, the outbreak of the Korean War in June 1950, and China's entry into that conflict in October that same year, served to solidify the Cold War structure in East Asia. The Ministry of Foreign Affairs of the Central People's Government called for the strengthening of control over American companies in China, and first laid out a policy of implementing military control over public utilities in the "Preliminary Opinions on the Handling of Foreign Enterprises" (关于外资企业处理办法的初步

[14] Central Financial and Economic Committee (中央财政经济委员会), "Report on the Situation of Navigation after the Enemy's Blockade of Our Sea" (报告敌封锁我海航后之航务情况), October 30, 1949, Zhongguoshehuikexueyuan and Zhongyangdanganguan (1994, p. 445).

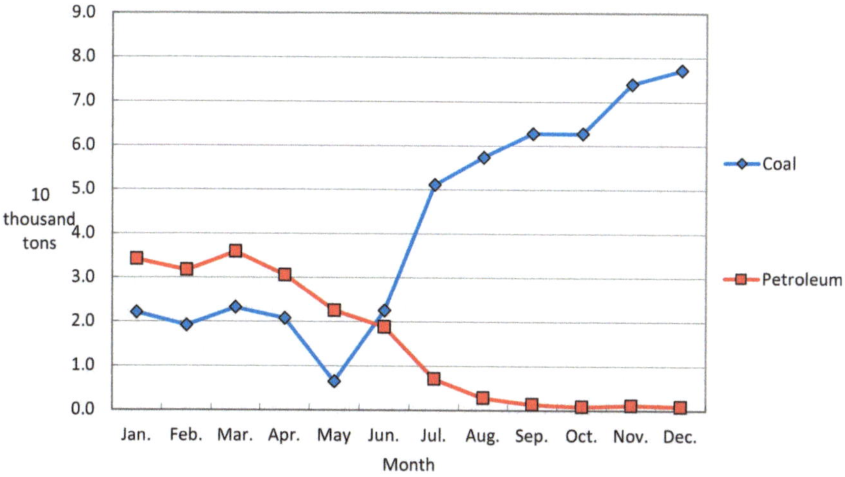

Fig. 11.1 Raw material consumption for electricity generation in Shanghai, January to December, 1949. *Source* Shanghaishi renminzhengfu mishuchu (publication year unknown), category "Public services," pp. 183, 199–200

意见) presented on November 5, 1950. At the same time, it decided to immediately and forcibly purchase the petroleum held by foreign companies, and when necessary, to confiscate and manage the companies themselves.[15]

What was even more crucial for foreign companies in China was the freezing of assets of both China and the US, which was implemented by the respective rivals in December 1950. On December 16, 1950, the US government announced the control of public and private property of the PRC within US jurisdiction, as well as the prohibition of all ships registered in the US from sailing to Chinese ports, in parallel with the implementation of an embargo against China. In response, on December 28, 1950, the Government Administration Council (政务院) issued an order on the "Control of American Property in China and the Freezing of American Deposits in China" (关于管制美国在华财产冻结美国在华存款的命令), which declared that "all property of the US government and US companies within the PRC will be controlled by the local people's government, and a detailed investigation will be conducted."[16]

This control and freezing of American assets in China became the direct trigger for the military control of the Shanghai Power Company. Immediately after the order by the Government Administration Council, on December 30, 1950, the Shanghai Military Control Committee decided that it was necessary to have military control over

[15] Ministry of Foreign Affairs, "Preliminary Opinions on the Handling of Foreign Enterprises" (关于外资企业处理办法的初步意见), November 5, 1950. For this document, refer to Liu (1997, p. 314).

[16] Government Administration Council, "Order on the Control of American Property in China and the Freezing of American Deposits in China" (关于管制美国在华财产冻结美国在华存款的命令), December 28, 1950, Zhongyangrenminzhengfu fazhiweiyuanhui (1952, p. 204).

the Shanghai Power Company, and declared the implementation of this decision mere days later on January 2, 1951 (Shanghaishi dianligongyeju shizhibianzuanweiyuanhui 1994, p. 21). At the same time, similar measures were taken against 115 American companies, including Texaco and Shanghai Telephone Company (上海电话公司). On July 11, 1951, part of the assets of Standard, Cathay, and Texaco were requisitioned, and all of their oil was forcibly purchased. Through this process, 94.5% of the total assets of American companies in China had been placed under governmental control by the end of 1952 (Liu 1997, p. 314).

Thus, triggered by China's entry into the Korean War and the accompanying control and freezing of American assets in China, the Chinese government decided to implement military control over the Shanghai Power Company. By so doing, the government was able to forcefully recover the exclusive business rights of foreign power companies, which had been the biggest bottleneck in the regional integration of the Shanghai power industry.

11.2.2 Regional Integration Through the Socialist Transformation

The military seizure of the Shanghai Electric Power Company, which had long held the dominant position in the Shanghai power industry, led to a rapid progression of local government-oriented integration of the industry. First, in June 1951, the Shanghai Municipal Government issued the "Temporary Regulations on the Unified Price of Shanghai's Electricity Supply Business" (上海市供电事业划一价格暂行办法), standardizing the electricity prices within the city (which had previously varied by power company) to 820 yuan per kWh (equivalent to 0.082 new RMB yuan), and 2,460 yuan per kWh for lighting (equivalent to 0.246 new RMB yuan).[17]

The unification of the power grid in Shanghai was also promoted. With the temporal power interchange among power companies in Shanghai due to the bombing by Nationalist fighter planes on February 6, 1950, as a catalyst, the Dispatch Team (调度组), which was in charge of power interchange management, was established under the Shanghai Municipal Bureau of Public Utilities in March 1950. Furthermore, a ring-shaped power transmission line, as shown in Fig. 11.2, was completed by erecting 33 kV contact lines between each power company in 1951 to connect them all together. This ring-shaped power transmission line was raised to 35 kV in 1953, and modified to a mixed form of 110/35 kV in 1960. In 1967, a 220 kV ring-shaped power transmission line was completed (Shanghai dianwangdiaodushi bianweihui 2004, pp. 19–36).

[17] Shanghai Municipal Government, "Temporary Regulations on the Unified Price of Shanghai's Electricity Supply Business," Shanghaishi dianligongyeju shizhibianzuanweiyuanhui (1994, p. 211). The price is in old RMB (denomination was implemented in 1955 at a rate of 1 new RMB: 10,000 old RMB).

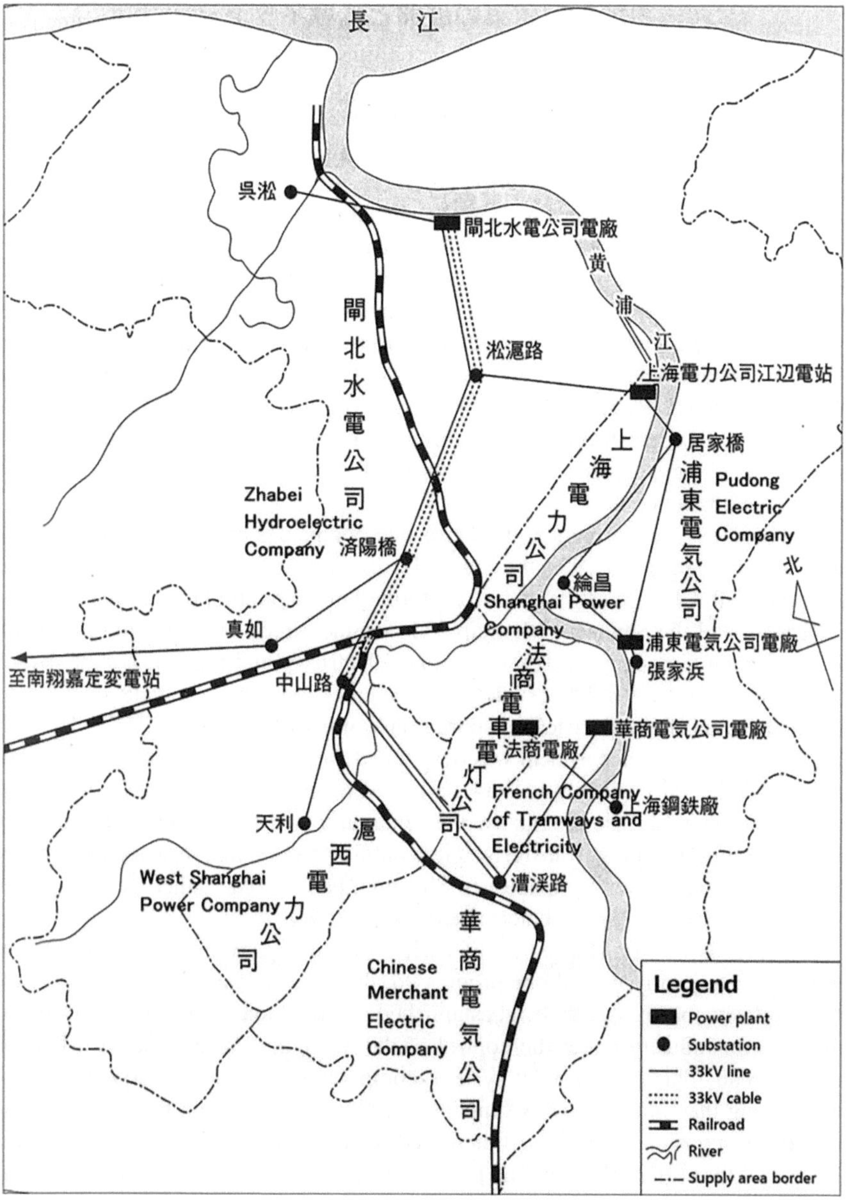

Fig. 11.2 Supply area of each power company and transmission networks, 1951. *Source* Created by author based on Shanghai dianwangdiaodushi bianweihui (2004, p. 27)

Based on such advances in operational unification, the Power Department of the Shanghai Municipal Bureau of Public Utilities (上海市公用局电力处) and the General Office of the Shanghai Electric Power Company (上海电力公司总办事处) merged to establish the Shanghai Power Industry Management Bureau of the Ministry of Fuel Industry (燃料工业部上海电业管理局) on February 20, 1953. On April 1, 1954, the Central Dispatch Office was established under this bureau to serve as an organization for centrally managing the Shanghai power industry. Consequently, military control over the Shanghai Power Company ended on February 2, 1954, and it was incorporated under the supervision of the Shanghai Power Industry Management Bureau. Moreover, the company was renamed the Shanghai Power Industry Management Bureau Yangshupu Power Plant (上海电业管理局杨树浦发电厂) in November 1954, and four years later in 1958 renamed again, to the Shanghai Yangshupu Power Plant (上海杨树浦发电厂). At this point, the Shanghai Power Company, which had been the core entity in the Shanghai power industry for so much of its history, had ceased to exist as a truly distinct entity and was completely under government control.

The socialist transformation of other power companies progressed almost simultaneously. On January 1, 1953, the Zhabei Hydroelectric Company, the largest power company with Chinese capital, was transformed into a public-private jointly-owned enterprise, and the Shanghai Municipal Government took over the entire property of the French Company of Tramways and Electricity and made it a state-owned enterprise on November 2 that same year. The latter company eventually became the South Shanghai Hydroelectric Transportation Company (沪南水电交通公司), while its power generation department was designated the South Shanghai Power Department (沪南电力处). On July 1, 1954, both the Chinese Merchant Electric Company and the Pudong Electric Company, the remaining two power generation companies, were simultaneously transformed into public-private jointly-owned enterprises. At this point, all power companies in Shanghai had become either state-owned or public-private jointly-owned enterprises.

In short, as the transformation of each power company into a state-owned or public-private jointly-owned one progressed, the government effectively reclaimed their exclusive business rights and established a unified management system for the city's power industry under the control of the Shanghai Power Industry Management Bureau. This management system, compared to the earlier postwar plan for establishing the United Power Company, was likewise based on the great demand for industrial power during eras of increased construction (postwar reconstruction in the case of the earlier plan, and the First Five Year Plan, 1953–57, in the case of the later one); similarly, both plans aimed at the establishment of a circular power grid by connecting existing power plants. However, a major difference between the two plans was that, while the United Power Company plan in the early postwar years was driven by a foreign company, the Shanghai Power Company, the management system put into place by the Shanghai Power Industry Management Bureau in the 1950s was a government-led initiative that occurred in a context of the aforementioned company being under military control, and resulted in it being ultimately placed under the control of a central government organization, the Ministry of Fuel Industry.

11.3 The Formation of Interregional Networks

11.3.1 Development of the Shanghai Power Industry During the Planned Economy Period

This section takes up the development of the Shanghai power industry, having been integrated through the socialist transformation, during the planned economy period, from a perspective that compares it with the national-level development of the Chinese power industry.

Looking at the changes in electricity generation capacity in Shanghai shown in Table 11.3, it is evident that there was a gradual increase until 1958, a sharp increase from 1958 to 1961, which coincided with the Great Leap Forward period (1958–60), and then a trend of overall increase thereafter despite several stagnations. However, compared to the growth rate of national-level electricity generation capacity, the growth of Shanghai's industry was generally slower, and the share of Shanghai to the national total also gradually and consistently decreased from its peak in 1952. As for the actual power generation, in line with the generation capacity this showed a gradual increase until 1957, surged in 1959 and 1960, and then experienced a growth trend thereafter, with its growth rate increasing year by year since 1968. Just as was the case with electricity generation capacity, the growth rate of Shanghai was slower than that of the industry at the national level, and the ratio of Shanghai to the national total gradually decreased. These figures suggest that the concentration of the power industry in Shanghai, which had developed from the end of the Qing Dynasty through the Republican period, had gradually eroded over time, dovetailing with how the integration of Shanghai's power industry progressed after the establishment of the PRC.[18]

This trend was largely related to the central government's industrial development strategy based on the planned economy. During the First Five Year Plan period, despite the increase in industrial production, large-scale power plants were not established in Shanghai due to the central government's policy of not prioritizing investment in coastal areas. In fact, only one piece of equipment was added to each of the power plants in Nanshi (南市), Yangshupu (杨树浦), and Zhabei (闸北) (Shanghai dianwangdiaodushi bianweihui 2004, p. 22). In the subsequent Great Leap Forward era, power generation facilities were expanded to cope with the sudden increase in industrial demand. It is noteworthy that they had achieved the goal of a power generation capacity of 700,000 kW by 1961, which had earlier been set by the United Power Company plan of 1947 to be achieved within 15 years. However, at the same time, these facilities which were rapidly expanded during the Great Leap Forward period also suffered from many technical problems.[19]

---

[18] For the national-level development of the Chinese power industry after the establishment of the PRC, refer to Li (1984), Zhang (1998), and Tajima (2003).

[19] On the development of the power industry in Shanghai during the Great Leap Forward, refer to Zhonggongshanghaishiwei gongyegongzuoweiyuanhui et al. (2003, pp. 94–111).

Table 11.3 Power industry production of China and Shanghai, 1949–1978

Year	Electricity generation capacity (10 thousand kW)			Electricity generation (100 million kWh)			Raw material consumption (10 thousand tons)					
							Coal			Petroleum		
	China	Shanghai (%)		China	Shanghai (%)		China	Shanghai (%)		China	Shanghai (%)	
1949	184.9	26.0	14.0%	43.1	10.1	23.4%	…	51.6	…	…	19.0	…
1950	186.6	23.6	12.6%	45.5	8.8	19.4%	…	76.3	…	…	0.7	…
1951	188.3	26.6	14.1%	57.5	11.9	20.7%	…	90.5	…	…	0.7	…
1952	196.4	29.8	15.2%	72.6	13.2	18.2%	…	96.6	…	…	0.2	…
1953	235.0	30.1	12.8%	92.0	15.8	17.2%	485.4	108.1	22.3%	…	0.5	…
1954	259.8	30.2	11.6%	109.9	17.1	15.6%	531.0	108.7	20.5%	…	0.3	…
1955	299.7	31.2	10.4%	122.8	15.3	12.4%	652.5	96.0	14.7%	…	0.1	…
1956	388.1	34.3	8.8%	165.9	18.9	11.4%	836.4	124.3	14.9%	…	0.5	…
1957	463.5	34.4	7.4%	193.4	18.9	9.8%	…	121.2	…	…	0.2	…
1958	628.8	40.6	6.5%	275.3	23.4	8.5%	…	142.2	…	…	0.9	…
1959	953.7	58.0	6.1%	422.9	31.8	7.5%	…	235.6	…	…	2.3	…
1960	1,191.8	65.2	5.5%	594.2	39.8	6.7%	2,876.3	298.1	10.4%	…	1.8	…
1961	1,285.6	72.7	5.7%	480.5	32.2	6.7%	…	178.5	…	…	27.7	…
1962	1,303.7	72.8	5.6%	458.0	30.1	6.6%	…	133.1	…	…	34.0	…
1963	1,332.9	72.8	5.5%	489.8	37.4	7.6%	…	163.3	…	…	34.0	…
1964	1,406.1	73.1	5.2%	559.8	40.8	7.3%	…	197.6	…	…	25.6	…
1965	1,507.6	72.3	4.8%	676.0	51.3	7.6%	…	273.8	…	…	16.5	…
1966	1,701.8	87.4	5.1%	825.2	58.0	7.0%	…	302.0	…	…	16.9	…
1967	1,799.3	87.5	4.9%	773.8	56.6	7.3%	…	234.9	…	…	42.8	…
1968	1,916.3	87.5	4.6%	715.9	60.4	8.4%	…	129.6	…	…	120.3	…

(continued)

Table 11.3 (continued)

Year	Electricity generation capacity (10 thousand kW)			Electricity generation (100 million kWh)			Raw material consumption (10 thousand tons)					
							Coal			Petroleum		
	China	Shanghai (%)		China	Shanghai (%)		China	Shanghai (%)		China	Shanghai (%)	
1969	2,103.6	102.5	4.9%	904.3	66.4	7.3%	…	94.4	…	…	160.4	…
1970	2,337.0	101.7	4.4%	1,158.6	74.4	6.4%	4,417.2	30.0	0.7%	…	273.9	…
1971	2,628.2	103.4	3.9%	1,383.6	84.5	6.1%	…	51.1	…	…	232.1	…
1972	2,950.1	132.4	4.5%	1,524.5	95.6	6.3%	…	63.5	…	…	253.2	…
1973	3,392.5	145.2	4.3%	1,667.6	101.8	6.1%	…	49.2	…	…	276.8	…
1974	3,810.8	157.9	4.1%	1,688.5	115.0	6.8%	…	15.7	…	…	327.0	…
1975	4,340.6	182.8	4.2%	1,958.4	123.1	6.3%	…	26.4	…	…	344.0	…
1976	4,714.7	197.8	4.2%	2,031.3	128.9	6.3%	7,967.0	27.7	0.3%	1,892	361.8	19.1%
1977	5,145.1	195.6	3.8%	2,234.0	127.9	5.7%	…	38.5	…	…	337.9	…
1978	5,712.2	197.7	3.5%	2,565.5	139.7	5.4%	11,084.0	145.5	1.3%	2,013	305.2	15.2%

Note "…" means figure unavailable

Sources Shanghaishi dianligongyeju shizhibianzuanweiyuanhu (1994, pp. 44–45), Zhang (1998, pp. 270–271, 296), Zhonghuarenmingongheguo guojiatongjiju gongyetongjisi (1958, p. 62), and Zhang et al. (1994, p. 97)

As for power generation fuel, the industry mainstream continued to be coal in the 1950s. Although petroleum consumption for electricity generation in Shanghai increased slightly in the early 1960s due to the results of existing oil resource development, coal continued to remain the main fuel until crude oil production surged in the late 1960s as a result of the development of the Daqing Oil Field (大庆油田). On the other hand, it should be noted that the proportion of Shanghai's coal consumption to that of China as a whole had been gradually decreasing through the 1950s. In the early years after the establishment of the PRC, coal was preferentially allocated to Shanghai for the purpose of maintaining industrial production. However, such a concentrated allocation of coal to Shanghai decreased in the latter half of the 1950s, a fact which also speaks to how the concentration of the power industry in Shanghai was gradually decreasing.

11.3.2 The East China Power Grid and the Shanghai Power Industry

Along with the relative downsizing of the Shanghai power industry, it is noteworthy that a power transmission network called the East China Power Grid, which connected Shanghai and its neighboring provinces, was developed from the latter half of the 1950s.

The East China Power Grid was an interregional transmission network that connected Shanghai with Jiangsu, Zhejiang, and Anhui Provinces, as shown in Fig. 11.3. Its direct origin was the completion of a 110 kV transmission line connecting Wangting Power Plant (望亭电厂) in eastern Jiangsu Province and Shanghai West Substation (上海西郊变电站) in 1957.[20] This connected the Shanghai power industry with the Sunan Power Grid (苏南电网), which had already begun to take form during the Republican period, and expanded from the Nanjing Xiaguan Power Plant (南京下关电厂, formerly the Capital Power Plant, 首都电厂), to the east to Qixia Mountain–Danyang–Changzhou–Qishuyan–Wuxi (栖霞山—丹阳—常州—戚墅堰—无锡), and to the west to Ma'anshan–Tongling (马鞍山—铜陵) in Anhui Province, in the 1950s (Huadong dianwangdiaodushi bianweihui 2004, p. 11). In 1960, a 220 kV transmission line was constructed from the Xin'anjiang Hydropower Plant (新安江水电厂) in Zhejiang Province to Shanghai via Hangzhou (杭州), creating a basic framework connecting the three provinces. In 1973, a 220 kV transmission line that connected Hefei (合肥), Wuhu (芜湖), Nanjing (南京), and Jianbi (諫壁, a power plant on the outskirts of Zhenjiang City, Jiangsu Province, which started power generation in 1965) began operation. Based on the development of these transmission lines connecting neighboring provinces, the East China Power Industry Administration of the Ministry of Water Resources and Electric Power (水

[20] Before the Second Sino-Japanese War, the Qishuyan Power Plant (戚墅堰电厂) had planned to build a power plant with a scale of 15,000–20,000 kW in Wangting (望亭) on the coast of Lake Tai, and the land acquisition was already completed. See Kanemaru (1994, p. 190).

利电力部华东电业管理局) was established in 1962.[21] It was after this long series of developments that the East China Power Grid came into operation.

Looking at the situation of the power industry within the East China Power Grid, the power generation capacity at the end of 1962 when this power grid officially came on line was 1,844,200 kW, of which thermal power accounted for 80.8% and hydroelectric power accounted for 19.2% (Huadong dianwangdiaodushi bianweihui 2004, p. 12). The power generation capacity of Shanghai in that same year was 728,000 kW, according to Table 11.3, reaching 39.5% of the total capacity of the East China Power Grid. This illustrates how Shanghai still contributed a large proportion of the capacity within the East China Power Grid, even as its share of the national total had relatively declined. Furthermore, according to Table 11.4, which shows the electricity generation and consumption of each city and province within the East China Power Grid, the scale of Shanghai's power generation consistently exceeded the other three provinces despite it being a single city. This structure had not fundamentally changed during the planned economy period, even in the face of the increasing trend of power generation in each province, especially after around 1970.

However, it is also important to note here the electricity supply and demand relationship within the East China Power Grid. In this power grid, electricity was mainly directed to several industrial cities and mining areas. According to the statistics for 1963, Shanghai, Nanjing, Hefei, Hangzhou, the Huainan Mining Area (Anhui Province), and the Juzhou Chemical Industrial Zone (巨州化学工业区, Zhejiang Province) accounted for 81.6% of the total electricity consumption of the East China Power Grid, with Shanghai's share reaching 56.4% (Huadong dianwangdiaodushi bianweihui 2004, p. 13).

On this point, taking a look at Fig. 11.4, which graphically indicates the supply–demand balance based on the difference between electricity generation and consumption in each city and province, it is clear that Shanghai and Jiangsu Province consistently had consumptions exceeding generation, indicating that they were receiving supply from other provinces within the East China Power Grid, while the electricity generation in Anhui and Zhejiang Provinces generally exceeded consumption. Shanghai in particular, despite leading the provinces in electricity generation, had suffered, as mentioned earlier, from a supply shortage from the late 1950s, when mutual power exchange began within the East China Power Grid, until the early 1970s. The proportion of supply from other provinces in Shanghai's power consumption reached a significant 10–26% throughout the period. Indeed, supplying electricity to Shanghai was considered an important task for the entire East China Power Grid at the time (Huadong dianwangdiaodushi bianweihui 2004, p. 14). This was likely due to factors such as the consistent increase in industrial electricity demand under the socialist system and the expansion of the Shanghai administrative area in 1958.

[21] The East China Power Management Bureau (华东电业管理局) existed from April 1952 to January 1955, and managed power bureaus in Nanjing, Sunan, Xuzhou, Huainan, and so on. However, the management of the East China Power Management Bureau at that time was likely limited to the individual management of each area, just as it was before the establishment of the interregional power network. Refer to Huadong dianwangdiaodushi bianweihui (2004, p. 48).

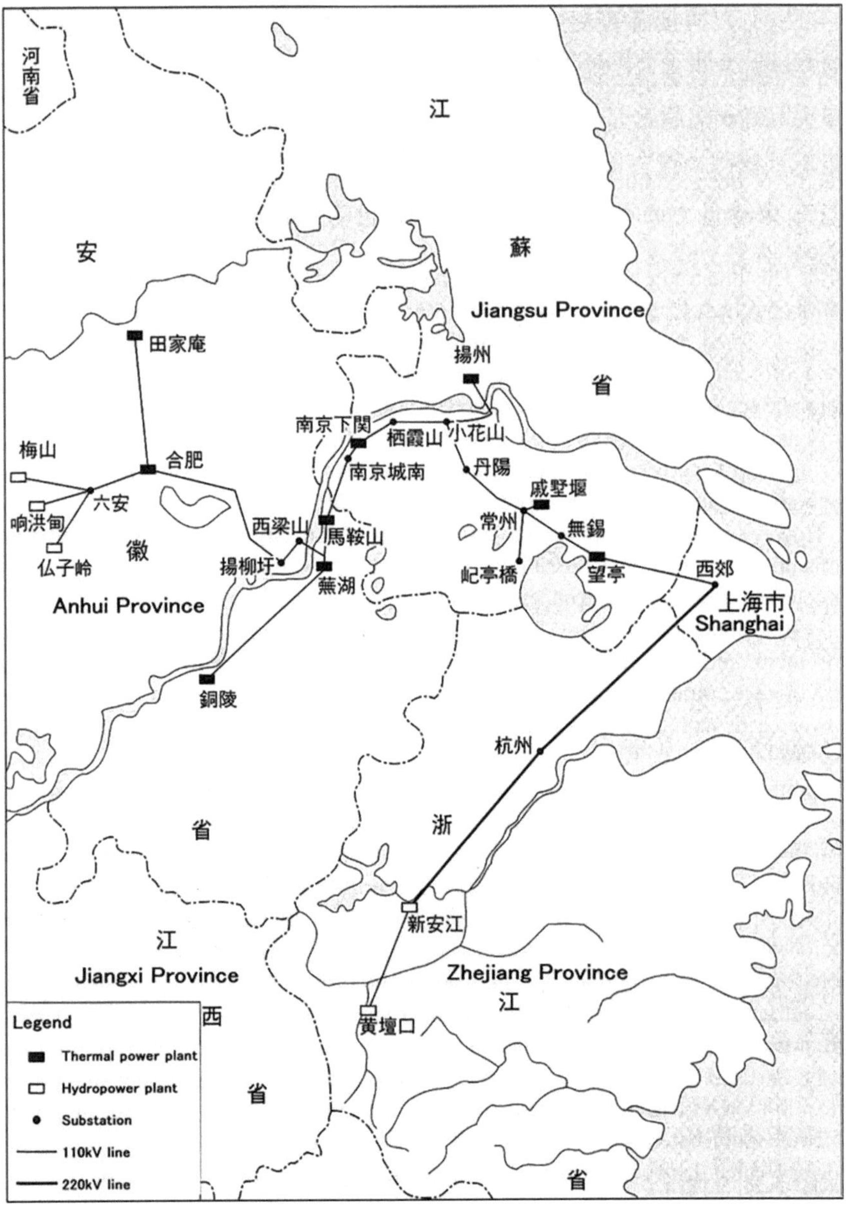

Fig. 11.3 Transmission networks of the East China Power Grid, around 1962. *Note* This figure was created based on various sources on the major power stations and transmission lines comprising the East China Power Grid around 1962, meaning the transmission lines here do not necessarily entirely coincide with the routes of the real lines. *Sources* Created by author based on Huadong dianwang-diaodushi bianweihui (2004), the map of East China 500 kV transmission networks (华东500千伏电网地理位置接线意图) on opening pages, pp. 9–15; Jiangsusheng difangzhi bianzuanweiyuanhui (1994, pp. 82–100); Anhuisheng dianligongyeju (1995, pp. 69–81), Zhejiangsheng dianligongyezhi bianzuanweiyuanhui (1995, pp. 118–127)

Table 11.4 Electricity generation and consumption of Shanghai and East China provinces, 1949–1978 (Unit: 100 million kWh)

Year	Shanghai		Jiangsu		Zhejiang		Anhui	
	Generation	Consumption	Generation	Consumption	Generation	Consumption	Generation	Consumption
1949	10.1	10.1	2.2	2.2	0.6	0.6	0.2	0.2
1950	8.8	8.8	2.5	2.5	0.6	0.6	0.3	0.2
1951	11.9	11.9	3.4	3.3	0.8	0.8	0.4	0.3
1952	13.2	13.9	4.1	4.1	0.9	0.9	0.5	0.4
1953	15.8	15.8	4.7	4.7	1.1	1.1	0.8	0.7
1954	17.1	17.0	5.2	5.4	1.3	1.5	1.3	0.9
1955	15.3	15.2	5.0	5.2	1.3	1.4	1.7	1.3
1956	18.9	18.8	6.3	6.5	1.6	1.8	2.2	1.8
1957	18.9	18.7	6.4	6.9	1.9	1.9	2.8	2.2
1958	23.4	26.4	9.2	10.6	3.5	3.4	4.2	3.7
1959	31.8	39.9	14.0	16.0	6.1	5.9	8.6	7.7
1960	39.8	52.1	20.5	22.9	10.6	9.5	14.8	12.4
1961	32.2	43.4	17.6	20.4	15.0	9.4	14.9	12.0
1962	30.1	39.2	15.4	20.0	16.7	10.1	12.5	9.2
1963	37.4	44.7	16.9	21.0	12.7	10.7	12.5	10.0
1964	40.8	53.0	20.2	24.3	19.4	13.2	13.5	11.4
1965	51.3	63.2	25.7	30.5	21.2	17.4	15.5	13.2
1966	58.0	70.3	32.8	39.3	29.0	21.9	20.1	17.6
1967	56.6	64.4	29.7	36.2	26.4	20.1	15.1	…
1968	60.4	67.0	28.3	34.7	21.1	18.0	15.4	…
1969	66.4	79.6	32.9	42.1	33.5	25.1	22.5	…
1970	74.4	84.9	50.1	57.3	33.2	30.2	29.3	24.7

(continued)

Table 11.4 (continued)

Year	Shanghai		Jiangsu		Zhejiang		Anhui	
	Generation	Consumption	Generation	Consumption	Generation	Consumption	Generation	Consumption
1971	84.5	94.0	69.8	74.8	39.5	37.7	35.0	29.8
1972	95.6	99.5	74.6	83.9	33.3	41.4	41.5	33.8
1973	101.8	108.6	79.6	95.7	51.0	45.9	51.1	39.8
1974	115.0	112.2	67.1	88.9	47.1	41.0	46.1	38.2
1975	123.1	120.4	85.6	105.5	46.8	42.2	55.5	48.0
1976	128.9	125.1	96.9	118.7	42.5	46.9	60.7	52.2
1977	127.9	131.9	105.1	129.6	50.7	57.8	68.5	55.6
1978	139.7	147.7	127.4	145.9	50.6	69.8	83.4	66.7

Notes (1) "…" means figure unavailable. (2) According to Shanghaishi dianligongyeju shizhibianzuanweiyuanhui (1994, p. 193), the consumption of Shanghai is the total of electricity generation by all power stations in Shanghai plus the imports from the East China Power Grid. (3) The consumption of other provinces is in all likelihood calculated in the same way. (4) As for the electricity generation of Shanghai, this table adopts the data from Shanghaishi dianligongyeju shizhibianzuanweiyuanhui (1994, pp. 44–45) referring to Shanghaishi tongjiju (1984, p. 97) although Huadong dianligongyeshi bianjishi (2004, pp. 178–181) indicates figures exceeding those of this table

Sources Shanghaishi dianligongyeju shizhibianzuanweiyuanhui (1994, pp. 44–45, 193), Jiangsusheng difangzhi bianzuanweiyuanhui (1994, pp. 71–72, 173), Zhejiangsheng dianligongyezhi bianzuanweiyuanhui (1995, pp. 63, 196), Huadong dianligongyeshi bianjishi (2004, pp. 182–183), and Anhuisheng dianligongyeju (1995, pp. 10–11, 134)

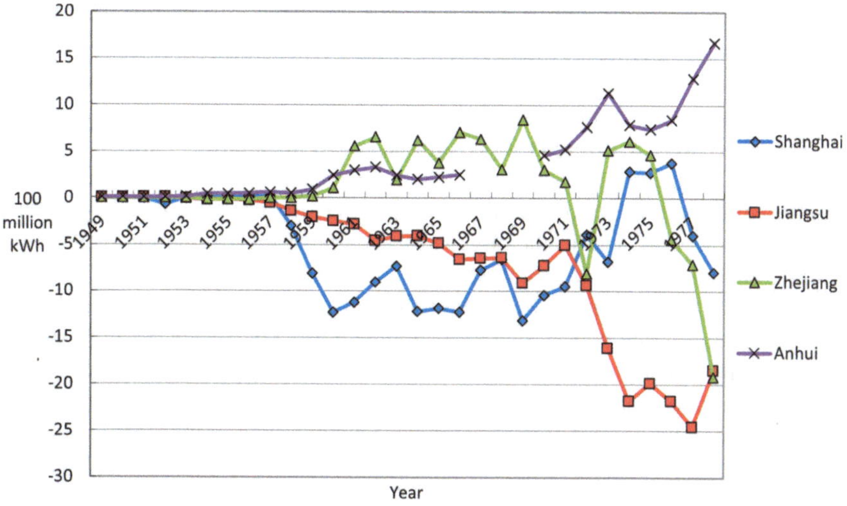

Fig. 11.4 Balance of electricity generation and consumption of Shanghai and East China provinces, 1949–1978. *Source* Table 11.4

These interregional electricity supply–demand relationships marked a major shift from the situation of the Shanghai power industry during the Republican period, when Shanghai possessed an overwhelming power generation capacity and essentially met its demand with its own supply within the city. Shanghai's power industry, while still dominant in terms of electricity generation capacity against the backdrop of the national strategy of prioritizing industrial development, had become an importer of electricity due to its having been incorporated into the East China Power Grid, which prioritized the power supply for industrial and mining areas with lines connecting them.

This chapter has aimed at examining the formation of an interregional network under the Chinese socialist system, focusing on the case of the Shanghai power industry from the immediate postwar period to the planned economy period.

Since before the Second Sino-Japanese War, the Shanghai power industry, which possessed a rich electricity generation capacity while being independent from neighboring regions, was characterized by a situation in which multiple power companies coexisted within the city. Based on the city's power shortage after the war, a plan for establishing the United Power Company initiated by the Shanghai Power Company, a company funded by US capital, represented a long-term and large-scale vision to explore new business developments backed by abundant petroleum resources, while sharing interests with the Shanghai Municipal Bureau of Public Utilities, which desired unified management of the city's power industry, and the Shanghai Municipal Representative Council, which desired a stable power supply. However, this plan was rejected by the National Government, which insisted that the entry of foreign capital into public utilities was nothing other than an infringement of sovereignty, and so ultimately the plan did not come to fruition.

After the occupation of Shanghai by the People's Liberation Army in 1949, the environment surrounding the Shanghai power industry changed significantly, and the foundation built on Western power companies gradually disappeared. Prompted by China's participation in the Korean War, the Shanghai Power Company's exclusive business rights were recovered by the Chinese government through military control, and a unified management system within Shanghai, led by the local government, was established through the unification of power prices, the establishment of a unified transmission network within the city, and the socialist transformation of the other power companies. However, from the 1950s to the 1970s, although the development of the power industry progressed nationwide in response to increased industrial investment, large-scale power source development was not carried out in Shanghai. Moreover, the primary power generation fuel of Shanghai's power industry shifted from petroleum to coal allocated by the Ministry of Fuel Industry. The sum of these points indicate how the relative scale of the Shanghai power industry nationwide under the integration led by the government had shrunk compared to the Republican period.

Under such circumstances, the East China Power Grid, an interregional network connecting Jiangsu, Anhui, Zhejiang, and the city of Shanghai, was developed. Since the late 1950s, the Shanghai power industry had consistently maintained a power generation capacity exceeding that of the other three provinces in the East China Power Grid. However, under the national strategy of connecting mining and industrial regions with lines and prioritizing electricity distribution for them, Shanghai instead became an importer of electricity from other provinces within the grid, and indeed supplying electricity to Shanghai was understood to be one significant task of the grid.

The implication of this process is that the interregional network connecting Shanghai and neighboring provinces, which was formed for the first time by government-led efforts after the establishment of the PRC, was strongly determined by the national industrial development strategy due to its government-led nature. It was developed in a fundamentally different way from the process of forming a wide-area monopoly system, which was what had come about in Japan in the 1920s as a result of the behavior of private companies. By contrast, in a government-led interregional network like what had been established in the PRC, the characteristics of the Shanghai power industry that had developed during the Republican period had no choice but to undergo a dramatic transformation.

References

Chinese Language

Anhuisheng dianligongyeju, ed. 1995. *Anhuisheng dianligongyezhi* (安徽省电力工业志, Anhui Provincial Power Industry Chronicle). Beijing: Dangdai zhongguo chubanshe

Huadong dianligongyeshi bianjishi, ed. 2004. *Zhonghua renmingongheguo dianligongyeshi huadongjuan* (中华人民共和国电力工业史 华东卷, The History of Power Industry in the People's Republic of China, East China Volume). Beijing: Zhongguo dianlichubanshe

Huadong dianwangdiaodushi bianweihui, ed. 2004. *Huadong dianwangdiaodushi* (华东电网调度史, The History of East China Power Grid Dispatch) . Beijing: Zhongguo dianlichubanshe

Jiangsusheng difangzhi bianzuanweiyuanhui. 1994. *Jiangsushengzhi, dianligongyezhi* (江苏省志 电力工业志, Jiangsu Province Chronicles, Power Industry Chronicles). Nanjing: Jiangsu kexuejishu chubanshe

Jinwan, Yuyi (Kanemaru, Yuichi). 1999. Tongjibiaozhong zhi jiangsudianye: yi 'jianguo shinian' shiqi wei zhongxin de taolungao (统计表中之江苏电业:以"建國十年"时期爲中心的讨论稿, Jiangsu Electricity Power Industry in Statistics: A Discussion Centered on the 'Decade of Nation Building' Period). *Ritsumeikan keizaigaku* (立命馆经济学, The Ritsumeikan Economic Review) 48(5): 885–901. https://doi.org/10.34382/00001452

Li, Daigeng, ed. 1983. *Zhongguo dianligongyefazhan shiliao: jiefangqian de qishinian* (中国电力工业发展史料:解放前的70年, Historical Materials on the Development of China's Electric Power Industry: The 70 Years Before Liberation). Beijing: Shuilidianli chubanshe

Li, Daigeng, ed. 1984. *Xinzhongguo dianligongye fazhanshi* (新中国电力工业发展史, History of the Development of the Power Industry in New China). Beijing: Qiyeguanli chubanshe

Lin, Meili. 1990. Waizi dianye de yanjiu (外资电业的研究 (1882–1937年), Research on Foreign Capital Power Industry: 1882–1937). Master's Thesis, Taipei: Institute of History, National Taiwan University

Liu, Songbin. 1997. *Zhongguo gongchandang dui dachengshi de jieguan: 1945–1952* (中国共产党对大城市的接管 (1945–1952), The Chinese Communist Party's Takeover of Large Cities: 1945–1952), Beijing: Beijing tushuguan chubanshe

Shanghaishi dianligongyeju shizhibianzuanweiyuanhui, ed. 1994. *Shanghai dianligongyezhi* (上海电力工业志, Shanghai Power Industry Chronicle). Shanghai: Shanghai shehuikexueyuan chubanshe

Shanghaishi dianligongyeshi bianweihui, ed. 2003. *Zhonghuarenmingongheguo dianligongyeshi shanghai juan* (中华人民共和国电力工业史 上海卷, The History of Power Industry in the People's Republic of China: Shanghai Volume). Beijing: Zhongguo dianlichubanshe

Shanghai dianwangdiaodushi bianweihui, ed. 2004. *Shanghai dianwangdiaodushi* (上海电网调度史, A History of Shanghai Power Grid Dispatch). Beijing: Zhongguo dianlichubanshe

Shanghaishizhengfu tongjichu, ed. 1947. *Shanghaishi tongjizongbaogao: minguo 35 nian* (上海市统计总报告 (民国35年), Shanghai Statistical General Report: Republic of China 35th Year). Publisher unknown

Shanghaishizhengfu tongjichu, ed. Publication year unknown. *Shanghaishi tongjizongbaogao: minguo 36 nian* (上海市统计总报告 (民国36年), Shanghai Statistical General Report: Republic of China 36th Year). Publisher unknown

Shanghaishi dianligongsi. 1946. *Shanghaishi dianliwenti* (上海市电力问题, The Issues of Power in Shanghai). Publisher Unknown

Shanghaishi tongjiju, ed. 1984. *Shanghai tongjinianjian 1983* (上海统计年鉴 1983, Shanghai Statistical Yearbook 1983). Shanghai: Shanghai renmin chubanshe

Wang, Shuhuai. 1991. Zhongguo zaoqide dianqishiye, 1882–1928: Donglixiandaihuazhiyi (中国早期的电气事业,1882–1928:動力现代化之一, China's Early Electric Power Industry, 1882–1928: A Modernization of Power). In *Zhongguo xiandaihua lunwenji* (中国现代化论文集, Collection of Essays on China's Modernization), ed. Institute of Modern History, Academia Sinica, 443–476. Taipei: Institute of Modern History, Academia Sinica

Zhang, Lin et al., eds. 1994. *Dangdai zhongguode dianligongye* (当代中国的电力工业, Contemporary China's Electric Power Industry). Beijing: Dangdai zhongguo chubanshe

Zhang, Lin, ed. 1998. *Zhongguo dianligongyezhi* (中国电力工业志, China Electric Power Industry Chronicle). Beijing: Dangdai zhongguo chubanshe

Zhejiangsheng dianligongyezhi bianzuanweiyuanhui. 1995. *Zhejiangsheng dianligongyezhi* (浙江省电力工业志, Zhejiang Province Electric Power Industry Chronicle). Beijing: Shuilidianli chubanshe

Zheng, Youkui, Cheng Linsun and Zhang Chuanhong. 1991. *Jiuzhongguo de ziyuanweiyuanhui: Shishi yu pingjia* (旧中国的资源委员会:史实与评价, Old China's Resources Committee: History and Evaluation). Shanghai: Shanghai shehuikexueyuan chubanshe

Zhonggongshanghaishiwei gongyegongzuoweiyuanhui, Zhonggongshanghaishi dangshiyanjiushi, and Shanghaishidanganguan, eds. 2003. *'Dayuejin' shiqi de shanghaigongye* ("大跃进"时期的上海工业, Shanghai Industry during the 'Great Leap Forward' Period). Shanghai: Shanghai kexuepuji chubansh

Zhongguo gongyejingjiyanjiusuo, ed. 1949. *Shanghai shachang de shengchanxiaolüwenti, Shangmianfangzhigongye de dianligongyingwenti* (上海纱厂的生产效率问题、上海棉纺织工业的电力供应问题, The Production Efficiency Problem of Shanghai Cotton Yarn Factory and the Power Supply Problem of Shanghai Cotton Textile Industry), Gongyejingji diaochabaogao, Xin 2 hao. Shanghai: Gongshang jingji chubanshe

Zhongguoshehuikexueyuan and Zhongyangdanganguan, eds. 1994. *Zhonghuarenmingongheguo jingjidanganziliaoxuanbian 1949–1952: Duiwaimaoyi juan* (中华人民共和国经济档案资料选编 1949–1952 (对外贸易卷), Selected Economic Archive Materials of the People's Republic of China 1949–1952: Foreign Trade Volume). Beijing: Jingjiguanli chubanshe

Zhonghuarenmingongheguo guojiatongjiju gongyetongjisi, ed. 1958. *Woguo gangtie dianli meitan jixie fangzhi zaozhi gongye de jinxi* (我国钢铁、电力、煤炭、机械、纺织、造纸工业的今昔, Past and Present of Our Country's Steel, Electricity, Coal, Machinery, Textile, and Paper Industries). Beijing: Tongji chubanshe

Zhongyang danganguan, ed. 1992. *Zhonggong zhongyang wenjianxuanji* (中共中央文件选集, Selected Documents of the Chinese Communist Party Central Committee), Volume 18, Jan. – Sep. 1949. Beijing: Zhonggong zhongyangdangxiao chubanshe

Zhongyangdangbu guominjingjijihuaweiyuanhui, ed. 1937. *Shinianlaiz zhi zhongguo jingjijianshe* (十年来之中国经济建设, China's Economic Construction in the Past Ten Years). Nanjing: Nanjing fulun ribaoshe

Zhongyangjuanbianjibu, ed. 1992. *Zhongguo zibenzhuyigongshangye de shehuizhuyigaizao: zhongyangjuan* (中国资本主义工商业的社会主义改造 (中央卷), The Socialist Transformation of China's Capitalist Industry and Commerce: Central Volume), Volumes I and II. Beijing: Zhonggongdangshi chubanshe

Zhongyangrenminzhengfu fazhiweiyuanhui, ed. 1952. *Zhongyangrenminzhengfu falinghuibian: 1949–1950* (中央人民政府法令汇编 (1949–1950), Compilation of Laws and Regulations of the Central People's Government: 1949–1950). Beijing: Renmin chubanshe

Japanese Language

Hashimoto, Jurō. 1977–78. 'Godai denryoku' taisei no seiritsu to denryokushijō no tenkai (『五大電力』体制の成立と電力市場の展開, Establishment of the 'Five Major Power' System and Development of the Power Market) *Reports of the University of Electro-Communications* (電気通信大学報) 27(2): 335–347, 28(1): 137–150, 28(2): 347–362

Hori, Kazuo. 1987. 'Manshūkoku' niokeru denryokugyō to tōseiseisaku (『満洲国』における電力業と統制政策, Electric Power Industry and Control Policy in 'Manchukuo'). *Rekishigaku kenkyū* (歴史学研究, Journal of historical studies) 564: 13–30, 58

Kajima, Jun. 2006. "Sengo kara jinminkyōwakokushoki ni kaketeno shanghai denryokusangyō no tōgōkatei" (戦後から人民共和国初期にかけての上海電力産業の統合過程, Integration Process of Shanghai Electric Power Industry from Postwar Period to the Early Years of the People's Republic of China), *Chūgoku kenkyū geppō* (中国研究月報, Monthly Journal of Chinese Affairs) 60(3): 28–40

Kajima, Jun. 2008. “Shanghai denryokusangyō no tōgō to kōiki network: Dainiji sekaitaisengo kara keikakukeizaiki ni kakete” (上海電力産業の統合と広域ネットワーク——第二次世界大戦後から計画経済期にかけて, Integration of Shanghai Electric Power Industry and Intra-regional Network: From the Post-World War II period to the Planned Economy Period), *Gendai chūgoku no denryokusangyō: ‘Fusoku no keizai’ to sangyōsoshiki* (現代中国の電力産業——「不足の経済」と産業組織, The Electric Power Industry of Contemporary China: ‘Economy of Shortage’ and Industrial Organization), ed. Tajima Toshio, 91–114. Kyoto: Shōwadō

Kanemaru, Yūichi. 1992. Kōbukyoku denkisho no teiden mondai: 1925 nen 7 gatsu 6 nichi zengo (工部局電気処の停電問題——1925年7月6日前後, The Power Failure Problem of the Shanghai Municipal Council Electricity Department: Around July 6, 1925). *Chikaki ni arite* (近きに在りて, Being Nearby) 21: 3–22

Kanemaru, Yūichi. 1993. Chūgoku ‘minzoku kōgyō no ougonjidai’ to denryoku sangyō: 1879 nen – 1924 nen no shanghaishi kōsoshō wo chūshinni(中国『民族工業の黄金時代』と電力産業——1879年-1924年の上海市・江蘇省を中心に, Electric Power Industry and ‘The Golden Age of National Industries’ in China: A Comparative Study of Shanghai and Jiangsu, 1879–1924). *Ajia kenkyū* (アジア研究, Asian Studies) 39(4): 29–84. https://doi.org/10.11479/asianstudies.39.4_29

Kanemaru, Yūichi. 1994. Kōhoku niokeru denryoku sangyō no seichō: ‘Kigyō jōkamachi nantsū no kēsu (江北における電力産業の成長——「企業城下町 (Kigyo-Jokamachi)」南通のケース, The Growth of the Electric Power Industry in Jiangbei: The Case of ‘Company Town (Kigyo-Jokamachi)’ Nantong). *Teikyō shigaku* (帝京史学, Teikyo Journal of History) 9: 27–50

Kanemaru, Yūichi. 2002. Chūgoku kōgyō chōsa: Denryokusangyōshi no jirei kara (中国工業調査——電力産業史の事例から, China Industrial Survey: From the Case of Electric Power Industry History). In *Kōain to senji chūgoku chōsa* (興亜院と戦時中国調査, Koain and the survey on China during the wartime), eds. Honjō Hisako, Uchiyama Masao, and Kubo Tōru, 128–152. Tokyo: Iwanami shoten

Kanemaru, Yūichi. 2005. ‘Shinajihen’ chokugo, nihon niyoru kachūdenryokusangyō no chōsa to fukkyūkeikaku (『支那事変』直後,日本による華中電力産業の調査と復旧計画, The Investigation and Restoration Plan for Central China’s Electric Power Industry by Japan after the Outbreak of ‘the Second Sino-Japanese War’). *The Ritsumeikan Economic Review* 53(5)-(6): 574–596. https://doi.org/10.34382/00001504

Kubo, Tōru, Kajima Jun, Kigoshi Yoshinori. 2016. *Tōkei de miru chūgoku kingendai keizaishi* (統計でみる中国近現代経済史, Economic History of Modern China: An Approach Based on Statistical data). Tokyo: University of Tokyo Press

Tajima, Toshio. 2003. Jūkōgyō: Ikōkeizaiki no ‘goshō kōgyō’ (重工業——移行経済期の『五小工業』, Heavy Industry: ‘Five Small Industries’ in the Transition Economy). In *Chūgoku no taiseitenkan to sangyōhatten* (中国の体制転換と産業発展, China’s Industries in Transition), Institute of Social Science Research Series No.6. Tokyo: Institute of Social Science, University of Tokyo

Tajima, Toshio, ed. 2008. *Gendai chūgoku no denryoku Sangyō: ‘Fusoku no keizai’ to sangyōsoshiki* (現代中国の電力産業——「不足の経済」と産業組織, Electric Power Industry in Contemporary China: ‘Economy of Shortage’ and Industrial Organization). Kyoto: Shōwadō

Zaishanghai chūgokutsūshinsha chōsabu. 1937. *Shanghaidenryokugaisha no soshiki to jigyō* (上海電力会社の組織と事業, Organization and Business of Shanghai Power Company), Chūtsū shiliō 67. Shanghai: Chūgokutsūshinsha chōsabu

Unpublished Primary Sources

B1, Shanghaishi renminzhengfu dangan (上海市人民政府档案, Shanghai People’s Government Archives)

B1-2-389, Shanghaishi renminzhengfu gongyongju (上海市人民政府公用局, Shanghai Municipal People's Government Public Utilities Bureau) "Gongyongju lianggebanyue de gongzuobaogao" (公用处两个半月的工作报告 (1949年5月28日-8月23日), Report of Public Affairs Office's Two and a Half Months Work from May 28 to August 23, 1949), Date of creation unknown

Q1, Shanghaishi zhengfu dangan (上海市政府档案, Shanghai Municipal Government Archives)

Q1–14–456a, "Lianhe dianligongsi quanyue caoan" (联合电力公司权约草案, Draft of the United Power Company Rights Contract), date of creation unknown, attached document to "Hansong lianhedianligongsian ji canyihui gonghan dengjian qingyinfayou" (函送联合电力公司案及参议会公函等件请印发由, Request for Print and Distribution of the Letter on the United Power Company Case and Senate Official Letter etc., from Shanghaishi gongyongju mishushi (上海市公用局秘书室) to Shanghaishi zhengfu (上海市政府), Letter, Shi gong mi (市公秘) (36) 386, September 23, 1947

Q1–14–456b, "Chao jingjibu deng huicheng" (抄经济部等会呈, Carbon Copy of the Detailed Report by the Ministry of Economic Affairs and Other Ministries), date of creation unknown, attached document of "Jingjibudeng liubuhui huitonghefu shanghailianhedianligongsi yingye-quanqiyuecaoan yijian qingchazhaofuyou" (经济部等六部会会同核复上海联合电力公司营业权契约草案意见请查照核复由, Request for Investigation and Reply to the Ministry of Economic Affairs and Other Six Ministries' Jointly Review and Reply to the Shanghai United Power Company Business Rights Contract Draft Opinion), from Xingzhengyuan mishuchu (行政院秘书处) to Shanghaishi zhengfu (上海市政府), Official Letter No. 9995, March 1, 1948

Q5, Shanghaishi gongyongju dangan (上海市公用局档案, Shanghai Municipal Bureau of Public Utilities Archives)

Q5-3-5469, Shanghaishi gongyongju (上海市公用局) "Chouzu lianhedianligongsijuan" (筹组联合电力公司卷, Preparation of the United Power Company Volume), date of creation unknown

Shanghaishi renminzhengfu mishuchu, ed. Publication year unknown. *1949 nian shanghaishi zonghe tongji* (1949年上海市综合统计, Comprehensive Statistics of Shanghai in 1949). Publisher unknown

Chapter 12
Conclusion

Abstract This chapter concludes the discussion by first outlining the development of Shanghai's economy following the beginning of the Reform and Opening-up Policy in 1978, which fundamentally transformed the basic elements of the socialist system, before finally reexamining the historical significance of the Chinese socialist system in context.

Keywords Reform and Opening-up Policy · Socialist system · Shanghai economy · Local governments · Central control in principle · De facto local autonomy

This study set out to discuss the formation and structure of the Chinese socialist system and its impact on the Chinese economy and society through focusing on the case of Shanghai. It is apt to conclude the discussion by first outlining the development of Shanghai's economy after the beginning of the Reform and Opening-up Policy in 1978, which fundamentally transformed the basic elements of the socialist system, and finally examining the historical significance of the Chinese socialist system in context.

12.1 The Reform and Opening-Up Policy and Shanghai's Economy

China's Reform and Opening-up Policy is generally considered to have originated from the 3rd Plenary Session of the 11th Central Committee of the Chinese Communist Party in December 1978. The internal system "reform" and external "opening up" processes implemented after 1978, unlike the institutional reforms attempted several times during the planned economy period, changed the fundamental elements of the socialist system (Okamoto 2013, pp. 267–269). Specifically, these processes entailed nothing other than, on the one hand, a transition from resource allocation based on planning to resource allocation through the market, and on the other hand, a transition

J. Kajima, *Shanghai under the Socialist System*, Studies in Economic History,
https://doi.org/10.1007/978-981-95-3225-4_12

from a system based primarily on public ownership of the means of production to one that accepted private ownership.

Firstly, regarding the transition from a planned economy to a market economy, resource allocation based on planning had been decreasing throughout the 1980s, with supply through the market becoming normative, as seen in the case of cement in Chapter 10. As for the ownership of the means of production, the introduction of the agricultural production contracting system (家庭联产承包责任制), which allowed individual farmers to engage in management to a certain extent, led to the dismantling of collective agriculture, and the people's communes, which were the symbols of collective ownership in rural areas, were reorganized into township-level governments (乡镇政府). Furthermore, while reform of the state-owned enterprise system progressed with the acceptance of corporate autonomy, township and village enterprises based on the collective enterprises of the planned economy period and private enterprises emerged. On top of this, the acceptance of private ownership of the means of production was also significantly bound up with promotion of the Opening-up Policy, in the sense that it provided a basis for permitting foreign companies to enter China. All of these changes showed how the breakdown of the socialist system, as defined in this book, was already underway in China in the 1980s.

However, it would be a mistake to think that Shanghai's economy changed completely as a result of the government's policy shift in 1978. Rather, it would be more accurate to argue that in the years after 1978 the Shanghai economy entered a new phase. What had a particularly significant impact on the Shanghai economy in terms of opening up to the outside world was the construction of the Shanghai Baoshan Steel General Factory (上海宝山钢铁总厂), which had its origins in a plant purchase contract signed with Nippon Steel Corporation (新日本製鐵) in April 1978, prior to the start of the Reform and Opening-up Policy (production started in 1985). However, Shanghai lagged behind Guangdong and Fujian Provinces, where the "opening up" proper had been preceded by the introduction of foreign capital through the establishment of four Special Economic Zones (经济特区), in Shenzhen, Zhuhai, Shantou, and Xiamen. Shanghai's own opening-up process was boosted by the start of the development of the Pudong New District (浦东新区) in 1990, and by Deng Xiaoping (邓小平)'s Southern Tour speech (南巡讲话) in 1992, which dispelled the chill in foreign investment caused by the 1989 Tiananmen Square incident. The development of the Pudong New District, which was given preferential treatment equivalent to or greater than that of the special economic zones by the central government, was a major project intended to redevelop Shanghai. Subsequently, the Pudong New District accepted many foreign companies and came to be regarded as a symbol of economic development in the Yangtze River Basin, serving as a node in the T-shaped development strategy connecting the Yangtze River Delta (Shanghai, Suzhou, Wuxi, Changzhou, Nantong, Hangzhou, etc.) and the cities along the Yangtze River, from Wuhu in Anhui Province to Chongqing in Sichuan Province (Seki 1997, pp. 132–162; Amako et al. 1999, pp. 54–55, 1154–1155).

Not only did Shanghai lag in opening to foreign capital, but moreover, the city was not in any particular hurry to move to reform the socialist system. At the initial stage of the Reform and Opening-up Policy, Shanghai essentially carried on the structure of the planned economy period discussed in this book, with local state-owned enterprises accorded a significant presence. Looking at the situation of Shanghai's industrial enterprises in 1982, out of a total of 8,368 units, only 148 belonged to the central government, and the output of 3,161 units of local state-owned enterprises directly managed by the municipal government amounted to 52.271 billion yuan, accounting for 82% of the total industrial output of 63.670 billion yuan in Shanghai, overwhelming central government-affiliated enterprises and collective-owned enterprises (enterprises affiliated with administrative units below Shanghai Municipality, including urban resident organization enterprises, township enterprises, etc.) in terms of economic scale.[1] Although this structure gradually changed with the increase of collective-owned enterprises, foreign enterprises, and private enterprises in the 1990s (Seki 1997, pp. 68–79), local enterprises affiliated with the Shanghai Municipal Government, which were strongly tied to the municipal public finance through the socialist fiscal system during the planned economy period, remained important economic entities even in the Reform period when the market economy was revived.

As for the development of Shanghai's economy after the Reform and Opening-up Policy, Huang (2008) highlights the importance of intensive urban infrastructure construction and foreign investment introduction driven by local governments, the large presence of state-owned enterprises, the relative lack of development of private enterprises compared to other regions, and the preferential treatment received from the central government since the top national leaders, Jiang Zemin (江泽民) and Zhu Rongji (朱镕基), themselves came from Shanghai (Huang 2008, pp. 175–232). This suggests that the influence of the government, both local and central, remained strong in Shanghai even as the Reform period got underway. From a long-term perspective, the character of Shanghai's development after 1978 was significantly different from that during the previous time it had been open to foreign and private investment and entrepreneurship, namely the Republican period, which had been so strongly based on private and foreign enterprises. In this sense, the introduction of the socialist system from the 1950s to the 1970s left a deep, entrenched impact on Shanghai's economy that could not easily be overcome.

[1] The number and output of the industrial enterprises under the direct control of the Shanghai Municipal Government was calculated by the following method: city total−(central state-owned industries [中央工业] + collectively-owned industries [集体所有制工业] + other economic type industries [其他经济类型工业]) based on the figures provided by Shanghaishi tongjiju (1984, pp. 77, 85). Also see Osaka shiritsudaigaku keizaikenkyūjo (1986, pp. 134–139) and Seki (1989, pp. 40–46).

12.2 The Historical Significance of the Chinese Socialist System

Taking into account the status of Shanghai's economy during the Reform and Opening-up Policy period, outlined above, if one were to sum up the analysis of the relationship between local governments and enterprises in Shanghai in this book, it could be encapsulated in the following key points.

12.2.1 The Emergence of Local Governments as Economic Entities

The first significant change brought about by the introduction of the socialist system was the emergence of local governments as economic entities due to the public ownership of the means of production. As pointed out in Chapter 3, former studies on the socialist transformation have focused on how private enterprises were transformed into public (state-owned or public-private jointly-owned) enterprises. These studies analyzed the process through which the government's control over private enterprises was fundamentally established within the framework of a public-private sector dichotomy. In other words, scholars have approached the socialist transformation as a process by which private enterprises were driven into extinction. However, as the analysis in this book has revealed, the establishment of dominant economic control by the government was in actuality only one aspect of the changes brought about by the socialist transformation. Equally significant is the fact that while previous studies have depended on a rather simple or united "public" conception, there were various levels within what comprised the "public," "state," or "government" sector, and the socialist transformation made all of the diverse economic entities that had existed until that point into state-owned or public-private jointly-owned enterprises belonging to various levels of government. This process is illustrated in Fig. 12.1.

Of course, state-owned or public enterprises existed in China before the socialist transformation. During the Republican period, state-owned enterprises essentially referred to companies directly under the central government, and there were several state-owned entities under the National Government Resources Committee established in the mid-1930s, in industries such as machinery, coal and petroleum, and electricity throughout the Second Sino-Japanese War and postwar periods. There was also the China Textile Construction Company, established after the war and based on former Japanese textile factories, which was an enormous state-owned enterprise that owned about half of the cotton spinning and weaving production facilities in China at the time. At the local level, meanwhile, there were public enterprises established by Yan Xishan (阎锡山) in Shanxi Province and Chen Jitang (陈济棠) in Guangdong Province during the Republican period (Uchida 1984; Kang 1996).

However, what the present study sought to emphasize is that the socialist transformation of 1956, which was uniformly implemented nationwide irrespective of

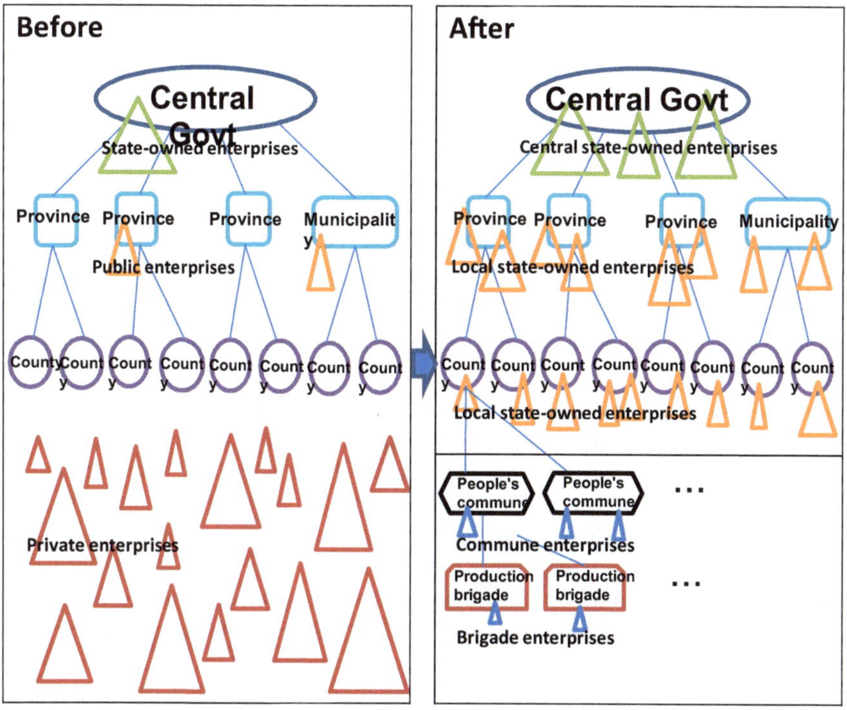

Fig. 12.1 Relationships between governments and enterprises before and after the socialist transformation. *Notes* (1) "Municipality" refers to a direct-administered municipality. (2) Units under "People's commune" were formed after 1958. *Source* Created by author

regional differences and the size of enterprises, had a broad impact, distinct from the establishment of individual state-owned/public enterprises or the nationalization of private enterprises seen up through the Republican period. As the analysis in Chapter 4 shows, large private enterprises were gradually and individually reorganized into state-owned or public-private jointly-owned ones and belonged to the central government after 1949, while the socialist transformation of 1956 transformed all private enterprises, regardless of their size and relative importance from the perspective of the central and local governments, and allocated them to various levels of government. What determined the relationship between local governments and enterprises within their respective regions was the devolution of central enterprises to local governments in 1958, and following this, despite subsequent backlashes, a system was established in which local governments managed enterprises, except for some central enterprises, within their regions.

In the historical context of Shanghai, the formation of such relationships between local governments and enterprises within the city marked a significant shift in the process of economic development since the late nineteenth century. This is because the relatively large economic scale of Shanghai during the Republican period was the result of the accumulation of various private enterprises, including foreign capital, under the aegis of the city's special status as a hub of domestic and foreign trade due to the opening of the port and the existence of foreign concessions. The direct relationship between the municipal government and enterprises at the time was basically limited to local tax collection, business registration, and other such matters. Therefore, as seen in Chapter 6, the fact that the Shanghai Municipal Government and countless private enterprises were directly linked financially in the early years of the PRC meant that the municipal government's control over the Shanghai economy had dramatically expanded compared to before. This was, so to speak, a process in which the vast economic city of Shanghai, having evolved through a complex historical process involving multiple and varied entities, was internally integrated and brought under the control of a single administrative body, the Shanghai Municipal Government.

From another perspective, the impact of the socialist transformation varied depending on the particular trajectory of historical economic development of each region up to 1956. What is unique in the case of Shanghai was the large number of private enterprises that had evolved, and therefore their transformation into local state-owned or public-private jointly-owned enterprises had a wide-ranging and lasting impact on the economic makeup of the city. However, as clarified in Chapter 7, the extent to which each region's finances depend on Enterprise Revenue varied considerably, and this diversity was likely related to the degree of enterprise development in each region at the time that the socialist system was put into place.

However, it should also be noted that the relationships between local governments and enterprises had been maintained as a basic principle under the socialist system since the completion of the socialist transformation in 1956. As seen in the case of the cement industry in Chapter 10, the means of production (factories and mines) newly formed in the region after the socialist transformation did not come under the jurisdiction of the higher-level government but instead belonged to the local government of the region. This is a key point related to the matter of regional integration by local governments, which will be discussed next.

12.2.2 Regional Integration by Local Governments and Interregional Division

The second major change brought about by the introduction of the socialist system was the regional integration by local governments and the division between regions.[2] Regional integration by local governments was essentially formed by combining the socialist transformation as outlined above with the introduction of a planned economy

[2] Donnithorne (1972) named the self-sufficient economy based on people's communes and production brigades seen during the Cultural Revolution period a "cellular economy." The regional integration and interregional division mentioned here are somewhat close to this image. However, the author holds that its institutional framework was formed in the establishment process of the socialist system in the 1950s, and that, moreover, this concept is one that could be applied to all levels of government at the time, not just that at the level of people's communes.

as a nationwide system, and by local governments coming to occupy a monopolistic position in resource distribution and economic management within their respective regions. As seen from the examples of the rubber processing industry in Chapter 9 and the cement industry in Chapter 10, private enterprises that were transformed into state-owned or public and private jointly-owned ones by the socialist transformation were reorganized under the Shanghai Municipal Government's organizations or specialized companies, and these various governmental organs became the main actors in later economic management. It was this system, in which a local government managed various economic entities within the region in question in a unified manner that made regional integration possible.

Regarding this regional integration, one may recall the similarities with the formation of the open port market networks (开港场市场圈) that occurred from the end of the nineteenth century to the beginning of the twentieth century, as well as the trend of provincial-level separation (Kuroda 1994, Chapter VIII, Chapter IX; Kigoshi 2012, Chapter 2). However, while the trend of provincial-level separation had political and policy aspects, such as the local government's response to the central government's fiscal policy (mainly regarding the enforcement of indemnity loan sharing), the formation of the open port market zones was essentially caused by economic changes such as the expansion of foreign trade. In contrast, regional integration under the socialist system was significantly different on the point that it was primarily caused by government-led institutional changes, namely the socialist transformation and the introduction of a planned economy. Moreover, unlike the provincial-level separation, which shook the Qing Dynasty's political system and led to the Xinhai Revolution in 1911, it should be noted that regional integration under the socialist system developed within a framework designed by the central government.

Another important aspect of regional integration under the socialist system is that it was accompanied to a degree by a division among regions. While an economic management system headed by a local government would be established within the respective region, free economic activities, such as trade with other regions, were restricted. For example, the distribution of important materials, as the examples in Chapters 9 and 10 show, was basically controlled by the central government's distribution organization, and trade between regions was only conducted in a limited form through administrative routes. A key backdrop against which this regional division in resource allocation occurred was the restriction of foreign trade and its centralization within the central government's trade department, triggered by changes in international relations in the early 1950s, as the example of raw rubber control in Chapter 9 illustrates. Especially for Shanghai, which had historically been the center of foreign trade of China, this represented a major structural change.

Moreover, it was not only the distribution of materials that was divided. As seen in Chapter 9, the ownership of assets such as sales networks and factories, which companies had expanded nationwide until the Republican period, was also regionally divided. Particularly representative was the case of the Guangzhou branch factory of the Dazhonghua Rubber Factory, which was confiscated by the local government, the Guangzhou Municipal Government, after the socialist transformation in 1956, in a clear case of the trend of local governments establishing territorial control of resources through the conversion of ownership. In the case of Chapter 10, the assets that the Shanghai Cement Factory held in other regions during the Republican period were confiscated by local governments after 1949, and the factories newly built in other regions during the planned economy period were also eventually transferred to the local governments governing the regions where said factories were located. Such phenomena, all but universal constants in the process of forming a socialist system, served to sever the interregional economic activity networks of each industry and company that had been developed up through the Republican period, and greatly regulated economic behavior.

However, this division between regions did not necessarily mean that there were no economic relations across regions. As seen in the state distribution of cement in Chapter 10 and the case of interregional networks in power supply in Chapter 11, there were indeed economic relations across regions under the socialist system. Further, the fiscal transfers through remittances to the central government and subsidies from the central government, discussed in Chapters 6 and 7, were also a form of interregional movement of funds via central finance. However, this was not caused by autonomous economic relations between regions but was instead limited to routes based on the central government's plan.

The case of the power industry is unique in that the regional integration was implemented under the leadership of the central government, which used the change in the international environment triggered by the Korean War as a pretext to recover the exclusive business right of foreign companies, especially the Shanghai Power Company. Industries of high importance for the national industrialization strategy, such as the power industry and the military industry, were largely under the strong supervision of the central government. In that sense, the central government's leading position in overall economic management remained unchanged. Rather, it should be emphasized here that the interregional resource movement across regions that existed before the formation of the socialist system was in principle unified into distribution routes based on the central plan. However, the fact that this resource allocation by the central government, which would normally be expected to be extremely important under a planned economy, was not fully carried out in practice, lead to the emergence of a structure of "central control in principle and de facto local autonomy," which will be discussed next.

12.2.3 Central Control in Principle and De Facto Local Autonomy

In addition to the two points mentioned above, the final point to discuss is the formation of a structure involving the fundamental control of the central government on the one hand, and the de facto autonomous response of local governments to said control on the other. It is well known that the phenomenon of local governments responding independently to central government policies is an enduring phenomenon seen in

China in previous eras, including the Qing Dynasty, the Republican period, and the Reform and Opening-up Policy period. However, what needs to be emphasized here is that the responses of local governments took unique forms under the socialist system due to its institutional characteristics, and can moreover be said to have characterized the economic management of the Chinese socialist system.

This is most evident in the case of the cement industry in Chapter 10. There, the central government's sudden industrial production promotion policy drove demand for cement in Shanghai. However, due to a lack of cement distribution from the central government, the Shanghai Municipal Government had to carry out its own cement procurement activities, such as the construction of small-scale cement factories, using its own investment. What is particularly important here is that the central government also recognized the imperfection of its own planned material distribution and allowed local governments to exercise a certain amount of discretion. In other words, the central government was utilizing the autonomy of local governments to bridge the gap between its own policies and planned resource allocation capabilities by deliberately creating loopholes in the planned economy system it had developed. The slogan "self-reliance" perfectly encapsulated this intention on the part of the central government.

The principle of control by the central government and the corresponding de facto autonomy of local governments became the core elements that characterized China's decentralized socialist system in contrast to the systems deployed in the Soviet Union and Eastern European socialist countries, along with the aforementioned emergence of local governments as economic entities and the regional integration and interregional division by those governments.

The implementation of such a socialist system during the planned economy period strongly affected the Chinese economy after the start of the Reform and Opening-up Policy, when the socialist system effectively began to collapse. Many studies on the Chinese economy after 1978 emphasize the role of local governments as economic entities, and point out that local governments led economic growth for a certain period of time after the start of the Reform and Opening-up Policy (e.g., Katō and Kubo 2009). However, it would be a mistake to simply put all of these phenomena regarding local governments into a framework contrasting decentralization in the Reform period and centralization in the planned economy period, as if a decentralized situation were somehow occurring for the first time in the wake of the Reform and Opening-up Policy.

The present study has shown that, by contrast, local governments as economic entities were already developing during the planned economy period. Furthermore, the factors that strengthened the presence of individual local governments after the start of the Reform and Opening-up Policy can be summarized as follows: (1) local governments were able to monopolistically manage resources within their respective regions, depending on what remained of the socialist system framework given that the reform policy was only proceeding gradually; (2) there were almost no other powerful economic entities at the regional level at the initial stage of the Reform and Opening-up Policy; and lastly, (3) the resources that local governments could use within their regions dramatically increased compared to the planned economy period through the progression of marketization, leading to the autonomous elements of the local governments in the "central control in principle and de facto local autonomy" framework becoming more actively demonstrated.

Of course, as the Reform and Opening-up Policy proceeded, the relative superiority of local governments based on these particular institutional elements of the socialist system also came to fade. It is also important to consider other economic entities, such as foreign companies, advancing into China, globalizing central state-owned enterprises, and private enterprises showing strong growth, to fully grasp the Chinese economy after 1978. However, more recent issues involving local governments' monopolies on the supply of land use rights within their regions and the pursuit of rent through such systems[3] can be traced back to the institutional framework of the socialist system, formed in the 1950s with the public ownership of the means of production. Moreover, in the longer term, securing land ownership is one of the most important issues in the establishment of modern private property rights. However, a situation in which land ownership was virtually monopolized by the local government of a region had never been anticipated, whether in Shanghai or in other regions, during the Republican period.

The foregoing has significant implications for the question of the historical significance of the Chinese socialist system, which was raised at the beginning of this study. It is the author's contention, from the standpoint of viewing the socialist system as an economic system, that the historical significance of the Chinese socialist system lies in the fact that it once halted the trend of modern economic system development in China, which had been gradually advancing in a manner compatible with the integration into the world economy since the opening of the port of Shanghai, and that this system, moreover, reconstructed the system of property rights and resource allocation according to what was deemed necessary for the operation of the socialist system. This, in turn, turned local governments into important economic entities in each region and left the formation of economic institutions—which might otherwise have promoted private companies and households to engage in economic activities, such as private property rights—in a relatively underdeveloped state due to the principle of the socialist system that government decisions were always prioritized. As was the case with the aforementioned land ownership issue and the serious public debt problems experienced by local governments, some of the problems that China faced after 1978 can be clearly seen as rooted in these institutional factors of the socialist system. In this sense, the formation of the Chinese socialist system had a significant impact on the long-term developmental process of the Chinese economy from the second half of the nineteenth century to the present day.

[3] Kajitani (2011, Chapter 7). Strictly speaking, there is a division whereby urban land is state-owned and rural land is collectively owned, and the supply of the former is managed by the local government of the region in question.

References

English Language

Donnithorne, Audrey. 1972. China's Cellular Economy: Some Economic Trends since the Cultural Revolution. *China Quarterly* 52: 605–619. https://doi.org/10.1017/S0305741000048116

Huang, Yasheng. 2008. *Capitalism with Chinese Characteristics: Entrepreneurship and the State.* New York: Cambridge University Press. https://doi.org/10.1017/CBO9780511754210

Chinese Language

Shanghaishi tongjiju, ed. 1984. *Shanghai tongjinianjian 1983* (上海统计年鉴 1983, Shanghai Statistical Yearbook 1983). Shanghai: Shanghai renmin chubanshe

Japanese Language

Amako, Satoshi et al., eds. 1999. *Gendai chūgoku jiten* (現代中国事典, Encyclopedia of Contemporary China). Tokyo: Iwanami shoten

Kajitani, Kai. 2011. *Gendai chūgoku no zaiseikinyū shisutemu: Gulōbaluka to chūō-chihō kankei no keizaigaku* (現代中国の財政金融システム——グローバル化と中央—地方関係の経済学, Financial and Monetary System of Contemporary China: Economics of Globalization and Central–local Relations). Nagoya: The University of Nagoya Press

Kang, Jin-a. 1996. 1930 nendai kanton chinsaitō seiken no seitōgyōkensetsu (1930年代広東陳済棠政権の製糖業建設, The Construction of the Sugar Industry by the Chen Jitang Regime in Guangdong province in the 1930s). *Chikaki ni arite* (近きに在りて, Being nearby) 30: 78–97

Katō, Hiroyuki, and Kubo Tōru. 2009. *Shinka suru chūgoku no shihonshugi* (進化する中国の資本主義, Evolving Chinese Capitalism). Tokyo: Iwanami shoten

Kigoshi, Yoshinori. 2012. *Kindai chūgoku to kōikishijōken: kaikantōkei niyoru macro teki apurōchi* (近代中国と広域市場圏——海関統計によるマクロ的アプローチ, Inter-regional Trade of Modern China: A Macroeconomic Analysis of China Maritime Customs Statistics). Kyoto: Kyoto University Press

Kuroda, Akinobu. 1994. *Chūka teikoku no kōzō to sekaikeizai* (中華帝国の構造と世界経済, Structure of the Chinese Empire and World Economy). Nagoya: The University of Nagoya Press

Okamoto, Takashi, ed. 2013. *Chūgoku keizaishi* (中国経済史, Chinese Economic History). Nagoya: The University of Nagoya Press

Osaka shiritsudaigaku keizaikenkyūjo, ed. 1986. *Shanghai: Sekai no daitoshi 2* (上海 世界の大都市2, Shanghai: World's Major Cities 2). Tokyo: University of Tokyo Press

Seki, Mitsuhiro. 1997. *Shanghai no sangyō hatten to nihon kigyō* (上海の産業発展と日本企業, Industrial Development in Shanghai and Japanese Companies). Tokyo: Shinhyōron

Seki, Mitsuhiro. 1989. Shanghai ni okeru chūshōkikaikinzokukōgyō no kisokōzō: jirei nimiru shūdankigyō to kokueikigyō (上海市における中小機械金属工業の基礎構造——事例にみる集団企業と国営企業, Structure of Small and Medium-sized Machinery Metal Industry in Shanghai: A Case Study of Collective Enterprises and State-owned Enterprises). *Kikai keizai kenkyū* (機械経済研究, Machine Industry Economic Research Report) 20: 37–69

Uchida, Tomoyuki. 1984. 1930 nendai niokeru enshakuzanseiken no zaiseiseisaku (1930年代における閻錫山政権の財政政策, Fiscal Policies of the Yan Xishan Government in the 1930s). *Ajia keizai* (アジア経済, Asian Economy) 25(7): 11–39

Name Index

B
Bo, Yibo, 74, 75, 80

C
Chen, Yun, 48, 52, 57, 64, 75, 78

G
Gu, Zhun, 114

J
Jiang, Zemin, 2, 275

K
Kajima, Jun, 1, 21, 37, 63, 95, 129, 145, 169, 189, 209, 243, 273

L
Liu, Hongsheng, 218, 219
Liu, Yongkang, 191
Li, Weihan, 80

M
Mao, Zedong, 8, 80

S
Shi, Zhishan, 191

W
Wu, Guozhen, 21, 252

X
Xu, Dixin, 48, 49, 52, 54, 57
Xue, Fujii, 191

Y
Yu, Zhiqing, 191

Z
Zhu, Rongji, 275

J. Kajima, *Shanghai under the Socialist System*, Studies in Economic History,
https://doi.org/10.1007/978-981-95-3225-4

Subject Index

B

Business tax, 47, 97–100, 102, 103, 105, 114, 121, 122

C

Cement industry, 14, 209–211, 218–220, 230, 236–238, 243, 278, 279, 281
Centralization, 8, 9, 12, 95, 99, 102, 146, 279, 281
Central Remittance Expenditure, 103, 134, 138, 145, 148–151, 153–155, 157, 159, 160, 162, 163
Central Subsidy Revenue, 148–151, 153, 155, 157, 159, 160, 163
Central tax, 96–99, 103, 112
China Construction Materials Company, 222, 224, 229
China Textile Construction Company, 42, 44, 175, 190, 276
Chinese Communist Party (CCP), 2, 8, 10, 27, 32, 37–42, 45, 48, 49, 52, 53, 63–65, 73–75, 77, 79, 80, 84, 85, 96, 102, 105, 111, 133, 190, 206, 219, 220, 253, 254, 273
Chinese economy, 2–5, 10–13, 21, 25, 27, 273, 281, 282
Cold War, 1, 13, 254
Commodity tax, 99, 103, 105, 114
Cultural Revolution, 4, 8, 215, 278

D

Dazhonghua Rubber Factory, 191, 193–195, 200, 201, 203, 204, 279
Decentralization, 8, 9, 12, 29, 138, 142, 146, 147, 210, 213, 216–218, 228, 229, 281

E

East China Power Grid, 245, 262–264, 266–268
Economic Construction Expenditure, 104, 129, 134, 145, 150, 160, 161, 163
Enterprise Revenue, 105, 119, 120, 123, 129–131, 133, 134, 138, 145, 148, 150, 160–163, 169, 177, 180, 182, 183, 185, 278

F

First Five Year Plan, 2, 37, 75, 76, 84, 104, 112, 138, 141, 210, 213, 215, 226, 227, 258, 259
Fiscal and taxation system, 96, 97, 102, 104, 105, 111, 122, 123, 129, 142
Fiscal structure of Shanghai, 96, 121, 130, 133, 163
Five Anti, 38, 73–77, 87, 88, 123, 200, 202
Five small industries, 217, 236, 238

G

General Line of the Transition Period, 38, 80, 85, 87
Government Administration Council, 48, 50, 65, 73, 75, 85, 123, 130, 131, 213, 255
Great Leap Forward, 4, 8, 28, 30, 138, 141, 146, 161, 183, 213, 215, 226, 227, 230, 235, 259

J. Kajima, *Shanghai under the Socialist System*, Studies in Economic History, https://doi.org/10.1007/978-981-95-3225-4

Guomindang, 27

H
Heavy industry, 4, 13, 29, 30, 33, 41, 45, 51, 77, 84, 85, 170, 172, 173, 179, 184, 185
Heavy-industry-priority Strategy, 4, 14, 33, 95, 170, 173, 176, 184, 185
Hong Kong, 3, 11, 49, 64, 65

I
Income tax, 97, 99, 102, 103, 106, 108, 114, 121, 131
Industrial and commercial tax, 102, 105, 122, 123
Industrialization, 3–5, 10, 25, 30, 53, 161, 170, 172, 185, 226, 227, 230, 280
Industrial organization, 14, 189, 191, 209

J
Japan, 3, 6, 10, 11, 26, 32, 41, 49, 65, 174, 191, 192, 194, 197, 198, 215, 244, 268
Japanese companies, 26, 192, 244

K
Korean War, 13, 31, 33, 38–40, 57, 63–67, 73, 74, 87, 88, 104, 112, 176, 190, 197, 198, 206, 254, 256, 268, 280

L
Local enterprise, 12, 14, 129, 133, 138, 140, 141, 150, 160, 163, 169, 170, 182, 275
Local government, 8, 9, 12, 13, 40, 87, 88, 95–97, 99, 102, 103, 105, 111, 112, 134, 138, 142, 146, 147, 149, 150, 153, 159–161, 163, 169, 170, 182, 204, 206, 209–211, 213, 216–218, 221, 228–230, 235, 236, 238, 243, 256, 268, 275–282
Local tax, 96, 98, 103, 112, 121, 122, 133, 134, 278

M
Machinery industry, 54, 170–172, 174–178, 180–185
Manchukuo, 13, 25, 30, 31, 160, 198, 244
Material management, 212, 213, 215–218, 229, 236, 238

N
National Government, 22, 25–27, 30, 41, 42, 49, 51, 64, 96, 97, 99, 101, 102, 105, 114, 130, 131, 175, 192, 193, 196, 244–246, 252, 253, 267, 276
New Democracy, 37, 45, 51, 80, 85
New Democratic Economy, 45, 47, 48

P
People's Republic of China (PRC), 4, 11–14, 22, 28, 37–40, 43–48, 51, 53, 70, 73, 84, 87, 96, 97, 102–105, 111, 112, 114, 121, 123, 130, 131, 134, 138, 170, 173, 191, 196, 197, 211, 218, 227, 245, 255, 259, 262, 268, 278
Planned economy, 2, 9, 37, 210, 220, 228, 236, 238, 259, 274, 278–281
Planned economy period, 3–6, 10, 11, 13, 21, 28–33, 96, 138, 141, 146–150, 153, 157, 159, 162, 170, 172–174, 177, 179, 180, 182–185, 189, 198, 211, 213, 215, 217, 222, 224, 229, 230, 234, 236–238, 245, 246, 259, 263, 267, 273–275, 280, 281
Private enterprise, 11–13, 25, 37–40, 43–47, 49–51, 56, 57, 63, 66, 67, 70, 71, 73–77, 79, 80, 84–88, 131, 141, 160, 169, 190, 196, 200, 201, 203, 253, 274–279, 282
Processing orders, 40, 44, 47–49, 51–57, 63, 67–74, 76–80, 84, 85, 87, 88, 200–202, 206
Public ownership of the means of production, 2, 37, 220, 274, 276, 282
Public-private jointly-owned enterprise, 80, 84, 86–88, 169, 182, 190, 203, 204, 222, 258, 276, 278

Q
Qing Dynasty, 97, 244, 250, 259, 279, 281

R
Reform and Opening-up, 2, 3, 6, 33, 215, 236, 273–276, 281, 282
Reform period, 4, 5, 7, 28, 32, 149, 275, 281

Republican period, 4, 5, 11–13, 28, 29, 31–33, 40, 42, 54, 79, 87, 88, 96, 97, 102, 111, 112, 114, 121, 122, 130, 133, 145, 160, 170, 172, 173, 175, 177, 180, 184, 185, 189, 197, 204, 211, 215, 218, 219, 244, 245, 254, 259, 262, 267, 268, 275–277, 279, 281, 282
Republic of China (ROC), 4, 22, 25, 26
Resources Committee, 41, 246, 252, 276
Rubber processing industry, 54, 189–194, 196–198, 200–206, 209, 243, 279

S
Second Sino-Japanese War, 26, 27, 41, 48, 98, 102, 111, 121, 175, 176, 192, 219, 244–246, 252, 262, 267, 276
Second World War, 1, 3, 21, 22, 26, 28, 190, 193, 194, 218, 246, 247, 251
Shanghai Cement Factory, 221, 222, 224, 227–230, 233, 235, 236, 280
Shanghai Municipal Bureau of Chemical Industry, 204
Shanghai Municipal Bureau of Finance, 112, 134
Shanghai Municipal Bureau of Industry and Commerce, 40, 43, 48–51, 53, 56, 57, 66, 67, 70–72, 76, 88
Shanghai Municipal Bureau of Public Utilities, 246, 251, 254, 256, 258, 267
Shanghai Municipal Bureau of Tax, 112, 121
Shanghai Municipal Government, 54, 55, 57, 66, 87, 88, 103, 122, 129–131, 134, 138, 141, 142, 151, 169, 193, 196, 197, 211, 222, 228–230, 235, 236, 238, 246, 251, 253, 256, 258, 275, 278, 279, 281
Shanghai Power Company, 244–252, 255, 256, 258, 267, 268, 280
Shanghai Power Industry Management Bureau, 258
Shanghai Rubber Industry Company, 204
Shortage economy, 12, 210, 236, 239
Small Third Front, 225
Socialist fiscal system, 95, 130, 163, 275
Socialist market economy, 2
Socialist system, 1–10, 12, 28, 30, 32, 33, 37–40, 63, 87, 88, 95, 169, 170, 173, 182, 185, 190, 206, 209–212, 218, 220–222, 224, 243, 245, 246, 263, 267, 273–276, 278–282
Socialist transformation, 2, 3, 11–13, 37–40, 75, 84–88, 130, 131, 133, 141, 160, 169, 202–206, 209, 220, 245, 258, 259, 268, 276, 278, 279
Soft budget constraint, 12
Soviet Union, 1, 7, 8, 10, 31, 75, 84, 102, 104, 105, 176, 235, 281
State Council, 212–214, 217
State-owned enterprise, 9, 12, 38, 40, 42–44, 47, 48, 52–57, 66, 67, 69, 71, 74, 87, 88, 99, 105, 160, 169, 196, 200, 201, 203, 206, 210, 212, 213, 246, 253, 258, 274–276, 282
State plan, 47, 212, 217, 221, 222, 228, 238
State Planning Commission, 210, 212–214, 237

T
Taiwan, 3, 6, 10, 11, 26, 41, 148
Taxation, 13, 96, 97, 99, 102–105, 111, 112, 114, 129
Textile industry, 30, 45, 54, 77, 82–84, 170, 172–180, 182–185, 190
Third Front Construction, 29, 161, 172, 234
Three Anti, 39, 73, 74, 76, 77, 87, 88, 123, 134, 200

U
United Power Company, 250–252, 258, 259, 267
United States (US), 10, 22, 32, 38, 64, 67, 105, 194, 197, 215, 235, 236, 247, 248, 255, 267

V
Vertical shortage, 210, 211, 238

Z
Zhengtai Rubber Factory, 191–195, 200, 201, 203, 204

MIX
Papier aus verantwortungsvollen Quellen
Paper from responsible sources
FSC® C105338

If you have any concerns about our products,
you can contact us on
ProductSafety@springernature.com

In case Publisher is established outside the EU,
the EU authorized representative is:
Springer Nature Customer Service Center GmbH
Europaplatz 3, 69115 Heidelberg, Germany

Printed by Libri Plureos GmbH
in Hamburg, Germany